Culture and Psychology

David Matsumoto is an Associate Professor of Psychology and Director of the Intercultural and Emotion Research Laboratory at San Francisco State University. He earned his B.A. from the University of Michigan and his M.A. and Ph.D from the University of California, Berkeley. He has studied emotion, human interaction, and culture for over 15 years and is a recognized expert in this field. He is the author of over 90 works on culture and emotion, including original research articles, paper presentations, books, chapters in books, videos, and assessment instruments. He has been invited to address professional and scientific groups in the United States and abroad, including the Russian Academy of Sciences in Moscow. He also serves as an intercultural consultant to various domestic and international businesses.

Dr. Matsumoto brings his expertise in intercultural relations to the arena of the Olympic sport of judo. He currently serves as the Chairman of National Coaching and Training and the National Coaching Staff for United States Judo, Inc., the national governing body of judo in the United States. He is the designated team leader for the judo team representing the United States at the 1995 World Championships in Chiba, Japan, and in the 1996 Summer Olympic Games in Atlanta, Georgia.

Related Titles by David Matsumoto

People: Psychology from a Cultural Perspective
Cultural Influences on Methods and Statistics
A World of Diversity video with student workbook and facilitator's guide

Culture and Psychology

David Matsumoto
San Francisco State University

Brooks/Cole Publishing Company

I(T)P™An International Thomson Publishing Company

Pacific Grove ▪ Albany ▪ Bonn ▪ Boston ▪ Cincinnati ▪ Detroit ▪ London ▪ Madrid ▪ Melbourne
Mexico City ▪ New York ▪ Paris ▪ San Francisco ▪ Singapore ▪ Tokyo ▪ Toronto ▪ Washington

Sponsoring Editor: *Marianne Taflinger*
Marketing Team: *Carolyn Crockett, Romy Fineroff*
Marketing Representatives: *Linda Schaeffer,*
  Liz Gilley
Editorial Assistant: *Laura Donahue*
Production Editor: *Nancy L. Shammas*
Production Service: *Scratchgravel Publishing Services*
Manuscript Editor: *Kay Mikel*
Permissions Editor: *May Clark*

Interior Design: *Anne Draus, Scratchgravel*
  Publishing Services
Interior Illustration: *Greg Draus, Scratchgravel*
  Publishing Services
Cover Design: *Renée Tafoya*
Indexer: *James Minkin*
Typesetting: *Scratchgravel Publishing Services*
Printing and Binding: *Malloy Lithographing, Inc.*

For more information, contact:

BROOKS/COLE PUBLISHING COMPANY
511 Forest Lodge Road
Pacific Grove, CA 93950
USA

International Thomson Publishing Europe
Berkshire House 168-173
High Holborn
London WC1V 7AA
England

Thomas Nelson Australia
102 Dodds Street
South Melbourne, 3205
Victoria, Australia

Nelson Canada
1120 Birchmount Road
Scarborough, Ontario
Canada M1K 5G4

International Thomson Editores
Campos Eliseos 385, Piso 7
Col. Polanco
11560 México D. F. México

International Thomson Publishing GmbH
Königswinterer Strasse 418
53227 Bonn
Germany

International Thomson Publishing Asia
221 Henderson Road
#05-10 Henderson Building
Singapore 0315

International Thomson Publishing Japan
Hirakawacho Kyowa Building, 3F
2-2-1 Hirakawacho
Chiyoda-ku, Tokyo 102
Japan

Printed in the United States of America

10   9   8   7   6   5   4   3   2   1

Library of Congress Cataloging-in-Publication Data
Matsumoto, David Ricky.
    Culture and psychology / David Matsumoto.
      p.   cm.
    Includes bibliographical references and index.
    ISBN 0-534-23220-5 (pbk. : alk. paper)
    1. Culture.   2. Cross-cultural studies.   I. Title.
HM108.M38   1996
  306—dc20   95-8728
                                                    CIP

To my mom, Mitsuno Matsumoto, and the memory of my dad, Paul Matsumoto

Contents

15 Conclusion   305

Preface

Cultural diversity is one of the most important topics facing psychology today. The world around us has become increasingly diverse and pluralistic—at work, at school, and at home. Diversity brings with it a challenge to all of us in our everyday lives. Many colleges and universities have met this challenge by infusing their curricula with a new or renewed emphasis on diversity. New courses that focus on issues of human diversity have been developed in various disciplines and departments. Existing courses have been revamped and redesigned to include components on human diversity.

Most college psychology departments in the United States have responded to these developments in a couple of ways. First, more and more are offering specific classes in cross-cultural psychology. Indeed, cross-cultural research in psychology has a substantial history, and the empirical and theoretical work that contributes to its literature have important implications for our understanding of human behavior across cultural contexts. Second, many departments and instructors are incorporating cross-cultural material into their existing courses on clinical, social, developmental, and other areas of psychology, extending the traditional material in exciting ways.

The challenges of diversity have been viewed by many as somewhat of a nuisance. Culture, race, and ethnicity have often been considered "extraneous variables" in research—aspects of people that could be ignored. This book approaches the challenges of diversity with a different philosophy and perspective. I believe that with every challenge comes great opportunities to open new horizons in learning about behavior and psychology. Cross-cultural psychology holds one of the keys with which we can find ways to uncover new knowledge and new ways of viewing old knowledge. Cross-cultural research offers important additions to the entire research literature in psychology; it complements, not conflicts with, traditional psychological research. Through cross-cultural research and psychology we are able to forge new roads and build new bridges in our quest for understanding the human mind in all contexts around the world.

Very few textbooks on cross-cultural psychology and cultural influences on human behavior have been aimed specifically at undergraduate courses in psychology. There is, however, a great need for such resources, as it becomes increasingly important for students to learn about the role of human diversity across a broad range of topics that apply to their everyday lives and are not limited to a single discipline or context.

The goal of this book is to provide that resource. *Culture and Psychology* presents current knowledge about human diversity and its influence on human behavior across a wide range of topics and areas relevant to psychology. The overall purpose of this book is to highlight crucial information we have gained through systematic and scientific research across cultures—looking at human behavior in a variety of contexts and settings and from different disciplines and approaches. I hope that readers get from this book a sense of the subtle yet strong influence of culture in all aspects of our lives and that they learn to apply this knowledge in our multicultural and pluralistic world, dealing with people from diverse backgrounds. I also hope that readers gain some appreciation for how this material can be used to raise questions about our existing knowledge and theories in psychology, adding to or revising those theoretical frameworks when appropriate.

How This Book Works

I organized this book so that all the areas of psychology that have a sufficient amount of cross-cultural research literature could be presented and discussed in a meaningful way. The topics span areas traditionally covered in social, clinical, developmental, and personality psychology. I have also included two chapters specifically relevant to communication processes, which are extremely important in cross-cultural psychology. I have included a chapter on the definition of culture, which has often been overlooked in studies of cross-cultural psychology. I have also included a chapter on cultural influences on the research process, which should give readers a sense of how culture influences the ways in which we gather information about the world.

- Chapter 1 provides an introduction to cross-cultural psychology and discusses the importance and relevance of this topic in our learning about psychology in general, especially in relation to our increasingly diverse world.
- Chapter 2 discusses definitions of culture and contrasts culture with race and ethnicity. This type of discussion has been sorely overlooked in cross-cultural research and theoretical work.
- Chapter 3 discusses cultural influences on concepts of self and personality, which form a foundation on which all other material in the book is based.
- Chapter 4 discusses cultural influences on research methods, providing an introduction to the influential biases researchers and research participants bring to the research process.
- Chapter 5 discusses how culture develops in us and how we can see the manifestations of cultural differences and similarities in several areas of development, including cognitive, moral, and socioemotional development.
- Chapter 6 discusses the impact of culture on work and our existence in work organizations. This material is especially relevant to those individuals who work in multicultural organizations; it provides an important practical framework from which cultural similarities and differences in psychology can be observed.
- Chapter 7 discusses the contributions of basic psychological processes to intergroup relations, especially with regard to ethnocentrism and stereotypes. The discussion focuses on categorization, memory, selective attention, and attributional bias and how they affect the development and maintenance of ethnocentric attitudes and stereotypes.
- Chapter 8 discusses cultural influences on social behavior with a focus on ingroup-outgroup interactions.
- Chapter 9 presents cross-cultural research on basic psychological processes, including perception, cognition, and intelligence.
- Chapter 10 focuses on cultural differences in gender and includes a discussion of the terms *sex, gender, sex roles,* and *gender roles.* I examine cross-cultural research that investigates the universality of gender-specific behavior patterns across cultures.
- Chapter 11 discusses cultural influences on physical and mental health and how cultural differences need to be incorporated in appropriate treatment plans. This chapter also includes a section on cultural and cross-national differences in health care systems.
- Chapter 12 discusses cultural similarities and differences in human emotion, contrasting the basic human emotions across cultures.

- Chapters 13 and 14 discusses cultural influences on the process of communication. Chapter 13 focuses on verbal communication and language, and Chapter 14 focuses on nonverbal communication. Both verbal and nonverbal communication are important components of the communication process, and both need to be viewed in relation to culture.
- Finally, Chapter 15 suggests some potential guidelines for how to engage with others in our pluralistic and multicultural world. I offer these as a platform from which we can have meaningful discussions about individual views on this important and practical topic.

You will find that the writing style of this book is geared for undergraduate courses. Despite the ease of reading, however, close inspection will reveal a heavy reliance on quality cross-cultural research that constitutes much of the published cross-cultural literature in psychology.

Who the Book Is For

Culture and Psychology will appeal primarily to instructors of courses specifically on cross-cultural psychology. This book fills a serious void in the resources needed to teach such a course. Much of the book assumes that students are already acquainted with basic psychology, and instructors should pay particular attention to any students who have little or no psychology background (although these students make some of the most interesting contributions in class!).

Culture and Psychology is also useful and relevant to instructors in other areas of psychology who wish to infuse their courses with material relevant to culture and cross-cultural research. Much material related to the main topics of psychology is interspersed throughout the text and can be assigned as specific readings for students or can serve as background information for instructors.

A Message to the Students

In my experience, people engage material concerning cultural similarities and differences in behavior in one of two ways. One approach is characterized by vindication—people selectively focus on ways to conclude that their own behavior and culture are the "best," therefore justifying their current beliefs and providing a reason not to change or improve. The second approach is characterized by investigation—people actively learn about similarities and differences equally and challenge themselves to find the best of all worlds for their own situation.

Learning about how people are different than we are can be challenging. Undoubtedly, there are good and bad, right and wrong, in every culture and in every approach. What is important to learn as our world becomes increasingly pluralistic and multicultural is not how to find ways to vindicate our own behaviors and existence but how to investigate the world around us and others in it so we can reap the benefits of diversity, turning the challenges of diversity into our best assets. If we approach the material with such a focus, we will find the way to learn this. What will determine success in this endeavor is not the amount of information we study or what it says but the degree to which our minds are open and the motivation with which we engage in the process.

Have an open mind, and investigate.

Acknowledgments

This book, like so many of my other projects, is the result of a collaborative effort between myself and numerous friends and colleagues. Although this book was conceived and written within approximately two years, it has received the benefit of the work and support of many people, even before its conception. My own research collaborators in the field of emotion—Paul Ekman, Wally Friesen, Klaus Scherer, Tsutomu Kudoh, and others—have helped me tremendously in my own growth as a scientist and a writer, and I will always be grateful for their collaboration.

Some of the material in this book comes from an earlier book of mine entitled *People: Psychology from a Cultural Perspective*. In that book, I was fortunate to work with some outstanding people who helped me gather and present information in specific areas of psychology. It is a tribute to Phil Hull, Shinobu Kitayama, Jeff LeRoux, Margaret Lynch, and Dawn Terrell that the material is again presented here in a larger context with their permission. I thank them for their past efforts, which have contributed to this present work.

I am always grateful to the wonderful and hard-working staff members in my laboratory at San Francisco State University. Without all their efforts, none of my works, including this book, would ever come to fruition. In particular, I would like to acknowledge the contributions of Deborah Krupp, Michael Biehl, Fazilet Kasri, Michiko Tomioka, and Michelle Weissman, who worked on the project team that inspired me to develop our ideas into this book. Mike, Michelle, and Sachiko Takeuchi also put in many hours of work on the references for this book, tracking down articles and other books, and I am eternally grateful to them. My thanks to all of them and the rest of my lab members.

As usual, the people at Brooks/Cole Publishing Company have put forth a stellar effort in helping me complete this project. The integrity and sincerity with which this company, and the individuals who comprise it, meet the challenges that face our universities today make collaboration a truly rewarding process. In particular, I would like to express my gratitude to Marianne Taflinger, senior editor at Brooks/Cole, for her patience, guidance, and support throughout this project. It has been a pleasurable experience working with her on this and other projects. I would also like to thank the reviewers of this book—Dennis Chesnut, East Carolina University; G. William Hill, Kennesaw State College; B. James Starr, Howard University; and John E. Williams, Wake Forest University—who took much time and spent much energy in providing thoughtful and incisive comments that helped me shape my ideas into a more presentable format. This book is a collaboration as much with them as with anyone else.

My continued thanks go to my wife, Nobuko, who gives me the love and support to make it through each and every day of my life. She helps me see each obstacle as a challenge, lends me the courage to meet those challenges, and gives me the wisdom, however little I may have, to turn those challenges into successes.

David Matsumoto

1

Introduction

Cultural diversity is one of the most important topics in the United States today. All of us are continually being thrust into an increasingly diverse world—at school, at work, and at home—and misunderstandings can lead to confusion and anger. Identifying yourself with a particular group may produce a feeling of protectionism for the group to which you belong. Diversity is a buzzword for "difference," and conflicts and misunderstandings often arise because of these differences.

Cultural diversity is our biggest challenge. Corporate America is attempting to address that challenge through workshops, seminars, and education in diversity throughout the workforce. The educational system has addressed diversity by hiring and retaining faculty of color and infusing material related to different cultures throughout the curriculum. Government has attempted to deal with diversity through policies such as affirmative action, equal employment opportunities, and the like.

The challenges that face us in the names of cultural diversity and intercultural relations also represent our biggest opportunities. If we can meet those challenges and turn them to our favor, we can actualize a potential in diversity and intercultural relations that will result in far more than the sum of individual components that comprise that diverse universe.

It is with this belief (bias, if you like) that this book was written—to meet the challenge of diversity and somehow turn that challenge into opportunity. Still, doing so is not easy. Meeting the challenge of diversity requires that you take an honest look at your own cultural background and heritage and its merits and limitations in meeting the challenges of a diverse world. Fear, rigidity, and sometimes stubborn pride come with any type of honest assessment. Yet without that assessment, we cannot meet the challenge of diversity and improve intercultural relations.

In academia, that assessment brings with it fundamental questions about what is taught in our colleges and universities today. Indeed, understanding how cultural diversity can color the nature of the truths and principles of human behavior delivered in the halls of science questions the pillars of much of our knowledge about the world and about human behavior. From time to time, we need to shake those pillars to see just how sturdy they are. This is especially true in the social sciences, and particularly in psychology, which is by definition the science concerned with the nature of truth about the mental and behavioral characteristics of individuals and groups.

The Nature of Knowledge in Science

Human behavior is at the heart of many of the social sciences: psychology, anthropology, philosophy, and sociology. But it is also an important element in many other fields, including business, communication, economics, and even biology and chemistry. While each of these disciplines takes a different approach and has a unique viewpoint for understanding human behavior, they all have at least one thing in common—reliance on formal, systematic research as the primary method by which knowledge is generated.

Each scientific discipline has its own research approaches and utilizes a unique paradigm and theoretical framework to understand and interpret data. Psychology, for instance, relies heavily on scientific research through interviews and laboratory experiments involving human participants to generate knowledge about how and why people behave as they do. Observational research, case studies, bibliographic studies, and surveys are also important research tools in psychology. Despite the differences in approaches, the goals are similar: to uncover information about individuals. Researchers conducting psychological studies often attempt to interpret and understand their data on the level of the individual. This characteristic, among others, sets psychology apart from other social science disciplines concerned with human behavior.

All disciplines rely on scholarship and research at least to some degree to discover knowledge about the world and about human behavior. In evaluating the knowledge obtained, it is important to be assured that the research meets some minimal standards for scientific rigor. Strict adherence to scientific principles allows us to "trust" the information produced by the study. Indeed, if the methods of any study are compromised to the point that the results obtained in that study are biased, those results should not necessarily be believed, regardless of how attractive and personally appealing the results may be. Only when the methods used in a study meet objective and well-accepted standards for quality and rigor can the findings be accepted as making a statement about human behavior.

The findings from a single study are not sufficient to declare that a new truth or principle has been discovered. It is only when individual research findings are consistently repeated across studies that academia begins to believe that a finding can be generalized to many people. **Generalizations*** are comprised of truths or principles winnowed from multiple, systematic research efforts that are believed to be true for a larger group of people than those actually studied. In psychological research, consistent repetition of a finding across a number of studies is called **replication** of a result, and replication is an essential ingredient in our quest for truth about human behavior.

Still, it is important to recognize that the data obtained in research studies are heavily dependent on the methods and underlying philosophy used to generate those data. In fact, there is a very close connection between the methods used to conduct a study and the implicit biases conceded in the data obtained in that research. If, for example, researchers ask participants to view an ambiguous stimulus and choose from a list of ten items what they think they see in the stimulus, the researchers will obtain a finding about a perception that is limited to the ten choices provided. Using that same methodology, a researcher can then study how such perceptions may be related to other phenomena, or how the perceptions reflected in those choices differ across cultural or gender groups. A considerable amount of time and effort can be expended conducting such studies and developing elaborate theoretical frameworks concerning how and why such perceptions exist and are maintained. What is too often forgotten is that the very nature of the data derived in this set of studies is dependent on the way those data were obtained in the first place. It may very well be the case, for example, that the perceptions reported by the study participants were simply the best alternatives available from the restricted list of ten items. While it may be the case that the choices made by the participants were close to their actual perceptions, it may also be true that the choices had little to do with their actual perceptions. Participants may have selected the least wrong choice available, but not necessarily because it matched their actual perceptions of the stimulus. If the participants had been allowed to say whatever came to their minds about the stimulus in an open-ended format, they might have provided entirely different data. Data obtained in any research project are dependent on the methods used by the

---

***Boldface** terms are defined in the glossary at the end of the chapter.

researcher and the personal biases of the scientists who design and conduct those studies.

It follows, then, that what we know as truths in science and academia are heavily dependent on how the research that produced those "truths" was conducted. Because of the nature of research, all studies are conducted under specific conditions, with certain arbitrary parameters and limitations. Researchers make conscious decisions about what to study (the topic), the exact questions to be addressed (the hypotheses), how the data will be collected (procedures) and from whom (subjects), how to organize the data (analysis), and how to interpret the findings in relation to the topic and specific questions. Indeed, scientific research is not a process that occurs in a vacuum without human contact; quite to the contrary, it is heavily dependent on the conscious and deliberate decisions made by the person conducting the research. These decisions form the basis for the parameters, conditions, and limitations under which the research is conducted. Because data about people are gathered within this framework, the knowledge generated by research on people is bounded by these artificial parameters and limitations.

One of the prominent characteristics of most research conducted in the United States on human behavior in psychology and presented in colleges and universities today is that the research typically involves college or university students. There are many reasons why this is so. Among them is the ease by which researchers, often housed at universities, can gain access to student volunteers for research relative to the difficulty of obtaining volunteers for research outside the school environment among people on their own working and living. These dynamics, along with other considerations, make it fairly safe to assume that the majority of the information and research you read about in textbooks and in research articles published in scientific journals in psychology is based on studies involving college or university student participants or samples.

There is nothing wrong with such research per se, and the findings obtained from such samples are definitely true for those samples. These findings may be replicated across different samples, using different methodologies. In short, many findings may weather tests for scientific rigor that would render them acceptable as a truth or principle about human behavior. However, a basic question still remains: Is what we know as truth or principle about human behavior, which we have learned in our "traditional" or usual way, true for all people, regardless of gender, race, ethnicity, culture, class, or lifestyle? Certainly, some truths must be true for all; we call those truths universals. Still, there must be much about the world and about human behavior that is true for one culture but not for others. It may very well be the case, therefore, that despite the fact that a finding is replicated in studies involving subjects from this culture and society, it is not true for another culture or society, and vice versa. Truth and principle, in this sense, are not absolutes; they are, in fact, culturally relative and cultural bound. And, not only are the results of our research bound by our methods and culture, but the very standards of care we use when we evaluate the scientific rigor and quality of research are also bound by the cultural frameworks within which our science occurs (Pe-Pua, 1989).

The Cross-Cultural Approach and Its Impact on Truths about Human Behavior

A **cross-cultural approach** is a view of understanding truth and principles about human behaviors within a global, cross-cultural perspective. **Cross-cultural research** is any type of research on human behavior that compares behavior of interest across two or more cultures. It is a research approach primarily concerned with examining how our knowledge about people and their behaviors from one culture may be the same or different from that of people from another culture. In many senses, cross-cultural research not only tests similarities and differences in behaviors, thus expanding our knowledge about people, but also tests possible limitations of our traditional knowledge by studying people of different cultures. In its narrowest sense, cross-cultural research simply involves including participants from different cultural backgrounds and testing possible differences between these different groups of participants. In its broadest sense, however, cross-cultural approaches are concerned with understanding truth and psychological principles as either **universal** (that is, true for all people of all cultures) or **culture-specific** (that is, true for some people of some cultures).

In the United States, psychology is segmented into specific topic areas, such as clinical, social, developmental, personality, and the like. Cross-cultural psychology and cross-cultural approaches in general are not necessarily topic-specific. Cross-cultural researchers are interested in a broad range of phenomena related to human behavior—from perception to language, child-rearing to psychopathology. Cross-cultural psychologists and cross-cultural research can be found in any specific area or subdiscipline within psychology. What delineates a cross-cultural approach from a traditional or mainstream approach, therefore, is not the phenomenon of interest but the commonality of testing limitations to knowledge by examining whether that knowledge is applicable to or obtainable from people of different cultural backgrounds.

Although cross-cultural research has existed for many years in fields such as psychology and anthropology, it has especially gained in popularity over the last few years. No doubt much of the popularity of a cross-cultural approach is due to our current focus on cultural diversity and intergroup relations. But, in a much larger sense, an increased interest in cross-cultural psychology is a normal and healthy development, questioning the nature of the truths and principles amassed to date and searching for ways to provide an even more accurate picture of human behavior across people of different cultural backgrounds. As psychology has matured and such questions have been raised, many scientists and writers have come to recognize that much of the research and the literature once thought to be universal for all people is indeed culture bound. The increasing importance and recognition of cross-cultural approaches in the social sciences, and in psychology in particular, represents our reactions to this realization. Much of this research and scholarship has had a profound impact on our understanding of truths and principles about human behavior.

Even without considering knowledge added using a cross-cultural approach, a great mass of information about people has already been developed. Indeed, an enormous body of information in the social sciences is considered as truth by American scientists, professors, and students. The comprehensiveness of most social science textbooks and the density of most course syllabi attest to the fact that there is a great deal out there to be learned. Why, you may ask, should it be necessary to go beyond information that currently exists?

Despite the wealth of knowledge that has been gathered, it is vitally important for us to incorporate a cross-cultural approach to our knowledge and learning base, for at least two reasons. The first has to do with what we may call **scientific philosophy**. Scientific philosophy here simply refers to what we have been discussing all along in this chapter—the need to evaluate our truths in terms of the parameters under which those truths were obtained. More simply put, we need to examine whether the information we have learned about (or will learn in the future) is applicable to *all* people of *all* cultures or only to *some* people of *some* cultures. Scientific philosophy refers to the notion that we have a duty and an obligation to ask these questions about the scientific process and about the nature of the truths we have learned, or will learn, about human behavior.

The second reason it is important for us to incorporate a cross-cultural approach is much more practical. One of the goals of studying cultural similarities and differences is to help us in our real-life, everyday interactions and dealings with others. As we come more and more in contact with people from different cultural backgrounds, it becomes increasingly important to learn about universals and cultural-specifics in our truths—that is, in the beliefs we hold about people and the way they are. More importantly, we need to use those universals and specifics in helping us formulate guiding principles that can be used as resources in our relations with those people. To be ignorant of such resources would render us inflexible in our ability to deal with those around us in our dynamic, ever-diversifying world.

Incorporating cross-cultural issues in our learning of human behavior means that we need to ask some very basic, yet extremely important, questions about the nature of the truths taught in classes across the United States today. Those questions are best addressed by a cross-cultural approach.

Gaining a Global Perspective

When we think of cultural diversity and intercultural relations in the United States, some of the most pressing concerns have to do with interethnic and interrace relations in our own states, cities, and communities. Very few universities in today's world are totally free from intergroup conflict regarding issues of race, ethnicity, or culture. Congruent with such concerns, most students want to learn about cultural diversity as it relates to them within this perspective; that is, with a focus on ethnic and racial minorities and intergroup relations among races within the United States. Indeed, as you will discover in the remaining chapters of this book, a considerable number of studies conducted in the United States pertain to ethnic differences in a variety of behaviors.

This book has a broader perspective, however, focusing not only on those questions but also on work from other countries and cultures, providing students with a perspective about the United States and American culture in relation to the rest of the world. At the same time, much of the information and many of the principles learned in this process can be applied to better our understanding of ethnic and racial groups within the United States. Gaining a larger perspective on our own intracountry differences in relation to the rest of the world will take much of the "heat" off relationships among different groups here in this country. Oftentimes, the problems we think are huge because they are right in our faces seem smaller when we understand that they are part of a larger picture of cultural diversity that occurs throughout the world.

Even as we obtain a global perspective, we need to realize that we in the United States have a special role with regard to how we deal with cultural diversity and intercultural conflict. The United States is a microcosm of the world; peoples of many different cultures coexist here, mirroring the world, but on a smaller scale. The problems, issues, and pitfalls that face the entire world face us now, and many of the problems we face are, or will be, faced by others in the future. The rest of the world is watching us, because they feel that how the United States fares is how the world will fare. We cannot fail.

The Goal of This Book

Still, as we dive into cross-cultural research and psychology, we must realize that it is neither a panacea nor a utopia of human knowledge. Cross-cultural research suffers from its own troubles and limitations. Research examining ethnic and cultural differences among groups within the United States are typically not considered cross-cultural and have generally remained separate from the cross-cultural literature. The politics of looking at such differences within the United States has made relevant literature more difficult to assimilate. In cross-cultural research, it is much easier to find or conduct studies that compare Americans as a whole against the Japanese or Germans rather than blacks versus whites or Hispanics versus Asians. The former studies often suffer because they assume Americans are homogeneous in comparison to other cultural groups in other countries. The subjects that participate in this research are usually middle-class Americans of European ancestry.

But the existence of these problems should not deter us from our quest for the truth about human behavior. Just as we need to take what we can from previous, culture-bound research, we must do so as well with the cross-cultural literature. We must recognize the limitations and the parameters under which the information was derived and somehow build a foundation from little bits and pieces of information that will come together into a larger, coherent structure.

After all is said and done, what do I intend that you gain from this book? In challenging the traditional, I definitely do not mean to disregard its importance or the importance of the work that produced that knowledge. Indeed, to disregard or ignore that material or the work that produced it would demonstrate a level of insensitivity that should have no place in our academic work. Instead, I seek to raise questions about the traditional, mainstream knowledge of human behavior. I want to know whether what we know of organizations, development, personality, emotion, communication, and the like is applicable to people of all cultural backgrounds. I want to challenge the traditional by seeking out answers to these questions in the cross-cultural literature. And if we discover that the research suggests that people are different from what is typically presented, I want to find better ways to understand those differences than are available today.

I offer this book to you, the readers, as a way to understand and appreciate cultural diversity and its influence on human behavior. In this book, there should be no right and wrong, no good and bad. In learning about others—in meeting the challenge of cultural diversity—our biggest challenge is within ourselves.

 # Glossary

cross-cultural approach   A viewpoint for understanding truth and principles about human behaviors across cultures.

cross-cultural research   Any type of research on human behavior that compares specific behaviors across two or more cultures. This approach is primarily concerned with testing the possible limitations of knowledge gleaned from one culture by studying people of different cultures.

culture-specific   A research finding considered to be true for some people of some cultures but not for others.

generalization   A research finding that is considered true for a larger group of people than those actually represented in the study or studies that produced the finding.

replication   A consistent finding that is obtained across a series of studies involving different methodologies or samples.

scientific philosophy   The need to evaluate our truths and principles against the parameters under which those truths were obtained.

universal   A research finding considered to be true for all people of all cultures.

2

Understanding Culture

What Is It?

Before embarking on the task of learning about cultural influences on behavior, it is important and useful to tackle the question of what the word *culture* means. Differences observed across studies and theories in various psychological disciplines are often related to differences in the usage of culture not only as a theoretical or explanatory concept but also as an empirical construct in research. A researcher's definition of culture, whether explicit or implicit, ultimately has an impact on how he or she views culture as influencing people's lives, and my own views are no exception. Thus, in presentations of cross-cultural material such as those found in this book, it is imperative to make explicit my own biases and definitions about the word *culture.*

One word of caution is in order here. When defining culture, as I will shortly attempt, it is almost unavoidable and inevitable that the discussion be oversimplified for the sake of making a clear presentation. Culture is a complex, dynamic, and fascinating phenomenon. Any attempt, the present one included, to reduce it to a definable, labeled construct demystifies that which is indeed mystic in the first place. While it is important to attempt such a definition, it is equally important to acknowledge at the outset that such attempts do not do justice to the complexity of culture in its fullest meaning.

A Definition of Culture

Common Usages of the Word *Culture*

We use the word *culture* in many different ways in everyday language and discourse. Sometimes we use the word *culture* to mean race, nationality, or ethnicity. For example, we often refer to people of African American ancestry as coming from African American culture, or Chinese people as coming from Chinese culture. We use the word *culture* to reflect trends in music or art. We use the word *culture* to refer to food or clothing. We use the word *culture* to refer to rituals, traditions, and heritage. In short, we use the word *culture* to mean many different things about people—physical and biological characteristics, behaviors, music, dance, and other activities.

In American English, *culture* has been used in many different ways. Kroeber and Kluckhohn (1952) and later Berry, Poortinga, Segall, and Dasen (1992) described six general categories in which culture is discussed:

- *Descriptive* uses highlight the different types of activities or behaviors associated with a culture.
- *Historical* definitions refer to the heritage and tradition associated with a group of people.
- *Normative* uses describe the rules and norms that are associated with a culture.
- *Psychological* descriptions emphasize learning, problem solving, and other behavioral approaches associated with culture.
- *Structural* definitions emphasize the societal or organizational elements of a culture.
- *Genetic* descriptions refer to the origins of a culture.

While these ways of using the word *culture* and talking about it may be true for American English, the word *culture* may have different meanings or emphases in other cultures. Used in the ways described above, culture has become increasingly fashionable in the United States in the last few years; we speak of cultural diversity, cultural pluralities, and multiculturalism in many avenues of life, including school and the workplace. People of other cultures, however, do not necessarily envision culture the way we do. If you refer to culture in Japan, for instance, a Japanese person may first think of flower arranging or a tea ceremony rather than the aspects of culture we would normally associate with the word. In this respect, our understanding and definition of culture is as much a product of American life and American science as it is a product of the world.

Still, all peoples of the world have culture. While learning about culture in this book, it is important to remember that this view of culture is only one view, and other cultures may have other views. As studies of culture and cultural differences have become popular in the last few years in the United States, we have assumed that our views and studies of culture are culture-free and universal, just because we happen to be studying it. Do not forget that our studies of culture and the ways in which we understand cultural influences on behavior conceptually (this book included) all stem from a particular view of culture—one that is rooted in American thinking and science.

Because we use *culture* to refer to so many different things about life, it is no wonder there is much confusion and ambiguity about it. We can get a better understanding of the complex nature of culture if we look at all the aspects of life referred to by the word *culture*.

Aspects of Life Touched on by Culture

Culture is used in so many different ways because it touches on many aspects of life. In an early work, Murdock, Ford, and Hudson (1971) described 79 different aspects of life that culture had something to do with. This list was rearranged by Barry (1980) into eight broad categories of life activities, which were also reported by Berry et al. (1992). These eight categories are:

- general characteristics
- food and clothing
- housing and technology
- economy and transportation
- individual and family activities
- community and government
- welfare, religion, and science
- sex and the life cycle

These broad categories make it very clear that culture is a complex concept that can be found in many aspects of life and living. Some of these aspects refer to material things, such as food and clothing. Some refer to societal and structural things, such as government organization and community structure. Some refer to individual behaviors. Some refer to reproduction. Some refer to organized activities, such as religion and science.

Culture, in its truest and broadest sense, cannot simply be swallowed in a single gulp (Malpass, 1993)—not in this book, not in a university course, not in a training program. Although I will attempt to bring you closer to a better understanding of what culture is and how it influences our lives, we must begin by recognizing and admitting the breadth and scope and enormity of culture. Culture cannot possibly be contained within the pages of a book or the confines of a university semester or quarter. Culture, in all its richness and complexity, is huge.

Culture as an Abstraction

How can we get a better handle on culture? Culture refers to so much of life and living. Yet, can you see it? Can you feel it? The answer to these questions is "no." Culture cannot be seen or felt or heard or tasted. What is concrete and observable to us is not culture per se but the differences in human behavior we see in actions, thoughts, rituals, traditions, and the like. We see the *manifestations* of culture, but we never see culture itself.

For example, look at the cultural differences in greeting behaviors. In American culture, we learn to shake hands when we greet others, and handshaking has become ritualistic and automatic for many of us. Yet, people of other cultures have different ways of greeting people. People of some cultures, for example, greet each other with a slight bow of the head. Some cultures encourage this bow with hands together in front as in prayer. Some cultures encourage a bow from the waist with the face lowered out of sight. Some cultures engage only in an eyebrow flash. We can witness these actions, and many other behavioral manifestations of culture, but we never see culture itself. Instead, we infer that a cultural difference underlies these various behaviors and that because the culture is different the behaviors are different. I have used culture as an explanatory concept to describe the reason we see differences in behaviors such as greetings.

In this sense, culture is an abstract concept. It is a theoretical or conceptual entity that helps us understand why we do the things we do and explains the differences in the behaviors of different groups of people. As an abstract concept, culture is not much more than a label. But like many labels it has a life of its own. Just as similarities within groups and differences between groups give rise to what we know as culture as an abstract concept, that abstract concept feeds back on those behaviors, reinforcing our understanding of those similarities and differences. Culture, in whatever way we come to know it, helps to reinforce, promulgate, and strengthen the behavioral similarities and differences that produced it in the first place, producing a cycle of reciprocity between actual behaviors and our theoretical understanding of them as culture (see Figure 2.1).

This reciprocal relationship helps to explain why we are taught to do many things simply because "that is the way they have always been done and it is how they should be done." Learning to eat a certain way, with a certain etiquette, with certain foods, with certain utensils, in a certain order, simply because "that's the way things are done" is just one of many examples of how the abstract concept of culture drives behaviors. Engaging in those behaviors, of course, further reinforces these aspects of culture. It is in this fashion that culture and actual behaviors share a close, intimate relationship. While it may appear throughout this book that culture is an abstract theoretical concept

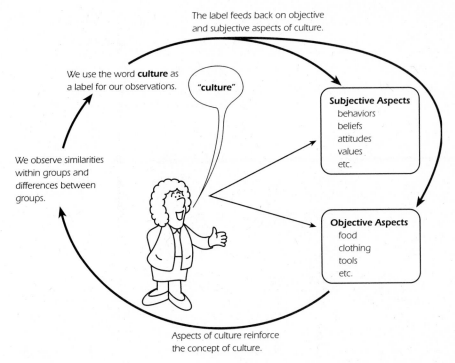

Figure 2.1 Cycle of reciprocity: Observing, labeling, feedback, and reinforcing. When something is labeled *culture,* it *becomes* culture; then the culture reinforces the label.

that sits above people and mysteriously influences our behavior, that is not the case. As an explanatory concept that people have created, culture shares a close relationship with behaviors.

Interestingly, changing behaviors will necessarily force a change in culture. Because culture is a concept we produce to help us explain actual behaviors, a discrepancy between behavior and culture produces tension in this relationship that often leads to a change in culture. Therefore, as your behaviors change during the course of your life, however slightly, these changes may be related to changes in culture within yourself and across people of the same generation. Differences in behaviors between younger and older generations surely signal differences in the underlying culture of these two groups and contributes to what we call the "generation gap."

In fact, it is probably safe to say that there is always some degree of discrepancy between behaviors mandated by culture and the abstract concept of culture. That is, there is never a one-to-one correspondence across people in the behaviors mandated by an underlying culture and the actual behaviors that occur. Instead, there will always be some degree of discrepancy, however small, between behaviors and culture, despite their close and intimate relationship. Thus, there is always a dynamic tension in this relationship. In this sense, even as an abstract concept or principle, culture is never a static entity. It is always dynamic and changing, existing within a tensive relationship with the actual behaviors it is supposed to explain and predict. In fact, the degree of tension between culture as an underlying construct and the behaviors that it mandates may be an important aspect of culture itself. Some cultures may be characterized by a high degree of tension, while others may be characterized by relatively less tension. This difference in the degree of tension is most likely related to Pelto's (1968) distinction of tight versus loose societies.

A Definition of Culture for This Book

Given the enormity of culture, how are we to study and understand it? The approach I have taken in researching the literature, in conducting my own research program involving cross-cultural issues, and in writing this book involves adopting a single definition of culture that I believe is most germane and relevant for its study in the context of understanding the influence of culture *to each person individually*. Even with these parameters (constraints may be a better word), culture is a rather difficult concept to define formally. For our purposes, I define **culture** as the set of attitudes, values, beliefs, and behaviors shared by a group of people, but different for each individual, communicated from one generation to the next.

This definition of culture is similar to Rohner's (1984) but differs in important ways. Two concepts in particular are central to this definition: first, sharing some aspects of life and behavior, and second, those things that are shared. By sharing, I refer to the degree to which individuals within a particular group have or hold the same value, attitude, belief, norm, or behavior. This does not necessarily refer to sharing in the physical sense; rather, this sharing refers to a psychological sharing of an attribute among members of the culture.

The attributes that are shared are the second crucial part of this definition. Again, these are not necessarily physical, observable attributes. This definition of culture does not refer to sharing tools, homes, utensils, or other physical objects. It does not refer to sharing physical attributes, such as skin color, facial morphology, and the like. It does not refer to sharing of citizenship or living space within a particular area or region. Rather, it is the sharing of ideas, attitudes, values, beliefs—the contents of the minds of each and every individual who lives in that culture. Moreover, not only are these ideas in the minds of people, but they also exist as a social conscious-ness above and beyond each and every individual. The behaviors that are shared are indeed observable and are often seen in rituals or common, au-tomatic behavior patterns that arise because of shared cultural values and norms for behavior.

This definition of culture is "fuzzy." By that I mean that there are no hard and fast rules of how to determine what a culture is or who belongs to that culture. In this sense, culture is a sociopsychological construct, a sharing across people of psychological phenomena such as values, attitudes, beliefs, and behaviors. What distinguishes members of the same culture is whether they share these psychological phenomena. What separates members of one culture from another is the absence of these shared phenomena.

It is also useful to distinguish what this definition of culture clearly does not refer to. This definition of culture is not rooted in biology; that is, cul-ture is not race. Two people of the same race can share the same values and behaviors (culture), or they can be very disparate in their cultural makeups. It is true that people of the same racial heritage may share the same social-ization processes and may be **enculturated** in similar ways. When we speak of a Hispanic culture or an African American culture or an Asian culture, our conceptions of those groups may be quite accurate. But it is also true that there need not be a one-to-one correspondence between race and culture. Just because you are born a certain race does not necessarily mean you adopt the culture that is stereotypic of that race. Culture is learned behavior.

As a side note, it is also important to realize that race is not as clear a con-cept as many people think it is. Confusion abounds about whether race is even real and, if so, whether it is biologically rooted and genetically encoded. Even among scholars who acknowledge the existence of race, there is con-troversy as to how many "basic" races exist—two, three, four, or five—their origins, and their associated biological differences. Much less clear, of course, are the psychological characteristics associated with such differences. (See Yee, Fairchild, Weizman, & Wyatt, 1993, and Zuckerman, 1990, for some excel-lent discussion on this issue; see also Betancourt and Lopez, 1993, for a dis-cussion of the implications of using the terms *culture, race,* and *ethnicity* interchangeably.)

Culture is not nationality. Just because a person is from France, for ex-ample, does not necessarily mean that he or she will act in accordance with what we would consider the dominant French culture or with our stereo-types of French people. Just as culture does not necessarily conform to race or racial stereotypes, culture does not necessarily conform to nationality or citizenship. In fact, there is ample and growing evidence to suggest that a small but substantial portion of the population in many countries does not "match" the dominant cultural stereotype of that country (Triandis, 1992).

Culture as an Individual Construct
and as a Social Construct

We speak of the culture of a group as if it were a single, unitary concept true for all members of that group in exactly the same ways. When we speak of the Middle Eastern culture, for example, we often assume that all the people that have roots in the Middle East are relatively homogeneous with regard to some psychological trait, characteristic, or behavior. This assumption is also prevalent in cross-cultural research. When a study compares people from the United States, Brazil, and Puerto Rico, there is an implicit assumption that the individuals within the groups are relatively homogeneous. (I will discuss this topic more fully in Chapter 4.) There is little doubt that this must be true at some level; that is, in the definition given here, culture is relevant for all members of the group that comprise that culture. But the definition of culture adopted in this book also suggests more than a single, unitary concept that is inflexible across people. The definition of culture used here suggests that culture is as much an individual, psychological construct as it is a social construct. To some extent, culture exists in each and every one of us individually as much as it exists as a global, social construct. Individual differences in culture can be observed among people in the degree to which they adopt and engage in the attitudes, values, beliefs, and behaviors that, by consensus, constitute their culture. If you act in accordance with those shared values or behaviors, then that culture resides in you; if you do not share those values or behaviors, then you do not share that culture.

While the norms of any culture should be relevant to all the people within that culture, it is also true that those norms will be relevant in different degrees for different people. It is this interesting blend of culture in anthropology and sociology as a macroconcept and in psychology as an individual construct that makes understanding culture difficult but fascinating.

Our failure in the past to recognize the existence of individual differences in constructs and concepts of culture has undoubtedly aided in the formation and maintenance of stereotypes. Stereotypes are generalizations about the culture of a group of people that we impose on the individuals within that group. (Chapter 7 has a more complete discussion on this topic.) There is often some bit of truth to stereotypes. But they are also often wrong because individuals within a culture may not all harbor those cultural values and norms to the same degree.

Culture versus Personality

The fact that there can be individual differences in culture leads to an interesting question: What is the difference between culture and personality? Some people may ask, "If culture exists as a psychological phenomenon, and if different people harbor it to different degrees, then aren't we really talking about personality and not culture?" The definition of culture I have adopted does indeed have some similarities to personality. The fact that I have defined culture as a sociopsychological phenomenon blurs the distinction between culture and personality. Many personality traits are sociopsychological in nature. Also, the fact that culture is an abstract phenomenon and is not based on physical characteristics or national citizenship contributes to this ambiguity. And the fact that culture, as defined here, can be different for different people contributes to this ambiguity. Many attributes shared across members of a cultural group are psychological in nature and are common referents in discussions of personality as well.

But, there are important distinctions between my definition of culture and what is traditionally considered personality. The first has to do with the fact that culture is a conglomeration of attributes that are shared with other members of a cultural group. Although there can be individual differences in the degree to which members of a cultural group harbor those attributes, existence of the attribute is true for all members of the group. This is not necessarily true for personality traits, which by definition refer to individual differences in traits across people and not to differences in the degree to which an attribute is shared.

A second important distinction between my definition of culture and that of personality concerns the stability of culture. An important aspect of culture is stability, as defined by cross-generational education and transmission of cultural values and behaviors. Parents, extended families, and peers serve as human socialization and enculturation agents across generations, ensuring that rituals, customs, beliefs, and norms are communicated to younger generations in much the same way as they were learned before. Schools, businesses, government agencies, laws, and the like serve as institutional agents in enculturation and fill the same role toward similar outcomes as do human agents. Consequently, there is a great deal of consistency in culture across time (albeit concomitant with the ever-present tension between culture-behavior relationships). This is not necessarily true for personality traits. Personality is usually discussed in terms of traits or attributes of individual people within their own lifetimes.

A final distinction between culture and personality revolves around the existence of culture as a macroconcept, a social phenomenon. As discussed earlier, not only does culture exist in each and every individual but it also exists as a social phenomenon, a label depicting the programmed patterns of life we have learned and become accustomed to. As such, culture as a social label has a life of its own, and feeds back to and reinforces the behaviors it influences. These behaviors then feed back onto the social label of culture, so that the label is reinforced as well. Culture has a cyclical nature between its properties as a social label and individual behaviors amongst its members.

Concepts of personality do not share commonality with social labeling, nor with the cyclical nature of a social label (although it can be said that a personality label can cycle with individual behaviors and vice versa).

While there are several commonalities between my concept of culture and that of personality, there are also important distinctions between them. Having a clearer picture of those similarities and differences is important for improving our understanding of both concepts.

Pancultural Principles versus Culture-Specific Differences: Emics and Etics

One way of conceptualizing principles in cross-cultural studies is by using the concepts of *emics* and *etics*. These terms define the tension that often exists when studying cultures and cultural differences. **Etics** refer to aspects of life that appear to be consistent across different cultures; that is, etics refer to universal or pancultural truths or principles. **Emics**, in contrast, refer to aspects of life that appear to be different across cultures; emics, therefore, refer to truths or principles that are culture-specific. These terms originated in the study of language (Pike, 1954), with phonetics referring to aspects of language and verbal behaviors that are common across cultures, and phonemes referring to aspects of language that are specific to a particular culture and language. Berry (1969) was one of the first to use these linguistic concepts to describe universal versus culturally relative aspects of behavior.

The concept of emics and etics is powerful because of their implications for what we may know as truth. If we know something about human behavior and we regard it as a truth, and it happens to be an etic (that is, universal) trait, then the truth as we know it is truth for all, regardless of culture. If that something we know about human behavior and regard as truth happens to be an emic (that is, culture-specific) trait, then what we regard as truth is not necessarily what someone from another culture regards as truth. In fact, these truths may be quite different. In this sense, truth is relative, not absolute. This definition of truth should force us all to reconsider what we believe is true and not.

There are many examples of emics and etics in cross-cultural studies. Indeed, one of the major goals of the study of cultures is to uncover exactly which aspects of human behavior are emic traits and which are etic traits. One fundamental and important point to remember when studying cultural differences in people and across cultural groups is that there are both etics and emics in the world.

Most cross-cultural psychologists would agree that there are just as many, if not more, emics as there are etics. That is, people of different cultures actually do find ways to differ with respect to most aspects of human behavior. In some sense, this is not surprising. Each culture evolves in its own distinctive way to "manage" human behaviors in the most efficient and appropriate fashion to ensure survival. The options chosen will differ depending on population density, availability of food and other resources, affluence, and what not. To the extent that each culture must meet different needs in the physical and social environment, each culture will develop different ways to address those needs. These choices are expressed as emic aspects by people within that culture.

That being said, it is also probably true that there are many more similarities between people from different cultures than we might think. In particular, there are considerable similarities between people of different cultures on the level of intention, good will, and the like. There can be many behavioral manifestations of these similar underlying constructs, which is what we observe in everyday discourse and what we tend to focus on in our thinking about culture and diversity because of their observability.

As described above, etics and emics refer to the tension between what we know of as universal versus culture-specific truths about the world. In other books and other classes, you may hear these constructs discussed in terms of universalism versus cultural relativism. Regardless of the jargon used, it is important to recognize that these ideas represent opposite poles with regard to human behavior, with universality on one pole and cultural relativity on the other. Unfortunately, when we polarize important concepts, there is a tendency to take an either-or approach to understanding differences. When observing behaviors and trying to interpret them, we often try to put them into either the etic or emic categories. This categorization process itself may be culture-bound, and the search for the one category to which we can classify some behaviors may reflect more of a Western or rather an American way of thinking. This way of thinking, or cognitive process, may have its roots in the American individualistic cultural value of searching for uniqueness in ourselves and translating that search to other objects and events in our environment.

There is another way of thinking, however, that may be more productive for understanding cultural influences on human behavior. Instead of considering whether any behavior we observe is etic or emic, we can ask how that behavior can be both etic and emic at the same time. Perhaps parts or aspects of that behavior are etic and other parts are emic. For example, suppose you are having a conversation with a person from a culture different from yours. While you talk to this person, you notice that she does not make eye contact with you when she speaks, and she does not look at you when you speak. On the few occasions when her eyes look your way, her gaze is quickly averted somewhere else when your eyes meet. From your cultural background, you may interpret that she does not feel very positive about you or your interaction. You may even begin to feel put off and reject any attempts at future interaction. You may not feel trusting or close to her. But she may come from a culture where direct gazing is discouraged or even a sign of arrogance or slight. She may actually be avoiding eye contact not because of any negative feelings but because of deference and politeness to you. Of course, these behavioral differences have real and practical implications in everyday life; think about this scenario occurring in a job interview, in a teaching-learning situation at an elementary school, at a business negotiation, or even in a visit with your therapist.

If we examine this behavior from an etic-emic polarity, we will undoubtedly come to the conclusion that gaze behavior must be a cultural emic; that is, cultures have different rules regarding the appropriateness of gazing at others when interacting with them. But, let's ask ourselves another question: Is there any aspect about this behavior that can be described as etic? The answer to this question may lie in the causes or roots of the cultural differences in the gaze. In the example described here, your partner wanted to show deference or politeness to you. Thus, she enacted gaze behaviors that were dictated by her cultural background in accordance with the underlying wish to be polite. If you are an American, your culture would have dictated a different gaze pattern, even with the same wish for politeness. Your culture dictates that you look your partner straight in the eye when talking and show interest and deference by looking directly at them when they speak. It is only the outward behavior manifestation that is different between the representatives of the two cultures however; the underlying reason is exactly the same. Thus, while the outward behaviors we can observe may rightly be called emic, the inner attributes that underlie those behaviors may in fact be etic.

It is in this way that etics and emics can coexist in relation to our behaviors. Our understanding of cultures and cultural influences on behavior will be vastly improved if we avoid tendencies to compartmentalize behaviors into one or the other category and, instead, search for ways in which any given behavior actually represents both tensions.

An Introduction to Ethnocentrism and Stereotypes

The existence of many emics, or cultural differences, is not problematic in and of itself. There is potential for problems, however, when we attempt to interpret the meaning underlying or producing those differences. Because we all exist in our own cultures with our own cultural backgrounds, we tend to see things through that background. Culture acts as a filter, not only when perceiving things but also when thinking about and interpreting events. We may interpret someone else's behavior from our own cultural background and come to some conclusion about that behavior based on our own beliefs about appropriate behavior. Our interpretation may be wrong, however, if the behavior we are judging originates from a different cultural orientation than our own. In some cases (more often than we all think), we may be way off in our interpretation of other people's behavior.

We do not always have the ability to separate ourselves from our own cultural background and bias so we can understand the behavior of others. This type of resistance forms the basis of what is known as **ethnocentrism**— viewing and interpreting the behavior of others through our own cultural filters. All people need to be aware of these biases and tendencies to understand the behavior of others of different cultural backgrounds.

Ethnocentrism is closely related to another important topic, stereotypes. **Stereotypes** are generalized attitudes, beliefs, or opinions about people who belong to cultures other than our own. Stereotypes may be grounded in fact but are often combinations of fact and fiction about people from a particular cultural group. Stereotypes are handy in helping people have a basis for judging, evaluating, and interacting with people of other cultures—an outline or framework of some sort—but they can be very dangerous and damaging when people adhere to them inflexibly and apply them to all people of that cultural background without recognizing the possible false basis of the stereotype as well as individual differences within that culture.

We often find that we are different from people of other cultures, either through research or through our everyday interactions and experiences. Our discovery of these differences can have severe and serious negative consequences. The potential for misuse occurs when values such as good-bad, right-wrong, and superior-inferior are attached to the behaviors of others that are different from our own expectations of appropriate behavior. Emics, etics, ethnocentrism, and stereotyping are all important concepts to learn about and remember when trying to understand the behavior of others. Indeed, Chapter 6 on intergroup relations is devoted exclusively to these topics. As you progress and learn more about cultural similarities and differences, it is important to have some idea of the potential pitfalls in this endeavor. Needless to say, making value statements and maintaining an inflexible ethnocentric attitude are not conducive to progress in this field.

A Dimensional Approach to Understanding Cultures

The definition of culture adopted in this book has no distinct biological or geographical boundaries. It is, in fact, a definition of culture that focuses on *subjective* rather than *objective* aspects of culture (Triandis, 1972). This focus on the subjective aspects of culture allows us to go beyond typical anecdotal or impressionistic approaches to understanding culture—more precisely, it *forces* us to do so.

If culture is more accurately represented by psychological markers, it may be possible to search for stable and meaningful sociopsychological dimensions to characterize cultures. If found, we can use them to understand cultural similarities and differences in behavior. If we can measure them, cross-cultural studies can address more sophisticated theoretical questions posed by our improved understanding of culture. Should such a measure of culture exist, then we can break free, to some degree at least, from the lock that stereotypes and anecdotes, derived from a reliance on country and race definitions, have on cross-cultural research.

The Search for Meaningful Dimensions of Cultural Variability

Many scholars have searched for meaningful dimensions of culture and provide a number of alternatives. The best-known dimension of cultural variability is arguably **individualism-collectivism** (IC). Anthropologists, sociologists, and psychologists alike have used this dimension to explain differences between cultures (Hofstede, 1980; Kluckholn & Strodtbeck, 1961; Mead, 1961; Triandis, 1972). IC refers to the degree to which a culture encourages, fosters, and facilitates the needs, wishes, desires, and values of an autonomous and unique self over those of a group. Members of individualistic cultures see themselves as separate and autonomous individuals. Members of collectivistic cultures, however, see themselves as fundamentally connected with others (Markus & Kitayama, 1991a). In individualistic cultures, personal needs and goals take precedence over the needs of others. In a collectivistic culture, individual needs are sacrificed to satisfy the group.

Other meaningful dimensions of cultural variability include work by Mulder (1976, 1977) and later Hofstede (1980, 1984) on **power distance** (PD), the degree of inequality in power between a less powerful individual (I) and a more powerful other (O). Matsumoto (1991) suggested a slightly modified version of PD called **status differentiation** (SD), the degree to which cultures maintain status differences among their members. Hofstede (1980, 1984) also proposed **uncertainty avoidance** (UA), the degree to which cultures develop institutions and rituals to deal with the anxiety concerning uncertainty and ambiguity, and **masculinity** (MA), the degree to which cultures foster traditional gender differences among their members. Pelto (1968) suggested that cultures could be classified along a dimension of **tightness**; that is, cultures were either "loose" or "tight" depending on the homogeneity within them. Hall (1966) suggested that cultures can be differentiated along a dimension of **contextualization**. High-context cultures, Hall argued, foster differential behaviors according to the specific context within which the behavior occurs. Low-context cultures, however, minimize differences in behavior due to context.

By far, most of the cross-cultural research and theorizing using a dimensional approach has focused on individualism-collectivism. This focus on IC is interesting in and of itself and may represent a bias among American researchers working and thinking in an American system and studying a concept so important to American culture—individualism—and its counterpart, collectivism.

Theoretical work on individualism-collectivism. There is already a considerable body of literature that demonstrates the theoretical relevance and empirical utility of the IC concept. Cultural dimensions such as IC are advantageous to theory and research because they can be used to predict and interpret cultural differences without relying on stereotypes, personal anecdotes, or impressions. Also, there is congruence in the conceptual understanding of IC across cross-cultural researchers around the world (Hui & Triandis, 1986). One of the best-known studies of IC was conducted by Hofstede (1980, 1984), who analyzed data from a questionnaire assessing IC tendencies to employees in an international corporation with sites in more than 50 countries. Each country was rank ordered by the degree to which people endorsed IC values. The United States, Australia, and Great Britain were the most individualistic. Pakistan, Colombia, and Venezuela were the most collectivistic (see Table 2.1).

Triandis, Bontempo, Villareal, Asai, and Lucca (1988) suggested that cultural differences on IC differ in self-ingroup versus self-outgroup relationships. (See Brewer and Kramer, 1985; Messick and Mackie, 1989; and Tajfel, 1982, for reviews of the ingroups-outgroups classification.) Individualistic cultures tend to have more ingroups. Because numerous ingroups are available to the individuals, members are not strongly attached to any single ingroup. Members of these cultures tend to drop out of groups that are too demanding, and their relationships within their groups are marked by a high level of independence or detachment. In collectivistic cultures, depending much more on the effective functioning of groups, a member's commitment to an ingroup is greater. Collectivists keep stable relationships with their ingroups no matter what the cost and exhibit a high level of interdependence with members of their groups. I will discuss this topic more fully in Chapter 8 on social behavior.

Triandis and colleagues (Triandis, Leung, Villareal, & Clack, 1985) have argued that IC orientations for individuals are both setting-specific and group-specific. They argue that collectivism must be viewed as a syndrome

Table 2.1 IC Scores across Countries in Hofstede's Study

Country	Actual IDV	Country	Actual IDV
U.S.A.	91	Argentina	46
Australia	90	Iran	41
Great Britain	89	Brazil	38
Canada	80	Turkey	37
Netherlands	80	Greece	35
New Zealand	79	Philippines	32
Italy	76	Mexico	30
Belgium	75	Portugal	27
Denmark	74	Hong Kong	25
Sweden	71	Chile	23
France	71	Singapore	20
Ireland	70	Thailand	20
Norway	69	Taiwan	17
Switzerland	68	Peru	16
Germany (F.R.)	67	Pakistan	14
South Africa	65	Colombia	13
Finland	63	Venezuela	12
Austria	55		
Israel	54	Mean of 39 countries	
Spain	51	(HERMES)	51
India	48		
Japan	46	Yugoslavia (same industry)	27

Work goal scores were computed for a stratified sample of seven occupations at two points in time. Actual values and values predicted on the basis of multiple regression on wealth, latitude, and organization size.

Source: G. Hofstede, *Culture's Consequences: International Differences in Work-Related Values*, p. 158. Copyright © 1980 Sage Publications. Reprinted by permission of Sage Publications, Inc.

relating to interpersonal concern rather than as a unitary disposition. The results from Triandis et al.'s (1988) study on IC values in the United States, Japan, and Puerto Rico support this position.

Empirical work on individualism-collectivism. Many studies demonstrate the utility of IC to explain cultural differences in behavior. For example, IC has been used to predict cultural differences in the expression, perception, and antecedents of emotion (Gudykunst & Ting-Toomey, 1988; Matsumoto, 1989, 1991; Wallbott & Scherer, 1988). Gudykunst et al. (1992) used IC to understand cultural differences in self-monitoring and predicted outcome value on communication in ingroup and outgroup relationships in four cultures. In the same vein, Lee and Boster's (1992) study demonstrated the dif-

ferential effects of speech rate on perceptions of speaker credibility in individualistic and collectivistic cultures.

Georgas (1989, 1991) used the IC dimension to explain changes in family
values in Greece. He found that the current transition of Greece from an ag-
ricultural, merchant economic society with an extended family system to an
industrialized, service-oriented society "is accompanied by the rejection of
collectivistic values and the gradual adoption of individualist values" (p. 90).

Hamilton, Blumenfeld, Akoh, and Miura (1991) compared teaching
styles in American and Japanese elementary classrooms. American teachers
directed their instruction toward individuals during both full class instruction and private study time. Japanese teachers, however, consistently addressed the group as a collective. Even when children were working individually, the Japanese teachers checked to make sure all of the children were
working on the same task.

Leung (1988) used IC to compare the United States and Hong Kong on
conflict avoidance. People rating high on collectivism were more likely to
pursue a dispute with a stranger, and Leung concluded that the cultural differences found were consistent with previous conceptualizations of IC.

These works highlight the importance of individualism-collectivism in
conceptualizing, predicting, and explaining cultural similarities and differences. A number of researchers have even gone beyond identifying the IC
concept in understanding cultural differences—they have developed ways of
measuring it.

Measuring individualism versus collectivism. Historically, when researchers
studied cultures, they generally adopted one of two approaches—ethnography or cross-culture comparison. **Ethnographies** are in-depth examinations
of a single culture that typically involve immersion of a researcher in that culture for an extended period of time. **Cross-cultural comparisons** generally involve sampling of individuals from at least two cultural groups, measuring some behavior of interest in both groups, and comparing the behaviors
between those groups. While ethnographies were common in anthropology,
cross-cultural comparisons have been very common in psychology and, to a
lesser extent, sociology. In recent years, there has been an interesting merging of research approaches across disciplines, with an increasing number of
scientists adopting comparative techniques for use in single-culture immersion research and comparative researchers adopting qualitative ethnographic
methods to bolster their traditional quantitative approach.

One of the major concerns in cross-cultural comparisons has been how
researchers defined and measured culture in their research. Most cross-
cultural studies **operationalize** culture by country. Samples from the United
States, Japan, Germany, and France usually constitute our cross-cultural

samples. Most studies are not actually cross–country studies; they are cross–city studies (for example, San Francisco versus Tokyo versus Frankfurt versus Paris). Also, many samples are really samples of convenience, meaning that the researcher has a friend in a university in these cities who will collect data for the project. Because many studies are conducted this way, researchers often have to resort to stereotype, impression, or anecdote to interpret observed differences.

One of the best-known attempts to measure IC came from Hofstede's (1980, 1984) study of IBM employees. His survey consisted of 126 questions clustered around four major themes: satisfaction, perception, personal goals and beliefs, and demographics. Hofstede's IC measurement method, however, was not designed to generate scores for individuals (this was not the purpose of his study); rather, countries were the unit of analysis. In comparative research, it is important to have a measure of IC on the level of the individual because we deal with a relatively small number of people in a cultural sample. By examining the influence of culture at the individual level, we can characterize a psychological culture underlying the samples in our research and examine its influence on other aspects of human behavior.

The most concerted effort to develop such a measure has been that of Triandis and his colleagues. Triandis and Hui (Hui, 1984, 1988) developed the INDCOL (individualism-collectivism, or IC) scale to measure an individual's IC tendencies in relation to six collectivities (spouse, parents and children, kin, neighbors, friends, and coworkers and classmates). This measure asks subjects to respond to seven key questions, each addressing a separate but theoretically important aspect of IC (for example, sharing or collective responsibility). This measure has been used with some degree of success.

A multimethod approach to measuring the degree of IC was compiled by Triandis, McCusker, and Hui (1990). Triandis and colleagues view IC as a cultural syndrome that cuts across values, beliefs, attitudes, and behaviors rather than as a single, unitary concept or tendency. Consequently, their comprehensive measure assesses each of these areas and includes methods taken from previous researchers, including Hui's INDCOL (1984) and value items suggested by Schwartz and Bilsky (1987). Triandis and colleagues' measure combines five methods, spanning social content of the self, value item ratings, and perceptions of social behavior as a function of social distance. Scores from each of the methods are combined to produce a single IC score for each person. On the individual level, Triandis et al. refer to individualism and collectivism as **idiocentric** and **allocentric** tendencies, respectively (Triandis et al., 1986).

One of the major advantages of the multimethod approach to IC measurement is its ability to measure IC tendencies in different psychological domains. This method combines IC tendencies across a wide range of phenomena in a single measurement technique. Still, it is important to be able to measure IC tendencies across different contexts as well in different psychological domains. Certainly, no single score can capture context-specific tendencies, either in terms of their conceptual implications or empirical applications. Indeed, as Triandis et al. (1988) have pointed out, IC differences should vary in different social contexts. People act differently depending on with whom they are interacting and the situation in which the interaction is occurring. A person could have collectivistic tendencies at home and with close friends and individualistic tendencies with strangers or at work, or vice versa. If a culture fosters collectivistic tendencies within self-ingroup relationships, it is unlikely that it would foster those same tendencies to the same degree in self-outgroup relationships. If it did, the meaning of collectivism, as defined by the ingroup-outgroup distinction, would be contrary to the fundamental definition of collectivism. This view of IC suggests the value of generating context-specific scores on IC rather than producing single scores collapsed across contexts. This view of IC also suggests that IC tendencies on the individual level should be understood as profiles of IC tendencies across contexts rather than as single scores that globally summarize IC tendencies.

Matsumoto and his colleagues (Matsumoto, Weissman, Preston, & Brown, 1995) have developed a measure of IC for use on the individual level that assesses context-specific IC tendencies. Their measure, called the IC Assessment Inventory (ICAI), includes a list of 25 items compiled from previous work on IC by Triandis et al. (1990), Hui (1984, 1988), and Schwartz and Bilsky (1987). The items are described in general value terms (for example, obedience to authority, social responsibility, sacrifice, and loyalty) rather than by specific statements tied to single actions. Universal values, such as love and security, are not included based on Schwartz's (1990) assertion that those "maturity" values serve both individualists and collectivists. The 25 items are presented in relation to four social groups of interactants: (1) family, (2) close friends, (3) colleagues, and (4) strangers. These four groups were selected based on their collective differences and the supposition that they maximized context-specific differences in a manageable number of contexts. All the items are rated twice, once in terms of general values as guiding principles for each person's behaviors and a second time in terms of the frequency of actual behaviors (see the box "Sample Items from the Individualism-Collectivism Assessment Inventory").

Matsumoto et al.'s (1995) ICAI measure has been used to demonstrate IC differences across different countries as well as across different ethnic groups within the United States. The availability of this measure and Triandis and colleagues' multimethod assessment technique described earlier clearly represent major advances for cross-cultural research and our understanding of the influence of cultural dimensions of variability on human behavior.

Sample Items from the Individualism-Collectivism Assessment Inventory (ICAI)

Below is a list of general descriptions of behavior. We want to know how important you believe each is as a *value* in relation to four social groups. Consider each of the descriptions as a general, hypothetical value. Also, consider the value separately in each of the four social groups. Please tell us how important each is in terms of being a *guiding principle* for you, regardless of whether you actually find yourself in these situations. Please make an attempt to answer each item.

Please use the following rating scale when giving your answers. Write the appropriate number in the space provided for each of the four social groups.

NOT IMPORTANT AT ALL						VERY IMPORTANT
0	1	2	3	4	5	6

	Family	Friends	Colleagues	Strangers
To comply with direct requests from	____	____	____	____
To maintain self-control toward	____	____	____	____
To share credit for accomplishments of	____	____	____	____
To share blame for failures of	____	____	____	____
To sacrifice your goals for	____	____	____	____
To sacrifice your possessions for	____	____	____	____
To compromise your wishes in order to act together with	____	____	____	____
To maintain harmonious relationships among	____	____	____	____

Source: "Context-Specific Measurement of Individualism-Collectivism on the Individual Level: The IC Assessment Inventory (ICAI)" by D. Matsumoto, M. Weissman, K. Preston, and B. Brown. Submitted for publication.

 Conclusion

Culture is an elusive, abstract concept that forms the basis for much of our understanding of life. It is the sum of all the learned ways of living that have been carried down from one generation to the next in the form of rituals, tra–

dition, heritage, and behaviors. Culture is the set of programmed responses that we and our ancestors before us have learned to adapt to our environment and to others around us in daily living. It is, in fact, the software of our minds.

While culture is one of the most important determinants and influences on our lives, it is probably the least thought of. We do not think about our culture every day, and we do not necessarily see culture. We see manifestations of our cultural heritage and that of others around us all the time, yet we do not readily stop to think about culture on a sociopsychological level even though culture helped to produce those similarities and differences we see around us. Because culture is invisible, we often latch onto other, more readily observable concepts to help us explain and understand people's behaviors. We may resort to using race or nationality to help us talk about behaviors that are affected by culture. These concepts are easier for us to use because they are observable; our minds can deal with this type of information more easily.

But focusing on the visible rather than the invisible has its limitations. By focusing solely on visible constructs like race or nationality to explain cultural differences, we lock ourselves into a pattern of understanding the world, a worldview, that is doomed to fail. Neither race nor nationality can explain the richness of the concept we know as culture. If we try to pigeonhole all of human behavior into fixed categories, we will find that much about life does not fit. Stereotypes and images cannot, and perhaps should not, cover the complexity of culture as a psychological phenomenon.

In the United States, it seems that there are two extremes when people talk about culture. On one hand, some people are desperately seeking culture—trying to find their roots, heritage, and tradition. On the other hand, some people consider culture as a foreign and irrelevant concept. To these individuals, culture is something that refers to groups and is shunned by many who reject the notion that groups can influence their behavior. American culture is characterized by a great deal of tension between culture-behavior relationships and the values related to concepts of culture.

Regardless of how we think about culture in our conscious, everyday lives, we cannot ignore the fact that much of our behavior is steeped in a tradition of culture, our own culture. For many people who reject the notion of culture, it is probably safe to say that their culture does not embrace notions of cultural heritage, of challenging traditions and the past. Interestingly enough, in challenging and rejecting culture, these people are indeed living their cultural mores and values.

The task of understanding culture and of understanding cultural influences on our own behavior is not an easy one. Remember that whenever you evaluate cultural influences, whether of your own or another culture, you look at those influences from your own cultural "eyes." An invisible filter exists that always influences how we perceive and evaluate things, regardless of whether we are aware of it or not. You are reading this text right now with that filter on and evaluating what I have to say with that filter. We make judgments about ourselves and others that are biased even though we are absolutely convinced that we are unbiased in making those judgments. For example, you may believe that you are rather interdependent or collectivistic, not independent and individualistic, and that your behaviors take social relations into account much more than your peers do. However, the culture in which you live may be, as a whole, more independent and individualistic than other cultures. While you are relatively interdependent within your own culture, you may still be very independent when viewed in comparison to the rest of the world. And yet you may absolutely believe that you are interdependent, because you cannot see the implicit standard of your own culture in relation to the standard provided by the rest of the world (see also Kitayama & Markus, in press b).

As you work through the rest of this book, it is important to consider the evidence provided about how cultures affect behaviors. But it is also important to pause and remember that we are thinking about these differences from the viewpoint of our own cultural biases and internal, implicit standards. Many years ago, Durkheim (1938/1964) wrote, "air is no less heavy because we do not detect its weight" (p. 5). Likewise, water is no less important to fish because they may not be aware of its existence. Culture is that air for us as water is for the fish.

 Glossary

allocentric   The collectivistic tendencies on the individual level.

contextualization   A cultural dimension that refers to the degree to which cultures foster differential behaviors according to the specific context within which those behaviors occur.

cross-cultural comparisons   A method of research that involves sampling individuals from at least two different cultural groups, measuring some behavior of interest in both groups, and comparing the behaviors between those groups.

culture   The set of attitudes, values, beliefs, and behaviors shared by a group of people, but different for each individual, communicated from one generation to the next.

emics   Aspects of life that appear to be different across cultures; truths or principles that are culture-specific.

enculturation   The process by which individuals learn and adopt the ways and manners of their culture.

ethnocentrism   Viewing and interpreting the behavior of others through your own cultural filter.

ethnographies   In-depth examinations of a single culture that typically involve immersion of a researcher in a culture for an extended period of time.

etics   Aspects of life that appear to be consistent across different cultures; universal or pancultural truths or principles.

idiocentric   Individualistic tendencies observed on the individual level.

individualism-collectivism   A dimension along which cultures differ that refers to the degree to which a culture encourages, fosters, and facilitates the needs, wishes, desires, and values of an autonomous and unique self over those of a group. In individualistic cultures, personal needs and goals take precedence over those of others. In a collectivistic culture, personal needs are sacrificed to satisfy the group.

masculinity   A cultural dimension that refers to the degree to which cultures foster traditional gender differences among its members.

operationalize   The way in which a variable in research is defined and measured.

power distance   A dimension along which cultures differ that refers to the degree to which cultures will foster or maintain inequality in power among people.

status differentiation   A cultural dimension that refers to the degree to which cultures maintain status differences among their members.

stereotypes   Generalized attitudes, beliefs, or opinions about people identified with or belonging to particular groups or cultures.

tightness   A cultural dimension that refers to the homogeneity within a culture.

uncertainty avoidance   A cultural dimension that refers to the degree to which cultures develop institutions and rituals to deal with the anxiety created by uncertainty and ambiguity.

3

Culture, Self, and Personality

The Influence of Culture on Our Sense of Self and Personality

While culture is generally considered a macrolevel construct, culture operates both on the social level and on the personal and individual level, as was discussed in Chapter 2. All of us operate in our worlds as individual agents of culture, bringing our implicit, underlying psychological culture to every situation, context, and interaction. We bring this culture to school, to work, and to meetings with our friends and family. It is a basic part of our selves. Because culture fulfills such a basic and fundamental role, it is important to examine exactly how culture plays that role in our lives. Because culture plays a major role in shaping our sense of self and identity, it has a pervasive influence on all our behaviors across all contexts. It is imperative that we go beyond the material presented in Chapter 2 that defined culture and examine how culture comes to play such a dominant role in shaping our core sense of self. Then we can explore how that sense of self, fundamentally interrelated with culture, affects our feelings, our thinking, and our motivations.

In psychology, the concepts we have been discussing here are related to self-concept, self-construal, and personality. Our sense of self and personality are important guides to understanding our own behavior as well as understanding and predicting the behavior of others. Personality is a core aspect of our being, a framework for understanding our relationships and our behaviors with others and with the environment.

In this chapter, we will explore how concepts about personality are different in different cultures. We will examine cultural differences in conceptions about the self in relation to others and look at cross-cultural research that has analyzed a variety of personality traits we deem important in the United States. In a final section this chapter, I will discuss indigenous personalities and how recognition of the existence of them is important to understanding cultural differences in personality. I hope you will come to a better understanding of how culture influences the fundamental, core nature of our selves and how we carry this core with us in our daily lives.

Culture and Concepts of Self

One of the most powerful and pervasive concepts in the social sciences in the United States is the **self-concept**. Scholars have wondered and written about the "self" for many years. We may not consciously think about our self very much, yet how we understand or construe our sense of self is intimately and fundamentally tied to how we understand the world around us and our relationships with others in that world. Whether conscious or not, our concept of self is an integral and important part of our lives.

Think about some descriptions of yourself. You may believe you are an optimist or a pessimist, extroverted or introverted. These descriptive labels supposedly describe something about ourselves, and in fact, we use these labels as shorthand descriptions to characterize ourselves. Suppose a young woman tells you she is "sociable." An array of underlying meanings are attached to this description that go beyond just this single word. Descriptions like this usually imply (1) that we have this attribute within us, just as we possess other attributes such as abilities, rights, or interests; (2) that our past actions, feelings, or thoughts have close connections with this attribute; and (3) that our future actions, plans, feelings, or thoughts will be controlled or guided by this attribute and can be predicted more or less accurately by it. In short, if someone describes herself as "sociable," we automatically know that her concept of self is rooted in and supported and reinforced by a rich repertoire of specific information concerning her own actions, thoughts, feelings, motives, and plans. As such, the concept of her self as "sociable" may be central to her self-definition, enjoying a special status as a salient identity (Stryker, 1986) or self-schema (Markus, 1977).

These assumptions about the meaning and importance of self are rooted in a particularly Western or individualistic way of thinking (see Chapter 2 for a review of the individualism versus collectivism distinction). In individualistic, middle-class culture, the self is seen as a bounded entity consisting of a number of internal attributes that include needs, abilities, motives, and rights.

Each individual carries and uses these internal attributes in navigating his or her thought and action in different social situations. A noted anthropologist, Clifford Geertz (1975), observed two decades ago that the self is seen as

> a bounded, unique, more or less integrated motivational and cognitive universe, a dynamic center of awareness, emotion, judgment, and action organized into a distinctive whole and set contrastively both against other such wholes and against a social and natural background. (p. 48)

As you can imagine, a sense of self is critically important and integral to how we view the world and ourselves and others in that world, including our relationships with other people, places, things, and events in that world. Americans have a certain sense of self, or self-construal, that influences their perception of the world. Our sense of self is at the core of our being, unconsciously and automatically influencing our every thought, action, and feeling.

What people actually mean and understand as the self is dramatically different in some other cultures. The sense of self we define in a predominantly individualistic American culture is not necessarily the same sense of self as that defined by other cultures, especially collectivistic ones. Just as our own sense of self has a powerful influence on our lives, the sense of self of people in other cultures influences their lives just as much. Our self-construals can be totally different from those of another culture. Yet, we do not think about these differences often because we are not very aware of our own sense of self and how much it influences our behavior. We only see these differences in the clashes that occur when people with different senses of self interact.

By raising the possibility that the individualistic concept of self may not make much intuitive sense to people of other cultures, I don't want to imply that students or experts in social psychology from other cultures fail to understand the notion of self as a theoretical concept in social psychology. To the contrary, they certainly can and do understand the notion as a theoretical construct. Yet the nature of their understanding is very different from that of the American undergraduate. People from other cultural backgrounds, particularly those in strongly collectivistic cultures, may understand Western concepts of self in the same way many Americans understand four-dimensional space. That is, they may understand the concept on a theoretical or cognitive level but have almost no experiential basis for that understanding. They don't feel that understanding emotionally.

In the remainder of this section, I will describe two fundamentally different senses of self. I will contrast the Western or individualistic construal of self as an independent, separate entity with a composite construal of self more common in many non-Western, collectivistic cultures, in which the individual is viewed as inherently connected or interdependent with others and inseparable from a social context. I will illustrate how these divergent forms of self are tied to differences in what people notice and think about, how they feel, and what motivates them (Markus & Kitayama, 1991b). Much of what is described in this section serves as a backdrop for material presented in later chapters. This general introduction provides a conceptual foundation upon which more specific information can then be built.

Of course, all cultures cannot be pigeonholed into one of these two categories, but we can use these categories as major guidelines along which cultures may foster substantial differences in the self-concept. Your job is to use these guidelines flexibly enough to understand different cultures and, more important, different people on their own bases rather than force them into conceptual categories based on theory alone.

An Independent Construal of Self

In the United States, standing out and asserting yourself is a virtue, so it is "the squeaky wheel that gets the grease." American politicians routinely credit their success to trusting their instincts, self-confidence, and the ability to make decisions and stick by them. In many individualistic cultures like ours, there is a strong belief in the separateness of individuals. The normative task in these cultures is to maintain the independence of the individual as a separate, self-contained entity.

In American society, many of us have been socialized to be unique, to express ourselves, to realize and actualize the inner self, to promote our own goals, and so on. These are the tasks provided by the culture for its members. These cultural tasks have been designed and selected throughout history to encourage the independence of each separate self. With this set of cultural tasks, our sense of self-worth or self-esteem takes on a particular form. When individuals successfully carry out these cultural tasks, they feel most satisfied about themselves and self-esteem increases accordingly. Under this **independent construal of self**, individuals focus on personal internal attributes—individual ability, intelligence, personality traits, goals, or preferences—expressing them in public and verifying and confirming them in private through social comparison. The independent construal of self is graphically illustrated in Figure 3.1. Self is a bounded entity, clearly separated from relevant others. Note that there is no overlap between the self and others. Furthermore, the most salient self-relevant information (indicated by bold Xs) are attributes thought to be stable, constant, and intrinsic to the self, such as abilities, goals, rights, and the like.

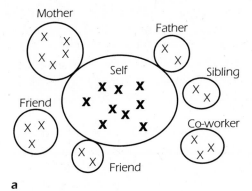

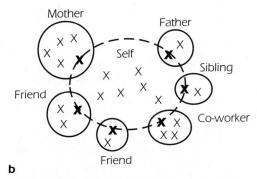

Figure 3.1 **(a)** Independent construal of self;
(b) interdependent construal of self

Source: "Culture and the Self: Implications for
Cognition, Emotion and Motivation," by H. Markus
and S Kitayama, 1991, *Psychological Review, 98,*
pp. 224–253. Copyright © 1991 American Psychological Association. Reprinted by permission of the
authors.

An Interdependent Construal of Self

Many non–Western, collectivistic cultures neither assume nor value overt
separateness. Instead, these cultures emphasize what may be called the "fundamental connectedness of human beings." The primary normative task is to fit
in and maintain the interdependence among individuals. Individuals in these
cultures are socialized to adjust themselves to an attendant relationship or a
group to which they belong, to read each other's minds, to be sympathetic, to

occupy and play their assigned role, to engage in appropriate actions, and the like. These cultural tasks have been designed and selected throughout history to encourage the interdependence of the self with others.

Given this construal of the self, self-worth, satisfaction, and self-esteem can have very different characteristics from those familiar to us. The self-esteem of those with interdependent construals of the self may depend primarily on whether they can fit-in and be part of a relevant ongoing relationship. Under this construal of self, individuals focus on their interdependent status with other people and strive to meet or even create duties, obligations, and social responsibilities. The most salient aspect of conscious experience is intersubjective, one rooted in finely tuned, interpersonal relationships. The **interdependent construal of self** is graphically illustrated in Figure 3.1b. The self is unbounded, flexible, and contingent on context. This is indicated by the substantial overlapping between the self and relevant others. The most salient information about the self (shown by bold *X*s) is aspects of the self in relationships, that is, those features of the self related to and inseparable from specific social contexts. This does not mean that those with interdependent selves do not have any knowledge about their internal attributes, such as personality traits, abilities, attitudes, and the like. They clearly do. However, these internal attributes are relatively less salient in consciousness and thus are unlikely to be the primary concerns in thinking, feeling, and acting.

Because of their collectivistic nature, many Asian cultures foster interdependent construals of self. In these cultures, if you stand out, you will most likely be punished; "the nail that sticks up shall get pounded down." In Japan, for example, political rhetoric sounds very different from that in the United States. A former vice prime minister of Japan once said that in his 30-year career in national politics he had given the most importance and priority to interpersonal relations. Similarly, Politics of Harmony was the sound bite a former Japanese prime minister used to characterize his regime in the 1980s.

Of course, considerable variation on independent versus interdependent construals of the self also occur within a single culture. People of different ethnicities within a culture, for example, may have different tendencies with regard to independent versus interdependent self-construals. Men and women may have different self-construals. Even within ethnic and gender groups, considerable variation in self-construals may, and often does, occur (Gilligan, 1982; Joseph, Markus, & Tafarodi, 1992). These intracultural differences are also important when considering cultural differences. In this chapter, I will describe general tendencies associated with independent and interdependent self-construals, acknowledging the limitations in representation within groups.

Consequences for Cognition, Motivation, and Emotion

Different concepts of self between cultures contributes to substantial cross-cultural differences in a variety of areas and behaviors. In this section, I will show how the two construals of the self affect our thinking, our feelings, and our behaviors. Cognitive, emotional, and motivational processes can vary dramatically with the construal of the self shared by a cultural group, and this has major implications for behavior.

Consequences for self-perception. Several studies (Bond & Tak-Sing, 1983; Shweder & Bourne, 1984) have shown how different self-construals are associated with differences in self-perception. In these studies, subjects wrote down as many of their characteristics as possible. Subjects typically generated several types of responses. One response type was abstract, personality-trait descriptions of the self, such as "I am sociable." Another response type was situation specific self-descriptions, such as "I am usually sociable with my close friends." Consistent with our knowledge of independent and interdependent selves, these studies show that American subjects tend to generate a greater number of abstract traits than do Asian subjects. These findings confirmed that people with an independent construal of self view their own internal attributes such as abilities or personality traits as the most salient, self-relevant information. Internal attributes are relatively less salient for those with interdependent selves who are more likely to think about the self in particular social relationships (for example, "me" with family members, or "me" with my boyfriend) or in specific contexts (for example, "me" in school, or "me" at work).

This, of course, does not mean that Americans have more knowledge about themselves than Asians or vice versa. Because the most salient information about self for the interdependent selves is context-specific, these individuals generally find it difficult or unnatural to state anything in abstract, noncontextual terms. Instead, those with interdependent selves are culture bound to define themselves in relation to context.

Consistent with this analysis, Triandis and colleagues (see Triandis, 1989, for a review) have shown that individuals from interdependent cultures (for example, China, Japan, and Korea) generate many more social categories, relationships, and groups to which they belong. Indeed, in a study done in the People's Republic of China, as many as 80% of all the responses given to the self-description task were about their memberships in a variety of different groups. This is a strong indication that specific relationships are very important for self-definition in this culture.

There is yet another interesting implication—interdependent people should be comfortable describing themselves in terms of abstract, internal attributes *once a specific context is specified*. Cousins (1989) provided evidence to support this analysis. He asked American and Japanese respondents to write down who they were in various specific social situations (for example, at home, in school, or at work). This instruction supposedly helped respondents to picture a concrete social situation, including who was there, what was being done to whom, and the like. The Japanese respondents generated a greater number of abstract internal attributes (for example, I am hardworking, I am trustworthy, or I am lazy) than did the Americans once the context was specified. American respondents tended to qualify their descriptions with phrases such as "I am more or less sociable at work" or "I am sometimes optimistic at home." It was as if they were saying that "this is how I am at work, but don't assume that this is the way I am everywhere." With this more contextualized task, the Americans may have felt awkward providing self-descriptions because their self-definitions typically are not qualified by specific situations.

Consequences for social explanation.   Self-construals also serve as a **cognitive template** for interpreting the behaviors of other people. (This process is related to the material on cultural differences in attributions in Chapter 8.) Those with independent selves assume that other people will also have a set of relatively stable internal attributes such as personality traits, attitudes, or abilities. As a result, when they observe the behavior of someone else, they draw inferences about the actor's internal state or disposition that supposedly underlies and even caused that behavior. Research done primarily in the United States supports these claims. For example, when subjects read an essay supporting Fidel Castro in Cuba (Jones & Harris, 1967), they inferred that the author must have a favorable attitude toward Castro. Furthermore, such dispositional inferences occur even when obvious situational constraints are present. The subjects in this study inferred a pro-Castro attitude even when they were explicitly told that the person was assigned to write a pro-Castro essay and no choice was given. The subjects ignored these situational constraints and erroneously drew inferences about the author's disposition. This bias toward inference about the actor's disposition even in the presence of very obvious situational constraints has been termed the **fundamental attribution error** (Ross, 1977).

Fundamental attribution error may not be as robust or pervasive among people of interdependent cultures as it is in people from independent cultures. People in interdependent cultures share assumptions about the self that are very different from those in Western cultures. This self-construal includes the recognition that what an individual does is contingent or dependent on and directed or guided by situational factors. These individuals are more inclined to explain another's behavior in terms of the situational forces impinging on the person rather than internal predispositions.

Miller (1984) examined patterns of social explanation in Americans and Hindu Indians. Both Hindu and American respondents were asked to describe either someone they knew well who did something good for another person or someone they knew well who did something bad to another person. After describing such a person, the respondents were asked to explain why the person committed that good or bad action. American respondents typically explained the behavior of their acquaintances in terms of general dispositions (for example, "She is very irresponsible"). Dispositional explanations, however, were much less common for the Hindus. Instead, they tended to provide explanations in terms of the actor's duties, social roles, and the like, which are by definition more situation-specific (see also Shweder & Bourne, 1984). The Hindu tendency toward situation-specific explanation did not depend on differences in social class or education. Thus, the situational, context-specific thinking common among Hindus was not due to an inability to reason abstractly (which has been suggested by some). Instead, the context-specific reasoning common in India seems to be due primarily to the cultural assumption of interdependence, a salient feature of Hindu culture. Given the interdependent construal of self, the most reasonable assumption to be made in explaining another's behavior is that this behavior is very much constrained and directed by situation-specific factors.

Consequences for achievement motivation. Western literature on motivation has long assumed that motivations are internal to the actor. A person's motives to achieve, affiliate, or dominate are salient and important features of the internal self—features that direct and energize overt behaviors. With an alternative, interdependent self-construal, however, social behaviors are guided by expectations of relevant others, felt obligations to others, or the sense of duty to an important group to which one belongs. This point is best illustrated by achievement motivation.

Achievement motivation refers to a desire for excellence. Such a desire, in this broad sense, is found quite widely across cultures (Maehr & Nicholls, 1980). In the current literature, however, desire for excellence has been conceptualized in a somewhat more specific manner—as individually or personally based rather than socially or interpersonally rooted. In two classic works in this area (Atkinson, 1964; McClelland, 1961), the desire for excellence is closely linked with an individual's tendency to push him- or herself ahead and actively strive for and seek individual successes. This notion of achievement, in fact, is congruent with the independent construal of the self shared widely in Western culture. From an alternative, interdependent frame, however, excellence may be sought to achieve broader social goals. These social forms of achievement motivation are more prevalent among those with an interdependent construal of the self. Interdependent selves have ever-important concerns that revolve around fully realizing the individual's connectedness with others. Thus, the nature of achievement motivation in these groups is quite different from that among those with independent construals of the self.

Yang (1982) distinguished between two forms of achievement motivation—individually oriented and socially oriented (compare with Maehr & Nicholls, 1980). Individually oriented achievement is commonly found in Western cultures such as the United States. It is for the sake of "me" personally that the individual strives to achieve. In Chinese society, however, socially oriented achievement is much more common. According to this form of achievement, the individual strives to achieve for the sake of relevant others such as family members. A Chinese student, for example, may work hard to gain admission to a prestigious university and then eventually to a top company. Behaviorally, there may be no difference between this Chinese individual and an American, who also strives to succeed both in school and at work. In the Chinese case, however, the ultimate goal in doing this may not be advancement of his or her personal career but rather a goal that is more collective or interdependent in character. Interdependent goals may include enhancing his or her family's social standing, meeting a felt expectation of family members, or satisfying his or her sense of obligation or indebtedness to the parents who have made enormous sacrifices to raise and support the student. In other words, the Chinese student's desire to achieve is much more socially rooted and does not necessarily reflect his or her desire to advance the quality or standing of "me" personally.

Supporting this notion, Bond (1986) assessed levels of various motivations among Chinese individuals and found that the Chinese show higher levels of socially oriented rather than individually oriented achievement motivation. Yu (1974) reported that the strength of the achievement motive in China is positively related to familism and **filial piety**. In fact, filial piety is a major social construct in many cultures influenced by Confucian and Buddhist teachings and philosophy, which tend to be more collectivistic than individualistic oriented. That is, those most strongly motivated to excel also take most seriously their duties and obligations to family members, especially to parents.

A similar observation is reported in Japan. K. Doi (1982, 1985) asked Japanese college students 30 questions designed to measure tendencies to persevere and pursue excellence (that is, achievement tendency). An additional 30 questions measured desires to care for and be cared by others (that is, affiliation tendency). The results suggested a very close association between achievement motivation and affiliation. Those high in achievement were also high in affiliation. This is in stark contrast to many Western findings, which indicate that these two dimensions of motivation are typically unrelated (cf. Atkinson, 1964). Both the Chinese study and the Japanese study indicate that achievement is closely related to people's social orientation of being connected and interdependent with important others in their lives.

Consequences for self-enhancement and effacement. We often hear how important it is to have a positive view of self. As early as four years of age, American children think they are better than most others. Wylie (1979) found that American adults typically consider themselves to be more intelligent and more attractive than average. In a national survey of American students, Myers (1987) found that 70% of the students thought they were above average in leadership ability; with respect to the ability to get along with others, 0% thought they were below average, and 60% thought they were in the top 10%. This tendency to *underestimate* the commonality of an individual's desirable traits has been called the **false uniqueness effect.** This effect appears to be stronger for males than for females in the United States (Joseph et al., 1992). It is one clear method of enhancing self-esteem. But is it true for people of different cultures?

Maintaining or enhancing the self may assume a different form for those with interdependent construals of self. Among those with interdependent selves, positive appraisals of the inner attributes of self may not be strongly linked with overall self-esteem or self-satisfaction. Instead, overall self-esteem or self-satisfaction are more likely to be derived from fulfilling roles of interdependence with others. Overall esteem or satisfaction about the self within an interdependent framework may result from the recognition that the individual is performing well in the cultural task of belonging, fitting in, engaging in appropriate action, promoting others' goals, maintaining harmony, and so on. It may also derive from the individual's capacity to regulate and coordinate his or her inner personal thoughts and feelings so they fit into the pursuit of interdependence with others. For the interdependent self, viewing yourself as unique or different would be unnecessary to maintain a sense of self-worth because the inner attributes of self contributing to an individual's perceived uniqueness are less self-defining. Being unique is undesirable, akin to being the nail that stands out, because it isolates the person from the ever-important relationship.

In an initial examination of cultural variation in the tendency to see the self as different from others, Markus and Kitayama (1991a) administered questionnaires containing a series of false uniqueness items to Japanese and American college students. The questions were in the form of: What proportion of students in this university have higher intellectual abilities than you? The questionnaire items were from one of three categories—abilities (intellectual, memory, and athletic), independence (independent, hold more

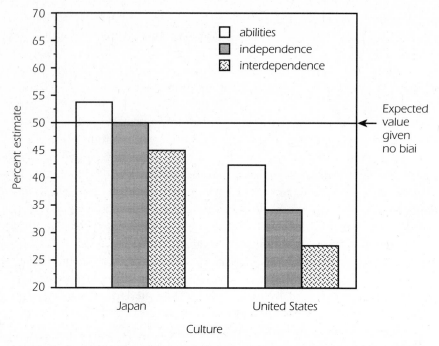

Figure 3.2 Estimates of the percentage of people who are better than oneself in three categories of behavior

Source: Data from H. R. Markus and S. Kitayama, "Cultural Variation in Self-Concept." In G. R. Goethals and J. Strauss (Eds.), *Multidisciplinary Perspectives on the Self* (New York: Springer-Verlag, 1991).

strongly to their own view), and interdependence (more sympathetic, more warmhearted). The data are summarized in Figure 3.2. The most striking aspect of these data is the marked difference between the Japanese and the American students in their estimations of their own uniqueness. American students assume that only 30% of people on average would be better than themselves on various traits and abilities. The Japanese students, however, showed almost no evidence of this false uniqueness. In most cases, they claimed that about 50% of students would be better than they are. You might suspect that these results occurred because the Japanese students tended to use 50% as their preferred answer. This was not the case; the variability in the data was virtually identical for both Americans and Japanese. This finding is typical and predictable for such a sample of college students evaluating themselves free of the need to establish their own uniqueness.

Consequences for the social connotation of emotion. Emotions can be classified into those that encourage the independence of the self from others from those that encourage interdependence with others (Kitayama, Markus,

& Matsumoto, 1995). Some emotions, such as pride or feelings of superiority, occur when you have accomplished your own goals or desires or have confirmed desirable inner attributes, such as intelligence and wealth. The experience of these emotions tends to verify those inner attributes. Similarly, some negative emotions, such as anger or frustration, result primarily from blocking your own internal attributes, such as goals or desires. When experienced, they highlight the fact that those inner goals or desires have been interfered with. In both cases, your inner attributes are made salient and contrasted against the relevant social context. These emotions tend to separate or disengage the self from social relationships. They also simultaneously promote the perceived independence of the self from the relationship. Kitayama, Markus, and Matsumoto (1995) have called these types of emotions **socially disengaged emotions.**

In contrast, other positive emotions, such as friendly feelings and feelings of respect, act very differently in this regard. These emotions result from being part of a close, more or less communal, relationship. Once experienced, they further encourage this interpersonal bond. Some types of negative emotions, such as feelings of indebtedness or guilt, act in a similar manner. These emotions typically result from failure to successfully participate in an interdependent relationship or from doing some harm to the relationship. Once experienced, you are motivated to restore the harmony in the relationship by compensating for the harm done or by returning your debt. These behaviors further engage and assimilate the self in the relationship and enhance the perceived interdependence of the self with relevant others. These emotions can be called **socially engaged emotions**.

All people experience both types of emotions. What is unique about these types of emotions is that people with interdependent self-construals typically experience socially engaged emotions differently from people with independent self-construals. These emotions may be more intense and internalized for the interdependent selves than for independent selves, because socially engaged emotions have different implications for interdependent selves than they do for independent selves. In contrast, those with independent self-construals may experience socially disengaged emotions internally and more intensely.

Consequences of social connotation and indigenous emotions. Although many emotions are common across cultures, others are relatively unique to particular cultures (Russell, 1991). These emotions are called **indigenous emotions.** Several anthropological studies have suggested that the social connotation of emotions I have just descried are salient in the organization of emotions in some non-Western cultures to a degree that is unheard of in the West. Lutz (1988) studied the emotions of people in the Micronesian atoll of Ifaluk and suggested that an emotion of *fago* is central in this culture. According to Lutz, *fago* can be roughly described as a combination of compassion, love, and sadness. This emotion is likely to motivate helping behaviors and to create and enhance close interpersonal relationships. In our terminology, *fago* is a highly socially engaged emotion. In contrast to *fago,* another emotion in Ifaluk, *ker,* translated as a combination of happiness and excitement, is perceived as "dangerous, socially disruptive" (p. 145). Ifaluk people regard *ker* as a highly socially disengaged emotion.

A similar analysis applies to another non–Western culture. T. Doi (1973) has suggested that the emotion *amae* is pivotal in understanding the Japanese culture. *Amae* refers to a desire or expectation for others' indulgence, benevolence, or favor. According to Doi, its prototypic form can be found in a mother-infant relationship, whereby the infant feels a desire for "dependency" on the mother and the mother provides much needed unconditional care and love to the infant. This prototype is subsequently elaborated to an adult form of *amae,* which is much more differentiated and sophisticated and is applicable to nonkin relationships, such as work relationships between a supervisor and his or her subordinates. Subordinates may feel *amae* toward the supervisor for his or her favor and benevolence. A reciprocal action from the supervisor would increase and consolidate the affectionate bond between them. The supervisor's refusal to do this could lead to negative emotions on both sides. As in the Ifaluk concept of *fago*, social engagement seems to define this emotion for the Japanese culture.

These anthropological studies fit well with the two construals of the self I have described here. For people with interdependent self-construals, public and intersubjective aspects of the self are elaborated in conscious experience. For those with independent selves, however, private and more subjective aspects are highlighted. Compare Figures 3.1 and 3.2. Because social connotation is a relatively public and intersubjective aspect of emotion, it is especially salient in the emotional experience of non-Western, interdependent people in collectivistic cultures. By contrast, in Western, individualistic cultures that foster independent senses of self, the more internal, private aspects of emotion, such as good and bad feelings or moods, may be more salient (Kleinman, 1988). This is true even though people of individualistic cultures recognize the social connotations of different emotions.

Consequences for happiness.   *Happiness* refers to the most generic, unqualified state of feeling good. Terms such as *relaxed, elated,* and *calm* are used to describe this generic, positive state. People across cultures share the general notion of happiness as defined in this way (Wierzbicka, 1986). However, the specific circumstances of happiness, and the meanings attached to it, depend crucially on the construal of the self as independent or as interdependent.

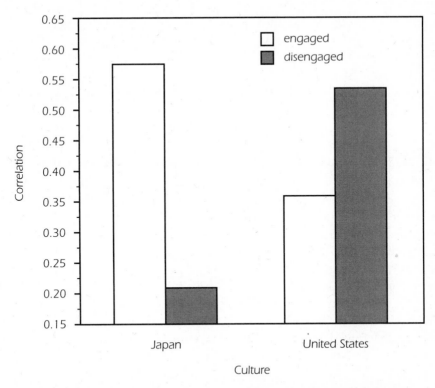

Figure 3.3 Cultural differences in the correlation between general positive feelings and engaged and disengaged emotions in the United States and Japan
Source: Data from S. Kitayama, H. R. Markus, M. Kurokawa, and K. Negishi, *Social Orientation of Emotions: Cross-Cultural Evidence and Implications* (unpublished manuscript, University of Oregon, 1993).

Kitayama, Markus, Kurokawa, and Negishi (1993) asked both Japanese and American college undergraduates to report how frequently they experience different emotions, including three types of positive emotions. Some terms used to describe the emotions were generic, such as *relaxed, elated,* and *calm.* Others had more specific social connotations either as socially engaged (such as, *friendly feelings, feelings of respect*) or disengaged (*pride, feelings of superiority*). An interesting cross-cultural difference emerged when correlations among these three types of emotions were examined (see Figure 3.3).

For the Americans students, generic positive emotions were associated primarily with experiencing the disengaged emotions. That is, those who experienced the emotions that signal success in cultural tasks of *independence* (socially disengaged emotions such as pride) were most likely to feel "generally good." This pattern was completely reversed among the Japanese students. Those who experienced the emotions that signal success in cultural tasks of *interdependence* (socially engaged emotions such as friendly feelings) were most likely to feel "generally good." The exact meanings or connotations of "feeling good" are shaped through culture and are linked very closely with the cultural imperatives of independence (in the United States) and interdependence (in Japan).

Summary

In this section we have discussed how cultures shape and mold fundamental, core aspects of our senses of self and how these self-construals have implications for the ways in which we think, feel, and act. Across cultures, the form of self varies considerably, as do various social phenomena and processes. Indeed, much of this entire book is based on this assumption. It is very important to examine carefully whether and to what extent various principles of understanding behavior, most of which have been advanced in the Western world, can travel across cultures to account for behaviors of people of other cultures. Self-construals provide a powerful framework for understanding and analyzing cultural differences in personality and their consequences for cognition, emotion, and motivation.

Culture and Personality Traits

In additions to studies of cultural influences on the self-concept and self-construals, another major area of cross-cultural research in psychology has focused on cultural similarities and differences in personality. As with self-concept, personality can be considered a core aspect of being and, as such, can be influenced by culture as a larger, social construct. Personality influences many behaviors across a wide range of contexts and also acts as a fundamental aspect of each individual. Research that examines cultural influences on personality should be of great interest in our quest for understanding human variation.

The first thing we need to do in examining the relationship between culture and personality is to understand the differences in definitions of personality. In American psychology, personality is generally considered to be a set of relatively enduring behavioral and cognitive characteristics and predispositions. We believe in a fundamental or "core" personality that people take with them to different situations and contexts and interactions with different people. Thus, in American psychology, personality is based on stability and consistency across contexts, situations, and interactions. This notion of personality has a long tradition in U.S. and European psychology. The psychoanalytic work of Freud and the neoanalytic approaches of Jung and Adler share this definition of personality. The humanistic approach of Maslow and Rogers, the trait approach of Allport, the behavioral approach of Skinner, and the cognitive approach of Rotter, Bandura, and Mischel also share this notion. While these approaches differ in their conceptions of how personality develops, there is consistency across them in what personality is and its fundamental nature and characteristics (that is, stable and enduring across contexts and situations).

Other cultures have different notions of personality. One particularly useful way of understanding these differences is by using the concept of *contextualization* (Hall, 1966). High-context cultures place little value on cross-context consistency, allowing (and necessitating) behaviors and cognitions to be quite different according to context or situation. Low-context cultures, in contrast, discourage cross-context differences, emphasizing instead consistency and stability across contexts. American culture is relatively low context, emphasizing stability. It is only within a cultural context such as this that we can even conceive of personality as a set of enduring characteristics with stability and consistency across cultures.

My recognition of cultural influences on conceptions of personality is not new and could be said to have received considerable aid from criticisms of psychoanalytic theory. In evaluating that theory of personality, many writers have pointed out that Freud dealt mainly with patients from middle- and upper-class Austrian society. As socialites who lived in a generally repressed society, many of these people found little opportunity to channel their anxiety and tension. Freud developed "talking theory," which served as the basis for the development of psychoanalysis. We were relatively quick to realize the type of culture that provided this framework—not only the people he dealt with as patients but also his own way of thinking about the world. Freud's theory was culture bound, just as are other prevalent theories of personality in American psychology.

Not only do we need to be wary of how we conceptualize personality across cultures but we also need to be concerned with how we measure it. As you will discover in Chapter 13, language has some effect on our worldview; this translates into real differences in personality. Some language research has shown that multilinguals give different responses to personality test questions when taking those tests in different languages. The implications of this finding are significant, especially when we consider that monolingual Americans are a minority in the world. Most people are fluent in at least two languages.

Context specificity effects can also be seen within monolingual American respondents. Recently, I conducted a simple study with a small group of students ($n = 40$). The study consisted of the students completing a personality test in two conditions. The personality test was the Big Five Inventory-54 (John, 1989), which assesses five traits thought to be "universal" (McCrae & Costa, 1987):

- extroversion–introversion
- agreeableness–antagonism
- conscientiousness–undirectedness
- neuroticism–stability
- openness to experience

Students completed this measure once in the usual way with general directions and a second time with context-specific directions (that is, complete this test responding as if you were interacting with your best friend). Even with this simple context manipulation, an analysis of the data indicated that students' responses differed substantially under the two conditions. For example, students gave significantly higher ratings in the second condition than the first on extroversion and agreeableness, $F(1,38) = 18.90$, $p < .001$ and $F(1,38) = 12.70$, $p < .001$, respectively. They gave significantly lower ratings in the second condition on neuroticism, $F(1,38) = 16.85$, $p < .001$. Thus, context-specificity in personality assessment can be obtained with American participants as well, which further challenges our traditional notions of personality.

Because the field of psychology has a long tradition of research on personality, many researchers have attempted to use the tools developed in this research to study cross-cultural differences in personality. Many cross-cultural studies have centered not on examining certain types of personality but rather have been driven by the types of personality tests available to the researcher. Most of the personality tests available have been developed in the United States by American researchers, and cross-cultural research in personality has typically been conducted by "exporting" these various tests—objective and subjective alike—to other countries and other cultures, resulting in assessments of "national character." With information gathered in this fashion, there is always the concern that findings across cultures using these tests are confused by the fact that the tests may be meaningful only to American subjects. It may very well be that findings using these tests in different cultures do not mean what we think they mean.

One of the most widely studied personality concepts across cultures is **locus of control**. This concept was developed by Rotter (1954, 1966), who suggested that people differ in how much control they have over their behavior and their relationship with their environment and with others. According to this schema, locus of control can be perceived as either internal or external to the individual. People with an internal locus of control see their behavior and relationships with others as dependent upon their own behavior. For example, you might believe that your grades are mostly dependent on how much effort you put into study. This is an example of an internal attribution of locus of control. People with an external locus of control see their behavior and relationships with the environment and others as contingent upon forces external to themselves, outside of and beyond their control. If you believed your grades were mostly dependent on luck, the teacher's benevolence, or the ease of the tests, you would be exemplifying an external locus of control.

Research examining locus of control has shown both similarities and differences across cultures. In general, Americans seem to be quite similar in locus of control to Europeans but quite different from people in the Far East. In particular, while Americans and other Westerners tend to view themselves with an internal locus of control, Asians, especially the Japanese, tend to view themselves with an external locus of control. A number of other findings across groups speak to differences on this variable. For example, men have generally been shown to have more of an internal locus of control than do women; people in industrialized nations appear to have a more internal locus of control than do people in developing countries. Dyal (1984) showed that European Americans appear to be characterized by a more internal locus of control than do African Americans.

A large number of cross-cultural studies have also been conducted with other personality tests, such as the Minnesota Multiphasic Personality Inventory (MMPI), the California Psychological Inventory (CPI), and the Eysenck Personality Questionnaire (EPQ). In general, however, the findings have not led to a clear picture about personality differences across cultures (Berry et al., 1992). The lack of consistency in findings on these other measures may be a product of the fact that these tests were developed in the United States with American subjects and may not have the same meaning or relevance in other countries.

Culture and Indigenous Personalities

In the United States, we tend to think of personality as a conglomeration of enduring and stable traits that describe certain types of personality dispositions across contexts. We use terms such as *friendly, outgoing, sociable,* and *introverted* to describe patterns of behavior that we come to associate with an individual. But in examining personality across cultures, keep in mind the fact that different cultures may have fundamentally different views about exactly what personality is. Unfortunately, relatively few studies of this perspective have been attempted, undoubtedly because most personality research is driven by research conducted within an individualistic framework and history and with a particular bias toward not only doing research but also thinking about research, culture, and personality. What we do know about indigenous personalities, however, challenges our traditional notions of personality.

Indigenous personalities are conceptualizations of personality developed in a particular culture that are specific and relevant only to that culture. Berry et al. (1992) examined three such indigenous personality concepts, each of which is fundamentally different from American or Western concepts. The model of African personality, for example, views personality as consisting of three different layers, each layer representing a different aspect of the person. The first layer, found at the core of the person and personality, includes a spiritual principle; the second layer involves what we may consider a psychological vitality principle; and the third layer involves what is considered a physiological vitality principle. The body forms the outer framework that houses each of these basic, fundamental layers of the person. In addition, family lineage and community affect different core aspects of the African personality (Sow, 1977, 1978, cited in Berry et al., 1992; see also Vontress, 1991).

Amae has been postulated by Doi (1973) as a core concept of the Japanese personality. The root of this word means "sweet," and loosely translated, *amae* refers to the passive, childlike dependence of one person on another. It is said to find its roots in mother–child relationships. According to Doi, all Japanese relationships can be characterized by *amae,* as it serves as a fundamental building block of Japanese culture and personality. This fundamental interrelationship between higher and lower status people in Japan serves as a major component not only of individual psychology but of interpersonal relationships, and it does so in ways that are difficult to grasp from an American individualistic point of view.

These are just two of many examples around the world of how people of different cultures view and understand personality within their own cultures. I hope these examples make it clear that these perspectives differ substantially from what we typically consider when defining personality in psychology as practiced and studied in the United States. Despite these apparent differences, it may also be true that people, regardless of culture, share many characteristics of personality that American as well as other views of personality suggest are important. Culture may serve to verbally formalize what is important in that particular culture concerning an understanding of personality, highlighting some aspects and calling it personality while ignoring others. These choices inform us about what those cultures deem to be important in their understanding of people, and they inevitably lead to fundamental differences in how people view themselves and the rest of the world.

Conclusion

Culture is a macrolevel, social construct that identifies the characteristics and attributes we share with others. But culture also influences the very core nature of our beings as individuals. Because culture shapes and colors our experiences, behaviors, attitudes, and feelings, it helps mold our fundamental sense of self—our self-concept, self-construals, and self-identities. Culture influences the fundamental nature of how we view personality, the types of personality traits we harbor, and undoubtedly helps create what laypersons and previous scholars alike have termed "national character." In addition, some cultures have developed their own distinctive and unique definitions of personality, such as the African and Japanese concepts described in this chapter.

Culture influences these core aspects of our sense of self, and we carry these self-construals and personality traits with us in all aspects of life. Whether we consider the places where we work, go to school, or have fun, or the people with whom we interact, we take our culture and our culture bound sense of self and identity with us. These self-construals help us understand the world around us and others in it and guide us and our behaviors in ways we are not always aware of. They help us interpret the world around us and the behaviors of others in that world—even though we are not aware that we have those cultural filters on when we do so.

Because culture influences core aspects of self and personality, I deemed it necessary for you to understand its importance and pervasiveness before studying other cultural influences on behavior. Indeed, the information discussed in this chapter will have an impact on all the remaining information presented in this book. I hope you can carry this information with you as we continue our journey to learn how culture influences behavior.

 # Glossary

achievement motivation   A desire for excellence.

cognitive template   A logical framework that serves as the basis for understanding ourselves and others.

false uniqueness effect   The tendency for individuals to underestimate the commonality of desirable traits and to overestimate their uniqueness.

filial piety   A sense of duty and obligation to family members, especially parents. This sense is especially strong in Asian and other collectivistic cultures.

fundamental attribution error   A tendency to explain the behaviors of others using internal attributions but to explain one's own behaviors using external attributions.

independent construal of self A sense of self that views the self as a bounded entity, clearly separated from relevant others.

indigenous emotions Emotions relatively unique to particular cultures.

indigenous personalities Conceptualizations of personality developed in a particular culture that are specific and relevant only to that culture.

interdependent construal of self A sense of self that views the self as unbounded, flexible, and contingent on context. This sense of self is based on a principle of the fundamental connectedness among people.

locus of control A concept that refers to where people locate control over their behaviors and their relationship with their environment and with others. Locus of control is usually perceived as either internal or external to the self.

self-concept The way in which we understand or construe our sense of self or being.

socially disengaged emotions Emotions that tend to separate or disengage the self from social relationships. They also simultaneously promote the perceived independence of the self from relationships with others.

socially engaged emotions Emotions that lead to behaviors that will engage and assimilate the self in social relationships and enhance the perceived interdependence of the self with others.

4

Cross-Cultural Research Methods: Issues in the Conduct of Studies Across Cultures

Why It Is Important to Understand
Cross-Cultural Research Methods

In reading a book about cultural diversity in human behavior, you may be wondering why it is important to learn about cross-cultural research methods to understand human behavior. Indeed, when academics begin to talk about research methods (and statistics), many students think the material is either boring or irrelevant to what they *really* want to learn. But it is vital to learn about these methods in order to gain a good understanding of how we have come to know how and why people from different cultures are different.

We are all consumers of cross-cultural research, and most of the research findings presented in this book are the result of cross-cultural research. To be a critical consumer of these findings, you must have some basis by which you can understand the ways in which findings were produced. At the same time, you must also have some basis for evaluating those findings—whether you believe them or not. Oftentimes, this evaluation is based on your knowledge of the methods that produced those findings and whether or not you can detect some characteristic of the methods that compromised the quality or nature of those findings. You need to have at least a rudimentary knowledge of cross-cultural research methods to make such an evaluation. All in all, study of research methods has an impact on our final understanding of the nature of "truth" in science and how we obtain that truth.

The Nature of Truth in Science and the Importance of Research

Scholars and scientists in psychology who are interested in generating knowledge about cultural diversity and its influences on human behavior rely on research to generate that knowledge. Although there are many different types of research, all scientists interested in generating knowledge about cultural influences and testing their ideas about that influence will rely on some type of research to go about their work.

Research is the primary way academics and scientists uncover facts about the world. When replicated across studies, time, and scientists, these facts serve as the basis for what we know as truth or principle in psychology. Almost all academic fields related to human behavior rely heavily on scientific research to generate knowledge about how and why people behave as they do. Before we accept something as true, we have to be assured that the research that produced that truth met some minimal standards for scientific rigor. Thus, the truth that was borne from the research is a reliable and consistent truth that was not compromised or biased due to the way the findings were produced.

Truth and principle in psychology are never generated from a single study. No matter how well any single study was conducted, most scientists and scholars will not accept its results as a general truth, and for good reason. Every study on human behavior is conducted under certain conditions or research parameters. These conditions form the basis for the limitations to the knowledge generated in that study. The results obtained from any single study are bounded by those conditions and parameters.

For a result about human behavior to be considered a truth through the research process, virtually the same study must be conducted again, with different participants, under different parameters and conditions. If a researcher obtains the same finding, despite having changed a number of parameters of the research, we can say that the findings have been repeated over a number of different studies. These studies may be conducted by the same researcher or research team, but often these repeating studies are conducted by independent researchers. In either case, when the same, or virtually the same, result is obtained, we call this repeating finding a **replication**. Only when findings are replicated across a number of studies will scholars and scientists start to believe that the findings say something about human behavior. Replicated findings form the basis for "truths" in academia and science. Truth, therefore, is heavily dependent on how the research was conducted.

In addition to the scientists who actually do the research and conduct studies on human behavior, many teachers and students are active consumers of the research of others. These scholars play a major role in searching for research relevant to their interests, reading and evaluating the reports, and digesting them well enough to communicate their cumulative results to others. Research, therefore, plays a major role not only in generation of knowledge and testing of ideas but in communication of that knowledge to others. It follows, then, that to be an active, informed, and critical receiver of knowledge, you must gain some basic understanding of research methodology. Eventually we all need to make our own decisions concerning whether or not to believe what is being told to us, either by a teacher-scholar or through our own reading of a research report. To make this decision, you need to be able to evaluate the research on its own merits and form your own conclusions as to whether or not the procedures employed by the researchers produced data that are believable.

If, for example, you read or were told about a study that employed what you believed were faulty methods and procedures, you wouldn't (and shouldn't) believe the results of that study, no matter how attractive (or politically correct) those results appear. On the other hand, if those methods and procedures appeared to you to be problem-free and the data generated by those procedures believable, you could be certain that the results you heard or read were true. In either case, you—as an informed and critical reader and evaluator of knowledge—need to have some working understanding of research methods to make these decisions. This process begins with a better understanding of the general parameters and conditions under which most studies are conducted.

The Parameters and Conditions of Research

All studies on human behavior are conducted under specific conditions with certain parameters and certain limitations. These conditions exist because it is impossible to study *all* people on *all* behaviors in a single study. If that were possible, we wouldn't have to worry about parameters and conditions. But it's not. So researchers need to make decisions about many things when conducting a study. Everything that is decided forms the basis for the conditions and parameters of a study. These, in turn, also become the limitations to a study. All the knowledge generated by the research is bounded by these parameters and limitations.

If you ask researchers about the decisions they made in conducting a study, many will not be aware of just how many decisions were made because many of the decisions were made automatically because "it is the way things are generally done" or because "another study did it this way." In this way, psychological research and researchers themselves have their own sort of culture. As people gain more experience in conducting research and especially in thinking about how to conduct research, they become more aware of the many decisions made in conducting a study.

What are some of these decisions? In the following section, I will outline some of the major decisions researchers make when conducting a study. Remember that these are just a few of the many specific decisions that need to be made for that study to be conducted.

The Nature of the Question Being Asked

One of the first decisions researchers make when conducting a study concerns what question they want to answer. Every study is designed to answer or address a particular question. For example, a researcher may want to find out whether boys or girls in elementary school do better at a particular type of problem, or whether the number of people in a given area (population density) is related to certain types of health problems.

The usual way research proceeds is that researchers have a question they want to answer, then they design a study to answer it. Conversely, every study, by default, answers some question. Even if you do not know what question a researcher started out trying to answer, you should be able to surmise what that question was just by reading about what the study is trying to do. Sometimes, the question the researcher started out with is not addressed by the study he or she conducts. Researchers may believe (and tell you in the introduction of their report) that their study is addressing a certain question or testing a certain hypothesis, but close inspection of their methods may reveal that the data collected did not exactly match the question and hypothesis they had intended to test.

Research questions and hypotheses should enjoy a close relationship to each other, but sometimes this relationship is not as close as we would like. But in all cases, researchers had some question they wanted to answer. Just what question to ask is the first decision a researcher makes.

The Type of Research Paradigm Chosen to Address the Question

Once researchers decide what question they want answered, the next step is to select a general research approach or **research paradigm** to answer it. There are many different research paradigms to choose from. If you study research methodology in psychology, you will learn about case studies, longitudinal research, experimental research, correlational research, quasi-experimental research, and the like. Public health research may use an epidemiological approach to understanding the causes and nature of different types of health outcomes and diseases. Sociological research may use social markers and other institutions to delineate social changes and their impact on people. Anthropological research may use in-depth studies of single cultures, where researchers immerse themselves in the culture and try to learn everything about it (ethnographies). Research in economics and business may study the number and types of industries or look at changes in gross national products or other national economic indicators.

Many research paradigms are available to researchers, and they need to choose one to address the question they want to answer. The general approach is often linked to the question, so a researcher may not give much thought to which approach to "choose," assuming that the paradigm appropriate to the question is a "given." Nevertheless, the approach used to conduct the actual study is a decision made by the researcher, by default or not. This decision further defines and places conditions, restrictions, and limitations on the study and the information generated from it. The general research approach adopted frames the nature of the data obtainable as a result of these methods. The nature of these data will affect the type of information that can be dealt with as well as the interpretation and understanding of the phenomenon under study.

The Participants in the Study

In most studies on human behavior in psychology, the basic "unit" in a study—used to gather the primary information in the study—is a person (commonly referred to as a subject or participant), often referred to as the **unit of analysis**. Different research paradigms utilize different units of analysis. In psychology the unit of analysis is usually people, but other disciplines employ various units of analysis. Epidemiological surveys across countries, for example, may use country as the unit of analysis. Industries may be the unit of analysis in a study of the effects of different types of companies on the national economy. Researchers decide what the exact unit of analysis is in their studies. This places a further condition on the nature of the data generated in the study.

Even when a decision is made about what the unit of analysis of any study will be, it is impossible to survey or include all possible examples of that unit of analysis in the research. In psychology, for example, it is impossible to study all the people we would really want to study, even though we want to generate findings and principles of behavior that are true for as broad a range of people as possible. Thus, a researcher has to decide how to limit the units of analysis in a study to a manageable and realistic size. The final group of units included in a study is commonly referred to as the **sample**, and the procedures researchers use in determining their sample is called the **sampling procedure**.

Most studies require that several decisions, not one, be made to achieve a workable number of units. For example, a researcher may decide to study human behavior. Of course, it is impossible to study everyone in the whole wide world. Thus, the researcher may decide to limit his or her samples to university students in the United States because they are the most easily accessible to the researcher, many of whom happen to be housed, supported, and employed by universities. Even then, a researcher cannot possibly survey all university students in the United States in one study. The decision often made by psychology researchers is to study university students enrolled in introductory psychology courses in a single university, because they are the most easily accessed (that is, researchers can offer research participation as an alternative activity in partial fulfillment of class requirements). Even then, not all students enrolled in the course will participate; only a small number enrolled in the course at one particular time will participate. Thus, what started out as a research question applicable to many or all people of the world ends up including only a small, specially chosen sample of a limited nature. This example describes "typical" psychological research procedures in sampling, and most studies that have to do with human behavior must make similar types of limiting decisions, regardless of the unit of analysis. Whatever the unit of analysis, those types of choices are made. Those choices, in turn, place conditions and limitations on the nature of the information or data obtained in the study.

Conceptual and Empirical Definitions of Variables

In addition to decisions about samples, researchers make decisions about how to measure the variables they are interested in. The ways researchers decide to measure something is intimately related to the ways they *conceptually* define it. The way a variable is conceptually defined dictates how it should be measured. The method of measurement, in turn, places a limitation on the nature of the information obtained by that type of measurement. Conversely, every method of measurement defines the nature of what is being measured *by default*. That is, even if you don't know how a researcher conceptually defined something, you should be able to guess how he or she conceptually views it by knowing how it is measured. In recent years, researchers interested in intelligence have broadened their conceptual definition of intelligence to include such things as musical, artistic, and other creative abilities, and physical, sport-type abilities. These changes dictate changes in the ways these aspects of intelligence are measured.

The ways in which researchers conceptually define a variable (such as intelligence) identify how they understand that variable theoretically. This understanding suggests a certain way in which it will also be measured, which is known as **operationalization**. For example, researchers interested in studying intelligence need to have a conceptual definition about what they believe intelligence is. Most American psychologists studying intelligence in the past, for instance, believed that intelligence consisted mainly of cognitive skills related to verbal, analytic, and problem-solving abilities. These researchers used methods such as the Wechsler Adult Intelligence Scale (WAIS) to measure intelligence in their research. The WAIS has a total of 11 different types of tests; some are verbal and some are analytical. The verbal tests include a vocabulary test and a reading comprehension test. The analytical tests include a jigsaw puzzle picture completion test and a picture arrangement test where subjects arrange a set of pictures so that they tell a story.

The specific tasks, questionnaires, or instruments used to measure a variable (such as the WAIS) places further conditions and limitations on the nature of the information gathered by that method and the nature of the data generated by the study. The data obtained using such measures may only be obtainable using those measures; other measures may produce different data.

Environment and Setting

All research occurs in a location in a particular environment and setting, and these are further conditions of the research. Many studies in anthropology, for example, are done "in the field," with the researchers visiting and oftentimes living together with the people they are interested in studying. This type of in-depth immersion in a people or culture, called an **ethnography**, dictates that the research setting or environment be the actual environment in which the people being studied live. This defines the setting under which the data, collected by observation or interview, are gathered.

Many studies in psychology occur in laboratory settings. These involve participants being recruited by some means (visiting a classroom, or signing up in a "subject pool") and then appearing at a designated experimental or laboratory room. Participants are often met by an experimenter who explains the purpose and procedures of the experiment. The participants may view a movie screen, interact with a computer, or do a task, but this setting defines the environmental parameters under which the data are obtained.

Many studies of human behavior are observational in nature; that is, they involve experimenters recording their observations of certain types of behaviors in a particular setting. The setting may be the university student center, a home, a village, a shopping mall—just about anywhere. Wherever the research takes place, that setting describes an environmental condition under which the research is taking place and this condition outlines a parameter and limitation of the nature of the data obtained.

Procedures

Not only do researchers need to decide "important" things, such as the nature and measurement of the variables, the samples to be included, and the setting of the research, but they also need to decide more "mundane" things, such as the type of instructions to give to participants, the time of day to conduct the experiment, the books to look at to uncover historical or archival data, and so on. All of these characteristics associated with conducting the study, regardless of the type of study or the unit of analysis, further define conditions of the study. Many of the more mundane aspects of the research are not given much thought by some researchers, and even less by many consumers of the research. Nevertheless, they are there, and they define the conditions and limitations under which data are obtained and knowledge is generated. We need to give particular attention to how these procedures may constrict or affect the data obtained.

Analyzing Data

Once researchers conduct a study—design their questions, decide on methods, and gather data—they are not yet done. They have to decide how to analyze their data. In fact, the primary decisions about how to analyze data should be made in conjunction with the design of the study and its methods, not after the data have been collected. More often than not, the need to do something with the data in psychological research leads us to the land of statistics. In research, statistics are used to manipulate data so researchers can draw some meaning from the data. Simply counting the number of times a particular behavior occurs is a statistical manipulation (and it even has a fancy name, *frequency*). Getting an average of the number of times a response is obtained is also a statistical manipulation. In some studies, the statistical manipulations can be quite complex, involving a multiple-step process with different types of outcomes. Names such as analysis of variance, discriminant analysis, multiple regression, and correlation abound in the research literature. But regardless of the name and the complexity of the statistics, they all have the same purpose—to transform the data obtained in a study into something from which researchers can draw some meaning.

There are many different types of statistics, and they all do different things to different types of data. Researchers have many choices as to how to analyze their data. They can devise different ways of splitting their data files—using only parts of the data or the whole thing or whatever. Researchers can choose this statistic or that one. They can even choose not to use any statistics at all and base their findings entirely on their own inferences about the data. The specific ways researchers choose to analyze data dictate that the data will be presented in a particular way. This presentation, in turn, affects the types of meanings researchers and the consumers of that research draw from the data. Because the choices of analysis and statistics affect the nature of the presentation of the data, they form yet another condition or limitation on research.

Interpreting the Findings

In any study, be it psychological, sociological, or anthropological in nature, researchers need to draw conclusions on the basis of their data and findings. The interpretations a researcher draws from a study are dependent on a number of factors, including the researcher's own background and upbringing, his or her particular theoretical bend and biases, and the like. All interpretations are made under these conditions; that is, with whatever particular viewpoint researchers bring with them to the interpretation. Because these are conditions, they are yet another way limitations are placed on a study.

I have highlighted some of the major ways many different conditions act as limitations in studies of human behavior. This is equally true for other types of research, because similar decisions need to be made regardless of the research question being addressed or the specific paradigm used to answer the question. While these parameters and limitations are important for us to understand in all types of research, cross-cultural research on human behavior brings with it special problems and issues. The information I have presented should be used as a basic foundation on which we can build a better understanding of cross-cultural research methodology—how it differs from non-cross-cultural research and the special issues it raises.

Special Issues in Cross-Cultural Research

Doing research in different cultures and comparing the results in one culture against those found in another brings with it its own set of special issues. Just as it is important for the informed and critical reader to understand some basic issues pertaining to all types of research (as just reviewed), it is important for consumers of cross-cultural research to have some understanding of the basic issues with regard to cross-cultural research. By knowing about some of these basic issues in cross-cultural research, we will all be in a better position to understand and evaluate the information presented to us about cross-cultural similarities and differences, in this text, in our classes, and in other sources.

Many of the "special" issues in cross-cultural research are really extensions of issues pertaining to all types of research, but some issues pertain solely to the conduct of research in different cultures and countries, across different languages. In this section, you should get a flavor of just what these issues are and how they are especially important to cross-cultural studies.

The Nature of the Question Being Asked

As mentioned earlier, all researchers make a decision about answering or addressing some sort of question in deciding to conduct a study and do research. This is no different in cross-cultural work. But it is important to realize that researchers who formulate research questions have their own cultural upbringing and backgrounds. These backgrounds produce certain types of biases on the part of researchers, regardless of whether these biases are good or bad, right or wrong, conscious or unconscious. These biases influence the types of questions we think are important and, thus, those questions we believe should be studied in cross-cultural research.

Because the research questions we formulate originate from our own personal and cultural biases, a question that is important for us to answer may not be important, or as important, to someone from a different cultural background. For example, think about a hypothetical study in which researchers want to examine cultural differences in how quickly people can solve maze-type puzzles presented to them on a computer. It might be interesting and relevant to conduct this type of study in the United States, Hong Kong, and France and compare the results of the Americans, Chinese, and French participants. But this study might not be as relevant to preliterate cultures such as those indigenous to New Guinea. If these people were asked to participate in the research, they might be afraid to go near that mechanical-looking contraption (the computer).

Or suppose researchers decided to study cultural differences in problem-solving ability in the United States and among tribespeople in Africa. To do this, researchers might present subjects in both cultures with a device that had to be manipulated in some way to obtain a reward, such as money. The

Americans might be able to approach this task and be successful at it. The tribespeople, however, might believe this task to be entirely meaningless, might view the contraption with fear, and might not care one bit about money! In contrast, if the problem-solving task was to track different animals via the use of scents and foot marks, the tribespeople might respond very positively to the task. Imagine American subjects performing such a task!

While these examples may seem quite extreme, some studies from time to time seem to do just this. And even more studies are subtle in their approach to washing over cultural differences in the importance and meaning of the research questions.

Researchers simply cannot decide on their own which questions are important to study across cultures and then impose these questions on people of other cultures. More often than not, the questions a researcher comes up with are assumed to be equally important and have the same meaning in other cultures. This is an ethnocentric way of doing research that cannot be avoided if the researcher does the research single-handedly without checking out the validity of his or her biases first.

Definitions of Culture in Cross-Cultural Research

When cross-cultural researchers decide to do a study, they may decide to gather data from such places as the United States, Germany, Japan, and India. That is, they gather data from different *countries*. While different cultures undoubtedly underlie different countries, researchers often make an assumption, through their research methods, that countries equal cultures. This presents a dilemma for cross-cultural researchers. As discussed earlier, most cross-cultural scholars would agree that culture is the shared conglomeration of attitudes, values, behaviors, and beliefs communicated from one generation to the next via language. This definition of culture is subjective not objective, sociopsychological not biological. This is where the problem lies.

Despite this definition of culture, cross-cultural researchers have lacked an adequate way of measuring this "sharing" of psychological characteristics in their research. Because a way of measuring this sharing does not exist, researchers rely on "easier" aspects of people to measure. Most typically, these have included ethnicity (for example, European American, Chinese, Mexican, African American) or nationality (for example, American, Japanese, German, Brazilian). But culture is not necessarily contained in either of these attributes.

The inability of researchers to measure culture on the sociopsychological level, in accordance with our definition of culture, has meant that we have had to "trade off" in our ability to study cross-cultural differences. Most, if not all, of the studies conducted to date and presented in this book have measured culture by either race, ethnicity, or nationality. Still, we cannot and should not categorically dismiss these studies or their findings. They provide us with valuable information about possible cultural differences, because cultural differences *do indeed* underlie countries. These studies alert us to the limitations to what we know and regard as truth produced by research from mainstream academia. Thus, it is still important for us to consider these studies, but we must consider them with caution concerning the discrepancy between our definition of culture and the definition of culture used in the research. When we conduct research using these categories to classify people, we must do so with care concerning the presumed relationship between these categories and the underlying culture.

The Participants in Cross-Cultural Research

Sampling issues. More often than not, it is assumed that a group of people who participate in a cross-cultural study (the sample) are "good" representatives of that particular culture. For instance, in the simplest cross-cultural research design, researchers obtain a sample of people in one culture, obtain data from them, and compare those data to data collected in another culture or to known values. Let's say a researcher obtained a sample of 50 Americans as part of a cross-cultural study. Are the 50 Americans adequate representatives of American culture? If they were recruited from Beverly Hills in California, would that be the same as recruiting 50 participants from the Bronx in New York? Or 50 people from Wichita, Kansas? If the 50 participants were all of European descent, would they be an "adequate" sample? If not, what percentage of people of different racial and ethnic backgrounds would the researcher need to be satisfied? If the sample required 25% to be of African descent, could any African American be recruited to make 25%? What criteria would be used to decide whether the sample of 50 people were adequate representatives of American culture? What is the definition of "American" culture anyway?

These questions are endless. They are not easy questions to deal with, and they pertain to any sample of participants in any culture. Cross-cultural researchers need to pay particular attention to issues of sampling in the conduct of their research. Aside from being unable (most of the time) to measure culture on a subjective level, cross-cultural research too often simply assumes that the participants in their studies are adequate representatives of their culture, whatever it is. When differences are found, researchers assume that the differences are "cultural" because they assume that the samples are representatives of culture. Who knows? The differences a researcher obtains from a study of the United States, Japan, Brazil, and Mexico may be the same as the differences in a study of Minneapolis, Los Angeles, Miami, and Newark!

Equivalence issues.   Not only are there questions about whether samples in cross-cultural studies are adequate representatives of their cultures, but there are questions about whether the samples across the cultures are equivalent to each other. For the research to be methodologically sound, researchers need to make sure the samples they compare are somehow equivalent. If they are not equivalent on demographic or other types of variables, then those variables on which they are not equivalent would serve as *confounds* in the study. For example, a researcher may compare two groups of subjects from two different cultures that were matched for age, education, and religion but differed in socioeconomic status (SES). Should differences be found between these two samples, it would not be clear whether those differences were due to the underlying cultural differences between the two samples or to the differences in the SES of those samples. SES would confound culture. Ensuring that cross-cultural samples are equivalent is not easy.

As another example, imagine comparing data from a sample of 50 Americans from Los Angeles with sample of 50 preliterate members of the Fore tribe in New Guinea. Clearly, the Americans and the Fore come from entirely different backgrounds—different socioeconomic classes, different educational levels, different social experiences, the existence of various forms of technology, and the like. How can you know that any differences, if found, are due to culture rather than other factors? Clearly, comparing data from a sample of respondents in a major, international metropolis to the data from a sample preliterate tribe with minimal outside contact is very difficult. Would we obtain similar differences if we studied different socioeconomic classes within the United States?

While these examples are quite far-fetched, the question is still valid for more subtle cross-cultural samples. How would you establish equivalence between a sample from Los Angeles in a comparison against samples from Paris, Wien, and Singapore? Cross-cultural researchers need to establish some basis of equivalence among their samples to make cultural comparisons meaningful. Often this is not feasible due to realistic differences on many noncultural dimensions as well as cultural ones among the different samples in a cross-cultural study. When differences are found, researchers usually assume that the differences reflect cultural differences, but this is not necessarily the case. We, the consumers of this research, must be aware of other plausible interpretations of the data.

Cross-Cultural Equivalence in Methods and Procedures

Equivalence of conceptual and empirical definitions of variables. Different cultures may attach different meanings to the variables of interest in a study. If a concept means different things to people of different cultures, it is difficult to compare data on that concept across these cultures.

Cross-cultural studies of intelligence are a good example. As described earlier in this chapter, many researchers in the United States in the past have considered intelligence to consist mainly of verbal and analytical types of critical thinking skills. Tests (such as the WAIS) assessing these skills have been widely used in this research. This is fine for the United States (or is it?), but a different culture may have a different conception of just what constitutes intelligence. For example, let's say a culture considers nobility of character and sincerity as markers of intelligence. If we tested a sample of people from this culture on the WAIS and compared these data to American data, were we really studying cross-cultural differences in intelligence? Probably not. Another culture may consider the ability to have smooth, conflict-free interpersonal relationships a marker for intelligence. Yet another culture may consider creativity and artistic abilities indices of intelligence. Would comparisons of WAIS data from any of these cultures constitute cross-cultural comparisons of intelligence? Probably not. Of course, researchers may be interested in such specific traits; the problem occurs when we interpret them as a global concept of "intelligence" that is assumed to be true for everyone.

Beyond issues of conceptual definitions and understanding are questions concerning cross-cultural issues of measurement. Let's say, for example, that two cultures do indeed define intelligence in terms of verbal and analytic abilities, such as those measured by tests like the WAIS. Now let's look at the exact ways by which the WAIS measures this definition of intelligence. If there is a question about American presidents as part of the WAIS test, can we use this test in this study? Would it be fair to give subjects in France this test to measure their intelligence?

Researchers need to think critically about possible cultural differences in the conceptual definitions of different variables of interest in cross-cultural research; but researchers also have to examine *in detail* the exact methods they will use to measure those variables, down to the very wording of individual items on the tests. Cultural differences in either the conceptual definitions of variables or their measurement are very common, and we need to be aware of these possibilities.

Language and translation issues. Cross-cultural research generally cannot be conducted in English. If you were to compare the responses of an American sample to those from a Beijing sample on a questionnaire, you would need to have an English and a Chinese version of the questionnaire. How are we to know that the questionnaires themselves are equivalent? Cross-cultural researchers frequently use a procedure known as **back translation** to ensure equivalence in their research protocols (Brislin, 1970). Back translation involves taking the protocol in one language, translating it to the other language, and having someone else translate it back to the original. If the back-translated version is the same as the original, they are generally considered equivalent. If it is not, the procedure is repeated until the back-translated version is the same as the original.

The concept underlying this procedure is that the end product must be a translation equivalent to the original English. The original language (usually English) is **decentered** through this process (Brislin, 1970, 1993), with any culture-specific concepts of the original language eliminated or translated equivalently into the target language. Still, even if the words being used in the two languages are the same, there is no guarantee that those words have exactly the same meanings, with the same nuances, in the two cultures. If the English word *anger,* for example, were translated into another language, we might indeed find the best translation equivalent, but would it have the same connotations, strength, and interpretation in that language that it does in English? It is very difficult to obtain exact translation equivalents of most words. Cross-cultural researchers need to be aware of issues of language equivalence so language differences are not confused with any cultural differences they want to test. "Perfect" equivalence is never found between any two languages, and this fact should be considered when evaluating cross-cultural research.

The research environment, setting, and procedures.   In many universities across the United States, students enrolled in introductory classes are required to participate in research as subjects in partial fulfillment of class requirements or complete an alternative activity. Because this is an established institution, there is a certain expectation of U.S. students to participate in research as part of their academic experience. Indeed, many American students are "research-wise," knowing their rights as subjects in experiments, expecting to participate in research, and so forth. Many other countries do not have this custom. In some countries, research is simply forced on students because the professor of the class wants to collect the data. In some countries, students may be required to come to a research laboratory, and coming to a university laboratory for an experiment can have different meanings across cultures because of these exceptions.

All the decisions researchers make in any other type of study are made in cross-cultural studies as well. But those decisions can mean different things in different countries. Whether laboratory or field, day or night, questionnaire or behavior—all these decisions may have different meanings in different cultures. Cross-cultural researchers need to confront these differences in their work, and we consumers need to be aware of these differences when evaluating cross-cultural research.

Cross-Cultural Issues in Analyzing Data

You may think that once you have designed a study to be as culturally sensitive to the issues as possible and collected the data, you would be free from cultural influences on the research. That is not the case. Culture can influence the ways in which response scales are used in research, and this has implications for analyzing data.

Cultural influences on the use of response scales are typically known as **cultural response sets**. Response sets pertain to cross-cultural findings and not to the methods by which the study was conducted. Response sets refer to a cultural tendency to respond a certain way on tests (response scales) that is more reflective of the cultural tendency than the meaning of the actual scale. For example, participants in the United States and Hong Kong may be asked to judge the intensity of a certain stimulus, using a 7-point scale. When examining the data, the researcher may find that Americans generally scored around 6 or 7, while people from Hong Kong generally scored around 4 or 5. The researcher may then interpret that the Americans perceived more intensity in the stimulus than did the people from Hong Kong. But what if the people from Hong Kong actually rate everything lower than the Americans, not just this stimulus? What if they actually perceive a considerable amount of intensity in the stimulus but have a cultural tendency to use the lower part of the scale? This is not as far-fetched as it may seem. Some collectivistic cultures encourage their members not to "stick out." Other cultures encourage their members to be very unique and individual. These cultural differences may result in different uses of response alternatives on questionnaires or interviews. Some cultures may encourage extreme responses on a rating scale; others may discourage such extreme responses and encourage responses around the middle of a scale. Two cultures may respond in exactly the same ways on a questionnaire—except the data may be located on different parts of the scale.

Fortunately, statistical manipulations allow researchers to deal with the possible influences of cultural response sets. For them to be used, of course, researchers need to be aware of cultural response sets and the statistical techniques available to deal with them in the first place (see Matsumoto, 1994, for an introduction to these). And consumers of that research need to have a similar awareness of them.

Cross-cultural research has its own special set of issues that need to be addressed for the research to be valid. These and other issues have made cross-cultural studies tricky in the past and have probably discouraged some researchers from conducting these studies. Recognizing and understanding these issues are important to conducting good cross-cultural research. They are also important first steps in appreciating cultural differences.

Cultural Influences on the Interpretation of Findings from Cross-Cultural Studies

Just as culture can bias formulation of the research questions in a cross-cultural study it can also bias the ways researchers interpret findings. Most researchers will inevitably interpret the data they obtain (whether from questionnaires, responses to a task, or whatever) with their own cultural filters on. Of course, there are degrees to which this bias can affect the interpretation. Interpretation of group differences in means, for example, may simply indicate differences in degrees. If the mean response for Americans on a rating scale, for example, is 6.0, and the mean for Hong Kong Chinese is 4.0, one interpretation is that the Americans simply scored higher on the scale. Another interpretation may be that the Chinese are suppressing their responses.

This type of interpretation is common, especially in research with Asian samples. But how do we know the Chinese are suppressing their responses? What if it is the Americans who are exaggerating their responses? What if the Chinese mean response of 4.0 is actually the more "correct" one, and the American one is the one that is off? What if we surveyed the rest of the world and found that the mean for the rest of the world is actually 3.0, and found that *both* the Chinese and the Americans inflated their ratings? When you consider this situation carefully, any interpretation that the Chinese are suppressing their responses really requires you to assume implicitly that the American data are the "correct" data. I myself have made this ethnocentric interpretation of research findings in a study involving American and Japanese judgments of the intensity of facial expressions of emotion without really giving much consideration to other possibilities (Matsumoto & Ekman, 1989).

Examples such as this one are found throughout the cross-cultural literature. Any time researchers make a **value judgment** or interpretation of a finding, it is always possible that that interpretation is bound by a cultural bias. Interpretations of good or bad, right or wrong, suppressing or exaggerating, important or not important are all value interpretations that may be made in a cross-cultural study. And these interpretations may reflect the value orientations of the researchers as much as they do the cultures of the samples included in the study. As researchers, we may make those interpretations without giving them a second thought—and without the slightest hint of malicious intent—only because we are so accustomed to seeing the world in a certain way. As consumers of research, we may agree with such interpretations when they agree with the ways we have learned to understand and view the world, and we will often do so unconsciously and automatically.

 Conclusion

Research is the primary way by which scholars and scientists generate knowledge about the world. Knowledge discovered through the research process and repeatedly found across a number of studies is said to be replicated. Replicated findings and knowledge form the basis for what we know as "truth" about the world. It is this truth that is taught to you in schools and conveyed everyday in the classrooms and through your readings.

But, as I have discussed in this chapter, truth and knowledge are bounded by the conditions, parameters, and limitations placed on them by the studies and research that produced that knowledge. All studies are bounded in some fashion by these parameters, whether decisions about those conditions are made consciously by the researchers or by default. This is true for research in all social sciences, regardless of field or discipline. It is important for researchers and for consumers of that research to be aware of the types of conditions and parameters that exist and how they limit the knowledge produced by research.

Cross-cultural research brings with it its own special set of issues concerning the conditions and parameters of research. Many of these issues are merely extensions of general research issues into the cross-cultural arena. Some issues, however, are solely reflective of cross-cultural research. In learning about knowledge generated from cross-cultural research, it is imperative to learn about these issues and to be a critical reader and evaluator of the cross-cultural literature studies.

The critical reader needs to be on top of many issues. There are so many, in fact, that you might be wondering right now whether *any* cross-cultural study can tell us anything. You must be thinking that something limits every single cross-cultural study and that all studies must have some kind of imperfection to detract from their data. Well, the answer to this question is, yes. There is no perfect study, and every study has a considerable number of limitations associated with it. But that does not necessarily mean we cannot learn something from that study. The real question in thinking about and evaluating cross-cultural research is whether the flaws of a study so outweigh its procedures as to severely compromise the trust you might place in those data. If a study is so compromised by problems that you don't trust the data, you shouldn't believe it, whether it is cross-cultural or not. But if a study's problems are not so bad, you should be able to glean information from it about cultural differences. If you can do this over a number of studies in an area, they might *cumulatively* or *collectively* say something about that area, even though any single study might not.

Despite all the inherent difficulties, however, cross-cultural research offers a number of exciting and interesting opportunities not available with traditional research approaches, and it is equally important to recognize these opportunities. For example, through cross-cultural research we are able to test the limits and boundaries of our knowledge in psychology and about human behavior. We are able to push the envelope of knowledge and understanding about people in ways that are impossible with traditional research approaches. The cross-cultural enterprise itself offers a process by which scientists and laypersons from disparate and divergent cultures can come together and work toward common goals, thereby improving human relations across what otherwise may seem to be a considerable chasm. The findings from cross-cultural research offer scientists, scholars, and the public ways to further our understanding of human diversity that can serve as the basis for renewed personal and professional interrelationships and can help to focus public and social policy. Methodologically, cross-cultural studies offer researchers a way to deal with empirical problems related to the conduct of research, such as confounding variables present in traditional research approaches.

This process of evaluating the merits of each study in terms of the trust you would place in the data and then accumulating bits and pieces of information across the studies you trust is integral to learning about a field. While cross-cultural research has its own potential problems, it has advantages and potentialities that far outweigh its difficulties. I hope to show you this through the studies I have selected for use in understanding the field of cultural influences on human behavior as presented in this book.

 # Glossary

back translation A technique of translating research protocols that involves taking the protocol as it was developed in one language, translating it into the target language, and having someone else translate it back to the original. If the back-translated version is the same as the original, they are generally considered equivalent. If it is not, the procedure is repeated until the back-translated version is the same as the original.

cultural response sets   Cultural influences on the use of response scales. That is, the cultural tendency to respond a certain way on tests or response scales that is more reflective of the cultural tendency than the meaning of the actual scale.

decenter   The concept underlying the procedure of back translation that involves elimination of culture-specific concepts of the original language in the translation equivalent of the target language.

ethnography   A type of study of a culture that involves an in-depth immersion in the culture, often requiring the researcher to spend a considerable amount of time learning the ways and customs of that culture.

operationalization   The ways researchers conceptually define a variable and measure it.

replication   Research findings that are repeatedly and consistently found across several studies, not only in a single study.

research paradigm   An approach to doing research that is characterized by particular methodologies that address certain types of research questions.

sample   The final group of units that is included in a study.

sampling procedure   The procedures researchers use in determining their sample.

unit of analysis   The basic unit in a study that is used to gather the primary information. In most studies on human behavior in psychology, the unit is a person (commonly referred to as subjects or participants).

value judgment   An interpretation of data that involves attribution of a value, such as good or bad, right or wrong, based on your own cultural framework on findings that originate from another cultural framework.

5

Enculturation, Socialization, and Development

Cultural Differences in Development and Development of Culture

Childhood in any society is a period of considerable change and flux. It is a period that is probably subject to more cultural and environmental impacts than any other in the life span. Despite the great changes and events that can happen in a child's life, one thing that is probably constant across cultures is that people emerge from childhood with a wish to become happy, productive adults. The various ways children develop along the same trajectory is evidence of the ability to achieve positive outcomes that account for survival while maintaining and socializing children to the culture in which they live. Cultures differ, however, in exactly what they mean by "happy" and "productive." Despite the similarities among cultures in the overall goals of development, a tremendous degree of variability still exists.

Each culture has knowledge of the adult competencies needed for adequate functioning (Ogbu, 1981), but these competencies differ by culture and environment,. Children are socialized in ecologies that promote their specific competencies (Harrison, Wilson, Pine, Chan, & Buriel, 1990). For example, if you need a formal education to succeed in your culture, you are likely as a child to be exposed to these values early on. You may receive books and instruction at a young age. Children in other parts of the world may have to do spinning and weaving as part of their adult livelihood. These children are likely to be familiarized early on with those crafts. By the time we are adults, we are all truly integrated in our own societies and cultures. By the time we are adults we have learned many cultural rules of behavior, and we have practiced those rules so much that they are second nature to us. Much of our behavior as adults is influenced by these learned patterns and rules, and we are so well practiced at them that we engage in these behaviors automatically and unconsciously, without giving much thought to them.

Still, at some time in our lives we must have learned those rules and patterns of behavior. Culture, in its truest and broadest sense, involves so many different aspects of life that it is impossible to simply sit somewhere and read a book and learn about, let alone master, a culture thoroughly. Culture must be learned through a prolonged process over a considerable period of time, with much practice. In learning about culture we make mistakes along the way, but people or groups or institutions are always around to help us, and in some cases to force us, to correct those mistakes.

Socialization is the process by which we learn and internalize the rules and patterns of behavior that are affected by culture. This process occurs over a long period of time and involves learning and mastering societal and cultural norms, attitudes, values, and belief systems. The process of socialization starts early, probably from the very first day of life. Some people believe that the biological temperaments and predispositions we bring with us into the world at birth are actually part of the socialization process. While this is an interesting and intriguing idea, most of what we know about the socialization process and the effects of socialization concern life after birth.

Closely related to the process of socialization is the process called **enculturation**. This is the process by which youngsters learn and adopt the ways and manners of their culture. There is very little difference, in fact, between these two terms. Whatever difference exists lies in what is being referred to in each term. Socialization generally refers more to the actual process and mechanisms by which people learn the rules of society and culture—what is said to whom and in which contexts. Enculturation generally refers to the products of the socialization process—the subjective, underlying, psychological aspects of culture that become internalized through development. The similarity and difference between the terms *enculturation* and *socialization* are also related to the similarity and difference between the terms *culture* and *society*.

A close relative of enculturation is a term we hear often today—**acculturation**. This term refers to the process of adapting (and in many cases adopting) to a different culture than the one in which you were enculturated. We often talk and hear about acculturation in discussions of people from one culture who move to a foreign country and must live in another culture.

There are many **socialization agents** in our lives. These are the people, institutions, and organizations that exist to help ensure that socialization occurs. Parents are one of the first and most important of the socialization agents. They help instill cultural mores and values in their children, reinforcing those mores and values when they are learned and practiced well and correcting mistakes in that learning.

Parents, however, are not the only socialization agents. Siblings, extended families, friends, and peers are all important socialization agents for many people. Organizations such as school, church, and social groups such as the Boy or Girl Scouts also become important socialization agents. In fact, as you learn more and more about the socialization process, you will find that culture is enforced and reinforced by so many people and institutions that it is no wonder we all emerge from the process of socialization as masters of our own cultures.

In this chapter, I will examine research that has been conducted on cultural differences in socialization. Fortunately, there is a wealth of studies on cultural differences in developmental processes that should inform us about how cultures "do" socialization differently. There is also a considerable amount of research conducted on schooling and education in different cultures, and this knowledge base should also inform us about how culture is transmitted through a major institution in many people's lives. In recent years, there has also been an effort to examine the process of enculturation itself, looking at how our interactions with the various socialization agents in our lives help to produce our cultures as we know them. We begin our trek by first examining what we know about how children develop their thinking skills—cognitive development.

Cultural Similarities and Differences in Cognitive Development

Piaget's Theory

Cognitive development is a specialty in psychology that studies how thinking skills develop over time. Theories of cognitive development have traditionally focused on the period from infancy to adulthood. One theory has dominated this field during the latter half of the 20th century, and that is Piaget's stage theory of cognitive development. Piaget based his theories on observations of Swiss children. He found that these children of various ages tended to solve problems quite differently. To explain these differences, Piaget (1952) proposed that children progress through four stages as they grow from infancy into adolescence. The four stages identified by Piaget are as follows:

1. *Sensorimotor stage.* This stage typically ranges from birth to about 2 years of age. Anxiety in the presence of strangers—stranger anxiety—is common during this period. The most important achievement of this stage is the

acquisition of object permanency; that is, knowing that objects exist even when they cannot be seen. Early in this stage, children appear to assume that when a toy or other object is hidden (for example, when a ball rolls under a sofa) it ceases to exist. Later in this stage, children will search under the sofa for the lost ball, demonstrating that they have come to understand that objects exist continuously. Other cognitive developments also typically occur during this stage that have implications for later cognitive development and enculturation. Among these are such skills as deferred imitation, language acquisition, and mental imagery. Imitation and imagery are important cognitive components of observational learning, and language skills are necessary to ensure proper communication of verbal socialization processes.

2. *Preoperational stage.* This stage ranges from about 2 to 6 or 7 years of age. Piaget defines this stage in terms of five characteristics: conservation, centration, irreversibility, egocentrism, and animism. **Conservation** is the awareness (or in this stage, the lack of such awareness) that physical quantities remain the same regardless of whether they change shape or appearance. **Centration** is the tendency to focus on a single aspect of a problem. **Irreversibility** is the inability to imagine "undoing" a process. **Egocentrism** is the inability to step into another's shoes and understand the other person's point of view. **Animism** is the belief that all things, including inanimate objects, are alive. For example, children in the preoperational stage might regard a book lying on its side as "tired" or "needing a rest," or they might think that the moon is following them.

3. *Concrete operations stage.* This stage lasts from about 6 or 7 years until about 11 years of age. During this stage, children acquire new thinking skills to work with actual objects and events. They are able to imagine undoing an action, and they can focus on more than one feature of a problem. Children also begin to understand that there are different points of view from their own. This new awareness helps children master the principle of conservation. A child in the concrete operations stage will understand that six apples are always six apples, regardless of how they are grouped or spaced, and that the amount of clay does not change as a lump is molded into different shapes. This ability is not present in the preoperational stage. However, instead of thinking a problem through, children in this stage tend to rely on trial-and-error strategies.

4. *Formal operations stage.* This stage extends from around 11 years of age through adulthood. During this stage, individuals develop the ability to think logically about abstract concepts. These might include such concepts as peace, freedom, and justice. Individuals also become more systematic and thoughtful in their approach to problem solving.

The transition from one stage to another is often gradual as children develop new abilities alongside earlier ways of thinking. Thus, the behavior of some children may represent a "blend" of two stages during periods when the children are in a state of transition from one stage to another.

Piaget hypothesized that two primary mechanisms are responsible for movement from one stage to the next: assimilation and accommodation. **Assimilation** is the process of fitting new ideas into a pre-existing understanding of the world. **Accommodation** refers to the process of changing your understanding to accommodate ideas that conflict with existing concepts.

Piaget's Stage Theory in Cross-Cultural Perspective

Cross-cultural research on Piaget's theory has focused on four central questions. The findings to date show an interesting blend of how cultural similarities and differences may exist in various aspects of cognitive development that parallel Piaget's stages.

Do Piaget's stages occur in the same order in different cultures?   Studies that have addressed this question have convincingly demonstrated that Piaget's stages occur in the same fixed order in other cultures. For instance, a large cross-cultural survey that tested children in Great Britain, Australia, Greece, and Pakistan (Shayer, Demetriou, & Perez, 1988) demonstrated that schoolchildren in these different societies performed Piagetian tasks within the same stage of concrete operations. We do not find cultures where 4-year-olds typically lack an awareness of object permanency or where 5-year-olds understand the principle of conservation. Thus, we know that children from very different cultures do indeed learn groups of Piagetian tasks in a similar order.

Are the ages which Piaget associated with each stage of development the same in all cultures?   There are surprising cultural variations in the ages at which children in different societies typically reach the third and fourth Piagetian stages. In some cases, there can be differences of as much as 5 or 6 years. However, it has often been overlooked that children may have the potential to solve tasks sooner than their answers would indicate. For example, a child in the concrete operations stage will typically give the first answer that comes to mind during a test. If the child comes from a culture where he or she has had practice performing the task in question, this answer is likely to be correct. If the child has never thought about the concept before, he or she may well utter the wrong answer and only later realize the mistake. When researchers checked for this possibility by repeating tests a second time at the end of testing sessions, they found that many children corrected their previous answers on the second attempt (Dasen, 1982; Dasen, Lavallee, & Retschitzki, 1979; Dasen, Ngini, & Lavallee, 1979). Thus, the important point to remember from such findings is that performance on a task may not reveal actual cognitive competence or ability.

Are there cultural variations within, rather than between, Piaget's stages? There is considerable cultural variation in the order in which children acquire specific skills within Piaget's stages. In a comparative study of tribal children (the Inuit of Canada, the Baoul of Africa, and the Aranda of Australia), half of all Inuit children tested solved a spatial task at the age of 7 years; half of the Aranda solved it at 9 years. The Baoul, however, did not reach the halfway point until the age of 12 years (Dasen, 1975). On a test of the conservation of liquids, the order changed dramatically: half of the Baoul children solved the problem when they were 8 years old, the Inuit at 9 years, and the Aranda at 12 years. Why did the ages at which these children could perform the same task vary so much? One reason is that the Inuit and Aranda children live in nomadic societies where children need to learn spatial skills early because their families are constantly moving. The Baoul children, on the other hand, live in a settled society, where they seldom travel but often fetch water and store grain. The skills these children used in their everyday lives seem to have affected the order in which they were able to solve Piagetian tasks within the concrete operations stage.

Do non-Western cultures regard scientific reasoning as the ultimate developmental end point? Piaget's theory assumes that the scientific reasoning associated with formal operations is the universal end point of cognitive development. In other words, Piaget assumed that the thinking most valued in Swiss and other Western societies (in formal operations) was the yardstick by which other cultures should be judged. Piaget considered scientific reasoning to be the ultimate achievement. His stage theory, therefore, is designed to retrace the steps by which people arrive at scientific thinking. Indeed, it is probably safe to say that this perspective with regard to the ultimate end point of cognitive competence has been widely accepted within American psychology, and generally by the American public, at least until very recently.

Cross-cultural research indicates that the answer to this question is clearly "no." Different societies value and reward different skills and behaviors. For example, until recently the most respected scholars in traditional Islamic societies were religious leaders and poets. Although the Islamic educational system included science and mathematics, its primary goal was not to train people in the scientific method but to transmit faith, general knowledge, and a deep appreciation for poetry and literature. People from such cultures could be expected to be at a disadvantage when confronted with advanced Piagetian tasks, which are drawn almost exclusively from Western physics, chemistry, and mathematics.

Many cultures around the world do not share the conviction that abstract, hypothetical thought processes are the ultimate or desired end point in the cognitive development process. Many cultures, for example, consider cognitive development to be more relational—involving the thinking skills and processes needed to engage in successful interpersonal contexts. What Americans consider as "common sense" and not cognitive development per se is considered a much more desired outcome in many cultures. This is especially true among more collectivistic and group-oriented cultures. In fact, high-level, individualistic, abstract thinking is often frowned upon in such collectivistic cultures.

Summary and Discussion

It is important to carefully evaluate the meaning of cross-cultural studies of Piaget's stage of formal operations. In some cultures very few people are able to complete fourth-stage Piagetian tasks. Does this mean that entire cultures are suspended at a lower stage of cognitive development? To answer this question, we must first be able to show that Piagetian tasks are a culturally appropriate way of measuring an advanced stage of cognitive development. Unfortunately, such tests may not be meaningful in other cultures. Besides the issue of cultural appropriateness, there is also the issue of what is being tested. Tests of formal operations can tell us whether people can solve a narrow range of scientific problems, but they do not tell us whether people in different cultures develop advanced cognitive skills in areas other than those selected by Piaget. We can say with certainty, however, that people who have not attended high school or college in a westernized school system perform very poorly on tests of formal operations (Laurendeau-Bendavid, 1977; Shea, 1985). This again raises the question of the degree to which Piagetian tasks depend on previous knowledge and cultural values rather than cognitive skills.

It is also important to remember that there are considerable within-culture differences in cognitive development. These within-culture differences make it extremely difficult to draw valid conclusions or inferences about differences in cognitive development between cultures. For example, not only will members of non-Western cultures have difficulty with tests of formal operations but many adults in our own society also have such difficulties. Scientific reasoning does not appear to be as common in Western societies as Piaget thought, and it is frequently limited to special activities. Individuals who apply scientific logic to a problem on the job may reason quite differently in other situations.

Given the fact that large numbers of people are unable to complete Piagetian tasks of formal operations, it has not been possible to demonstrate the universality of the fourth stage of Piaget's theory of cognitive development. It is possible that most adults possess the potential to complete Piagetian tasks but fail to do so because they lack either the motivation or knowledge of how to demonstrate such ability. To successfully demonstrate success on a task purporting to measure some aspect of cognitive ability or intelligence, it is crucial that the test-taker and the test-maker agree on what is being assessed. Cultural differences in the desired end points of cognitive development as well as cultural differences in definitions of intelligence (see Chapter 9) contribute to this dilemma.

Other Theories of Cognitive Development

While Piaget's theory is the most influential theory in the United States, it is important to note that it is only one of many stage theories proposed by social scientists in the West. An earlier theory, for example, was proposed by the 18th century German philosopher, Hegel. Hegel ranked all societies on an evolutionary scale based on a classification of religious beliefs, with Christianity at the top. Stage theories multiplied in the 19th century after Darwin's theory of evolution became well-known. Several writers (for example, Morgan, 1877; Spencer, 1876; Tylor, 1865) proposed that humanity had progressed from savagery to civilization in a series of stages.

One of the most influential stage theories of the early 20th century was proposed by the French philosopher Levy-Bruhl (1910, 1922, 1949). In common with earlier scholars, Levy-Bruhl drew most of his conclusions from material related to the mystical and religious beliefs of non-Western peoples. Levy-Bruhl put forth the **great divide** theory, separating the thought of Westerners from that of people who lived in primitive societies. He described non-Western peoples as having a distinct way of thinking, which he attributed to the effects of culture. According to Levy-Bruhl, non-Westerners were not bothered by logical contradictions, and they lacked a clear sense of individual identity. More recently, some scientists (Goody, 1968, 1977; Hippler, 1980; Luria, 1976) have put forward new great divide theories. Although these researchers have various names for the two groups, their division of humanity breaks down along similar lines. In all of these theories, the cultural development or thought of non-Westerners is usually judged as deficient or inferior to that of Europeans.

Several points need to be made about these theories. First, it is probably more than coincidence that stage theories produced by Westerners judge people from other cultures (and minorities within their own countries) in terms of how closely they resemble Westerners, thereby placing themselves at a relatively superior level of development. The popularity of stage theories in the 19th century, for example, coincided with the colonial imperialism of the period. Stage theories provided justification for imposing European rule around the world, since it could be said that scholars had convincingly demonstrated the superiority of European civilization.

Other problems also existed. Stage theorists persisted in evaluating the rationality of non-Westerners in terms of their magical and religious beliefs, while the rationality of Western beliefs was usually not questioned. Levy-Bruhl's theory has been fiercely attacked over the years by field anthropologists who have objected to both his methodology and his conclusions. Levy-Bruhl based his work on stories told by missionaries and travelers, many of whom could barely speak native languages.

But Westerners are not the only ones who have ethnocentric assumptions. Cross-cultural studies have shown that people from many cultures prefer their own groups and rate them more positively than they rate outsiders. For example, a study that compared what people in 30 different East African societies thought of themselves and others demonstrated that members of each society rated themselves highly and judged outsiders to be "advanced" when they were culturally similar to their own group (Brewer & Campbell, 1976).

This brings us back to Piaget's theory, which has several strong points. Piaget's theory is considerably more sophisticated than earlier theories. By devising tasks to measure concepts in an experimental setting, Piaget established a new standard by which to gauge cognitive development, one appearing to be less vulnerable to ethnocentric bias. Piaget's tests can be, and have been, administered cross-culturally, with clear-cut results that do not rest on the subjective beliefs of the researcher (although the choice of the research instruments and the interpretation of the data are still clearly subject to researcher bias). Still, cognitive development is complicated, and it is unlikely that such tasks can capture all of its complexity.

Moral Reasoning

Another area of development crucial to our becoming functional adults in society and culture concerns moral judgments and reasoning. As they grow, children develop increasingly complex ways of understanding their world. These cognitive changes also bring about changes in their understanding of moral judgments. Why something is good or bad changes from the young child's interpretation of reward and punishment conditions to principles of right and wrong. In fact, morality and culture share a very close relationship, and moral principles and ethics provide guidelines for our behaviors with regard to what is appropriate and what is not. These guidelines are not developed "out of the blue," as it were, but rather are products of our cultures and societies—and handed down from one generation to the next. As products of our culture, morality is heavily influenced by our underlying, subjective, and implicit culture. Morality also serves as the basis of laws, which are formalized guidelines for appropriate and inappropriate behavior. In this way, culture also affects the laws of our societies. For these and other reasons, morality occupies a special place in our understanding of culture and cultural differences.

Our knowledge of the development of moral reasoning skills, at least in the United States, has been heavily influenced by the work of a psychologist named Lawrence Kohlberg. His model of moral reasoning and judgment is based in large part on Piaget's model of cognitive development.

Kohlberg's Theory of Morality

Kohlberg's theory of moral development (1976, 1984) suggests that there are three general stages of development of moral reasoning skills. Each of these three general stages can be further divided into two stages each, for a total of six substages of moral development. Kohlberg's three general stages of moral reasoning are:

1. **Preconventional morality,** with an emphasis on compliance with rules to avoid punishment, and with rules to get rewards. A person operating at this level of morality would condemn stealing as bad because you might get caught and be thrown in jail or otherwise punished. The focus of the justification is on the punishment (or reward) associated with the action.
2. **Conventional morality,** with an emphasis on conformity to rules that are defined by others' approval, or society's rules. A person operating at this level of morality would judge stealing as wrong because it is against the law and others in society generally disapprove of it.
3. **Postconventional morality,** with an emphasis on moral reasoning according to individual principles and conscience. A person operating at this level of morality would judge stealing within the context of either societal or community needs or his or her own personal moral beliefs and values that supercede perceived societal and community needs.

In the last decade, work by Gilligan and her colleagues (Gilligan, 1982) has challenged Kohlberg's theory by suggesting that the stages of Kohlberg's theory are biased toward the particular way in which males as opposed to females view relationships. She argues that male moral reasoning is equated with justice, while female moral reasoning is equated with obligations and responsibilities. Despite the fervor of the debate, however, reviews of the research seem to indicate that sex differences in moral reasoning have not been found (Walker, 1984). Cross-cultural research may shed more light on this issue.

Cross-cultural studies of moral reasoning.   The universality or cultural-specificity of moral principles and reasoning has been an area of interest for anthropologists and psychologists alike. A number of anthropological ethnographies have examined the moral principles and domains of different cultures (see review by Shweder, Mahapatra, & Miller, 1987). Many of these works have challenged traditional American views of morality, and for good reason. Culture, morality, ethics, and law share a close relationship.

A number of cross-cultural studies on moral reasoning raise questions about the universal generalizability of Kohlberg's ideas. One of the underlying assumptions of Kohlberg's theory is that moral reasoning according to individual principles and conscience, regardless of societal laws or cultural customs, represents the highest level of moral reasoning that exists. This underlying philosophy is grounded in the cultural milieu in which Kohlberg developed his theory, which had its roots in studies involving American males in the midwestern United States in the 1950s and 1960s. While democratic notions of individualism and unique, personal conscience may have been appropriate to describe his samples at that time and place, it is not clear whether those same notions represent universal moral principles applicable to all people of all cultures.

In fact, some researchers have criticized Kohlberg's theory for harboring such cultural biases (Bronstein & Paludi, 1988). Miller and Bersoff (1992) compared the responses to a moral judgment task by respondents in India and the United States. The Indian subjects, both children and adults, considered not helping someone a moral transgression more than did the American subjects, regardless of the life-threatening nature of the situation or if the person in need was related or not. These researchers interpreted the cultural differences as having to do with values of affiliation and justice, suggesting that Indians are taught a broader sense of social responsibility—individual responsibility to help a needy person. The issue of interpersonal responsiveness Miller and Bersoff (1992) raised is related to Gilligan's (1982) claims of gender bias in U.S. studies. It is entirely possible that Gilligan's findings are also influenced by cultural as well as gender differences.

Snarey (1985) completed a review of moral reasoning studies involving subjects from 27 different countries and concluded that moral reasoning is much more culture-specific than Kohlberg originally suggested. Kohlberg's theory, as well as the methodology for scoring moral stages according to verbal reasoning, may not recognize higher levels of morality as defined in other cultures. Should different cultures define those higher levels of morality along totally different dimensions, those differences would have direct implications for profound differences between people of those different cultures in judgments of moral and ethical appropriateness. Fundamental differences in the bases underlying morality and ethics across cultures are not at all an impossibility, given that they feed and are fed by subjective culture. Above all, those fundamental differences in morality as a function of culture form the basis for the possibility of major intercultural conflicts.

Socioemotional Development

In socialization, thinking and morality are only part of the total picture of the developing person. Another large part of the puzzle of development concerns what we know as social and emotional development. Indeed, this aspect of our lives is as important to us as the development of our thinking skills.

Erikson's Theory of Socioemotional Development

One of the dominant theories of socioemotional development was proposed by the noted scholar Erik Erikson (1950). Erikson's theory of socioemotional development is really a theory of socialization across the life span. Erikson views development as a continuing and ongoing process from birth until old age. Across this span of time, Erikson posits eight general stages of a person's life. Each stage is characterized by a conflict or tension that a person must resolve in his or her own way for him- or herself. Erikson's stages and their corresponding conflicts include:

1. *Basic trust versus mistrust* (infancy). In infancy, the major tension is one of trust versus mistrust. This tension is resolved in each person to different degrees as a function of how the infant interacts with his or her caretaker and others in the environment. Human infants are perhaps the most dependent of all newborn animals and must trust others to provide for their needs. It is in this interaction between the infant and the caretakers who meet the infant's needs that the infant will develop a sense of trust versus mistrust.

2. *Autonomy versus shame and doubt* (toddler). As infants develop motor skills and muscular coordination, they begin to operate in the world as autonomous beings. Mobility brings with it a sense of independence, competence, and mastery (just ask anyone who just received their driver's li-

cense). How caretakers and the environment around the developing toddler deal with these newfound skills forms the basis of the resolution to
the conflict that is associated with the development of these skills.

3. *Initiative versus guilt* (preschool). At this stage of development, youngsters
begin to coordinate their continuously developing motor skills with
planned goals to produce purposeful actions. How the environment
around these youngsters meets the new challenges produced by them
serves as the central conflict underlying this stage. Will efforts at initiation
be reinforced? Or will they be thwarted by caretakers or others? The answer to these questions forms the basis from which the youngsters' central core revolves around this issue.

4. *Industry versus inferiority* (young childhood, 6–12). In many societies and
cultures, this age range corresponds to the time when formalized instruction begins. In many societies, of course, this time period marks the beginning of elementary school. According to Erikson, it is this period of
life when youngsters find themselves addressing concerns about work
ethic and discipline, concepts related to a sense of industry. To the extent
that a sense of industry is not found in the youngsters, this period of life
can mark a sense of inferiority with regard to work ethic.

5. *Identity versus role confusion* (adolescence). Puberty brings with it biological and physiological changes in adolescents as well as profound
sociopsychological questions. This period of life is marked by the central
question of developing an individual identity, place, and role in life. Puberty forces all of us to ask and answer this question. To the degree to
which we address this question we can develop a sure sense of identity. If
not, we can be confused about our roles.

6. *Intimacy versus self-absorption* (young adulthood). Intimacy refers to the
degree to which individuals can develop close and intimate relationships
with others. The opposite of intimacy is self-absorption, the inability to
develop such relationships. Erikson's suggestion of the importance of this
stage of life highlights the social nature of his theory and of his understanding of people as social creatures.

7. *Generativity versus stagnation* (middle age). As adults, we face challenges in
later years regarding our productiveness in life. The degree to which we
feel we have been useful to society in some way, or productive in our
work or relationships, marks the degree of generativity of our lives. An
important aspect of generativity is the notion that something we have
done is meaningful to the next generation of people. An unsuccessful
resolution of this conflict brings with it feelings of stagnation and questioning of the purpose and utility of life.

8. *Integrity versus despair* (old age). The final stage of our lives is marked by
reflection over and across our life span. As we examine and reflect on our
lives, we question how we entered each stage of life and how we resolved

each question and conflict. To the extent that we can look back on our lives and be proud of how we entered and resolved each conflict, we develop a sense of integrity about our lives and about ourselves. The opposite, however, is marked with despair and disgust.

Erikson's Theory of Socioemotional Development in the Context of Enculturation

Erikson's theory of socioemotional development is important when considering cultural diversity in enculturation for several reasons. First, it is important to know that while Erikson developed his theory while he worked in the United States, the research that forms the basis for that work is by no means unicultural. Indeed, Erikson studied the development of individuals from many different cultures, including European, American, and Native American cultures. Erikson himself was not raised in the United States, but was born and raised in Europe. This fact in itself does not guarantee a multicultural focus, but it does at the very least provide the milieu within which cross-cultural comparison and experience could have contributed to his theory. Erikson's perspective enabled him to develop a theory of socialization and socioemotional development that he himself intended to be cross-cultural in nature. In general, cross-cultural and anthropological research on this theory has been supportive of it (Ferrante, 1992).

A number of other important points about this theory are helpful to our understanding of enculturation processes. First, the conflicts characterizing each stage do not pose either-or resolutions. Instead, they should be seen as labels on a continuum on which each individual marks him- or herself. Differences between people are understood as differences in degree, not as absolute differences in dichotomous resolutions to these conflicts.

Second, "successful" resolutions at one stage are partially dependent on successful resolutions at a prior stage. There is linkage in this work that connects life span issues together. Viewed in this way, enculturation can be considered a package of phenomena linked together by a series of resolutions across the life span.

Third, cultures may differ in how they define what a "successful" resolution is. For example, while our individualistic, American culture may view a sense of autonomy in Stage 2 as a preferred outcome, other cultures may not and may prefer children to be socialized to be less autonomous and more dependent on others. What is important in terms of Erikson's theory is not that it posits a preferred choice of resolution at each stage but that it posits the conflict individuals must go through. Different cultures provide differential tendencies for these conflict resolutions.

Fourth, you should not focus on the labels Erikson originally used to describe the conflicts underlying each stage. "Shame and doubt" may be the alternative to "autonomy," and these terms definitely have negative connotations in our language. These may be preferred outcomes in another culture, however, and that culture may choose to label that outcome differently. For example, people of collectivistic cultures that discourage individual autonomy and foster a sense of dependence on others may consider the alternative to autonomy to be "dependence" or "merging relations." Interestingly, shame is often used in these cultures as the social sanction to thwart against too much autonomy.

Finally, Erikson (1950) is clear that while the progression through these stages is somewhat ordered they need not be fixed in any sense. The conflicts described may, in fact, exist throughout the life span and may have particular relevance only at certain times throughout that span. This view of socioemotional development gives Erikson's theory a particularly useful flexibility in understanding socialization across cultures.

Erikson's theory provides a framework that can be used to understand the socioemotional context of development and the enculturation process and should be considered a companion set to the cognitive and moral contexts of development discussed earlier. By highlighting the emotional conflicts that children and adults must negotiate, this theoretical framework helps us realize that the processes of socialization and enculturation are filled with emotional conflicts that add important affective meaning to development.

Temperament, Attachment, and Child Rearing

Socialization and enculturation do not occur in a vacuum. Many other socialization agents and influences need to be considered to understand socialization and the development of culture. In this section, I will examine three areas of development related to children and their parents: temperament, attachment, and child rearing.

Temperament

Traditional knowledge. Any parent can tell you that no two babies are alike. It is not simply that they look different but that they are different from the very beginning with regard to what is called **temperament**. Each baby has its own way of being in the world—easy-going or fussy, active or quiet.

These qualities of responsiveness to the environment that we call tempera- ment exist from birth and evoke different reactions from people in the baby's world. Temperament is generally considered to be a biologically based style of interacting with the world that exists from birth.

Thomas and Chess (1977) have described three major categories of tem- perament: easy, difficult, and slow-to-warm-up. **Easy temperament** is defined by a very regular, adaptable, mildly intense style of behavior that is positive and responsive. **Difficult temperament** is an intense, irregular, withdrawing style generally marked by negative moods. **Slow-to-warm-up** infants need time to make transitions in activity and experiences. Though they may withdraw initially or respond negatively, given time and support they will positively adapt and react.

The interaction of a child's temperament with that of the parents seems to be a key to the development of personality. This is a concept known as **goodness of fit**. Parental reactions to their children's temperaments can pro- mote stability or instability in their children's temperamental responses to the environment. The interaction of the parents' responses to the child's tempera- ment will also affect subsequent attachment.

Cross-cultural studies on temperament. Several studies have examined whether or not children of non-American cultures have different general styles of temperament than those described for American infants. The im- plications of differences in temperament, if they exist, are large. If children of other cultures have different temperaments at birth than American chil- dren, they will respond to the environment differently. Moreover, they will themselves evoke responses by the environment and caregivers that are dif- ferent from what we would traditionally expect. These two fundamental differences that occur as a result of differences in temperament should pro- duce a fundamental difference in worldview and culture in the children as they grow older.

Indeed, Freedman (1974) found that Chinese American babies were calmer and more placid than Euro-American babies or African American ba- bies. When a cloth was placed on their faces covering their noses, the Chi- nese American babies lay quietly and breathed through their mouths. The other babies turned their heads or tried to pull the cloth off with their hands. Freedman found similar differences with Japanese American and Navajo ba- bies when compared to Euro-Americans. Likewise, Chisholm (1983) exten- sively studied Navajo infants and found that they were much calmer than Euro-American infants.

Chisholm (1983) argues that there is a well-established connection be- tween the condition of the mother during pregnancy (especially high blood pressure levels) and the irritability of the infant. This connection between maternal blood pressure and infant irritability has been found in Malaysian, Chinese, Aboriginal and white Australian infants as well as in Navajo infants (Garcia Coll, 1990). Garcia Coll, Sepkoski, and Lester (1981) found that the differences in the health of Puerto Rican mothers during pregnancy were related to differences in their infants' temperaments when compared to Euro-American or African American infants. The Puerto Rican babies were alert and did not cry easily. The African American babies scored higher on motor abilities—behaviors involving muscle movement and coordination. The temperament difference we find as characteristic of a cultural group may reflect differences in genetics and in reproductive histories.

Another important cultural factor to consider is the interaction between parents' responses and infant temperament. This interaction is certainly one of the keys in understanding the development of culture and socialization processes. The quiet temperament and placidity that are notable in infants from Asian and Native American backgrounds are probably further stabilized in later infancy and childhood by the response of the mothers. Navajo and Hopi babies spend long periods of time tightly wrapped in cradle boards; Chinese parents value the harmony that is maintained through emotional restraint (Bond & Wang, 1983).

Still, the difficulties inherent in interpreting temperament differences found in research such as that reported here is compounded by the difficulties in studying and making accurate interpretations of race and racial differences (Zuckerman, 1990). Considerable caution should be exercised in doing so. Nevertheless, these differences that occur from birth contribute to the cultural differences in personality we observe in adults of different cultures. It is important for us to realize the magnitude of these contributions as building blocks in the development of adult members of the cultures of the world.

Attachment

Traditional knowledge.   **Attachment** refers to the special bond that develops between the infant and the caregiver. Many psychologists feel that the quality of attachment has life-long effects on our relationships with loved ones. Attachment provides the child with emotional security. Once established, babies are distressed by separation from their mothers (separation distress or anxiety). The studies on attachment in rhesus monkeys by the Harlows (Harlow & Harlow, 1969) highlighted the importance of contact and physical comfort in the development of attachment. Bowlby (1969) concluded that infants must have a preprogrammed, biological basis for becoming attached to their caregivers. This program includes behaviors such as smiling and cooing that elicit physical attachment-producing behaviors on the part of their mothers.

Ainsworth, Blehar, Waters, and Wall (1978) have delineated three different styles of attachment—secure, avoidant, and ambivalent. Mothers of **securely attached** babies are described as warm and responsive. Mothers of **avoidant children**, who shun their mothers, are suspected of being intrusive and overstimulating. **Ambivalent** children are uncertain in their response to their mothers, going back and forth between seeking and shunning her attention. These mothers have been characterized as insensitive and less involved.

Attachment underpins the concept of trust. Erikson (1963) described the formation of basic trust as the important first step in the life-long process of psychosocial development. Poor attachment is a component of mistrust—the unsuccessful resolution of the needs of the infancy stage. Basic trust is presumed to affect our later relationships and the subsequent stages of development. Erikson described the other stages that occur in childhood as ones involving the tasks of establishing autonomy, initiative, and competency. All of these are parts of the developing self and are influenced by how mothers and important others in the child's life respond to him or her.

Cross-cultural studies of attachment. One of the assumptions about the nature of attachment in the United States is that secure attachment is the ideal. In fact, the very choice of term that Ainsworth and colleagues selected to describe this type of attachment, and the negative terms selected to describe others, reflects this underlying bias. Cultures differ, however, on their notion of "ideal" attachment. For example, German mothers value and promote early independence and regard avoidant attachment as the ideal. German parents see the "securely" attached child as "spoiled" (Grossmann, Grossmann, Spangler, Suess, & Unzner, 1985). Of Israeli children who are raised on a kibbutz (collective farm), half display anxious ambivalent attachments with only a third appearing to be securely attached (Sagi, Lamb, Lewkowicz, Shoham, Dvir, & Estes, 1985). Children raised in traditional Japanese families are also characterized by a high rate of anxious ambivalent attachment, with practically no avoidant types (Miyake, Chen, & Campos, 1985). These traditional mothers seldom leave their children and foster a strong sense of dependence in their children (which in itself is curious, because studies of this culture have shown that ambivalent infants generally are associated with mothers who are less involved). This supports the traditional cultural ideal of family loyalty. In nontraditional Japanese families where the mother may have a career, attachment patterns are found to be similar to those in the United States (Durrett, Otaki, & Richards, 1984).

Some cross-cultural studies also challenge the notion that closeness to the mother is necessary for secure and healthy attachment. Indeed, this notion is prevalent in traditional theories of attachment based on research in the United States. Studies involving an African tribe of forest-dwelling foragers known as the Efe (erroneously referred to by most people as the pygmies, a name they do not like) show a very different situation from that psychologists have come to accept as part of healthy attachment (Tronick, Morelli, & Ivey, 1992). Efe infants spend most of their time away from their mothers and are cared for by a variety of people. They are always within earshot and sight of about ten people. They have close emotional ties to many people other than their mothers and spend very little time with their fathers. The researchers found these children to be emotionally healthy despite having multiple caregivers.

Although this study demonstrated that closeness or proximity to their mothers is not necessary for healthy attachment, this is not necessarily the case for children of other cultures. And it is certainly not comparable to U.S. children who attend day-care centers. The Efe have large, extended families, and these families are permanent parts of the growing Efe children's lives. That is different from day care in the United States, where staff turnovers are typically high and relationships with children are not long term. What the Efe may be revealing is that multiple caregivers who remain stable in a child's life are a healthy alternative to our traditional ideas.

There is still much to be done to understand the attachment patterns in other cultures. The studies that do exist, however, are clear in suggesting that we cannot assume that what is seen most in Euro-American culture is best or most descriptive for all. Notions concerning the quality of attachment and the processes by which it occurs are qualitative judgments made from the perspective of each culture. Each culture has different but not necessarily better values than others.

Child Rearing, Parenting, and Families

Traditional knowledge.   Clearly, our parents play an important if not the most important role in our development. Parenting styles differ dramatically. Baumrind (1971) has identified three major patterns of parenting. The **authoritarian parent** expects unquestioned obedience and views the child as needing to be controlled. **Permissive parents** allow children to regulate their own lives and provide few firm guidelines. The **authoritative parent** is firm, fair, and reasonable. This style is seen as promoting psychologically healthy, competent, independent children who are cooperative and at ease in social situations. Other researchers (Maccoby & Martin, 1983) have identified a fourth type of parenting style called uninvolved. **Uninvolved parents** are often too absorbed in their own lives to appropriately respond to their children and may seem indifferent to them.

   Much of the influence on our development occurs in our relationships with people other than our parents. As children move out of early childhood, friendships change. These changes are in great part due to cognitive development. The new ability to think about themselves and others and to understand their world allows children to develop peer relations that have more depth and meaning.

Diversity in parenting as a function of economics.   One of the first things we need to recognize is that parenting and child rearing often occur in very different economic conditions in other countries and cultures as well as within this country. These diverse conditions produce socialization processes that are extremely varied from culture to culture. Child-rearing practices may differ not merely because of difference in beliefs but also because of marked differences in standards of living. Using a yardstick that we might apply to evaluating parenting in the United States could lead us to harsh conclusions about parenting in other countries and cultures. Consider the case of a slum-dwelling Brazilian mother who leaves her three children under the age of 5 locked in a bare, dark room for the day while she is out attempting to bring home basic needs of food and clothing. Certainly, we cannot judge the practices of others according to our own standards or those of any other single culture.

   It is common folklore that picking up a baby and bringing it to the shoulder reduces bouts of crying and that babies who are ignored and allowed to cry for fear of spoiling them actually cry more. However, in remote rural river regions of China, few-week-old infants are left for long periods of time while their mothers work in the fields. These babies are placed in large sacks of sand that support them upright and act as an absorbent diaper. These babies quickly cease to cry because they learn early that it will not bring about any response at all.

   If a society has a high rate of infant mortality, parenting efforts may concentrate on meeting basic, physical needs. Parents may have little choice but to disregard other developmental demands. Sometimes the response to harsh and stressful conditions brings about changes that we might consider positive. In the Sudan, for example, the mother traditionally spends the first 40 days after delivery entirely with her baby. She rests, and her relatives tend to her as she focuses all her energy on her baby (Cederblad, 1988).

   Levine (1977) has theorized that the caregiving environment reflects a set of goals that are ordered in importance. First is physical health and survival. Next is the promotion of behaviors that will lead to self-sufficiency; last are behaviors that promote other cultural values such as morality and prestige. Many families in the United States are fortunate in that they can turn their attention to meeting the second two goals. In many countries, the primary goal of survival is all important and often overrides the other goals in the amount of parental effort exerted. Indeed, this is true in many areas of the United States as well.

Extended families.   The structure of the family also has a large impact on child rearing and care giving. In many non-Euro-American cultures, extended families are prevalent. In the United States in 1984, for example, 31% of African American children lived in extended families, while only 19.8% of children of other races lived in such families (U.S. Bureau of the Census, 1985). Extended families are a vital and important feature of child rearing, even when resources are not limited. Many cultures view extended family child rearing as an integral and important part of their cultures. It can provide a buffer to stresses of everyday living. It is also an important process by which cultural heritage is transmitted from generation to generation.

Extended families can support and facilitate child rearing in ways that are completely different from the traditional, Euro-American nuclear family. Research on parenting tends to assume a nuclear family structure when delineating the style of parenting (for example, authoritarian, permissive, authoritative, neglectful). In the United States, ethnic minority families have been characterized as extended and generally more conservative than Euro-American families. For example, Japanese American families have been categorized as extended with strict age and sex roles and as having an emphasis on children's obedience to authority figures (Trankina, 1983; Yamamoto & Kubota, 1983).

Even though mothers are still seen as the primary caregiver, children experience frequent interaction with fathers, grandparents, godparents, siblings, and cousins in an extended family situation. Godparents are seen as important models for children in Hispanic and Filipino families. They are also sources of support for the parents. Sharing households with relatives is a characteristic of extended families and is seen as a good way of maximizing the family's resources for successful child rearing.

One need not look outside the United States to recognize the importance of extended families. One major difference, however, is that participation in child rearing via extended families in the United States is often seen as a consequence of poor economics rather than a desirable state of affairs. Limited resources are a reality, with 11.2 million children in the United States living below the poverty level in 1990. Many are born to single mothers, and here the extended family plays an important role in the child-rearing process. Grandmothers are more actively involved with their grandchildren when they live with their single adult daughters. These children experience a greater variety of main caregivers and have different social interactions than their traditional Euro-American counterparts. Compounding this picture is the reality that ethnicity also confounds social class.

Teenage parenting also forces us to think differently about traditional notions of parenting. The presence of the maternal grandmother in these families has been found to cancel out some of the negative results associated with teen mothering (Garcia Coll, 1990). The grandmother often serves as a valuable source of information about child development. She also tends to be more responsive and less punitive with her grandchildren than the teen mother is. The grandmother in these three-generation households plays a very important role as a teacher and role model to her daughter and can provide favorable, positive social interaction for her grandchild.

Extended families differ in their composition from one culture to another but have in common sharing of resources, emotional support, and care giving. The experiences of a child growing up in these situations can be quite different from those of a child in a traditional Euro-American household. In addition, we need to be aware that the "traditional" two parent household composition is changing for many Euro-American homes. Future studies will undoubtedly change the way we view parenting in this culture as well.

Cultural differences in sleeping arrangements.   Of the many different child-rearing behaviors people of different cultures engage in, one of the most representative of cultural differences concerns sleeping arrangements. One of the single greatest concerns of urban dwelling Western parents, especially Americans, is getting their baby to sleep through the night, and to do so in a room separate from the parents'. In the United States, we shun co-sleeping arrangements, with the underlying assumption that sleeping alone will help develop independence. Some assistance is offered to the child by way of "security objects" such as a special blanket or toy.

This value is not shared by many other cultures. In rural European areas, for example, infants sleep with their mothers for most, if not all, of their first year. This is also true for many other cultures in the world, and comfort objects or bedtime rituals are not common in other cultures. Mayan mothers allow their children to sleep with them for several years because of a commitment to forming a very close bond with their children. As a new baby comes along, older children move to a bed in the same room or share a bed with another member of the family (Morelli, Oppenheim, Rogoff, & Goldsmith, 1992). In traditional Japanese families, the child sleeps with the mother, either with the father on the other side or in a separate room by him- or herself.

Summary

The information presented in this section speaks to just a few of the many ways in which parenting and child rearing take place around the world. Perhaps what is most important to realize is that each culture's way of raising children, through parenting, preferred attachment styles, sleeping arrangements, and other concrete mechanisms, represents that culture's way of ensuring that its values and norms are transmitted to those children. In all cultures, these practices are ritualized so that this transmission of information can occur in generation after generation. Learning cultural values is as much a part of the process of socialization as it is an outcome of socialization.

In the final section of this chapter, I will examine cultural and socialization effects of the single most important formalized mechanism of instruction in many societies and cultures—the educational system.

Socialization and the Educational System

Socialization of Culture through Education

There is perhaps no more important institution that influences the development and socialization of our children in much of the world today than the educational system. Most of us think about the educational system solely as an institution that teaches members of a society about thinking skills and knowledge. But the educational system is probably the most important institution that socializes our children and teaches and reinforces important cultural values.

Our educational system imparts cultural values and socializes children in several ways. First, the content of what is taught in the schools reflects a priori choices by that culture or society regarding what it believes is important to learn. Different cultures believe different topics to be important. By teaching a certain type of content, the educational system reinforces a particular view of cognition and intelligence.

The environmental setting in which education occurs is yet another important factor to consider. Many industrialized societies have a formal educational system, with identifiable areas and structures (schools) and identifiable education agents (teachers) to "do" education. In other cultures, formalized education may be in small groups led by elders of the community. In yet other cultures, formalized education may be a family task (for example, the mother tutoring her own children in cognitive and other skills necessary for members of their community). Regardless of the environmental setting, the vehicle by which education occurs reinforces certain types of cultural values in its recipients.

The organization, planning, and implementation of lesson plans is another important cultural socializer. Some cultures encourage a didactic model of teaching, where an expert teacher simply gives information to students who are expected to listen and learn. Other cultures view teachers as leaders through a lesson plan, providing the overall structure and framework by which students discover principles and concepts. Some cultures view imparting of praise as an important process. Other cultures focus on mistakes made by students in the learning process. Some cultures (like ours) have special classes and mechanisms to deal with many different types of groups, for example, students with learning disabilities, physical handicaps, and the gifted. Other cultures tend to downplay such differences among their students, treating all students as equals.

Once in school, the majority of a child's life is spent away from the parents. The socialization process that began in the primary relationship with the parents continues with peers in play situations and in school. School institutionalizes cultural values and attitudes and is a significant contributor not only to the intellectual development of the child but as importantly to the child's social and emotional development.

Regardless of the way education occurs, the choices a society and culture make concerning its structure, organization, planning, and implementation all encourage and reinforce a certain view of culture. We are not always cognizant of our own cultural view because we are in the middle of it. To see our own biases and choices, we simply need to observe education in other cultures and compare what is done elsewhere to what we do. In doing so, the differences and the similarities often become quite clear.

Cultural Differences in Learning Mathematics

Mathematics learning occupies a special place in our understanding of culture, socialization, and the educational system. Of course, learning math skills is crucial to the ultimate development of science in any society, which is probably why so much attention is focused on it in research as well as funding from government and private sources. Still, math and culture have a very special relationship because, as Stigler and Baranes (1988) describe, math skills "are not logically constructed on the basis of abstract cognitive structures, but rather are forged out of a combination of previously acquired (or inherited) knowledge and skills, and new cultural input" (p. 258). Culture is not only a stimulator of math but is itself represented in math learning. That is, culture is represented in math and how a society teaches and learns it.

Not all cultures of the world rely solely on mathematics training in an institutionalized school setting to teach math. For example, important math skills are taught to Micronesian islanders in the Puluwat culture through learning navigation, to coastal Ghanans by marketing fish, and even by bookies in Brazil (Acioly & Schliemann, 1986; Gladwin, 1970; Gladwin & Gladwin, 1971). Of course, important math skills are imparted not only by extra-school activities in more "exotic" cultures but even through activities such as dieting and weight watching in the United States (Stigler & Baranes, 1988).

Cross-national research on math learning in schools has traditionally compared the math abilities of students around the world. An early study conducted by the International Association for the Evaluation of Education Achievement (IEA) (Husen, 1967), for example, measured math achievement scores in 12 different countries at the 8th and 12th grades. A later study compared 17 countries. Perhaps the best known of the findings is the relatively poor performance of American students in comparison to most other countries, but particularly Japan.

Since those earlier studies, the most concerted effort to pinpoint the root of these national differences in math abilities has been by the research programs of Harold Stevenson and James Stigler. Several of their studies have focused on a comparison among American, Japanese, and Chinese (Taiwan) elementary school students and have centered on three topics: documentation of cross-cultural differences in math performance, an examination of how math is taught in class, and cultural differences in the value and belief systems relating to math and schooling that may underlie those differences.

The findings in all three areas speak to the vast and complex relationship between culture and education. Even in first grade, the superiority of the Japanese and Chinese in math performance is already striking, and reaches "dynamic" proportions by fifth grade (Stevenson, Lee, & Stigler, 1986; Stigler & Baranes, 1988, p. 291). The relatively poor performance of American children has also been documented in comparisons with Korean children (Song & Ginsburg, 1987). Moreover, the differences were observed not only in computational tests but in all math tests produced and administered by the researchers.

Stigler and his colleagues then examined the classrooms to find the possible roots of these differences. Several major differences in the use of classroom time underlie math performance differences. The Japanese and Chinese spent more days per year in school, more hours per day in school, a greater proportion of time in school devoted to purely academic subjects, and a greater proportion of time devoted to math. The Japanese and Chinese teachers spent a greater proportion of time working with the whole class than did the American teachers. This difference is even more dramatic when you consider that the average size of American classes was smaller than those in Japan or China. As a result, American students spent less time working under the supervision and guidance of a teacher.

During class, it was also observed that American teachers tended to use praise to reward correct responses. Teachers in Japan, however, tended to focus on incorrect answers, using those as examples to lead into discussion of the computational process and math concepts. Teachers in Taiwan tended to use a process more congruent with the Japanese approach. This teaching difference speaks to the cultural emphasis in the United States of rewarding uniqueness and individualism and the emphasis in Japan and China on finding ways to engage in group process and sharing responsibility for mistakes with members of the group. Praise, while nice, often precludes such discussion.

Finally, a number of important differences in cultural values and belief systems among the Americans, Japanese, and Chinese were found to have an impact on education. These differences are also heavily rooted in culture. For example, Japanese and Chinese parents and teachers alike were more likely to consider all children as equal, with no differences between them. American parents and teachers are more likely to recognize differences and find reasons to treat their children as special. This difference is clearly rooted in a cultural tension between individualism and collectivism among the three cultures.

American parents and teachers are more likely to consider innate ability more important than effort; for the Japanese and Chinese, however, effort is far more important than ability. This difference is also rooted in cultural differences among the three countries and has enormous implications for education. American parents tend to be more easily satisfied at lower levels of competence than either the Japanese or the Chinese. Also, when problems arise, Americans are more likely to attribute of the cause of the problem to something they cannot do anything about (for example, ability). These cultural differences in attribution of causality are directly related to cultural differences in self-construals discussed in Chapter 3.

Believing that ability is more important than effort has yet another side to it—a belief that each child is *limited* in his or her abilities. Once this belief becomes a cultural institution, it dictates how the educational system should respond. The resulting emphasis in the case of the American system, for example, is to seek unique, innate differences among the students, to generate separate special classes for these unique groups of students, and to generally individualize the process of education. As a result, more time is spent on individualized instruction and less on whole group instruction.

Summary

Cross-national differences in any type of academic performance, and the cross-cultural differences that underlie them, are not solely a product of cultural differences in effort or abilities. The performance of students of any culture on any topic is the result of a complex interplay of economics, geography, resources, cultural values and beliefs, abilities, experiences, language, and family dynamics. Research by Stigler, Lee, and Stevenson (1986) demonstrated that cross-national differences among Chinese, Japanese, and American children in counting and memory exercises may be just as much a function of the Chinese, Japanese, and American languages related to counting and numbers than to anything else. For example, the numbering system in the Japanese language requires a unique verbal label for numbers 1 through 10. Number eleven is then 10-1, twelve is 10-2, twenty is 2-10, twenty-one is 2-10-1, and so forth. In English, however, we must learn a unique number for 1 through 19. All the decade numbers (20, 30, 40, and so forth) also have unique labels. This fundamental difference in language related to numbers may contribute to cultural differences in counting.

Still, it is important to remember that as a social institution, formalized educational experiences, whether in schools, communities, or in families, are an important and integral part of the socialization process of any culture. Differences in these institutions not only reflect but reinforce cultural differences in values, beliefs, attitudes, norms, and behaviors and help transmit this important cultural information from one generation to the next. As discussed earlier in this chapter with Erikson's socioemotional theory of socialization, the school-age period of life is indeed a critical time when culture is strongly reinforced in children by society as a whole. This process is pervasive.

Conclusion

Work in the fields of developmental psychology, education, sociology, and anthropology has all contributed to the vast knowledge we have concerning the influence of culture on development, sociocultural institutions of socialization, and education. We have gained a perspective of socialization not only through formative infant and childhood years but through adolescence, young adulthood, and throughout the life span. Cultural influences produce many similarities as well as differences in a variety of areas of life, including thinking skills, moral reasoning, and socioemotional life. Culture influences and is influenced by the educational institutions established to transmit cultural as well as intellectual knowledge to its members.

Each of these areas of study informs us about how culture influences development. But equally important, we must ask ourselves how it is that these processes, and the differences we observe as a result of these processes, come to ensure that our children are enculturated properly? Super and Harkness (1986, 1994) suggest that enculturation occurs within what they term a *developmental niche.* This niche forms the structural and subjective framework by which children come to learn the cultural values and mores important to their society. According to these authors, this niche includes three major components: the physical and social setting, the customs of child care and child rearing, and the psychology of the caregivers. The developing child is seen as receiving influence from all three components, or more precisely from the interaction of the three components with each other, all of which occurs within a larger environmental and human ecology. In this niche, the developing children are able to receive the influences of various socialization agents and institutions around them to ensure enculturation of the child to the culture, while the child also brings his or her temperamental disposition to the interaction.

Enculturation is not a quick process. While the process may start at a very early age, it takes time, effort, and energy by all components of the developmental niche to ensure that enculturation occurs successfully. Recent research by Bernal (1994) and her colleagues suggests that children acquire ethnic and cultural identities in stages across a span of years and that these stages differ considerably from the children's awareness of race and gender. In her research, Bernal found that preschool children have very limited awareness of their ethnic and cultural backgrounds. This awareness grows gradually as the children get older and their knowledge and understanding of their ethnic and cultural heritage increases. Even older children still do not grasp the meaning attributed to their culture and ethnic heritage as adults seem to. This long developmental process of enculturation is congruent with my view that culture is a subjective, psychological phenomenon consisting of a conglomeration of attitudes, values, beliefs, norms, and behaviors; it is history, and it is the present. It is not a fixed entity, and it is no wonder that it takes years for enculturation to occur.

The developmental differences discussed in this chapter all speak to how a sense of culture develops in each of us. As cultures exert their influences in their own special and unique ways, they produce specific tendencies, trends, and differences in their members when compared to others. When we are in the middle of a culture, as we all are, we cannot see those differences or how culture itself develops in us. Only when we look outside ourselves and examine the developmental and socialization processes of other cultures are we able to see what we are ourselves. Only then can we come to appreciate the fact that those differences and similarities are our culture, or at the very least are the manifestations of our culture. Thus, while cultures produces differences in development that we observe in our research, these differences contribute to the development of culture. Despite the subtle interplay of the wording in that last sentence, it is a very important point to recognize.

 # Glossary

accommodation   The process of changing your understanding to accommodate ideas that conflict with existing concepts.

acculturation   Refers to the process of adapting, and in many cases adopting, to a different culture than the one in which you were enculturated.

ambivalent attachment   A style of attachment in which children are uncertain in their response to their mothers, going back and forth between seeking and shunning her attention. These mothers have been characterized as insensitive and less involved.

animism   The belief that all things, including inanimate objects, are alive.

assimilation   The process of fitting new ideas into a pre-existing understanding of the world.

attachment   Refers to the special bond that develops between the infant and the caregiver. The quality of attachment has life-long effects on our relationships with loved ones.

authoritarian parent   A style of parenting in which the parent expects unquestioned obedience and views the child as needing to be controlled.

authoritative parent   A style of parenting that is viewed as firm, fair, and reasonable. This style is seen as promoting psychologically healthy, competent, independent children who are cooperative and at ease in social situations.

avoidant attachment   A style of attachment in which children shun their mothers, who are suspected of being intrusive and overstimulating.

centration   The tendency to focus on a single aspect of a problem.

cognitive development   A specialty in psychology that studies how thinking skills develop over time. The major theory of cognitive development is that by Piaget.

conservation   An awareness that physical quantities remain the same regardless of whether they change shape or appearance.

conventional morality   The second stage of Kohlberg's theory of moral development, it emphasizes conformity to rules that are defined by others' approval, or to society's rules.

difficult temperament   A type of temperament that is characterized by an intense, irregular, withdrawing style that is generally marked by negative moods.

easy temperament   A type of temperament that is defined by a very regular, adaptable, mildly intense style of behavior that is positive and responsive.

egocentrism   The inability to step into another's shoes and understand the other person's point of view.

enculturation   The process by which individuals learn and adopt the ways and manners of their culture.

goodness of fit   Refers to the interaction of children's temperament with their parents and is a key to the development of personality.

great divide theories   Theories of cognitive development that suggest that the thought of Westerners was superior than that of people who lived in primitive societies.

irreversibility   The inability to imagine "undoing" a process.

permissive parents   A style of parenting in which parents allow children to regulate their own lives and provide few firm guidelines.

postconventional morality   The third stage of Kohlberg's theory of moral development, which emphasizes moral reasoning according to individual principles and conscience.

preconventional morality   The first stage of Kohlberg's theory of moral development, it emphasizes compliance with rules to avoid punishment and with rules to get rewards.

secure attachment   A style of attachment in which babies are described as warm and responsive.

slow-to-warm-up   A type of temperament where infants need time to make transitions in activity and experiences. Though they may withdraw initially or respond negatively, given time and support they will positively adapt and react.

socialization   The process that occurs during development by which we learn and internalize the rules and patterns of behavior that are affected by culture. This process occurs over a long period of time and involves learning and mastering society's and culture's norms, attitudes, values, and belief systems.

socialization agents   The people, institutions, and organizations that exist to help ensure that socialization occurs.

temperament   Qualities of responsiveness to the environment that exist from birth and evoke different reactions from people in the baby's world. Temperament is generally considered to be a biologically based style of interacting with the world.

uninvolved parents   A style of parenting in which parents are often too absorbed in their own lives to appropriately respond to their children and often seem indifferent to them.

6

Cultural Influences on Organizations and the World of Work

Leadership, Management, and Productivity

We all spend an inordinate amount of time in our lives in organizations. In fact, most of you reading this book are probably doing so in one of the most important organizational systems that exist in this and other countries—the organization that we know of as school. The educational system is one type of organization that plays an important part in many people's lives and is an important agent of socialization in the development and maintenance of culture. But schools are not the only organization to which we belong in our lives. The companies that we work for are also organizations. Many of the extracurricular activities we engage in are supported by organizations, such as the YMCA, churches, sport clubs, and the like. And there are organizations that provide structure and services for us such as government and hospitals.

Culture influences organizations and how we operate within those organizations. Culture can have an impact on the structure of organizations as well as on their functions. Culture can also have an important impact on the relationships among people within organizations and between organizations. In this chapter, we will explore how culture influences organizations. While there are many different types of organizations in the world, I will focus on one particular type—work organizations. Work organizations have been the topic of many intercultural studies and provide the context for our knowledge of the effects of culture on organizations. The information gained in understanding the relationship between culture and work organizations can be useful in understanding other organizations as well. We will examine how cultures influence work and organizations and learn how work and organizations influence culture reciprocally as well.

Cultural Similarities and Differences in the Meaning of Work

When considering cultural similarities and differences in work and organizations, the first issue is to consider the possibility that the meaning of work differs across cultures. People construe themselves and their existence in relation to work differently across cultures, and these differences are related to meaningful dimensions of cultural variability. For example, as discussed in Chapter 3, people who are members of collectivistic cultures tend to have interdependent construals of their selves. That is, they tend to identify people around them, and their work organization itself, as fundamentally interrelated with themselves and as integral parts of their self-identities. This tendency is diminished in individualistic cultures, which tend to foster a view of self as independent, unique, and autonomous from others.

People of collectivistic cultures view their work groups and the work organizations (companies) to which they belong as a fundamental part of themselves. The bonds between these people and their work colleagues, and between themselves and their company, are stronger and fundamentally and qualitatively different from those for people with independent senses of self. Work, work colleagues, and the company become synonymous with the self.

People in individualistic cultures, however, have an easier time separating themselves from their jobs. They find it easier to distinguish between "work time" and "personal time." They make greater distinctions between company-based expense accounts and personal expenses. They make greater distinctions between social and work activities, with regard to both their work colleagues and their business associates (potential clients, customers, and so forth.).

As we examine the relationship between culture and work across different cultures, the first lesson is that a person's self-identification with work and with companies is fundamentally different, across cultures and these differences are intimately tied to differences in culture along dimensions such as individualism versus collectivism. Thus, there are fundamental differences in the definition and implication of work across cultures.

Cultural differences in the meaning of work can be manifest in other aspects of work as well. For example, in American culture, it is easy to think of work as a means to the accumulation of money (pay or salary) to make a living. In other cultures, especially collectivistic ones, work may be seen more as the fulfillment of an obligation to a larger group. In this situation, you would expect to find less movement of an individual from one job to another because of the social obligations the individual has toward the work organization to which he or she belongs and to the people comprising that organization. In individualistic cultures, however, it is easier to consider leaving one job and going to another because it is easier to separate jobs from the self. A different job will just as easily accomplish the same goals.

Much of the material in this chapter speaks to the notion that the meaning of work differs across cultures. Fundamental differences exist among people in relation to this important area of our lives. I will return briefly to this discussion at the end of the chapter.

Organizations and Culture

An organization is a structure created by people to achieve certain objectives. Organizations are generally composed of people who work collectively to address the overall goals of the organization. Different people or groups of people may have different specific goals within the organization, but theoretically they should collectively address a common goal (for example, building a car, selling groceries). Different people or groups of people may be specialized according to role, objective, or task, and they may be differentiated from each other by rank or status within a hierarchy.

In the past, it was probably easier than it is now to identify organizations relatively isolated from issues of culture. Previously in the United States, the general population was less racially and ethnically diverse than it is today. This characteristic of the population meant that much of the workforce in any company or work organization was less diverse culturally. With less cultural diversity within the workforce, the expectations of the members of any work organization were generally similar to each other. Communication, lines of authority, and hierarchical structure were established with less conscious awareness of differences underlying the people, because there were fewer cultural differences among the people in the first place. In many ways, we all had implicit, tacit knowledge about how to behave around each other and how to work together, because we all started with relatively similar cultural backgrounds.

Organizations were more isolated from issues of culture in yet another way, as many companies in the past were entirely domestic. Many of the work-related issues companies dealt with were limited to issues raised within this country and, therefore, within this culture. And most of the companies that cooperated with one another to do their work resided in the same country and culture. Competing companies were also from this same culture. Work was much more domestic than it was international. These characteristics of a national work environment have quickly become a thing of the past. Increasing ethnic and racial diversity in the American population in general has ensured that much of the workforce within American companies is culturally mixed and diverse. That diversity brings the richness of varied cultural heritages to the work context and provides challenges for many companies today.

Also, many companies are now influenced by the international arena. Today, there are unprecedented numbers of **multinational and international corporations**—work organizations that have subsidiaries and satellite offices and work units in more than a single country. More and more of these companies need to deal with people of diverse and varied backgrounds. Today, transfers from one business unit to another within the same company can mean a transfer from one country to another. Clearly, intercultural issues brought about by this type of internationalization of business bring with them more challenges of cultural differences in the work context than in the past.

Even domestic companies that are not multinational in their structure must face the challenge of internationalization of business and work and the resulting intercultural issues associated with it. With changes in trade laws, more and more of today's business competitors come from distant cultures. Conversely, increasing opportunities exist for opening markets in other countries and cultures. Recent legislation in the United States (North American Free Trade Agreement, NAFTA, for example) has made these opportunities and challenges a reality for many American companies.

Technological changes in communication—telephones, facsimile machines, videoteleconferencing, and electronic mail—have forced the issue of culture to the forefront of our work lives. The world and business are seen today as less distant and remote; indeed, we are living in a unitary global village. Within this global village, the exchange of goods, services, and resources knows few boundaries. In the United States, the issues that this global village raises can be seen within our borders as well as across borders. Many of these issues are cultural. Our ability to deal with these issues in an ever changing business world will dictate our success or failure.

Culture and Organizational Structure

Organizations are assemblies of people and resources that have their own structure. Like people, each organization is unique; like groups of people and cultures, groups of organizations have similarities we may equate as culture. In recent years, it has become fashionable to refer to this aspect of organizations as "organizational culture" (O'Reilly, 1989; O'Reilly, Chatman, & Caldwell, 1991). Some writers have suggested that organizations differ along certain stable dimensions. Robbins (1987), for example, suggests that organizations differ in complexity, formalization, and centralization. **Complexity** refers to the degree to which organizations foster a differentiation of tasks and activities within themselves. **Formalization** refers to the degree to which organizations provide structure and rules for their operations. **Centralization** refers to the degree to which organizations concentrate their operations and decision-making capabilities in a limited number of business units or people.

Berry et al. (1992) point out that a number of factors determine how organizations deal with these three dimensions. These factors include the size of the organization, the technology available to it, resources, and history. In addition to these variables, we need to account for the culture of the people comprising these organizations—the employees—and their worldview or ways of understanding and interacting with the world and with other people.

With these factors to take into consideration, it is no wonder that organizations differ on these dimensions according to the culture in which they exist. Several writers have used these differences to characterize the "national character" of organizations. Lammers and Hickson (1979) suggest the existence of three different types of national character in organizations: the **Latin type,** the **Anglo-Saxon type,** and the **Third World type.** The Latin type is characterized as a classic bureaucracy, with centralized power and decision making and many hierarchical levels. The Anglo-Saxon type is more or less the opposite, with less centralization, more diffusion of power and decision making, and less hierarchy in the bureaucracy. The Third World type is characterized by greater centralization of decision making, less formalization of rules, and a more paternalistic or traditional family orientation.

Lammers and Hickson's (1979) study is but one attempt to examine cultural differences in organizational structure. All the different types of organizations of the world cannot be pigeonholed into three (or any number of) limited classifications, just as it would be impossible to pigeonhole all people into neat categories of classification (no matter how hard psychologists may try!). But general tendencies of differences in organizational structure can be observed across countries, and these differences are most likely related to cultural differences in the people comprising the organizations and the countries in which they exist. As with people, each organization needs to be understood on its own terms. Many other countries, not only the United States, are dealing with increasing diversity in their populations. This diversity challenges us to begin questioning the validity of broad generalizations about people and organizations.

Organizational Culture

It has become quite fashionable of late to speak of **organizational or corporate culture**. These terms supposedly refer to aspects of an organization that serve as a macrolevel climate or atmosphere within which employees must operate. As a macrolevel variable, organizational culture has an impact on how people within an organization think, feel, and behave. Research on organizational climate or corporate culture as we know it, however, has not provided support for the existence or importance of this variable. Berry et al. (1992) reviewed several studies that examined correlations between organizational climate and actual employee attitudes and productivity. In general, very little correlation exists, which tends to minimize the importance of organizational culture as an important factor. Studies that do support the view of corporate culture as an important variable tend to be based on impressions or anecdotes of organizational behavior and life.

Undoubtedly, employees need to learn organizational rules concerning their proper behavior, but these rules are learned relatively late in their personal development. After all, people have been learning the rules of their culture since birth. Organizational culture as we know it may refer more to "shared daily practices" in the workplace (Berry et al., 1992, p. 322) than to shared values of life, which is more akin to our understanding of culture. Thus, it may be more accurate to suggest that employees of an organization all learn to temporarily engage in the organizational structure, or culture, while they are within the organization. That is, they learn to work and function within a "temporary culture" that is added to the cultural milieu within which people normally operate. This temporary culture exists as a separate entity from more basic, fundamental cultural values. The temporary cultures to which people acculturate do not necessarily change the fundamental self outside of the work environment. Rather, it is a limited and contextualized version of culture that people move in and out of in their daily lives. While a tangible climate exists within corporations and organizations, it does not replace or take away from culture as we know it.

Cultural Differences in Work-Related Values

People of different cultural backgrounds come to work with different values related to their work. These values range across broad topics such as individual orientation and attitudes about work itself, attitudes about the organization and company loyalty, the importance of personal relationships with other members of the company, and so forth. Cultural similarities and differences in value orientations related to work can be the source of overall growth and financial gain or of conflict, frustration, and organizational stumbling.

The best known study of work-related values was conducted by Hofstede (1980, 1984) in the 1960s and 1970s. His study involved employees at International Business Machines (IBM), a multinational corporation with branch offices and subsidiaries in many different countries. In his original study (1980), Hofstede reported data collected from workers in 40 different countries. In a later study (1984), he reported data from an additional 10 countries. Altogether, more than 116,000 questionnaires were distributed to workers in these various countries, spanning upwards of 20 different languages. In addition, 7 different occupational levels were included in the study.

The questionnaire itself contained approximately 160 items, of which 63 were related to work values. The questions clustered around four major themes: satisfaction, perception, personal goals and beliefs, and demographics. On the basis of the data he obtained, Hofstede identified four major dimensions of work-related values and computed overall scores for each country on each of these four dimensions. This approach allowed him to order the countries according to the score they had on each dimension. This approach, using country or group scores as the units of analysis, is called an ecological approach. This approach is slightly different from those that use individuals as the unit of analysis and can be used to identify and characterize national tendencies along these dimensions. However, a one-to-one correspondence with those same tendencies does not necessarily exist on the individual level within a country.

Hofstede called the four major dimensions in his study power distance (PD), uncertainty avoidance (UA), individualism-collectivism (IC), and masculinity (MA). IC was introduced in Chapter 2; indeed, Hofstede's study was a major impetus to viewing and understanding cultures using a dimensional approach. Each of these dimensions is related to concrete differences in attitudes, opinions, beliefs, and behaviors within work organizations and forms the basis for understanding certain societal norms that exist in each of the countries in Hofstede's studies. These dimensions also have consequences for organizational structure and interorganizational behavior and will be addressed separately in the next sections.

Power Distance

Status and power are sociological concepts associated with groups of individuals. In companies and organizations, vertical or hierarchical relationships based on status and power differences are common. Indeed, differentiating people according to their roles, functions, and positions within a company is vital to the successful operations of that organization. Work organizations are no different in this respect from any other organizations. The various statuses afforded different individuals within a hierarchy in a company come with certain benefits, rights, privileges, and power not afforded others. The "chain of command" within a company identifies the players and their roles. Each company decides these issues based on their importance for its continued functioning in the marketplace.

The basic hierarchical relationship is that between an immediate boss and his or her subordinate. In most cases, an employee is involved in both a hierarchical relationship with someone of higher status, and with others of lower status. Each culture, and all people within cultures, develops ways of interacting with different people according to the status differential that exists between the individual and the person with whom he or she is interacting. Power distance (PD) refers to the degree to which different cultures encourage or maintain power and status differences between interactants. Cultures high on PD develop rules, mechanisms, and rituals that serve to maintain and strengthen the status relationships among their members. Cultures low on PD, however, minimize those rules and customs, eliminating if not ignoring the status differences that exist between people.

In Hofstede's original study (1980), the Philippines, Mexico, Venezuela, and India had the highest scores on this dimension. These findings suggest that the cultures underlying these countries maintained strong status differences. Countries such as New Zealand, Denmark, Israel, and Austria, which had the lowest marks on PD, suggest that the cultures underlying these countries did the most to minimize status and power differentials. Spain, Pakistan, Japan, and Italy were right in the middle of the scores. The United States had slightly lower scores, reflecting some degree of minimizing of power differences.

The findings for the United States are somewhat surprising. You would think that American culture was developed to minimize power differences among people, treating all people as equals. Mulder (1976, 1977), however, has suggested that an unequal degree of PD exists in American culture. According to Mulder, people of lower status try to minimize power differences when interacting with someone of higher status. But people of higher status try to maintain power differences with subordinates. In a company, this interesting power differential can be observed by subordinates attempting to minimize power differences when interacting with their bosses, while their bosses try to maintain the power differential with their subordinates.

According to Hofstede, cultural differences on PD are related to individual differences in behaviors that have consequences for their work. Table 6.1 summarizes those characteristics Hofstede gleaned not only from his research but from that of others as well. For example, managers in organizations in high PD cultures are seen as making decisions autocratically and paternalistically. Managers in organizations in low PD cultures, however,

Table 6.1 Summary of Connotations of Power Distance Index (PDI) Differences Found in Survey Research

Low PDI Countries	High PDI Countries
Parents put less value on children's obedience.	Parents put high value on children's obedience.
Students put high value on independence.	Students put high value on conformity.
Authoritarian attitudes in students are a matter of personality.	Students show authoritarian attitudes as a social norm.
Managers seen as making decisions after consulting with subordinates.	Managers seen as making decisions autocratically and paternalistically.
Close supervision negatively evaluated by subordinates.	Close supervision positively evaluated by subordinates.
Stronger perceived work ethic: strong disbelief that people dislike work.	Weaker perceived work ethic: more frequent belief that people dislike work.
Managers more satisfied with participative superior.	Managers more satisfied with directive or persuasive superior.
Subordinates' preference for manager's decision-making style clearly centered on consultative, give-and-take style.	Subordinates' preference for manager's decision-making style polarized between autocratic-paternalistic and majority rule.
Managers like seeing themselves as practical and systematic; they admit a need for support.	Managers like seeing themselves as benevolent decision makers.
Employees less afraid of disagreeing with their boss.	Employees fear to disagree with their boss.
Employees show more cooperativeness.	Employees reluctant to trust each other.
Managers seen as showing more consideration.	Managers seen as showing less consideration.
Students have positive associations with "power" and "wealth."	Students have negative associations with "power" and "wealth."
Mixed feeling about employees' participation in management.	Ideological support for employees' participation in management.
Mixed feelings among managers about the distribution of capacity for leadership and initiative.	Ideological support among managers for a wide distribution of capacity for leadership and initiative.
Informal employee consultation possible without formal participation.	Formal employee participation possible without informal consultation.
Higher-educated employees hold much less authoritarian values than lower-educated ones.	Higher- and lower-educated employees show similar values about authority.

Source: G. Hofstede, *Culture's Consequences: International Differences in Work-Related Values,* p. 92. Copyright © 1980 Sage Publications. Reprinted by permission of Sage Publications, Inc.

are observed making decisions only after more extensive consultation with their subordinates.

The concrete behaviors listed in Table 6.1 are related to societal norms, which in turn have important consequences for organizational structure. In general, cultures high on PD foster organizations with greater centralization of organization and process, taller organizational pyramids, larger proportions of supervisory personnel, larger wage differentials, lower qualifications for lower strata of employees, and greater valuation of white collar as opposed to blue collar jobs. All these characteristics of work organizations and the nature of interpersonal relationships within companies can be considered as a natural consequence of social and cultural differences on power distance.

Uncertainty Avoidance

Uncertainty is a fact of life. No one can predict with 100% accuracy what the future holds for any of us. While this is true for each and every one of us as individuals, it is especially true for companies. Today's profits can easily turn into tomorrow's losses, and vice versa. How a market will react to a new product, revisions in old products, corporate restructuring, mergers and acquisitions, and all the other changes that occur within organizations and in the business world is a major source of uncertainty. With this uncertainty can come confusion, stress, and anxiety.

Every society and every organization develops its own unique ways to deal with the anxiety and stress associated with the uncertainty of the future. Oftentimes, these ways involve development of rituals, informal or written, concerning a code of conduct among employees, as seen in intracompany policies regarding communication or interpersonal relationships. These rules may also govern behavior between companies within a society, or across cultures, as witnessed in domestic and international laws governing business and interbusiness relationships.

Uncertainty avoidance (UA) is a dimension observed in Hofstede's (1980) study that described the degree to which different societies and different cultures develop ways to deal with the anxiety and stress of uncertainty. Cultures high on UA develop highly refined rules and rituals that are mandated and become part of the company rubric and normal way of operations. Companies in these cultures may be thought to be "rule oriented." In Hofstede's survey, Greece, Portugal, Belgium, and Japan were the four countries with the highest scores on this dimension. Cultures low on UA are less concerned with rules and rituals to deal with the stress and anxiety of uncertainty. Companies in these cultures have a more relaxed attitude concerning uncertainty and ambiguity and have comparably fewer rules and rituals mandated for their employees. In Hofstede's study, Sweden, Denmark, and Singapore had the lowest scores on UA.

Cultural differences on UA are directly related to concrete differences in jobs and work-related behaviors. Table 6.2 lists the characteristics of people associated with cultures high or low on UA. For example, cultures high on UA tend to be associated with greater job stress than cultures low on UA.

Table 6.2 A Summary of Connotations of Uncertainty Avoidance
Index (UAI) Differences Found in Survey Research

Low UAI Countries	High UAI Countries
Lower anxiety level in population.	Higher anxiety level in population.
Greater readiness to live by the day.	More worry about the future.
Lower job stress.	Higher job stress.
Less emotional resistance to change.	More emotional resistance to change.
Less hesitation to change employers.	Tendency to stay with the same employer.
Loyalty to employer is not seen as a virtue.	Loyalty to employer is seen as a virtue.
Preference for smaller organizations as employers.	Preference for larger organizations as employers.
Smaller generation gap.	Greater generation gap.
Lower average age in higher level jobs.	Higher average age in higher level jobs: gerontocracy.
Managers should be selected on other criteria than seniority.	Managers should be selected on the basis of seniority.
Stronger achievement motivation.	Less achievement motivation.
Hope of success.	Fear of failure.
More risk-taking.	Less risk-taking.
Stronger ambition for individual advancement.	Lower ambition for individual advancement.
Prefers manager career over specialist career.	Prefers specialist career over manager career.
A manager need not be an expert in the field he manages.	A manager must be an expert in the field he manages.
Hierarchical structures of organizations can be by-passed for pragmatic reasons.	Hierarchical structures of organizations should be clear and respected.
Preference for broad guidelines.*	Preference for clear requirements and instructions.
Rules may be broken for pragmatic reasons.	Company rules should not be broken.
Conflict in organizations is natural.*	Conflict in organizations is undesirable.
Competition between employees can be fair and right.	Competition between employees is emotionally disapproved of.
More sympathy for individual and authoritative decisions.	Ideological appeal of consensus and of consultative leadership.
Delegation to subordinates can be complete.*	However, initiative of subordinates should be kept under control.
Higher tolerance for ambiguity in perceiving others (higher LPC).	Lower tolerance for ambiguity in perceiving others (lower LPC).
More prepared to compromise with opponents.	Lower readiness to compromise with opponents.
Acceptance of foreigners as managers.	Suspicion toward foreigners as managers.
Larger fractions prepared to live abroad.	Fewer people prepared to live abroad.
Higher tolerance for ambiguity in looking at own job (lower satisfaction scores).	Lower tolerance for ambiguity in looking at own job (higher satisfaction scores).
Citizen optimism about ability to control politicians' decisions.	Citizen pessimism about ability to control politicians' decisions.
Employee optimism about the motives behind company activities.	Employee pessimism about the motives behind company activities.
Optimism about people's amount of initiative, ambition, and leadership skills.	Pessimism about people's amount of initiative, ambition, and leadership skills.

*Based on studies by Laurent (1978).

Source: G. Hofstede, *Culture's Consequences: International Differences in Work-Related Values,* pp. 132–133. Copyright © 1980 Sage Publications. Reprinted by permission of Sage Publications, Inc.

This is ironic, given that cultures high on UA are supposed to place greater emphasis on developing ways of dealing with the stress and anxiety produced by uncertainty. Perhaps the ways that are developed are so complex that they produce increased stress in the workers who have to abide by those rules and rituals!

Cultural differences on UA have concrete consequences for organizations and organizational structure. As described above, organizations located in cultures high on UA generally have more structured activities, more written rules, a greater number of specialists, more managers involved in details, more task-oriented managers, and more conformity in managerial style than do organizations in cultures low on UA. Organizations in high UA cultures also tend to have lower labor turnover, less ambitious employees, less risk-taking behaviors and ventures, and more ritualistic behavior.

Individualism-Collectivism

Individualism-collectivism (IC) is a dimension that has been used quite extensively to explain, understand, and predict cultural differences in a variety of contexts. IC refers to the degree to which a culture will foster individualistic tendencies as opposed to group or collectivistic tendencies. Individualistic cultures tend to foster development of autonomous, unique, and separate individuals. In these cultures, the needs, wishes, desires, and goals of individuals take precedence over group or collectivistic goals. Collectivistic cultures foster interdependence of individuals within groups. In these cultures, individuals sacrifice their own personal needs and goals for the sake of a common good.

IC is a very important dimension in relation to work organizations. Collectivistic cultural values foster more compliance with company policies and more conformity in group, section, or unit behavior. Collectivism also fosters a greater degree of reliance on group work and group orientation to company and organizational tasks. Harmony within groups, sections, or business units is valued more in collectivistic cultures, and members are more likely to engage in behaviors that ensure harmony and refrain from behaviors that threaten harmony.

In Hofstede's study, the United States, Australia, Great Britain, and Canada had the highest scores on IC. Workers in these countries were characterized as being the most individualistic of all workers in the study. It is interesting to note that each of these countries has a strong link to Great Britain in its history. Peru, Pakistan, Columbia, and Venezuela had the lowest scores on IC and were the most collectivistic.

IC differences between countries and cultures are associated with concrete differences in worker attitudes, values, beliefs, and behaviors about work and their companies. Table 6.3 summarizes the differences Hofstede gleaned from his and other people's studies. For example, people in individualistic cultures tend to regard their personal time as important and make clear distinctions about their time and company time. People in individualistic cultures place more importance on freedom and challenge in their jobs, and initiative is generally encouraged on the job. These tendencies are generally not

Table 6.3 Summary of Connotations of Individualism Index Differences Found in Survey and Related Research

Low IDV Countries	High IDV Countries
Importance of provisions by company (training, physical conditions).	Importance of employees' personal life (time).
Emotional dependence on company.	Emotional independence form company.
Large company attractive.	Small company attractive.
Moral involvement with company.	Calculative involvement with company.
Moral importance attached to training and use of skills in jobs.	More importance attached to freedom and challenge in jobs.
Students consider it less socially acceptable to claim pursuing their own ends without minding others.	Students consider it socially acceptable to claim pursuing their own ends without minding others.
Managers aspire to conformity and orderliness.	Managers aspire to leadership and variety.
Managers rate having security in their position more important.	Managers rate having autonomy more important.
Managers endorse "traditional" points of view, not supporting employee initiative and group activity.	Managers endorse "modern" points of view on stimulating employee initiative and group activity.
Group decisions are considered better than individual decisions.	However, individual decisions are considered better than group decisions.
Duty in life appeals to students.	Enjoyment in life appeals to students.
Managers choose duty, expertness, and prestige as life goals.	Managers choose pleasure, affections, and security as life goals.
Individual initiative is socially frowned upon: fatalism.	Individual initiative is socially encouraged.
More acquiescence in responses to "importance" questions.	Less acquiescence in responses to "importance" questions.
People thought of in terms of ingroups and outgroups; particularism.	People thought of in general terms; universalism.
Social relations predetermined in terms of ingroups.	Need to make specific friendships.
More years of schooling needed to do a given job.	Fewer years of schooling needed to do a given job.
More traffic accidents per 1000 vehicles.	Fewer traffic accidents per 1000 vehicles.
More traditional time use pattern.	More modern time use pattern.

Source: G. Hofstede, *Culture's Consequences: International Differences in Work-Related Values*, pp. 166–167. Copyright © 1980 Sage Publications. Reprinted by permission of Sage Publications, Inc.

found in collectivistic cultures. In fact, such issues as freedom, independence, and initiative are normally frowned upon in collectivistic cultures.

IC cultural differences across countries and societies produce clear consequences for organizational structure and work in general (Hofstede, 1980). For example, organizations in individualistic cultures are not expected to look after their employees across their life span. Organizations in collectivistic cultures, however, are expected to do so, as they are morally responsible for the welfare of their employees for most of their lives. As a result, employees in individualistic cultures tend to have a more calculating or analytic view of their relationship to their companies, while employees of collectivistic cultures tend to view their relationship with their companies as moral in nature. Likewise, in individualistic cultures, employees are expected to defend their own personal interests; employees in collectivistic cultures can expect their companies to have their best interests at heart.

On the level of organizational policy, companies in individualistic cultures generally have policies, rules, and guidelines that will allow and encourage individual initiative and freedom; collectivistic cultures do not. Promotion and organizational advancement in individualistic cultures are generally based on accomplishment or achievement; in collectivistic cultures, promotions are generally based on seniority regardless of accomplishment.

Masculinity

Biological differences between men and women are a given. The question that every society, culture, and individual has to deal with is the degree to which the biological differences translate, or should translate, to practical differences in social roles, functions, or positions. Traditionally, these differences have existed, at least in the United States, with men generally being more assertive, dominant, and the primary wage earner. Women have traditionally been perceived as more nurturing, caring, and primarily concerned with family and child care issues (see also Chapter 10). This picture has been changing rapidly in the United States and continues to be a source of conflict, controversy, and confusion. Values concerning equity and equality have been infused in the workplace, and many American companies are still in transition to provide gender equity in the workplace.

Each culture and society must deal with the issue of sex roles and gender differences. A fourth dimension emerged in Hofstede's study, which he labeled masculinity (MA). This label, however, implies gender differences and is somewhat problematic and misleading because almost all the employees who completed the questionnaire were male. Many of the items identified with this dimension, in fact, had more to do with materialism than relationships, and Hofstede interpreted this factor as identifying masculinity. Still, this dimension can be conceptually useful in understanding gender differences in the workplace. According to Hofstede, this dimension referred to the degree to which cultures would foster or maintain differences between the sexes in work-related values. Cultures high on MA—such as Japan, Austria, Venezuela, and Italy—were found to be associated with the greatest degree of sex differences in work-related values. Cultures low on MA—such as Denmark, Netherlands, Norway, and Sweden—had the fewest differences between the sexes.

As with each of the other dimensions Hofstede generated, cultural differences on MA were associated with very concrete differences between the workers and the organizations. Table 6.4 summarizes these differences. For example, managers in cultures high on MA valued leadership, independence, and self-realization; cultures low on MA placed less importance on these constructs. Employees in high-MA cultures regarded earnings, recognition, advancement, and challenge relatively more important than did employees in low-MA cultures. And, fewer women were in mixed-sex jobs in organizations in high-MA cultures than in low-MA cultures.

There are interesting consequences for both organizational structure and employee relationships in the company as a result of cultural differences on MA (Hofstede, 1980). For example, young men in high-MA cultures generally expect to make a career in their jobs, and those who don't see themselves as failures. In high-MA cultures, organizational interests, needs, and goals are viewed as a legitimate reason to interfere in the personal and private lives of employees. There are generally fewer women in more qualified and better paid jobs in high-MA cultures, and those women who are in more qualified jobs are generally very assertive. There is generally higher job stress in organizations located in high-MA cultures.

Other Dimensions of Work-Related Values

In addition to Hofstede's original work, other studies of international and cross-cultural differences in work-related values have pointed to yet another important dimension of cultural difference. Working in collaboration with Hofstede, Michael Bond and his colleagues (Chinese Culture Connection, 1987; Hofstede & Bond, 1988) studied the work-related values and psychological characteristics of workers and organizations in Asian countries in recent years. No doubt much of the impetus for this line of research has been the surge of industry and business success of many Asian nations such as Japan, Hong Kong, and Korea. These researchers have identified a fifth and important dimension of work-related values, **Confucian dynamism**. Many

Table 6.4 Summary of Connotations of Masculinity Index Differences Found in Survey and Related Research

Low MAS Countries	High MAS Countries
Relationship with manager, cooperation, friendly atmosphere, living in a desirable area, and employment security relatively more important to HERMES employees.	Earnings, recognition, advancement, and challenge relatively more important to HERMES employees.
Managers relatively less interested in leadership, independence, and self-realization.	Managers have leadership, independence, and self-realization ideal.
Belief in group decisions.	Belief in the independent decision maker.
Students less interested in recognition.	Students aspire to recognition (admiration for the strong).
Weaker achievement motivation.	Stronger achievement motivation.
Achievement defined in terms of human contacts and living environment.	Achievement defined in terms of recognition and wealth.
Work less central in people's lives.	Greater work centrality.
People prefer shorter working hours to more salary.	People prefer more salary to shorter working hours.
Company's interference in private life rejected.	Company's interference in private life accepted.
Greater social role attributed to other institutions than corporation.	Greater social role attributed to corporation.
HERMES employees like small companies.	HERMES employees like large corporations.
Entire population more attracted to smaller organizations.	Entire population more attracted to larger organization.
Lower job stress.	Higher job stress.
Less skepticism as to factors leading to getting ahead.	Skepticism as to factors leading to getting ahead.
Students more benevolent (sympathy for the weak).	Students less benevolent.
Managers have more a service ideal.	Managers relatively less attracted by service role.
"Theory X" strongly rejected.	"Theory X" (employees dislike work) gets some support.
In HERMES, more women in jobs with mixed sex composition.	In HERMES, fewer women in jobs with mixed sex composition.
Smaller or no value differences between men and women in the same jobs.	Greater value differences between men and women in the same jobs.
Sex role equality in children's books.	More sex role differentiation in children's books.

Source: G. Hofstede, *Culture's Consequences: International Differences in Work-Related Values,* pp. 200–201. Copyright © 1980 Sage Publications. Reprinted by permission of Sage Publications, Inc.

of the principles and values found to be important to Asian companies are thought to be rooted in Confucian thought and principle. For example, some key principles of Confucian thought are:

- Unequal status relationships lead to a stable society.
- The family is typical of all social organizations.
- Virtue in life consists of working hard, acquiring useful skills and as much education as possible, not being a spendthrift, and persevering when faced with difficult tasks. (Brislin, 1993)

These principles translate to abstract values that play an important role not only in interpersonal relationships in business but also as organizational goals and principles. These include values for persistence and perseverance, ordering relationships by status and preserving this order, having a sense of thrift, and having a sense of shame. Also important are values that enforce personal steadiness and stability; protecting face and outward stance; respect for tradition, custom, history, and heritage; and reciprocating favors, greetings, and gifts.

Summary

Clearly, the research reviewed in this section indicates that culture does play a major and important role in influencing work organizations as a whole and the people who are members of these organizations. Culture influences organizational goals, structures, and functions. Culture also influences employee attitudes, values, behaviors, and interpersonal dynamics. The dimensions that Hofstede, Bond, and others have identified are extremely useful in helping us understand exactly how and why these cultural differences exist. But keep in mind that ecological differences between countries and societies do not necessarily correspond with similar differences on the individual level. Instead, the five dimensions discussed in this section should be considered a general guide to understanding cultural influences on the macrolevel of organizations and work-related values.

Motivation and Productivity

One important issue all companies, work organizations, and businesses must address concerns the degree to which their employees will be productive in various types of work settings. Of course, all companies want to maximize productivity while minimizing personnel costs and the expenditure of other resources, thereby ensuring the greatest profit margins. This concern has led to an important area of research on productivity as a function of group size.

Research on group productivity in the United States has typically shown that individual productivity often declines in larger groups (Latane, Williams, & Harkins, 1979). These findings have contributed to coining the term **social loafing.** Two factors appear to contribute to this phenomenon. One is the reduced efficiency resulting from the loss of coordination among workers' efforts. As group membership increases, presumably the lack of coordination among the people works to reduce efficiency, resulting in lack of activity or duplicate activity. This results in loss of productivity. The second factor typically identified as a contributor to lack of group productivity involves the reduction in effort by individuals when they work in groups as compared to when they work by themselves. Latane (1981) and his colleagues (Latane et al., 1979) have conducted a number of studies investigating group size, coordination, and effort. They found that in larger groups a lack of both coordination and effort resulted in decreased productivity. Latane (1981) attributed these findings to a diffusion of responsibility in groups. That is, as group size increases, the responsibility for getting a job done is divided among more people and many group members ease up because their individual contribution is less recognizable.

Cross-cultural research on groups and their productivity, however, suggests that exactly the opposite phenomenon occurs in other cultures. Earley (1989) examined social loafing in an organizational setting among managerial trainees in the United States and in the People's Republic of China. Subjects in both cultures worked on a task under conditions of low or high accountability and low or high shared responsibility. The results were clear and indicated that social loafing was observed for the American subjects, whose individual performances in a group were less than that of a person working alone, but not for the Chinese.

Shirakashi (1985) and Yamaguchi, Okamoto, and Oka (1985) conducted studies involving Japanese participants in several tasks. They showed that not only did social loafing not occur but exactly the opposite occurred. That is, being in a group enhanced individual performance for their subjects rather than diminished it. Gabrenya, Wang, and Latane (1985) also demonstrated this **social striving** in a sample of Chinese schoolchildren.

Several authors have offered speculations concerning why social striving has been observed in other cultures. These explanations center around the culture's degree of collectivism or group orientation. Cultures that are more collectivistic (for example, China and Japan) foster interpersonal interdependence and group collective functioning more than does individualistic American culture. As a result, groups tend to be more productive in these cultures precisely because they foster coordination among in-group members. They also place higher values on individual contributions in group settings.

Interestingly, this trend may also be occurring in the United States. Several studies involving American subjects have begun to challenge the traditional notions of social loafing (for example, Harkins, 1987; Harkins & Petty, 1982; Shepperd & Wright, 1989; Weldon & Gargano, 1988; Zaccaro, 1984). Jackson and Williams (1985) showed that Americans working collectively improved performance and productivity. Thus, our notions of social loafing and group productivity are challenged not only cross-culturally but also within our own American culture. With increased American interest in the organizational and management styles of other countries, this topic is sure to gain even more attention in the future. A central question in these examinations is bound to revolve around the best ingredients (for example, group size, nature of the individuals, nature of the tasks) to ensure social striving among all participants and to minimize social loafing. Recent economic necessities have forced many companies and organizations to consider spending less in personnel costs, resulting in "downsizing" or, more recently, "rightsizing." With fewer people to do more work, people in successful business organizations are forced to reevaluate and then redefine their own identities within their work groups according to more traditionally collectivistic styles for their survival and for the success of the business unit.

Leadership and Management Styles

Given that organizations and the people who are members of them differ so much across cultures, it is no surprise that leadership and management styles of people in power in those organizations also differ. But before we can understand how leadership and management styles differ across cultures, we need to realize that the definition of leadership and management differs across cultures.

Cultural Differences in the Definition of Leadership

Different cultures define and conceptualize leadership and management differently, and the manifestations of these different definitions are different across cultures. In many industrialized cultures, for example, **leadership** may be defined as the "process of influence between a leader and followers to attain group, organizational, or societal goals" (Hollander, 1985, p. 486). Leaders can be thought of as basically autocratic, dictatorial, democratic, and the like. In common language, we speak of "strong" and "effective" leaders as opposed to "weak" and "ineffective" ones. In many work situations, especially in the United States, we look to leaders to have vision, authority, and power and to give subordinates tasks that have meaning in a larger picture. In American culture, leaders are expected to be decision makers, "movers and shakers" of organizations and people.

In other cultures, leaders may share many of these same traits, but their leadership and managerial styles are not necessarily seen as dynamic or action-oriented. For example, some of the most effective leaders and managers in organizations in India are seen as much more nurturing, taking on a very parental role within the company and in relation to their subordinates (Sinha, 1980). These leaders are seen as much more participative in their jobs and activities, guiding and directing their subordinates' tasks and behaviors as opposed to merely giving directives to complete tasks. Still, leaders and managers in India need to be flexible so that at times they can become very authoritative in their work roles. In this light, the optimal leadership style in India, according to Sinha, is somewhere between a totally participative and totally authoritative style.

Another way leadership and managerial styles differ across cultures is in the boundaries of that leadership. In American culture, for example, workers make a clear distinction between work and personal life. When 5:00 P.M. arrives and the bell to end work rings, many American workers consider themselves "off" from work and on their personal time. The boundaries between work and their personal lives are very clear. Leaders, bosses, and others in the company should have nothing to say about how members of the company live their personal lives (for example, where they should live or whom they should marry). In other cultures, however, the boundaries between work and personal life are not as clear. In fact, in many countries the individual's existence at work becomes an integral part of the self. Thus, the distinction between work and company on the one hand and one's personal life on the other is fuzzy and blurred. Needless to say, leaders in such cultures can request overtime work from their subordinates and expect to receive it with much less griping than in American culture.

As the distinction between work and self becomes blurred, so do the boundaries of jurisdiction for leaders. For example, leaders and managers in India and Japan are expected to look after their subordinates in terms of their work and existence within the company; but it is also not uncommon for leaders to be concerned with their subordinates' personal, private lives as well. Subordinates in these cultures will not hesitate to consult with their bosses about problems at home and seek advice and help from them about those problems. Leaders, more often than not, will see the need to help their subordinates with this part of their lives as an integral and important part of their jobs. In India and Japan, it is not uncommon for bosses to find marriage partners for their subordinates and to look after them inside as well as outside the company. There is a bond between them that extends well beyond the company.

Many of the cultural differences in the definition and boundaries of leaders and managers are related to differences discussed earlier in this chapter and elsewhere in this book concerning individualism-collectivism (IC). People in collectivistic cultures identify themselves more with their work organizations and companies; indeed, they see their work and their company as an integral part of themselves. The distinction between their company and their self is blurred; they are more or less one and the same. People in individualistic cultures, however, see themselves as unique and autonomous beings. As a result, the distinction between themselves and their company is clear-cut.

Leaders in collectivistic cultures such as India and Japan, therefore, see their responsibilities not solely as a function of work and the company's benefit; they extend beyond mere work and company and include their subordinates as people. Because the boundaries between the company and the people is less distinct, managers and leaders in collectivistic cultures have an obligation to care for their subordinates as people outside of their work environment to a much greater extent than managers in individualistic cultures. Collectivistic cultures view the responsibilities associated with the role, status, and position of boss and leader as integrally and fundamentally linked with duties and obligations to care for their subordinates as people outside of work and company as well. This tendency is not seen in individualistic cultures.

Cultural Differences in Decision-Making Processes in Companies

Making decisions is probably one of the most important things a company, or any organization, does. As with many other types of behaviors, culture quite heavily influences how a company makes decisions. Many companies in the United States use a democratic procedure in making decisions. One of the main characteristics of democratic procedures is that every person involved has a say in the decision, usually by way of a vote. Another main characteristic of this process is that once votes are all tallied, the side of the issue that has a majority prevails. There are, of course, advantages as well as disadvantages to this procedure. One of the major advantages to this procedure is that everyone is equal, and the one-person/one-vote rule is the equalizer. Every person with a vote has a formal say in the process. This process is heavily influenced by an individualistic cultural viewpoint, which tends to see each person as a separate, autonomous being. This viewpoint also fosters a view of equality among people, despite real or apparent differences.

One disadvantage to this process concerns the consequences of close votes. If, for example, one side of an issue wins with just a majority (51%), that means that the other 49% of the voting members were against the proposal. This oftentimes has dire consequences to the implementation of the decision because 49% of the voting members will not be as enthusiastic in implementing the decision as the winning 51% will be. Indeed, this characteristic can and has led to sabotage and disruption in many organizations. The democratic process can also lead to considerable red tape and bureaucracy. Many organizations, in fact, can be characterized not so much as a democracy but as an **oligarchy** (Ferrante, 1992). Oligarchies are organizational structures characterized by rule or decision-making power of a few. Decisions are typically made by people "at the top" who then impose their decisions on subordinates. Sometimes the size of an organization necessitates that they be oligarchies for the mere purpose of having decisions made. If everyone were to be involved with all types of decisions, the bureaucracy involved would be too unwieldy for decisions to be made in a timely fashion by a majority of participants. This top-down approach to business decisions is characteristic of many American companies.

There are interesting differences across cultures in decision making in companies, and one of the studied cultures is that of Japan, most likely because of its economic successes over the past few decades. (Similar decision-making procedures in other cultures are reviewed in Berry et al., 1992.) The Japanese process is known as the **ringi** system of decision making. In a Japanese company, there is no formal system by which every person is ensured a vote. Instead, a proposal is circulated among all people who will be affected by the proposal, regardless of status, rank, or position. Initiatives for proposals can come from top, middle, or lower management, or from subordinates within a business section. Even before proposals are formally circulated among all interested parties, there is often considerable discussion and debate about the proposal. All views are taken into account so that the proposal, when written and formally circulated, addresses concerns and negative consequences raised by as many parties as possible. There is considerable consultation on as broad a basis as possible about the proposal, and consensus is achieved before the proposal is ever formally put into action. This broad-based, consensus-building procedure is called **nemawashi**. If proposals do not achieve consensus by this procedure, they do not appear formally. Proposals that have gone through this procedure and have received the blessing from all those affected by them are then put in the form of a formal proposal on paper. A routing of the proposal involves all section chiefs and managers before it gets to the person or persons on top who can put their formal stamp of approval on it. Needless to say, by the time something gets to that stage, it has met the approval of many people beforehand.

Like all decision-making procedures, the Japanese system has advantages and disadvantages. One of the major disadvantages is the time-consuming nature of the decision-making process. In fact, the inability of Japanese managers to make a decision on the spot in international negotiation is often a source of frustration on the part of American negotiators who are used to dealing with single decision makers. The Japanese negotiator, however, must contact all the people within the company affected by the impending decision prior to making that decision. One of the advantages to the Japanese system, however, is the speed at which decisions can be implemented. While the Japanese typically take much more time making a decision, they can usually implement it relatively quickly. No doubt, having everyone briefed about the proposal in the first place aids in speedy implementation. Also, people in a collectivistic culture are more likely to get behind a decision that is for the good of the company despite their personal feelings about it.

Intercultural Conflicts in Business and Work

Cultural differences in the meaning of work, in work-related values, attitudes, and beliefs, and in leadership and managerial styles provide the potential for considerable dynamism within organizations. Unfortunately, this organizational dynamism is often translated into conflict and controversy between people and organizations. In this final section, I explore the nature of some conflicts and controversies that arise because of differences in culture.

Intercultural Issues within and among Multinational Corporations

International business for multinational corporations is not just international; it is inter*cultural*. As has been discussed throughout this chapter, business organizations and work companies are affected in many different ways by the cultures in which they reside. Organizational structures are different in different cultures; organizational decision-making procedures are different in different cultures; people are different in different cultures, with differences in definitions and views of work itself, of work-related values, of identification between self and company, and in rules of interacting with other workers. In today's business world, succeeding in international business requires that businesses, and the people within them, gain intercultural competence as well as business competence. In particular, there are three different situations in which intercultural differences manifest themselves in the business situation: international negotiation, overseas assignments, and receiving workers from other countries.

International negotiation. The dual influences of improving communications technologies and changes in trade and tariff laws among countries has resulted in an increasing interdependence among countries for economic and business survival. This means that today more than ever before there are considerable burdens placed on multinational corporations that do business in many different countries. Extra burdens are also placed on domestic companies that need to negotiate with companies in other countries to obtain resources, sell products, and conduct other business activities.

In the arena of international negotiation, negotiators come not only as representatives of their companies but of their cultures as well. They bring with them all the issues of culture—customs, rituals, rules, and heritage—as they come to the negotiating table. Things that we are not even aware of play a role in these negotiation sessions, such as the amount of space between the people, how to greet each other, what to call each other, and what kinds of expectations we have of each other. The "diplomatic dance" that has been observed between American and Arab negotiators because of differences in personal space is but one example. People from Arab cultures tend to interact with others at a much closer distance than Americans are accustomed to. As the distance shrinks, Americans unconsciously edge backward, with the Arabs unconsciously edging forward, until they are almost chasing each other around the room.

Even little cultural differences can have big effects on international business. In the Japanese language, for example, the word for *yes* (*hai*) is also used as a conversational regulator, signaling to another person that you are listening to what they are saying (but not necessarily agreeing). American negotiators have often heard this word being used as a regulator but interpreted it to mean yes. As you can imagine, considerable conflicts can arise, and have arisen, when a totally contradictory statement or refusal is given by the Japanese when they were using this word throughout the conversation. To the Japanese, they were merely saying "um hmm," while the Americans were interpreting this to be saying "yes." Such contradictions can lead to conflict, mistrust, the breakdown of negotiations, and the loss of business and good faith relations (see Okamoto, 1993).

One interesting arena in which cultural differences in negotiation occur is in entertainment. American businesspeople are used to "sitting down at the table and hammering out a deal." Japanese businesspeople may want to have dinner, have drinks, and play golf. The Japanese are more willing to engage in these activities because they are interested in developing a relationship with their business partners as people; it also gives them a good opportunity to make a judgment as to the character or integrity of potential partners, which is an important aspect of their business decisions. American businesspeople are primarily concerned with "the deal" and what is right for the company's bottom line. Many American business negotiators not used to the Japanese style of negotiating have become impatient with these activities, as it seems like they never get to talk business. Many Japanese negotiators have been put on the spot by American negotiators, feeling like they have been thrust into a situation and forced to make a decision they cannot possibly make. Needless to say, these cultural differences in negotiation styles have led to many a breakdown in international business negotiations.

Overseas assignments.   Many multinational corporations with subsidiaries and business partners in other countries are finding it increasingly necessary to send workers abroad for extended periods of time. In many cases, worker exchange and overseas assignments are the result of the need to train employees and business units in another country in skills that are resident only there. When someone is sent abroad on an overseas assignment, myriad potential problems arise. Of course, problems occur at work because of all the cultural differences discussed in this chapter. But an added problem is limited language skills on the part of both the person on assignment and his or her hosts. Differences in expectations of the person on assignment and his or her hosts can be a major stumbling block to efficiency and progress.

In the United States, we would not hesitate in today's world to send a woman on assignment, either in negotiation or long term. In some other cultures, however, a woman would not be taken as seriously as a man. This will play out in very frustrating ways, such as not being looked at during a conversation, or having questions directed to a man when the women is the recognized leader or expert on an assignment team.

Ironically, many of the most pressing problems for people on overseas assignments don't occur at work but in other aspects of living in a foreign country. There are oftentimes major differences in lifestyle, customs, and behaviors that overshadow cultural differences at work. If an individual goes on overseas assignment with his or her family, there is the added problem of their adjustment to the new culture, especially if children are involved and they need to be in school.

Despite the potential problems, there are also a number of advantages. People who go on overseas assignments have a tremendous opportunity to learn new skills and new ways of doing their work that can help them when they return. They may learn a new language and customs, which will broaden their perspectives. They may make new friends and business acquaintances, and this type of networking may have business as well as personal payoffs in the future. Foreign assignment is an important activity in today's international business world that promises to play an even larger role in the global village of the future. Our ability to complete these assignments to the best of our abilities requires us to understand all the influences of culture on these activities, both in and out of the workplace.

Receiving foreign workers. American companies are increasingly hosting workers from other countries. Joint ventures between American and Asian and European countries have increased over the past 10 years. One result is an influx of workers from these other countries, and cultures, to the United States. One good example of this that has grabbed the nation's attention in the past is the joint ventures between American and Japanese and American and German automobile manufacturers.

Many of the problems that arise when we send workers overseas exist when we receive foreign workers. Often, managers from another culture will come to oversee and supervise production or assembly. They bring with them all the expectations, customs, and rituals they learned and that were developed in their home country. Oftentimes, they find that those ways of business do not work here in the United States because the people are different and the system is different. And many of the problems for workers' families exist for workers who have come to the United States. One response by many Japanese companies in the Los Angeles area has been to establish little Japanese villages and apartments where the lifestyle and customs can be preserved to make transition easier. Of course, these are not without controversy. They serve to maintain barriers between people just as much as they are a solution for some problems.

Nevertheless, despite the potential problems associated with receiving foreign workers, many of the advantages that exist for overseas assignments exist for receiving people from abroad as well. The ability to reap these benefits, of course, depends on the openness of the host company and organization to learn and the goodwill and intent of the employee and the company to engage in a mutually beneficial partnership.

Issues of Cultural Diversity in Domestic Work Organizations

One of the hottest issues in corporate America today concerns diversity. No doubt this is such a crucial issue in the United States because of the diverse nature of the American population and workforce. The United States is home to people of many different races and ethnicities and cultures. Within this "mixed salad" of cultures come generational differences, with some first-generation immigrants and others with many generations of descendants in the United States.

Many of the issues raised in dealing with people across countries and cultures are relevant for domestic work organizations as well. People come to work with different expectations, and differences in expectations has led to intercultural clashes. Cultural differences in the management of time and people, in identification with work, and in making decisions all provide areas for conflict. People in the United States come to work with differences in work-related values and the degree to which they respect or minimize power and status differences between them. People come to work with differences in their preference with regard to sex differences and how to manage uncertainty.

The challenge facing most American companies today with regard to cultural diversity is due to the wide range of people and cultures that can exist within any single work organization or business section. The problems that can occur when two cultures clash can be magnified many times over when people from multiple cultures are thrust together to interact with each other toward a common goal. Indeed, this is a very difficult problem because, at its base, people from different cultural backgrounds differ on their perceptions of goals and on means to achieve those goals.

What solutions exist? Many successful companies have met this challenge by making explicit what kinds of communication styles, decision making, productivity, and worker behaviors are important for the success of the company. Above and beyond that, they have created temporary organizational cultures in which their employees can move and adapt without fear of losing themselves or their own personal cultures. Many companies have designed ways not only of avoiding problems but also of handling problems effectively and constructively when they do occur, having the realistic vision that such problems are inevitable when different people come together. While negotiating all this requires additional work and effort by companies and people just when resources seem to be getting scarcer and scarcer, organizations that have managed to do so generally realize greater benefits to the bottom line through their efforts.

 ## Conclusion

The world of work is an important part of all of our lives. As adults, we spend a major portion of our lives at work. Work takes on many different meanings for all of us. Despite differences in those meanings, few can doubt that we spend much time, effort, and energy in our lives at work and in business organizations. As time goes on, issues of culture and cultural differences with regard to work and organizations will become even larger and more important than today. The world is shrinking before our eyes, as improvements in communication and travel technology bring previously distant lands closer to us than ever before. The growing interdependence among countries and the businesses and industries that comprise those countries promises to bring companies increasingly together. And along with those companies and countries come people with different cultural backgrounds.

In the final analysis, business is people. Products, goods, services, and warranties are important, but business leaders in international as well as domestic companies, large and small alike, agree that the most important ingredient to successful business is people. Our "people" skills are our most important business asset. Our ability to manage, guide, and lead others is a reflection of people skills. Our ability to search for prospective customers, to develop relationships, to negotiate contracts, to close sales, and to follow up are all dependent on people skills. Our ability to interact with bosses, presidents, and chairpersons of the board is dependent on people skills. Excellent products, goods, and services make our jobs easier, but in the final analysis, *good business is good people.*

Yet the differences that people bring with them to the job, both internationally and domestically, present us with challenges unprecedented in the modern industrialized period of history. These challenges, of differences among people due to differences in culture, are being met by business, government, and private organizations in the form of more research and education about cultural diversity as it relates to work. There is a growing industry in intercultural communication and competence training and in business consulting with regard to managing diversity.

We face these challenges with a particular perspective. Unfortunately, this perspective is usually dominated by the thought that diversity has to be "managed" or "dealt with." But when diversity is managed, the underlying philosophy is often that diversity is an unwanted by-product of our work environment, a nuisance variable that has to be dealt with in order to be effective. As we move toward a greater appreciation of cultural similarities and differences, particularly those that contribute to the diversity we observe in the workplace, we will gain a better appreciation for the approaches to work, management, and leadership that have worked for different cultures. As we confront the challenges of diversity in the future, we need to move away from a perspective of managing a nuisance variable to viewing it as a potential resource for tapping into products, services, and activities that will make companies more efficient, productive, and profitable than before. By tapping into diversity rather than managing it, perhaps we can increase international and intercultural cooperation in business and among people in general.

 # Glossary

Anglo-Saxon type of organization   A work organization more or less opposite to the Latin type, with less centralization, more diffusion of power and decision making, and less hierarchy in the bureaucracy.

centralization   The degree to which organizations concentrate their operations and decision-making capabilities in a limited number of business units or people.

complexity   Refers to the degree to which organizations foster a differentiation of tasks and activities within them.

Confucian dynamism   A dimension of work-related values important to Asian companies and thought to be rooted in Confucian thought and principles.

formalization   The degree to which organizations provide structure and rules for their operations.

Latin type of organization   A work organization that is characterized as a classical bureaucracy, with centralized power and decision making and many hierarchical levels.

leadership   The "process of influence between a leader and followers to attain group, organizational, or societal goals" (Hollander, 1985).

multinational and international corporations   Work organizations that have subsidiaries and satellite offices and work units in more than a single country.

nemawashi   The broad-based, consensus-building procedure that occurs within the Japanese ringi system of decision making.

oligarchy   Organizational structures characterized by rule or decision-making power of a few. Decisions are typically made by people "at the top" who impose their decisions on subordinates.

organizational or corporate culture   Terms that supposedly refer to aspects of an organizational that serve as a macrolevel climate or atmosphere within which employees must operate. As a macrolevel variable, organizational culture has an impact on how people within an organization think, feel, and behave.

ringi   The Japanese process of decision making, involving circulation of a proposal among all people who will be affected by it, addressing concerns and negative consequences raised by as many parties as possible, considerable consultation on as broad a basis as possible about the proposal, and achievement of consensus before the proposal is ever formally put into action.

social loafing   The often observed finding in research on group productivity in the United States that individual productivity often declines in larger groups.

social striving   A term used to refer to the opposite of social loafing, where being in a group enhances individual performance rather than diminishes it.

Third World type of organization   A work organization characterized by greater centralization of decision making, less formalization of rules, and a more paternalistic or traditional family orientation.

7

Culture and Intergroup Relations

Cultural and Psychological Influences on Ethnocentrism and Stereotypes

Some of the most pressing issues of society today concern ethnocentrism and stereotypes. This is true domestically, within the United States, because of our increasingly diverse and multicultured society, and it is also true for us internationally, as borders between countries and cultures are more and more permeable due to advances in transportation, technology, and business. You cannot pick up a newspaper or magazine or turn on the television news without seeing a story about problems that have occurred because of ethnocentrism or racial or national stereotypes. These problems range from doing business cross-culturally or internationally to violence and wars based on racial or ethnic differences.

While it is very common for the mass media and the public to use the terms *ethnocentrism* and *stereotype,* they are often used without being clearly understood. The ambiguity associated with the use of these terms can, in fact, foster the problems they are supposed to be referring to in their use. These terms refer to differences between people and are often interpreted as being based in racial or nationalistic differences.

A great deal has been written about these topics in the social science literature, especially in disciplines such as sociology, ethnic relations, and the like. In this chapter, I will borrow from the existing literature in psychology to develop a psychological explanation of ethnocentrism and stereotypes based on our knowledge of fundamental psychological principles in the areas of memory, cognition, concept formation and categorization, attribution, and person perception. While there is relatively little direct research utilizing these topics to study ethnocentrism and stereotypes, I believe the extensive psychological literature on these topics can inform us about the nature and formation of ethnocentrism and stereotypes. The ultimate goal of this understanding is to improve our intergroup and interpersonal relationships by refining our use of ethnocentrism and stereotypes.

At the same time, I would like to focus the attention in this chapter on culture as I defined it earlier, and not necessarily on race, nationality, or ethnicity. Granted, many of the stereotypes we hold are based on categories such as race or nationality, and some of these will be used as examples in this presentation, but I believe it is culture as a subjective, psychological construct existing on the level of the individual that contributes the most to ethnocentrism and stereotypes. Many of the differences we observe between people are based on differences due to culture, rather than race or nationality. These cultural differences in behavior and our perceptions and interpretations of behavior, in turn, form the basis for stereotypes. Somewhere in the process, the cultural aspect of these bases are replaced by race or nationality, and we use these concepts in framing our stereotypes. Thus, we commonly speak of racial or national stereotypes, when in fact we are referring to cultural, not racial or national, differences. Unfortunately, we act on these stereotypes as if they are indeed factually based on race and nationality.

The first part of this chapter will review some research in basic psychological processes related to ethnocentrism and stereotypes, beginning with a discussion of person perception and impression formation.

Person Perception and Impression Formation

Person perception refers to the process of forming impressions of others. Social scientists have long realized the influence of impressions and perceptions of others in our interactions. Questions concerning the degree to which impressions influence actual behaviors and the extent to which people's expectations color their impressions of others fall within the purview of person perception. Social scientists are also concerned with questions concerning whether bad first impressions can be overcome. To gain the best perspective on how we form impressions and perceive others, we should probably review all the literature in this book. Virtually everything is indirectly related to these two processes. But person perception and impression formations have also been studied directly in their own right. Social psychology has explored specific lines of research in this area, and there have been a few studies of this topic cross-culturally as well. Research on person perception in the United

States has outlined several key factors that contribute to the formation of our impressions of others, including appearance, schemas, stereotypes, and selectivity in person perception.

Knowledge Based on U.S. Research

Appearance, especially physical attractiveness, influences judgments of personality. Research with American subjects has consistently shown that people tend to ascribe desirable personality characteristics to those who are good looking, seeing them as more sensitive, kind, sociable, pleasant, likable, and interesting than those who are unattractive (Dion, 1986; Patzer, 1985). Attractive people are also judged to be more competent and intelligent (Ross & Ferris, 1981).

Other aspects of appearance also influence our perceptions of others. For example, greater height, which is generally considered attractive, has been associated with leadership ability, competence, and high salary (Deck, 1968; Patzer, 1985). Adults with baby-face features tend to be judged as warm, kind, naive, and submissive; adults with more mature facial features tend to be judged as strong, worldly, and dominant (Berry & McArthur, 1985, 1986). People who are neat dressers are thought to be conscientious (Albright, Kenny, & Malloy, 1988). People with poor eye contact are often judged as dishonest (DePaulo, Stone, & Lassiter, 1985).

Research on person perception in the United States has also focused on the ways impressions are formed and the way information about others is stored. Much attention has been given to the study of **cognitive schemas** as organizational tools. A schema is a conceptual framework that people use to make sense of the world and people around them. **Social schemas** are organized clusters of ideas about categories of social events and people that have been shown to widely influence person perceptions (Markus & Zajonc, 1985). Much attention has also been given to the study of **stereotypes**— widely held beliefs about people's underlying psychological characteristics or personality traits—and their influence on our impressions of others. Finally, social psychologists have studied the influence of selectivity on our perceptions of others to either confirm or disconfirm beliefs and stereotypes.

Cross-Cultural Studies of Person Perception and Impression Formation

Many cross-cultural studies challenge our traditional notions of person perception in American social sciences. For example, cross-cultural studies of nonverbal behavior, including gaze, proximity, touching behaviors, verbal utterances, and facial expressions, all speak to the impact of culture on communication. Differences in these behaviors arising from differences in cultural upbringing undoubtedly influence our perception of people of different cultures. We are often unaware of or unprepared to deal with cultural differences, and it is easy to form negative perceptions of others because of cultural differences in these nonverbal behaviors.

Although the effects of attractiveness and physical appearance on the formation of positive impressions is well documented, cultures clearly differ on the meaning and definition of attractiveness. Beauty is a relative judgment, and people of different cultures can have quite different and distinct concepts of what is beautiful and what is not. Cultural differences in the definition of attractiveness can clearly influence the formation of impressions.

Cultural differences in facial expressions also speak to the impact of culture on person perception. In one study (Matsumoto & Kudoh, 1993), for example, American and Japanese subjects were asked to judge Caucasian and Japanese faces that were either smiling or neutral on three dimensions: attractiveness, intelligence, and sociability. The Americans consistently rated the smiling faces higher on all three dimensions, congruent with our traditional notions of person perception and impression formation. The Japanese, however, only rated the smiling faces as more sociable. There was no difference in their ratings of attractiveness between smiles and neutrals, and they rated the neutral faces as more intelligent.

Even when different cultures agree on overall dimensional judgments of others, they may disagree on what kinds of behavioral consequences those judgments may have. For example, Bond and Forgas (1984) presented Chinese and Australian subjects with a description of a target person varying across the dimensions of extroversion, agreeableness, conscientiousness, and emotional stability. Across both cultures, target person conscientiousness was linked with intentions of trust, while extroversion and agreeableness were linked to intentions of association. But the Chinese subjects were much more likely than the Australians to form behavioral intentions of trust and to form behavioral associations based on agreeableness. Thus, ample evidence exists to suggest that cultures differ in both the process and the meaning of person perception and impression formation. This area of social psychology is indeed germane to our understanding of cultures, stereotypes, and ethnocentrism because it forms the basis for such intergroup and interpersonal processes.

The Contribution of Other Basic Psychological Processes

Ethnocentrism and stereotypes are processes built upon other, basic psychological processes. To understand the basis upon which ethnocentrism and stereotypes are developed and maintained, it is important to have a basic understanding of these other psychological processes upon which they are built, among which are concept formation and categorization, memory, selective attention and appraisal, and attributions. Attributions were briefly discussed in Chapter 2; they will receive further attention in the discussion of culture and social behavior in Chapter 8. Likewise, categorization and memory will be discussed in more detail later in Chapter 9. Here I will try to limit the discussion to a basic presentation of these principles as they are related specifically to ethnocentrism and stereotypes.

Concept Formation and Categorization

We form concepts in our minds so we can evaluate information, make decisions, and act accordingly. Most psychologists would agree that a **concept** is a mental category we use to classify events, objects, situations, behaviors, or even people with respect to what we perceive of as common properties. (Cultures differ on exactly what these common properties may be; this is discussed more fully in Chapter 9.) We use these common properties to aid us in classification or categorization, which refers to the process by which psychological concepts are grouped together. In psychology, the study of concept formation refers to examinations of how people classify or categorize events, objects, situations, people, and the like into concepts.

Concepts and the process of concept formation via classification and categorization are extremely useful processes. In our everyday lives, we come across a multitude of stimuli—objects in the environment, people we meet, things we hear or say—and it is literally impossible for us to keep track of them all. Concepts provide us with a way to organize the diversity of the world around us into a number of finite categories. Those categories, in turn, are based on particular properties of the objects that we perceive or deem to be similar in some psychologically meaningful way. For example, we may classify all objects of a certain color together, all types of facial expressions of a particular emotion together, and so on. Once such concepts have formed, we can act upon the individual stimulus in our environment on the basis of our knowledge of the general category. We now have a certain degree of information about a class of events, objects, or phenomena—that is, a concept.

There are a variety of theories about how concept formation occurs. However, what is most germane to our discussion here is recognition of the existence of concepts and their general utility to us in organizing the world around us.

Memory, Selective Attention, and Appraisal

Memory refers to our ability to remember past events, actions, people, objects, situations, learned skills, and so forth. It also refers to how we store such information. Psychologists generally differentiate among three different subtypes of memory and memory-related processes: *sensory memory,* the initial coding of memory-related stimuli; *short-term memory,* the "working" memory that serves as an intermediate between sensory and long-term memory (Baddeley & Hitch, 1974); and *long-term memory,* storage and retrieval of information over long, sometimes indefinite periods of time.

Semantic memory is a special type of long-term memory for rules, ideas, and general concepts about the world, including other people, and is usually based on generalizations or images about events, experiences, and learned knowledge. Semantic memory can also be based in large part on verbal knowledge communicated from one person to the next without any basis in actual experience or interaction with the target of the memory. It refers to knowledge that is gathered over a long period of time and continually modified or reinforced as the individual engages with related facts, events, or experiences (Bahrick & Hall, 1991). These properties of semantic memory make it especially relevant to our understanding of stereotypes.

A closely related psychological process is **selective attention**. Generally studied by psychologists interested in perception, selective attention refers to the process by which we all filter out or attenuate the multitude of stimuli present in the environment or that we receive via our senses to reduce that number to a more meaningful, finite amount of information that we can then process. Because our sensation and perceptual systems have limited capacities, we must learn ways to limit the amount of information we need to process from the world around us. When filtering that information, a certain degree of bias is inherent in the selection process. The cocktail party phenomenon illustrates this selection process: People can often hear their own names across the room at a party even though there are myriad other sounds occurring at the same time.

Finally, some consideration needs to be given to the nature of the selection process itself. One useful psychological concept for study of the nature of this process is appraisal (compare with Lazarus, 1991). **Appraisal** refers to the process by which we evaluate the relevance of stimuli in terms of their meaning to our lives. On the basis of the appraisal process, we then make decisions concerning appropriate behavioral and emotional reactions, which Lazarus (1991) refers to as *coping.* The process of appraisal is relevant to our discussion of stereotypes and ethnocentrism because it provides a psychological mechanism by which we can, and do, actively operate on incoming stimuli and process it in terms of its meaning to us. While not the original intent of appraisal theorists, this process has been shown to work hand in hand with selective attentional processes to encode and "massage" information about people that, in turn, is handed to memory processes and contributes to perception and impressions.

Attributions

A final psychological process that influences the formation and maintenance of ethnocentrism and stereotypes is attribution. **Attribution** refers to the process by which we infer the causes of behavior, not only for others but for ourselves as well. (This process was discussed somewhat in Chapter 2 and will be discussed again in more detail in Chapter 9.) We all develop a number of ways of making attributions about our own and others' behaviors that are biased according to our culture; these inferences form the basis for errors in our attributions.

Attributions serve important functions in our lives. As with concept formation and categorization, attributions allow us to organize information in psychologically meaningful ways. This psychic organization is necessary at the very least because of the sheer number of events that occur around us. Some research has shown that attributions are related to control and that people who desire control are more likely than others to make attributions (Burger & Hemans, 1988). Attributions also help people to accommodate new information about their world and help resolve discrepancies between new and old ways of understanding the intentions and behaviors of others (Snyder & Higgins, 1988).

When we observe the behavior of others, we draw inferences (that is, make attributions) about the underlying causes of those behaviors. We may selectively attend to those behaviors we subsequently appraise in a certain way that produces certain types of attributions. Those attributions, in turn, reinforce preexisting concepts and categories or help us form new ones. Over time, attributions form the basis of semantic memory and ultimately influence how we perceive others as well as ourselves. These basic psychological processes provide the framework for the development and maintenance of ethnocentrism and stereotypes.

Culture and Ethnocentrism

As we grow up, we learn many rules about how to behave. These rules form the basis of culture, and culture can be considered to consist of the many rules concerning the regulation and control of our behavior via socially appropriate channels. For example, we learn that "big boys don't cry" and "you don't scratch yourself in public." As these rules shape our behavior, we learn that many rules come with sanctions for transgressing them. If a boy cries in public, for example, he may be ridiculed by his friends or family; he may be called a sissy or some other name.

When we are very little, these rules must be drilled into us. Our parents, friends, teachers, and other agents of socialization continually remind us of these rules. Many of these rules are transmitted by people, but rules are also transmitted and reinforced by organizations and institutions. All of these lessons contribute to the process of enculturation discussed in Chapter 5. As we get older, we need to be reminded less and less about these rules. We begin to act upon them with less and less conscious effort.

During adolescence, many people believe we begin to rebel against the rules. We begin to question authority and the rules that authority dictated to us. We begin to seek out new ways and rules of behavior. We search for "ourselves." Much of this is related to Erikson's stage of "identity versus role confusion" (discussed in Chapter 5). After adolescence, however, many people seem to come back to their roots, to the ways and rules with which they were brought up. Oftentimes, this happens after college or university life, when a person needs to step out into the workforce and relearn the rules of society. By this time, we have learned how to act according to those rules. Generally, no one around us needs to remind us of those rules as our parents, teachers, and friends did when we were little. Indeed, not only will we have internalized the rules of behavior by the time we are adults but we will also have learned them so well that we can act according to those rules automatically without thinking very much about them. Many of these rules governing our behavior make up what we know of as our culture. In large part, culture is the conglomeration of a set of rules that we have learned about how to behave and that we share with a group of people. To the extent that we share these rules about behavior, we share a certain culture with that group.

But rules of behavior are not the only things we learn as we grow. We also learn how to perceive others, how to interpret the behaviors of others, and how to make judgments of those behaviors. Because we share a set of rules with a certain group of people, we have a set of expectations about the kinds of behaviors people should exhibit. That is, we implicitly learn that the rules with which we were raised and that are true for us must also be true for others who share the same cultural heritage. This forms a basis of tacit knowledge that need not be spoken each time we, as adults, operate on that knowledge. It is similar to connecting two computers that can communicate with each other well because they have the same basic operating system resident in them that "speaks" the same language.

More important, not only do we have certain expectations about people's behaviors but we also have learned patterns of judgments about those behaviors. We also have emotional reactions associated with those expectations and judgments that range from acceptance and pleasure to outrage, hostility, and frustration. When we interact with someone of our own cultural background, we interact using the same "ground rules." Whatever discussions or negotiations we have will be held above and beyond those ground rules, because we both implicitly and tacitly share them. Thus, there will be a current of pleasant acceptance about those ground rules as we interact (although we may or may not like the discussion occurring above and beyond those ground rules). When we observe or interact with people who engage in transgressions to what we view as "normal" or "socially appropriate," we have negative reactions. We become upset or frustrated or annoyed because we have learned that those types of behaviors are not appropriate, and negative emotions have become associated with that learning. Of course, these types of reactions will be more common when interacting with people of different cultural backgrounds, because they operate with different ground rules. (But these reactions often occur when interacting with people of our own cultural heritage as well.)

Oftentimes our emotional reactions lead us to make judgments about others. When the behaviors we observe are what we would normally expect in a given situation, we make an implicit judgment that that person is a member of our culture or that the person is engaging in socially appropriate behavior. We may consider the individual to have been socialized "well" into our culture; they are "good." But when the behavior we observe is what we do not expect, we begin to question that person. Oftentimes, we interpret the behavior to mean that that person is "bad" or "stupid" or "had a bad upbringing" or something similar.

Often we make these judgments of good and bad, right and wrong, without a second thought. Indeed, why should we give those judgments second thought? The judgments are often rooted in our upbringing, and those are the only types of judgments we have learned to make. In fact, because we have learned to make those judgments since childhood, those are the only types of judgments we know exist; they are colored by our emotions, which serve as guidelines in helping us form opinions about ourselves and others.

As we become enculturated, not only do we learn how to act but we also learn how to perceive and interpret how other people act. Our learning is associated with strong emotions of acceptance and rejection and with moral judgments of good or bad or right or wrong, and with judgments of personality. These rules of perceiving and interpreting form the basis for our own "filters" that we use in seeing the world. As we become more and more enculturated, we add more layers to those filters. These filters have lenses that allow us to perceive the world in a certain way, from a certain angle, or from a certain color. By the time we are adults, we share the same filters, with the same prescription and color filtering, with other people in our cultural group. It is as if we all purchased a camera filter with the same properties. We have these filters on all the time—so much so, in fact, that by the time we are adults we hardly notice they are there. They become part of our self, inseparable and invisible. They are a normal part of our psychological composition because of the way we were enculturated. Culture exists in each and every individual as a set of psychological rules, attitudes, values, beliefs, and so forth, and strong associations exist between those rules and our emotions and judgments of morality and personality.

We have heard a lot about the term *ethnocentrism* in the past few years. Although this word is often used in a way that gives negative connotations, it need not have these connotations. I define **ethnocentrism** as the tendency to view the world through your own cultural filters. With this definition and the knowledge about how we obtain those filters, it follows that just about everyone in the world is ethnocentric. Everyone learns a certain way of perceiving and interpreting the behaviors of others, and it is in this way that we first perceive and make interpretations about others. In this sense, ethnocentrism per se is neither bad nor good; it merely reflects the state of affairs— that we all have our cultural filters on when we perceive others.

The term *ethnocentrism* is often used in a negative way to describe the inability to view the behaviors of others in a manner outside of your own cultural background. While this definition is somewhat related to my first definition of ethnocentrism, an important concept differentiates this second definition from the first: the *inability* to go outside your own cultural filters and perceive and interpret the behaviors of others from their own perspective. This inability has to do with the degree of flexibility versus rigidity in our own rule adherence. The more inflexible and rigid we are, the less able we are to view others from their own perspective.

It is important to consider ways to develop a considerable degree of flexibility when interacting with others while at the same time accepting our ethnocentrism. Looking at the work of several researchers (for example, Bochner, 1982; Boucher, Landis, & Clark, 1987; Brislin, 1993), there appear to be various ways to attain this degree of flexibility. First, it is important to know how our own culture filters reality, distorting, rotating, and coloring images so we see things a certain way. Second, it is important to recognize and appreciate the fact that people of different cultural backgrounds have different filters that produce their own distortions, rotations, and coloring of reality, and that their version of reality will seem as real and valid to them as ours is to us. And third, while knowledge of our own and other people's cultures and their influences on the filtering process is a necessary condition to gaining flexibility, it is not sufficient. We have to learn to deal somehow with the emotions, judgments of morality, and judgments of personality that are associated with our ethnocentrism and cultural filters. I am not suggesting that our potential negative reactions are not valid; what I am suggesting is that we must give ourselves a chance to go beyond those reactions and try to learn about other people's viewpoints. In doing so, we may have to force ourselves to have a crash course on cultural filters from different cultures that we superimpose over our own filters so we can come closer to seeing the world from another person's vantage point. Above all, this process suggests that we learn ways of putting our emotional reactions and moral judgments on hold, however briefly, even though we have learned them so well they are generally automatic.

All of this requires a substantial degree of learning and effort. These new filters are superimposed over and above our existing cultural filters, not substituted for them. Our own cultural filters become a permanent and fixed part of ourselves (although it is true that because they are learned we are constantly modifying them as we go along). We do not get rid of our own filters when learning to be flexible; we learn ways to add onto them to help us see things from different perspectives. We don't necessarily lose ourselves in this process—a realistic fear of many people—rather, we gain new skills and knowledge.

I think of this entire package of events as **flexible ethnocentrism**. It is important to realize that flexible ethnocentrism does not mean you must accept or like the other viewpoint. Some may argue, for example, that the criminal mentality constitutes a culture in itself. You can engage in flexible ethnocentrism to attempt to understand the criminal culture and viewpoint; accepting or liking it, however, is another matter entirely.

The alternative to the process of gaining flexibility is to have **inflexible ethnocentrism**. This term refers to our traditional notions of ethnocentrism as reflecting an inability to go beyond our own cultural filters in interpreting the behavior of others. Inflexible ethnocentrism may arise from ignorance of the processes necessary to gain a different cultural viewpoint, or it may arise from a refusal to engage in such a process. It is important to note the differences between these two terms to differentiate between ethnocentrism as a general process applicable to people of all cultures and the use of that ethnocentrism in positive or negative ways.

If you ask people which type of ethnocentrism they have, most will probably say they are flexible. But subjective judgments of ourselves and our own abilities must be tempered because of cultural influences as well (such as the "false uniqueness effect" discussed in Chapter 2). The best indicator of the type of ethnocentrism a person has is found in his or her responses to actual interpretations of the behaviors of others. If a person interprets the behavior of someone from a different cultural background solely from his or her own perspective, the person's probably inflexible and will attach value statements such as "they are terrible" or "that's why people hate them." If we interpret behavior from a flexible ethnocentric viewpoint, qualifying statements will be heard such as "that's the way they have learned to do things" and "we can't judge that right or wrong from our perspective."

As you were reading this section, you had your own cultural filters on. You probably didn't realize that, but you did. Most people have one of two types of reactions to this section. One type of reaction acknowledges these types of ethnocentrism (the "mm hmm" and "ah hah" type of reaction). The other type of reaction questions what was described in this section (the "is that really true?" reaction). Which type of reaction did you have? Which type of ethnocentrism do you think you operate with?

Stereotypes

The fact that we are ethnocentric and are influenced by a number of basic psychological processes contributes to the development of stereotypes. Stereotypes are generalized images that we have about people, particularly about their underlying psychological characteristics or personality traits. While some stereotypes may be positive in nature (for example, Asians as the "model minority"), most are negative in connotation. And despite their positive or negative connotation, stereotypes are generally limiting and in many cases discriminatory.

Stereotypes may develop from several different sources. For one, the development of stereotypes is often related to the development of our ethnocentrism. As discussed in the previous section, when we observe the behavior of others, we perceive that behavior and make interpretations (attributions) about underlying causes based on rules we have learned from our own cultural upbringing. Those interpretations serve as mental categories or concepts that help us organize and assimilate information about people. As we grow up, we may selectively attend to particular behaviors and even ignore the existence of evidence or behaviors to the contrary, which reinforces the mental categories we have created. These categories are stored as verbal labels in long-term memory and play a large role in the way we interact with the world. All of these processes may be influenced by personal preference, cultural factors, and the like, and they are all open to errors in the processing of information. Because of the cyclical nature of the interaction between basic psychological processes and our culturally based ethnocentrism, these processes form a feedback loop, reinforcing itself and its errors and creating and maintaining mental categories of people we come to know as stereotypes.

While these generally internal processes may play a large role in the creation and maintenance of stereotypes, they are definitely not the only contributing factors. Stereotypes may be created and perpetuated in individuals merely by communication of verbal labels from generation to generation with no actual interaction with the people who are the target of the stereotype

(Brislin, 1993). Stereotypes can be created and reinforced by television, movies, magazines, and other forms of media. Stereotypes may be formed through limited exposure to the target people or to exposure based on a "biased" sample. Whatever the reason, it is important to recognize that stereotypes can be formed and reinforced in a person on the basis of no exposure whatsoever to the target people, or by very limited exposure. The complex interplay of these external factors with our own cultural and psychological processes make stereotypes a difficult problem to deal with.

Sometimes the existence of a stereotype in us is a product of our own observation of something we have interpreted as negative. Because of our need to classify information about people and to verify such classifications based on selective attention and memory processes, we often associate our interpretations with inferred traits of the target person and generalize those traits to observable, *identifiable characteristics* of that person (for example, skin color) and then make a *generalizable statement* that can be used to describe all people sharing that identifiable characteristic. Thus, we come up with such statements as blacks, or Japanese, or Hispanics, or Jews are ————. To be sure, many stereotypes are associated with characteristics that are not visible, such as lawyers, homosexuals, and the like, and these stereotypes are equally limiting, intense, and resistant to change.

While stereotypes may be based on some degree of "factual" observation (Triandis, 1994, calls these *sociotypes*), it is important to remember that they can also be baseless in any fact. Because stereotypes can be perpetuated without direct observation of the behaviors of others, there is a danger that stereotypes may not have anything to do with the target people. Even when we convince ourselves that a stereotype is based on direct observations, we have to question the validity of those observations and the interpretations based on them because of the cultural and psychological biases inherent in those processes.

Despite their positive or negative connotations, stereotypes are generally limiting and potentially discriminatory. This is so because stereotypes as mental categories of people tend to take on a life of their own. Rather than using stereotypes as "best guess" generalizations of a group of people from which we will then interact with individuals and adjust accordingly, we often use stereotypes as a rigid set of knowledge about all people of that group, regardless of individual differences or evidence to the contrary. In this sense, people are used to approximate stereotypes instead of allowing stereotypes to approximate people. When we use stereotypes in this fashion, we are using people to vindicate our stereotypes, instead of to validate (or invalidate) them.

There is a fine line between using a generalization as a guide and using a stereotype to vindicate your personal view of the world. Vindicating your view of the world by using stereotypes rigidly and inflexibly allows you only a limited view of the world and the people and events in that world. Vindicating your view of the world by using stereotypes inflexibly also provides a framework by which prejudice and discrimination can occur. By being based on such vindication, prejudice and discrimination themselves are often based on nonfacts.

Stereotypes we hear about in our everyday language are usually the inflexible type. For example, a stereotype may be used to categorize all people sharing certain identifiable characteristics without any chance of deviating from the stereotype. A person operating with an inflexible stereotype will see people only in ways that match the stereotype; data (that is, actual observed behavior) will be "massaged" to the point where they can be used to support the stereotype. Data that simply cannot support the stereotype will be simply thrown out or discarded as random chance occurrences, a random blip on a screen. Indeed, as time goes on, it seems that people who hold inflexible stereotypes become more and more entrenched in those stereotypes. This is because all their experiences serve to reinforce the stereotype despite the actual nature of the data.

Baseless stereotypes, like many labels for people, have a way of gathering a life of their own. People can begin to adhere and believe in stereotypes inflexibly with no chance for adaptation or change. People can selectively choose the behaviors they observe in others to arbitrarily support their stereotypes. Likewise, they can selectively choose to ignore behaviors that challenge their stereotypes. Behaviors that are observed are increasingly stretched to support the stereotypes. When this happens, our observations of life begin to serve the survival of the label. Once this occurs, the process feeds on itself—as the label gets more support, it requires more and more observations that continue to support it. Once reinforced in such a way, it is very difficult to eliminate, regardless of how true or false it is. In short, the label of the stereotype has gathered a life of its own.

Stereotypes exist, even in the most pluralistic of people. What is important is how we may go beyond them, considering them only as basic guides to interacting with people of other cultural backgrounds. As guides, stereotypes are not written in stone but give us ideas, impressions, or images of people that can be used for an initial encounter, after which they can be discarded or reinforced depending on the exact nature of the interaction and behavior observed.

Going Beyond Stereotypes

We can learn to go beyond stereotypes by recognizing three key points about them:

- Stereotypes are based on an interpretation we produce based on our own cultural filters and background or from communication from external sources;
- Stereotypes are often associated with identifiable characteristics; and
- Stereotypes are generalizations about a group of people.

If we challenge each of these three points, we can find ways to use stereotypes more flexibly than we have in the past. Let's examine each of these three points in more detail.

Our interpretations may be wrong, based on wrong facts or no facts. Our stereotypes are based on an interpretation we have made about the underlying meaning, psychological characteristic, or personality trait of a person. These interpretations are based on the cultural rules we have learned that are applicable for ourselves and are made about behavior observed through our own cultural filters. Or stereotypes may not be based on facts at all, having simply been told to us by others or reinforced by the media.

Other people may engage in behavior we interpret to be rude or offensive, based on our own cultural filters. In fact, that behavior may not have been intended to be rude or offensive from the other person's viewpoint. In some cases, the behavior may have been intended to be polite or deferent, the exact opposite of rude or offensive. Furthermore, the behavior we observed may not even be the behavior that actually occurred because our cultural filters may have distorted our perceptions of it or because we selectively attended to parts of an action sequence but not the whole. Thus, it may very well be the case that not only are our perceptions of the actual event incorrect, but our interpretations of the underlying causes of those events may also be incorrect. When interacting with people of a culture that is obviously different from our own, the potential for being mistaken is much larger than when interacting with someone of the same culture.

On the other hand, your interpretations may be correct, despite the fact that you and the other person come from different cultural backgrounds. It may have been the case that the person was trying to be rude and offensive and was engaging in behavior that that person's culture would agree was rude and offensive. You may actually be correct in your perceptions and interpretations—or you may not be.

The point is that we don't really know. All we know is that we perceive events and behaviors and make interpretations about those events and behaviors based on our own cultural filters and rules. We may not know whether we are exactly correct in our perceptions and interpretations (although there are times when we are more sure of our interpretations than others). We usually feel that we are absolutely, entirely correct, and that this is entirely reasonable because we interpret the world through our own cultural filters. But the very fact that there is a possibility we may be incorrect should allow us to be more flexible in our assumptions about others and their behaviors. When we are mistaken in our judgments, the costs can be high, whether in business, love, or everyday relationships.

The characteristics we identify are often selected without reason. In making stereotypes, we generally associate our images and impressions with identifiable characteristics of a group of people. Oftentimes, these characteristics are racial or ethnic; thus, we hear that African Americans, Asians, or Hispanics are a certain way. We have all heard these kinds of stereotypes. But race and ethnicity are not the only types of visible characteristics for which we have stereotypes. Stereotypes also exist about other observable, physical characteristics. Thus, we hear stereotypes about blondes or redheads. Sometimes stereotypes are made on the basis of other characteristics that identify a group of people, such as lawyers, homosexuals, politicians, and the like.

Why do we define our stereotypes according to such characteristics that identify groups? We must look to basic psychological processes related to concept formation and categorization for an answer. With such categories, it is easier for us to summarize the wealth of information about the world around us. Indeed, it is impossible to keep track of all the possible information about people we come in contact with. One of the easiest ways groupings or categorizations can be made is according to observable, physical characteristics. Therefore, it is easy to make generalizations or stereotypes on the basis of race, because racial differences are generally visible and easy to verify. Because they are easy to verify, categorization via stereotypes can also be reinforced rather easily. In addition to distinctions such as race, it is also easy to make stereotypes about sex or class or occupation. Thus, we have stereotypes about men and women, rich and poor, lawyers, doctors, and others.

This aspect of stereotypes highlights how they are limited. The important elements of stereotypes are not the characteristics we can see but the aspects of the person we cannot observe. It is this invisible aspect of people that produces differences and diversity in the first place; this invisible aspect is culture. Indeed, it is culture as a sociopsychological phenomenon, and not race, sex, class, or occupation, that produces differences in behavior. Learned patterns of behaviors, rituals, values, attitudes, and opinions produce behavior differences. Neither race, sex, class, nor occupation per se can produce such differences; culture can and does. This notion is related to similar messages by other authors writing on ethnic and race relations, including Steele (1990), Taylor (1992), Sowell (1983), and Steinberg (1989), in their own ways and platforms. It is a message that is truer to that of Martin Luther King's "I have a dream . . ." message than what we ourselves now consider to be important.

Unfortunately, it is impossible to "see" culture, a psychological phenomenon, but it is easy to see race and gender and other physical characteristics. Thus, it is easier to use these other concepts to try to understand or explain differences in behavior. But these other concepts are mere approximations of the effects of culture and cannot come close to helping us understand true differences between people. In fact, our reliance on race, sex, class, or occupation often leads us down entirely wrong paths of understanding that in the long run probably do more harm than good.

Generalizations about a group may not describe any single individual within the group. Stereotypes are generalizations about a group of individuals sharing some identifiable characteristic. Aside from whether those generalizations are true, we must also realize that within any group there are considerable individual differences. For example, saying that African Americans, Asians, or Hispanics are ———— doesn't necessarily mean that each and every African American, Asian, or Hispanic person you meet is so, especially given that the stereotypes may be totally baseless in the first place. As with any other aspect of culture, there are bound to be individual differences in the degree to which any description about a culture or group of people is harbored in the individuals comprising that group. Just as some people will indeed be rude and offensive, others will be polite and deferent. Some will be untrustworthy and devious; others will be totally trustworthy and forthright.

A stereotype, or any statement about a group of people, *at best* merely reflects a summary of a tendency of the group as a whole. (At worst, it reflects a generalization about a group of people that has no basis in fact and serves as an excuse for discrimination.) As with any summary, there are bound to be people that summary fits and those it doesn't fit. And while group tendencies may differ substantially, individuals within a group may or may not differ at all, depending on their individual placements within their respective groups.

We need to challenge the basis for stereotypes and the generalizations underlying them about the characteristics of the groups to which they are associated. We need to recognize individual differences within groups and the fact that no stereotype can adequately describe all people within a certain group. Stereotypes are not likely to disappear. It is human nature to develop guidelines and to use categories and groups to store the wealth of information about people that we gain in our lives. We cannot ignore stereotypes, but we can realize their potential abuses and use them more wisely. Stereotypes should be used as guidelines for interaction, not as rigid and inflexible descriptors of people. We need to validate or invalidate stereotypes, not use them to vindicate ourselves. Only by understanding the bases for stereotypes can we begin the process of using them better.

Conclusion

Although only a few cross-cultural studies have focused directly on the issues of appearance, schemas, stereotypes, or selectivity in perception, the entire field of cross-cultural psychology speaks strongly to our overall understanding of person perception. Moreover, much of the knowledge in basic psychology regarding memory, selective attention, concept formation, and attribution contribute directly to our understanding of the formation and maintenance of ethnocentrism and stereotypes. And all these topics contribute to what we know of as intergroup relationships.

Improving our understanding of the dynamics of person perception and its influence on the development and maintenance of stereotypes is extremely important in today's world. Despite the steps we have taken to close the gap between different groups of people in the last few decades, especially among the races, the 1992 riots in Los Angeles and the cries to "Buy American!" in the last few years both speak to the pervasive and strong sentiments of group identification that can have negative or positive effects.

One of the first steps to improving our knowledge and understanding of intergroup relationships is improving our understanding of culture, and understanding the influence of culture on basic psychological processes and the formation and maintenance of ethnocentrism and stereotypes. Improving our understanding of culture and its influences, however, is only one of many steps along the road. We need to search our own culture to discover the reasons these stereotypes have persisted and how our own culture may be fostered or facilitated by their maintenance. We need to recognize the existence of considerable individual variability within groups and cultures. We need to recognize the limitations of our own ethnocentrism, and of vindictive, inflexible stereotyping. By recognizing group and individual differences and by acknowledging rather than ignoring their influences, we are free to allow ourselves to engage with people on a common ground rather than predetermining their actions, behaviors, and reasons via stereotypes entirely from our ground or theirs.

The study of culture informs us about the importance of cultural background, upbringing, and heritage and their impact on our behaviors. Many of our behaviors as adults are not only shaped by culture but also draw their meaning from culture. Recognizing the important contributions of culture to the actions, behaviors, and reasons of causality for these behaviors helps us to understand, respect, and appreciate those differences when we observe them in real life.

One final note. I have found the material in this chapter to be some of the most difficult to write about, both here and elsewhere. There is no doubt in my mind that the material in this chapter is charged, and almost everyone you talk with will have an opinion, sometimes a strong one, about these issues. These issues are so charged, in fact, that my perception of this area of psychology is that we all become quite afraid to engage in what could be healthy discussion for fear of offending others or revealing supposed "biases" on our part. Although the material presented here is undoubtedly influenced by my views on these topics, the more important point is that this presentation can serve as a springboard for healthy discussion about these most difficult topics. Whether you agree with the material presented here or not, I hope the interactions that result from the thoughts stimulated here mirror the type of tolerance for widely divergent opinions that the topic deserves.

 # Glossary

appraisal   The process by which we evaluate the relevance of stimuli in terms of their meaning to our lives.

attribution   The process by which we infer the causes of behavior, not only of others but for ourselves as well.

cognitive schemas   Clusters of ideas, thoughts, or mental representations of the world that help us organize the world around us.

concept   A mental category we use to classify events, objects, situations, behaviors, or even people with respect to what we perceive of as common properties.

ethnocentrism   The tendency to view the world through our own cultural filters.

flexible ethnocentrism   Ethnocentrism in which people can learn ways of putting on hold, however temporarily, their ethnocentrism and perceptions of and reactions to reality based on their cultural filters and interpret the behaviors of others from the others' perspective.

inflexible ethnocentrism   Ethnocentrism that is characterized by an inability to go outside one's own perspective and add a view of the behavior of others from the others' cultural background.

person perception   The process of forming impressions of others.

selective attention   The process by which we filter out or attenuate the multitude of stimuli present in the environment or received via our senses to reduce that number to a more meaningful, finite amount of information that we can then process.

semantic memory   A special type of long-term memory for rules, ideas, and general concepts about the world, including other people; it is usually based on generalizations or images about events, experiences, and learned knowledge.

social schemas   Organized clusters of ideas about categories of social events and people that widely influence person perceptions.

stereotypes   Generalized images we have about people, particularly about their underlying psychological characteristics or personality traits.

8

Culture and Social Behavior

Intergroup Behavior, Attributions, and Stereotypes

Humans are social animals, and much of our everyday lives involve interactions with and influences of others. In the United States, there is a saying that goes "every man for himself" (which should probably be rephrased as "every person for him- or herself" in today's jargon), but it is difficult to think of an existence devoid of any contact with others. Especially in the United States, we struggle with the tension between being unique, separate individuals with few or no ties to others and being fundamentally connected to each other ("no man is an island").

Social scientists have long been concerned with our perceptions, interpretations, and relationships with others. In the United States as well as in other countries, social behavior and relationships are often the focus of intense study in psychology, sociology, and other disciplines. Among the topics relevant to social behavior are inter- and intragroup behavior, attributions of the behaviors of the self and others, love and interpersonal relationships, conformity and compliance, group productivity, aggression, and person perception and stereotypes. Some of these topics are covered in this chapter, others in other chapters. Each topic is not only an area of active inquiry in psychology but also of great concern in terms of its real implications for our lives in society.

Culture exerts considerable influence in the social arena. The ways we interact with others, perceive others, and work with others—all are areas of our lives influenced by the culture in which we live. We have all learned a particular way of behaving, perceiving, and working based on our own cultural upbringing and milieu. Just as this is true for us, it is also true for people of other cultures. They, too, have learned particular ways or styles of behaving, perceiving, and working. We may believe our way is the way people of all cultures should behave and interact; but this is not true. Indeed, what is true for us is often not true for people of other cultural groups.

Of course, problems can occur when we arbitrarily impose our standards on others when trying to understand them. Nowhere is this more apparent than in social behavior and relationships. The very fact that we are social beings and that most of our lives are spent in contact and interaction with one another makes it imperative that we understand how culture influences our lives as members of a society.

In this chapter, I will review some of the most relevant and well-documented issues concerning cultural differences in social behavior, including our attributions of ourselves and others; interpersonal attraction and love; and conformity, compliance, and obedience. The goal of this chapter is to set the stage for learning about other aspects of cultural influences on social behaviors covered in later chapters. The first topic in this chapter, cultural differences in intergroup behavior, sets the stage for understanding cultural influences on our behavior with others.

Cultural Differences in Intergroup Behavior

Culture influences social behavior in many different ways. We all live with others, forming attachments, bonds, and relationships. We are close to some people and distant from others. We make friends, acquaintances, and even enemies. Some of the people we see every day we know well, yet other people we see every day we don't know at all. Strangers, family members, friends, coworkers, acquaintances—the list of people in our everyday world is long.

One way social scientists have learned to understand our relationships with different people is by classifying them into categories that approximate the psychological categories we create. Especially important to understanding self-other relationships and pertinent to understanding cultural differences in social behavior is the category of ingroups and outgroups.

Ingroups and Outgroups

The ingroups-outgroups classification is one of the oldest and best studied social classifications in social psychology and sociology (see Brewer & Kramer, 1985; Messick & Mackie, 1989; and Tajfel, 1982, for reviews and more complete descriptions of this distinction). Most of us intuitively know the difference between ingroups and outgroups. **Ingroup relationships** are relationships characterized by some degree of familiarity, intimacy, and trust. We feel close to the people around us we consider to be in our ingroup. Self-ingroup relationships develop through bonds that tie the ingroup together through common friendship or relationships or goals.

Outgroup relationships are just the opposite. Outgroup relationships lack the familiarity, intimacy, and trust afforded to relationships with ingroup others. Ingroup relationships may be associated with feelings of closeness, but outgroup relationships may lack such feelings altogether and may even involve negative feelings of hostility, aggression, aloofness, or superiority. A bond exists that binds ingroup relationships together, but no such bond exists for our relationships with people on the outside. These people simply exist and are barely in our consciousness. They do not have any special relationship with us.

The ingroup-outgroup distinction is dichotomous, allowing us to characterize or classify everyone in our world into one of these two categories. But social scientists know the world is not that simple. Our social relationships cannot be neatly classified into two categories. There are differing degrees of intimacy, familiarity, and closeness even within one category. Classification schemes like ingroups-outgroups are simply aids that help us understand our behavior with others while acknowledging that greater complexity exists in those relationships.

Much of socialization and enculturation—the time of growing and learning about the rules and standards of our society and culture—is spent learning which people constitute our ingroup and our outgroup. From birth (and arguably before), we are busy building relationships with the people around us. As we go to school, make friends, find jobs, fall in love, and generally go through life, we develop relationships with many different people. Explicitly or implicitly, we categorize those relationships in our own minds according to the dimensions that define our ingroups and outgroups.

The ingroup-outgroup distinction is useful in describing our relationships with others in our culture and is applicable to all cultures and societies of the world. People of all cultures must learn to differentiate among the people they have relationships with, just as we must. This fact makes this distinction very useful indeed in understanding social behavior around the world and how that social behavior may be influenced by culture.

People of different cultures differ in exactly how these relationships develop, and with whom. The people we generally consider to belong to our ingroup may not be the same people that members of another culture consider to be in their ingroup. The same is true for outgroups. And regardless of whether the same people can be classified as ingroup or outgroup across cultures, the particular shapes, forms, and meanings of those relationships may be entirely different. Understanding and recognizing the existence of ingroup and outgroup relationships and the possibilities for how they may differ forms the basis for understanding how culture can influence these relationships and guide our social behaviors.

Cultural Differences in Ingroup-Outgroup Relationships

Cultural differences in the structure and format of ingroup-outgroup relationships. I have already touched on how people of different cultures can differ in their self-ingroup and -outgroup relationships. My own observations suggest that people of different cultures may not consider the same types of people and relationships when defining ingroups and outgroups. Just because a certain type of person (a friend at school, or a work colleague) is an ingroup (or outgroup) member, we cannot assume that people from another culture will interpret and act on those relationships in exactly the same way. And we cannot interpret the relationships of others as we do our own, because they may be entirely different.

Cultures differ in the formation and structure of self-ingroup and self-outgroup relationships in other ways as well. It is not uncommon for ingroup and outgroup membership to change in some cultures as referents to the groups change. This may be particularly difficult for us to understand from our traditional American way of thinking. In our own culture, ingroup and outgroup membership is stable, no matter what we are talking about, to whom we are talking, or where we are talking. Our friends are our friends no matter what. But in another culture, some people may constitute your ingroup in one circumstance or situation but *the same people* may constitute your outgroup in another. It is not uncommon for businesspeople in many Asian cultures, for example, to consider each other outgroups and competitors when talking about domestic business issues. But when the discussion turns to international business competition, those same outgroup competitors may band together to form an ingroup. This type of switching of ingroup-outgroup relationships is not limited to Asian or collectivistic cultures; it is present in many, if not all, cultures. When former President Bush visited Japan in 1991 with the chief executive officers of many different American companies, they all represented ingroup "Americans," even though those companies and officers would consider each other outgroup rivals in relation to domestic issues. Like many cultural differences, cultures differ in terms of degree but not necessarily presence or absence of this switching phenomenon. That is, the exact depth and meaning of those relationships may differ substantially across cultures.

Cultural differences in the meaning of ingroup-outgroup relationships. Some scientists have done a considerable amount of work on cultural differences in self-ingroup and -outgroup relationships. Triandis and his colleagues (1988) have done an especially nice job of elucidating how self-ingroup and self-outgroup relationships differ across cultures by using the cultural dimension known as individualism versus collectivism to understand cultural differences in social behavior.

Individualism-collectivism (IC) is one of the most important social psychological dimensions of culture (see Chapters 2 and 6). Many writers across the social science disciplines have used this dimension to understand differences in social behaviors across the cultures they have studied (e.g., Hofstede, 1980, 1983; Kluckholn & Strodtbeck, 1961; Mead, 1961; Triandis, 1972). IC refers to the degree to which a culture promotes individual needs, wishes, desires, and values over group and collective ones. Individualistic cultures encourage their members to become unique individuals; hierarchical power and status differences are minimized, while equality is emphasized. Collectivistic cultures stress the needs of a group; individuals are identified more through their group affiliation than by individual position or attributes. Hierarchical differences and vertical relationships are emphasized, and role, status, and appropriate behaviors are more clearly defined by position.

Self-ingroup and self-outgroup relationships differ in individualistic and collectivistic cultures. And these differences in the meaning of ingroup and outgroup relationships produce differences in the types of behaviors people engage in when interacting with others. In individualistic cultures, for example, a person may belong to many ingroups, and indeed, many people in individualistic cultures belong to multiple ingroups. In our culture, for instance, which is traditionally quite individualistic, many of us belong to several ingroups—music groups, sport groups, church groups, social groups, and so forth. Children in America today may belong to football teams during football season, basketball teams during basketball season, and baseball teams during baseball season. They may take swimming lessons, piano, or violin lessons, be members of Boy or Girl Scouts, and generally just be the busiest people around. This is not the case in collectivistic cultures. Members of collectivistic cultures belong to fewer ingroups. People in many Asian and South American cultures do not belong to all the different sports, music, and social groups that people in individualistic cultures like ours do.

This characteristic of individualistic and collectivistic cultural differences in ingroup membership has important consequences to the commitment people have to different groups. In general, in exchange for belonging to fewer groups, people in collectivistic cultures have greater commitments to the groups to which they belong. They also identify more with the groups to which they belong; that is, the groups themselves become an integral part of each individual's self-concept and identity. This makes sense because by definition collectivistic cultures depend on groups to a much greater degree, and subjugating personal goals in favor of collective goals is a necessity.

Members of individualistic cultures do not necessarily collapse their sense of self-identity and self-concept into the groups to which they belong. They have fewer commitments to their ingroups and move much more easily from ingroup to ingroup. While groups take on special importance in collectivistic cultures, the same degree of importance does not exist for group membership in individualistic cultures.

It follows that collectivistic cultures require a greater degree of harmony, cohesion, and cooperation within their ingroups and place greater burdens on individuals to identify with the group and conform to group norms. Sanctions usually exist for nonconformity. Individualistic cultures, however, depend less on groups and more on the uniqueness of their individuals. The pursuit of personal goals rather than collective ones is of primary importance. As a result, individualistic cultures require less harmony and cohesion within groups and place less importance on conformity of individuals to group norms.

These differences in the meaning of self-ingroup relationships between individualistic and collectivistic cultures have consequences for behavior. In collectivistic cultures, for example, you would expect people to make more individual sacrifices for their ingroups in pursuit of group goals. You would expect to see people trying harder to cooperate with each other, even if it means that the individual must suppress his or her own feelings, thinking, behaviors, or goals to maintain harmony and cohesion. You would expect people to try to find ways of agreeing with each other more, downplaying and minimizing interpersonal differences for the sake of harmony.

Self-ingroup relationships in individualistic cultures have different consequences for behavior. In these cultures, you would expect people to make fewer sacrifices of their own individual goals, needs, and desires for the sake of a common good. You would expect people to be more expressive of their own feelings, attitudes, opinions, without as much fear or worry about the consequences to group harmony or cohesion. You would expect people to bring up interpersonal concerns, problems, and conflicts more freely.

Not only do self-ingroup relationships differ between individualistic and collectivistic cultures but self-outgroup relationships also differ. In collectivistic cultures, the primary focus of attention is on ingroup relationships. For that reason, relationships with outgroup people are marked by a relative lack of concern. To the degree to which members of collectivistic cultures focus on harmony, cohesion, and cooperation in ingroup relations, distancing, aloofness, and even discrimination with regard to self-outgroup relationships also exists. The opposite is true in individualistic cultures. People of individualistic cultures are more likely to treat outgroup persons more equally, with relatively less distinction between ingroups and outgroups. Members of individualistic cultures engage in positive, relationship-building behaviors with outgroup others that members of collectivistic cultures would reserve only for ingroup others. These concepts are summarized in Table 8.1.

Cultural differences in the meaning of self-ingroup and self-outgroup relationships have particular meaning for the emotions expressed in social interactions (see Matsumoto, 1991, for an extended discussion). In general, the familiarity and intimacy of self-ingroup relations in all cultures provide the safety and comfort to express emotions freely along with tolerance for a broad spectrum of emotional behaviors. Part of emotional socialization involves learning who are ingroup and outgroup members and the appropriate behaviors associated with them.

Collectivistic cultures foster more positive and fewer negative emotions toward ingroups because ingroup harmony is more important to them. Positive emotions ensure maintenance of this harmony; negative emotions threaten it. Likewise, individualistic cultures foster more positive and less negative emotions toward outgroups. It is less important in individualistic cultures to differentiate between ingroups and outgroups, and thus they allow expression of positive feelings and suppression of negative ones toward outgroup members. Collectivistic cultures, however, foster more negative expressions towards outgroups to distinguish more clearly between ingroups

Table 8.1 Characteristics of Self-Ingroup and Self-Outgroup Relationships in Individualistic and Collectivistic Cultures

| | Type of Culture | |
	Individualistic	Collectivistic
Self-ingroup relations	more emphasis on personal and individual needs, goals, and desires	more emphasis on group goals and maintenance of harmony, cohesion, and cooperation
Self-outgroup relations	more likely to treat them like ingroup members	more likely to make distinctions from ingroups and use distancing and discrimination against them

Table 8.2 Consequences for Personal Emotions in Self-Ingroup and Self-Outgroup Relationships in Individualistic and Collectivistic Cultures

	Type of Culture	
	Individualistic	Collectivistic
Self-ingroup relations	okay to express negative feelings; less need to display positive feelings	suppress expressions of negative feelings; more pressure to display positive feelings
Self-outgroup relations	suppress negative feelings; okay to express positive feelings as would toward ingroups	encouraged to express negative feelings; suppress display of positive feelings reserved for ingroups

and outgroups and to strengthen ingroup relations (via the collective expression of negative feelings toward outgroups). These consequences for personal emotions are summarized in Table 8.2

Summary

People in all cultures and societies grow up learning to make distinctions among others in terms of ingroups and outgroups. Culture exerts considerable influence not only over the structure and format of those self-ingroup and self-outgroup relationships but also over the very meaning of those relationships. And cultural differences in the meaning of those relationships produces real, observable differences in the behaviors, thoughts, and feelings of the individual when interacting with ingroup and outgroup others.

One of the most important ramifications of this discussion is that how we conceptualize and act on our relationships with others can be dramatically different from culture to culture. Indeed, if we engage in interaction and try to interpret the social behaviors of others from our own limited cultural framework, it is very possible that we will misunderstand and misinterpret those behaviors. Good intentions may be seen as bad; innocuous behaviors may be seen as threatening or aggressive.

Research on other aspects of social behavior also informs us about how culture influences our interpretations of the world around us. One topic that is related to how we perceive and interpret the social behavior of others is attribution.

Cultural Differences in Our Interpretations of the World Around Us: Cross-Cultural Research on Attributions

 Attributions are the inferences people draw about the causes of events and their own and others' behaviors. Attributions are an important part of social interaction, because they represent the ways we understand the world around us. Attributions also represent the ways we understand the behavior of others. You might attribute your friend's failure to show up for a date as a sign of irresponsibility or too much traffic or forgetting. You might attribute your success on an exam to your effort or to luck. Attributions allow us to examine the biases people have when explaining others' behavior, which in turn affects their own behavior.

The study of attributions has a rich history in social psychology. In general, research on attributions in the United States has centered around several issues. One issue is the type of attributions people make, especially in relation to the locus of causality. Another popular concept in attribution research concerns the distinction between internal and external attributions. Internal attributions specify the cause of behavior within a person; external attributions locate the cause of behavior outside a person. Attributions have been widely studied in achievement situations, ranging from academic settings to sports and occupational contexts. These studies have led to development of several major theories of attribution. And research on attribution bias has led to several popular concepts in American social psychology: fundamental attribution error, defensive attributions, and self-serving bias.

Traditional American Patterns of Attributions

One of the most popular models of attribution in American psychology is Kelley's covariation model (1967, 1973). This model assumes that people attribute behavior to causes that are present when the behavior occurs and absent when the behavior does not occur. According to this theory, people consider three types of information—consistency, distinctiveness, and consensus—when making attributions. **Consistency** refers to whether a person's behavior in a situation is the same over time. **Distinctiveness** refers to whether a person's behavior is unique to the specific target of the behavior. **Consensus** refers to whether other people in the same situation tend to respond in the same manner. Behaviors that have high consistency but low distinctiveness or consensus produce internal attributions. Behaviors that have high consistency, high distinctiveness, and high consensus produce external attributions.

Another major theory of attribution in American psychology is Weiner's theory (1974; Weiner et al., 1972). This theory focuses on the concept of stability. According to Weiner, stability cuts across the internal-external dimension, creating four types of attributions for success and failure (stable and unstable, internal and external). For example, if you failed to get a job you wanted, you might attribute your failure to stable internal factors (lack of ability or initiative), stable external factors (too much competition), unstable internal factors (lack of effort), or unstable external factors (bad luck). Using Weiner's model of attribution, the types of emotions and behaviors that will probably occur in consequence to these attribution types can be predicted.

Studies conducted on attributional styles with people in the United States have shown a number of different ways we may be biased in interpreting the world around us and the behavior of others and the culture-bound nature of attributions in our culture. **Fundamental attribution error** refers to a bias toward explaining the behavior of others using internal attributions but explaining our own behaviors using external attributions (Jones & Nisbett, 1971; Watson, 1982). It is not uncommon to hear students attribute a friend's bad grade to low intelligence or ability (internal). At the same time, however, you may attribute your own bad grade to the teacher's bad choice of test questions or to bad luck (external).

Self-serving bias is the tendency to attribute your successes to personal factors and your failures to situational factors (Bradley, 1978). If you fail an exam, for instance, you may attribute your failure to a poorly constructed test, lousy teaching, distractions, or a bad week at home (external). If you ace an exam, however, you are more likely to attribute that to effort, intelligence, or ability (internal).

Defensive attributions refer to the tendency to blame victims for their misfortune. Some scientists have suggested that we engage in defensive attributions so we don't feel as likely to be victimized in a similar way (Thornton, 1984). If you attribute others' misfortunes (for example, burglary, rape, loss of a job) to the victim rather than to circumstance, it is easier to not consider that the same misfortunes may happen to you.

These attributional styles and theories have an impact both on our own behavior and on our understanding of the behavior of others. Many of you can probably recognize some of these attributional tendencies in your own behavior. The attributional styles and biases I have described are derived from research conducted almost exclusively in the United States with American participants. Research conducted in other cultures shows that people of other cultures do not interpret their world the way we do; that is, they do not share the same attributional biases.

Attributional Styles across Cultures

Many studies show how people of other cultures differ from Americans in their attributions. Several studies have found that the self-serving bias that tends to characterize American students is not found in students from other cultures. For instance, Hau and Salili (1991) asked junior and senior high school students in Hong Kong to rate the importance and meaning of 13 specific causes of academic performance. Effort, interest, and ability were rated the most important causes, regardless of success or failure. These are all internal attributions. Likewise, Moghaddam, Ditto, and Taylor (1990) showed that Indian women who had immigrated to Canada were more likely to attribute both successes and failures to internal causes. American research would have hypothesized that the subjects would attribute only successes to internal causes and attribute failures to external causes.

Two studies with Taiwanese subjects also challenge our notions about self-serving attributions. Crittenden (1991) showed that Taiwanese women used more external and self-effacing attributions about themselves than did American women. Crittenden suggested that the Taiwanese women did this to enhance their public and private self-esteem by using an attributional approach that conformed to a feminine gender role. Earlier, Bond, Leung, and Wan (1982) showed that self-effacing Chinese students were better liked by their peers than those who adopted this attributional style less often.

Other cross-cultural studies on attribution pepper the literature with findings that challenge our notions of attribution. Kashima and Triandis (1986) showed that Japanese people use a much more group-oriented, collective approach to attributional styles with regard to attention and memory achievement tasks. Unlike their American counterparts, Japanese subjects attributed failure to themselves more and attributed success to themselves less. Kashima and Triandis (1986) interpreted this finding as suggestive of American and Japanese cultural differences in the degree of responsibility taking.

Forgas, Furnham, and Frey (1989) documented broad cross-national differences in the importance of different types of specific attributions for wealth. Their study included 558 subjects from the United Kingdom, Australia, and the Federal Republic of Germany. The British considered family background and luck the most important determinants of wealth. The Germans also considered family background the most important determinant. The Australians, however, rated individual qualities the most important determinant of wealth. In yet another study, Romero and Garza (1986) reported similar findings between Hispanic and Anglo women in their attributions concerning occupational success and failure.

As these studies exemplify, attributional styles are quite different across cultures. We need to discover why those differences occur. It may be the case that the way Americans have conceptualized attributions, success, and failure has a lot to do with the differences found in cross-cultural research. Duda and Allison (1989) suggested that our definitions of success and failure are ethno-centrically biased. How Americans view success and failure—that is, in terms of personal achievement on the basis of competition with others—is differ-ent from how people of other cultures define them. They also suggested that the meanings of the specific elements in theories and research on attribution may differ among cultures (for example, effort, work, luck). Different mean-ings assigned to these elements have implications for the meanings of the at-tributions associated with them. Finally, Duda and Allison also suggested that the use of bipolar dimensions in research may be extremely limited. Cultural differences in the dimensions that are important for understanding and pre-dicting attributions may lead to entirely different expectations of attribution styles.

Cultural differences in attributional styles have several possible negative consequences. Wong, Derlaga, and Colson (1988) asked 40 white and 40 black undergraduates to read stories about the performance of either a black or a white child. The students were then asked to (1) explain why the child failed or succeeded, (2) describe questions in their mind concerning the child's performance, and (3) predict the child's performance on other tasks. All subjects, regardless of their race, generated more questions and causal ex-planations for the performance of a black rather than a white target. And, all subjects expected the white student to do better than the black student on other tasks.

Tom and Cooper (1986) examined the attributions of 25 white elemen-tary school teachers for the performance of students varying in social class, race, and gender. The results indicated that the teachers were more likely to take account of the successes of middle-class, white students and discount their failures, relative to students of other social classes or race.

Fortunately, the news about the consequences of cultural differences in attributional style is not entirely negative. Hall, Howe, Merkel, and Leder-man (1986) asked teachers to make causal attributions about the perfor-mance of black and white students. Their findings suggested that the teach-ers all believed that the black females exerted the greatest amount of effort (although the teachers also believed that black males exerted the least). Gra-ham and her colleagues (for example, Graham, 1984; Graham & Long, 1986) have also shown that there is considerable overlap in the attributions of the black and white subjects in their studies and that these attributions are often equally adaptive. In addition, these researchers have also found that attributions are influenced by social factors such as class as well as race and culture.

Cross-cultural research on attributions does not yet provide a consistent picture of the nature of attributions or the attributional processes across all cultures and races. But its message to date is quite clear: People of different cultures have different attributional styles and biases, and these differences are deeply rooted in cultural background and upbringing. A sufficient number of studies across cultures question many of the popular notions concerning attributions found to be true in the United States. Self-serving biases, defensive attributions, and fundamental attribution error do not exist in the same way or have the same meaning in other cultures.

These findings are especially important in furthering our understanding of intercultural interactions. The consequences for incorrect attributions are potentially severe. Correctly interpreting the causes of behavior accurately, especially with regard to intentions and good will, is important to the success of *any* type of social interaction. Intercultural interactions are no exception. Don't be too quick to attribute another person's behavior to ill will or negative feelings, when that behavior may actually be rooted in a cultural dynamic that fosters that behavior with no ill will. We should leave room for the influence of cultural factors on behavior in our attributions of others as well as our own. Then we will have taken an important step toward improving intercultural understanding and relationships.

Interpersonal Attraction: Love, Intimacy, and Intercultural Marriages

As our world gets smaller and smaller, the frequency of interacting with people of ethnic and cultural backgrounds different from your own increases. As these intercultural interactions increase, so does the likelihood that people will become attracted to each other, fall in love, get married, and have families. Indeed, whereas intercultural and interracial relationships were a rarity in the past, they are now more and more frequent. With this increase in intercultural and interracial relationships comes increased tension, frustrations, worries, and joys.

Psychologists use the term "interpersonal attraction" to encompass a variety of experiences, including liking, friendship, admiration, lust, and love. U.S. research on interpersonal attraction and love has produced a number of interesting findings, mainly focusing on the factors that contribute to attraction. At the same time, cross-cultural research gives us important clues to cultural differences in attraction and love, and an increasing number of studies on intercultural relationships point to the pitfalls and possible solutions.

Interpersonal Attraction and Love in the United States

Studies conducted by psychologists even in the 1950s (for example, Festinger, Schachter, & Back, 1950) showed that proximity influences attraction—people who live close to each other are more likely to like one another. Despite the fact that these first studies were conducted more than 40 years ago, findings from recent studies support this notion. In the late 1970s, for instance, Ineichen (1979) showed that people who lived close together were more likely to get married.

In the United States, physical attractiveness is an important ingredient of interpersonal relationships (Patzer, 1985), but attractiveness may be more important for females than for males (Buss, 1988). Most people surveyed in the United States prefer physically attractive partners in romantic relationships. But a **matching hypothesis** also suggests that people of approximately equal physical characteristics are likely to select each other as partners. Likewise, a **similarity hypothesis** suggests that people similar in age, race, religion, social class, education, intelligence, attitudes, and physical attractiveness tend to form intimate relationships (Brehm, 1985; Hendrick & Hendrick, 1983). Certainly, there is something safe about similarities in a relationship that make similar partners particularly attractive for romance and love. Another important concept in understanding interpersonal attraction in the United States concerns a **reciprocity hypothesis**, which suggests that people tend to like others who like them (Byrne & Murnen, 1988).

Few people in the United States would discount the importance of love in the development and maintenance of long-term relationships like friendships and marriage, and love has been a particularly well-studied topic in American psychology. Hatfield and Berscheid's (Berscheid, 1988; Hatfield, 1988) theory of love and attachment proposes that romantic relationships are characterized by two kinds of love. One is **passionate love**, involving absorption of another that includes sexual feelings and intense emotion. The second is **companionate love**, involving warm, trusting, and tolerant affection for another whose life is deeply intertwined with your own. Sternberg's (1988) theory is similar to Hatfield and Berscheid's but divides companionate love into two separate components: intimacy and commitment. Intimacy refers to warmth, closeness, and sharing in a relationship. Commitment refers to an intention to maintain a relationship in spite of the difficulties that arise. In Sternberg's theory, eight different forms of love can exist, depending on the presence or absence of each of the three factors: passionate love, intimacy, and commitment. When all three factors exist, Sternberg calls that relationship **consummate love**.

Another well-studied area of interpersonal attraction concerns intimacy. In research conducted in the United States, intimacy is usually closely tied with a concept known as *self-disclosure* (for example, Adamopoulos, 1991; Altman & Taylor, 1973; Helgeson, Shaver, & Dyer, 1987). This concept refers to the degree to which people will disclose information about themselves to others. In the United States, intimate relationships are characterized by high levels of self-disclosure. According to social penetration theory, relationship development is based on four stages of increasing disclosure, where partners can describe themselves fully in the final stage.

Interpersonal Attraction, Love, and Intimacy across Cultures

While theories about love and attraction are prevalent and popular in American psychology, I know of no research across cultures that directly tests their validity. There is sufficient information from cross-cultural research, however, to suggest how the concepts of attraction, love, and intimacy differ across cultures. It is important to consider first how different cultures may view love. In the United States, we generally feel that love is a necessary and sometimes sufficient ingredient for long-term romantic relationships and marriage. We tend to marry people whom we love. This makes sense in our culture, just as it does not make sense to marry someone you don't love. "Love conquers all," as the saying goes. But love does not enjoy the same consideration for long-term relationships and marriage in many cultures as it does here in the United States. I remember talking to a person from another culture about the supposed "divorce rate problem" of the United States. We were discussing how sociological data seem to indicate that the frequency of divorce is higher than it is has ever been in American history and that it continues to rise. He commented to me that there is no such problem in his country. "The reason for this difference," he said, "is quite clear. You Americans marry the person you love; we love the person we marry."

Indeed, arranged marriages are quite common in many cultures of the world, including Japan, China, and India. Sometimes marriages are arranged by parents far before the age at which the couple can even consider marriage. In other cases, marriage meetings are held between prospective couples, who may then date for a while to decide whether to get married or not. Love is often not part of this equation but is something that should grow in the marriage relationship.

Findings from some cross-cultural studies show how people of different cultures think differently about love and romance. Ting-Toomey (1991) compared ratings of love commitment, disclosure maintenance, ambivalence, and conflict expression by 781 subjects from France, Japan, and the United States. Love commitment was measured by ratings of feelings of attachment,

belongingness, and commitment to the partner and the relationship; disclosure maintenance by ratings of feelings concerning the private self in the relationship; ambivalence by ratings of feelings of confusion or uncertainty regarding the partner or the relationship; and conflict expression by ratings of
frequency of overt arguments and seriousness of problems. The French and
the Americans had significantly higher ratings than the Japanese on love commitment and disclosure maintenance. The Americans also had significantly
higher ratings than the Japanese on relational ambivalence. The Japanese and
the Americans, however, had significantly higher ratings than the French on
conflict expression.

Simmons, vom–Kolke, and Shimizu (1986) examined attitudes toward
love and romance among American, German, and Japanese students. The results indicated that romantic love was valued more in the United States and
Germany than in Japan. These researchers suggested that this cultural difference arose because romantic love is more highly valued in less traditional cultures with few strong, extended-family ties, and less valued in cultures where
kinship networks influence and reinforce the relationship between marriage
partners. This would certainly explain the differences they found between the
Americans, the Germans, and the Japanese.

In another study, Furnham (1984) administered the Rokeach Value Survey to groups of South Africans, Indians, and Europeans. The Europeans valued love more than did the South Africans and the Indians. The South Africans, however, placed higher value on equality and peace.

Despite differences in the definitions and importance of attraction, love,
and romance, however, some research suggests that there may be amazing
cross-cultural agreement in sex differences with regard to mate selection. The
most well-known studies on this topic include that by Buss (1989). In this
study, over 10,000 respondents in 37 different cultures drawn from 33 countries completed two questionnaires, one dealing with factors in choosing a
mate and the second dealing with preferences concerning potential mates. In
36 of the 37 cultures, females rated financial prospects as more important
than did males; in 29 of those 36 cultures, females also rated ambition and in-
dustriousness as more important than did males. In all 37 cultures, however,
males preferred younger mates, while females preferred older mates; in 34 of
the cultures, males rated good looks as more important than did females; and
in 23 of the cultures, males rated chastity higher as an important variable in
choosing a mate than did females. Buss (1989) concluded that females valued
cues related to resource acquisition in potential mates more highly than did
males, whereas males valued reproductive capacity more highly than did females. These findings were predicted, in fact, on the basis of an evolutionary-
based framework that generated hypotheses related to evolutionary concepts
of parental involvement, sexual selection, reproductive capacity, and certainty

of paternity or maternity. The degree of agreement in sex differences across cultures has led Buss (1989) and his colleagues to view these mate selection preferences as universal and developed on the basis of different evolutionary selection pressures on males and females.

Intercultural and Interracial Marriages

Given the cultural differences in attitudes toward love, interpersonal attraction, and marriage, it is no wonder that intercultural and interracial marriages and relationships bring with them their own special problems and issues. As the frequency of interacting with people from many diverse cultures and ethnicities increases in our everyday lives, so too will the number of such relationships increase over time.

Intercultural marriages have been the topic of study by a few researchers (for example, see Franklin, 1992, for a review). These studies have generally shown that conflicts in intercultural marriages arise in several major areas, including the expression of love and intimacy, the nature of commitment and attitudes toward the marriage itself, and the nature of child-rearing when couples have children.

It is no wonder that couples in intercultural marriages experience conflicts around intimacy and love expression. As described in Chapter 12, people of different cultures already have considerable differences in the expression of basic emotions such as anger or frustration or happiness. And emotions such as love and intimacy are not seen as such important ingredients to a successful marriage in many other cultures. These differences arise from a fundamental difference in attitudes toward marriage. Americans tend to view marriage as a lifetime companionship between two people in love. People of many other cultures, however, view marriage differently. Many other cultures view marriage much more as a partnership formed for succession (that is, for producing offspring) and for economic and social bonding. Love rarely enters the equation in the beginning for people in these cultures. However, there is usually a tendency to develop a love relationship with the marriage partner. This is the opposite order from American custom. With such fundamental differences in the nature of marriage across cultures, it is no wonder that intercultural marriages are often among the most difficult of relationships.

Sometimes the differences between two people involved in an intercultural marriage are not seen or experienced until they have children. Oftentimes, major cultural differences emerge around issues of child-rearing. This is no surprise, either, because of the enormous differences in socialization practices and the role of parenting in the development of culture, as was discussed in Chapter 5.

In many ways, intercultural marriages are the prime example of intercultural relationships. For them to be successful, both partners need to be flexible, compromising, and committed to the relationship. If these three ingredients are in the pot, the couples will often find ways to make their relationships work out. Despite these difficulties, anecdotal evidence suggests that these types of marriages are not necessarily associated with higher divorce rates than intracultural marriages. Perhaps it all comes down to how much both spouses are willing to work to negotiate differences, compromise, and stay together.

Cultural Differences in Conformity, Compliance, and Obedience to Groups

Few words and concepts are associated with such negative connotations in American social psychology and social behavior as conformity, compliance, and obedience to the group. These words often stir up forceful images of robots and automatons lacking any individuality. Without doubt, these images strike at the heart of the "rugged American individuality" that is not only central but vital to our outlook on ourselves and our peers. **Conformity** refers to people yielding to real or imagined social pressure. **Compliance** is generally defined as people yielding to social pressure in their public behavior, even though their private beliefs may not have changed. **Obedience** is a form of compliance that occurs when people follow direct commands, usually from someone in a position of authority. Whether we like it or not, these issues are very real in all of our lives. Research on these topics in the United States has shown that not only does conformity, compliance, and obedience exist but their effects are pervasive.

U.S. Research on Conformity, Compliance, and Obedience

Two of the best-known studies in American social psychology on conformity, compliance, and obedience are the Asch and Milgram studies. Asch's studies were conducted quite some time ago, but are very relevant in today's world as well. In the earliest experiments, Asch (1951, 1955, 1956) examined a subject's response to a simple judgment task when experimental confederates responding before the subject all gave an incorrect response. For example, a subject would be placed in a room with others, shown objects (lines, balls, and so forth), and asked to make a judgment about the objects where the answer was often obvious, but where subjects gave their answers only after a number of experimental confederates gave theirs. The basic finding from these simple experiments was that more often than not the subjects would give the wrong answer, even though it was obviously wrong, if the people answering prior to them gave that same wrong answer. Across studies and trials, group size and group unanimity were major influencing factors. Conformity would peak when the groups included seven people and the group was unanimous in its judgments (even though the judgments were clearly wrong).

In Asch's studies, compliance resulted from subtle, implied pressure. But in the real world, compliance can occur in response to explicit rules, requests, and commands. We can only imagine how forceful and pervasive group pressure to conform and comply are in the real world if they can operate in a simple laboratory environment among people unknown to the subject and about a task that has relatively little meaning.

Another well-known study on this topic in American social psychology is that of Milgram (1974). In that study, subjects were brought into a laboratory to presumably study the effects of punishment on learning. Subjects were instructed to provide shocks to another subject (actually an experimental confederate) when the latter gave the wrong response or no response. The shock meter was labeled from "slight shock" to "DANGER: Severe Shock," and the confederate's behaviors ranged from simple utterances of pain through pounding on the walls, pleas to stop, and then deathly silence. No shock was actually administered. Despite these facts, 65% of the subjects obeyed the commands of the experimenter and administered the most severe levels of shock.

The Asch experiments were rather innocuous in the actual content of the compliance (for example, judgments of the length of lines). The Milgram studies, however, clearly highlighted the potential negative and harmful effects of compliance and obedience. To this day, it stands as one of the best known studies in American social psychology. It is unlikely to be attempted today because of restrictions based on ethics and university standards of conduct, but its findings speak for themselves of the power of group influences.

Conformity, Compliance, and Obedience in Other Cultures

One of the first things to consider when thinking about cultural differences in conformity, compliance, and obedience concerns our cultural bias against these terms. Clearly, these terms carry negative connotations in our culture. These negative connotations actually gain strength through research such as the Milgram studies described above, because these studies clearly showed how blind obedience to authority can have severe, drastic, and dramatic consequences. To be sure, these studies focused on simple behaviors that could be produced in the laboratory under different obedience or conformity conditions. Yet much of our and the scientific community's reactions to these studies have concerned the value of conformity and obedience as social constructs. This transformation from behaviors in a study to discussions of social constructs is interesting and important in its own right. But we need to understand that our feelings about conformity, compliance, and obedience are rooted in our own culture. American culture emphasizes individuality and shuns groupism and conformity. To be a conformist in our culture means that you are "bad" or somehow "lacking" in something.

If we can see that these feelings and connotations about conformity are heavily rooted in our cultural upbringing, then it clearly follows that different cultures will have different feelings about conformity, obedience, and compliance. Whereas these topics are viewed negatively in our own culture, they may very well be attractive aspects of social behaviors in other cultures. A number of cross-cultural studies have been conducted on this topic and do indeed show that people of other cultures view conformity, obedience, and compliance positively, which is a striking contrast to our American view. Some studies have shown that Asian cultures in particular not only engage in conforming, compliant, and obedient behaviors to a greater degree than Americans but that they also *value* conformity to a greater degree. For example, Punetha, Giles, and Young (1987) administered an extended Rokeach Value Survey to three groups of Asian subjects and one group of British subjects. The British subjects clearly valued individualistic items, such as independence and freedom, whereas the Asian subjects endorsed societal values including conformity and obedience.

Studies involving other Asian and American comparisons have generally produced the same results. Hadiyono and Hahn (1985) showed that Indonesians endorsed conformity more than Americans did. Argyle, Henderson, Bond, Iizuka, and Contarello (1986) showed that the Japanese and Hong Kong Chinese endorsed obedience more than did British and Italian subjects. Buck, Newton, and Muramatsu (1984) showed that the Japanese were more conforming than Americans. Valuing conformity and obedience is not limited to Asian cultures. Cashmore and Goodnow (1986) demonstrated that Italians were more conforming than Anglo-Australians. And El-Islam (1983) documented cultural differences in conformity in an Arabian sample.

Two cross-cultural studies on child-rearing values speak to the strength of these values in socialization and as products of enculturation. Not only Asians but also Puerto Rican subjects value conformity and obedience as child-rearing values (Burgos & Dias-Perez, 1986; Stropes-Roe & Cochrane, 1990). A number of anthropological works on the Japanese culture (for example, Benedict, 1946; Doi, 1985) indicate the importance of obedience and compliance in child rearing in that culture.

These findings are undoubtedly related to cultural differences in values regarding groupism versus individualism. Traditional American culture fosters individualistic values, endorsing behaviors and beliefs contrary to conformity. To conform in American culture is to be "weak" or somehow deficient. But this is not true in other cultures. Many cultures foster more collectivistic, group-oriented values, where concepts of conformity, obedience, and compliance enjoy much higher status and a positive orientation. In these cultures, conformity is not only viewed as "good" but necessary for the successful functioning of the culture, its groups, and for interpersonal relationships of the members of that culture.

Still, we may wonder why research conducted in the United States has such negative findings. While the Asch studies described are rather innocuous, clearly the Milgram studies are powerful statements of how things can turn sour because of obedience. We need to ask ourselves why the best known studies of conformity and obedience are regarded so negatively. Have any studies been conducted by American social psychologists that show positive outcomes because of conformity or compliance or obedience? If not, perhaps we need to examine the possible biases of American social scientists in not wanting to conduct such studies and the possible biases of people who make unreasonable requests of others.

 # Conclusion

Humans are social animals. By nature we bond with others, live with others, work and play with others. Our whole lives are spent in some kind of interaction or relationship with other people. No matter how we look at it, we cannot ignore the fact that we are fundamentally connected with other people in our world around us. Our behaviors, thoughts, and feelings are all influenced by others. In turn, we influence those around us. Certainly individuals have different degrees of influence and reciprocation.

As we grow in our own cultures and societies, we learn certain ways of behaving, interacting, feeling, and interpreting with relation to the world around us. By the time we are adults, we are so well practiced at these ways that we often don't think about how or why we do the things we do. Our attributions, interpersonal and romantic relationships, and group behavior are all influenced strongly by the culture in which we live.

We need to recognize that culture plays a major role in shaping our behaviors with others. And we need to recognize that what is true and valid for us in our own social behavior may not be true or valid for other people from other cultures. While we may frown on conformity to group norms or obedience to authority, many cultures view them as positive aspects of social behavior. While we may believe that our successes are due to internal attributes and our failures to external ones, people from other cultures may equally attribute successes and failures to themselves personally. While we may not feel anything is wrong in expressing negative feelings toward ingroup others, people from other cultures may feel that is indeed the worst thing that someone can do.

These are just a few of the examples of how culture can influence social behavior. The most important thing to remember is that just as how we think and feel and act is valid for us, how people from other cultures think and feel and act is equally valid for them within their own cultural background, no matter how different their behaviors are from ours. Validity, of course, is a different question from acceptance or liking, but it is the first step toward those goals as well.

Many of the issues raised and discussed in this chapter are relevant to other topics covered in this book. I hope the material presented here can serve as a background and a springboard for inquiring further about how culture can influence our behaviors and perceptions of groups, organizations, communities, and society as a whole.

Glossary

attributions   The inferences people draw about the causes of events and their own and others' behaviors.

companionate love   Love that involves warm, trusting, and tolerant affection for another whose life is deeply intertwined with your own.

compliance   People yielding to social pressure in their public behavior, even though their private beliefs may not have changed.

conformity   People yielding to real or imagined social pressure.

consensus   One of the dimensions thought to influence the nature of attributions; it refers to whether other people in the same situation tend to respond in the same manner.

consistency   One of the dimensions thought to influence the nature of attributions; it refers to whether a person's behavior in a situation is the same over time.

consummate love   Love that is characterized by passionate love, intimacy, and commitment.

defensive attributions   The tendency to blame victims for their misfortune.

distinctiveness   One of the dimensions thought to influence the nature of attributions; it refers to whether a person's behavior is unique to the specific target of the behavior.

fundamental attribution error An attributional bias to explain the behavior of others using internal attributions but explaining your own behaviors using external attributions.

ingroup relationships Relationships characterized by some degree of familiarity, intimacy, and trust. We feel close to people around us we consider to be in our ingroup. Self-ingroup relationships develop through bonds that tie the ingroup together through common friendship or relationships or goals.

matching hypothesis A hypothesis about love relationships that suggests that people of approximately equal physical characteristics are likely to select each other as partners.

obedience A form of compliance that occurs when people follow direct commands, usually from someone in a position of authority.

outgroup relationships Relationships that lack the familiarity, intimacy, and trust afforded to relationships with ingroup others.

passionate love Love that involves absorption of another and includes sexual feelings and intense emotion.

reciprocity hypothesis A hypothesis about love relationships that suggests that people tend to like others who like them.

self-serving bias The tendency to attribute your successes to personal factors and your failures to situational factors.

similarity hypothesis A hypothesis about love relationships that suggests that people similar in age, race, religion, social class, education, intelligence, attitudes, and physical attractiveness tend to form intimate relationships.

9

Culture and Basic Psychological Processes

Perception, Cognition, and Intelligence

Perception and cognition are basic psychological processes. **Perception** refers to how we perceive and gather information about the world around us. **Cognition** is related to perception and refers to the way we process that information.

These processes describe the most elemental ways we receive and process information about the world and our relationship to it. Both have rich traditions of research and theory in psychology, and as with other psychological processes, they are heavily influenced by our cultural backgrounds. Recognition of the pervasive influence of culture on human behavior must be extended to these basic processes as well.

In this chapter, we explore how culture influences perception and then cognition. I will review some of the traditional information about these topics. However, some of the topics of interest to this discussion have not been addressed in cross-cultural research, so only selected topics will be addressed.

Later in this chapter, I will discuss cultural influences on definitions and measurement of another basic psychological process—intelligence. I hope this information will give you a flavor of how culture contributes to our perceptions, cognitions, and views of intelligence.

Culture and Perception

Perception and Experience

Before considering how culture affects our perceptions, we must first realize that regardless of culture, our perceptions of the world do not necessarily match the physical realities of the world, or of our senses. Consider how visual perception may not be absolutely factual. All of us have a **blind spot** in each eye. This is a spot with no sensory receptors because the optic nerve goes through the layer of receptor cells at that spot on its way back toward the brain. Close one eye; you probably won't experience a hole in the world. There is no blind spot in our conscious perception, even though we have no receptors receiving light from one area of the eye. Our brains fill it in so it looks as if we see everything. It is only when something comes at us out of this spot that we get some idea that something is wrong with our vision in this particular location. Many of you may have performed a brief experiment in an introductory psychology course that illustrates the existence of the blind spot. The point here is that our perception of the world as "complete" does not actually match the physical reality of the sensation we receive in our visual system. Everyday experiences with temperature and touch also highlight this distortion in perception. If you filled three bowls with water—one with hot water, one with ice water, and one with lukewarm water—and put your hand in the hot water for a few seconds and then in the lukewarm water, the lukewarm water will feel cold. Wait a few minutes, then put your hand in the ice water and then the lukewarm water, and the lukewarm water will feel warm. The lukewarm water will not have changed its temperature; rather, it is our perception of the water that has changed (compare with Segall, 1979).

Once we begin to question our own senses, we want to know their limits. We want to know what influence our experiences and beliefs about the world have on what we perceive. We also want to know if other people perceive things the same as we do. If others do not see things as we do, what aspects of their experiences and backgrounds might explain those differences?

One thing we know about our perceptions is that they change. One way they change was noted in our perception of the temperature of the bowls of water. Our perceptions also change when we know more about a particular thing. We all have experienced seeing something complex, like a piece of machinery, for the first time. Can you remember the first few times you looked under the hood of a car? To most people it seems like an immense jumble. But for those who learn about the engine, it becomes familiar and differentiated into specific parts: a carburetor, an engine block, an alternator, and so forth. But to those who don't know much about mechanics, the engine looks like one big thing. So, clearly, the way we "see" things changes with our experiences with them.

How might someone with a very different background "see" something that is very familiar to us? How might we "see" something that is very familiar to them and less so to us? A teacher visiting in Australia related an interesting anecdote that highlights these cultural differences in perception. She was teaching at a school for aborigine children in Australia and was trying to teach the aborigine children to play a schoolyard game called "Who touched me?" In this game, everyone stands in a circle and the person who is "it" is blindfolded. Then another person from the circle quietly walks around the outside of the circle, touches the blindfolded person, and then returns to her or his place. The blindfold is removed, and the person who is "it" has to guess who touched him or her. The teacher found that the aborigine children didn't really want to play, but they cooperated because she was the teacher. Later, in the classroom, she found the students to be uncooperative and reluctant to try anything she suggested. They refused to make any effort to try to learn the alphabet. She began to think they were being stupid or naughty.

Later, to her surprise, she found out that the children thought that *she* was the stupid one. Aborigine children can tell whose footprint is on the ground behind them with a casual glance. So the teacher had them playing a game that was completely silly to them; it was so easy as to make no sense at all as a game. In fact, when the aborigine children realized the teacher couldn't tell people's footprints apart, they thought she was the stupid one, so there was no point paying attention to her. They just humored her so they wouldn't get into trouble, but they wouldn't take her or her ideas about what they should learn seriously.

Cultural Influences on Visual Perception

Most of what we know about cultural influences on perception comes from cross-cultural research on visual perception. Much of this excellent work has been based on testing differences in optical illusions by Segall, Campbell, and Hersokovits (1963, 1966). **Optical illusions** are perceptions that involve an apparent discrepancy between how an object looks and what it actually is. Optical illusions are often based on inappropriate assumptions about the stimulus characteristics of the object being perceived. One of the best-known optical illusions is the Mueller-Lyer illusion (see Figure 9.1). Research has shown that subjects viewing these two figures typically judge the line with the arrow pointing in as longer than the other line. This is an illusion, however, because the lines are actually the same length. Another well-known illusion is the horizontal-vertical illusion (see Figure 9.2). When subjects are

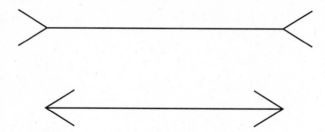

Which line is longer? To most people the top line appears longer than the bottom line. The lines are actually identical in length.

Figure 9.1 The Mueller-Lyer illusion

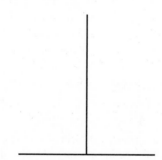

Which line is longer? To most people the vertical line appears longer than the horizontal line although both lines are the same length.

Figure 9.2 The horizontal-vertical illusion

asked to judge which line is longer, they typically respond that the vertical line is longer, which is also false. A third well-known illusion is the Ponzo illusion (see Figure 9.3). When subjects view this image, they typically report that the horizontal line closer to the originating point of the diagonal lines is longer than the one away from the origin. Of course, they are in actuality the same length.

Several important theories have been developed to explain why optical illusions occur. One of these is the **carpentered world theory**, which suggests that people (such as most Americans) are used to seeing things that are rectangular in shape. We live in a world where many things are made in rectangular shapes with squared corners. Living in such a squared environment, we unconsciously come to expect things to have squared corners. If we see a house from an angle and the light reflected off it does not form a right angle

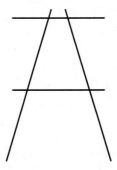

Which horizontal line is longer? To most people the upper line appears longer although both are the same length.

Figure 9.3 The Ponzo illusion

on the eye, we still perceive it as a house with squared corners. We interpret what we see as having squared corners. We have been doing this for so long that we are no longer aware that we are interpreting things as being square even when the physical object does not form a right angle on our eye. We simply "see" it as square. Thus, in the Mueller-Lyer illusion, we tend to see the figures as having square corners that project in depth toward or away from us. We know that things that look the same size to our eyes but are at different distances are truly different sizes, and we learn to interpret a set length of line as longer when it seems to project away from us and shorter when it seems to project toward us.

The **front-horizontal foreshortening theory** suggests that we interpret vertical lines as horizontal lines that exist in the distance. We then interpret the vertical line in the horizontal-vertical illusion as a line extending away into the distance. Again, we would guess that a line would be longer if it were further away in space, so we see the vertical line as extending into space and thus longer than the horizontal line, which we do not see as extending out into the distance.

These two theories share some common characteristics. For example, they both assume that the way we see the world is developed over time through our experiences. What we see is a combination of the way the object reflects light to our eyes and our learning about how to see things in general. Although learning helps us see well most of the time, it is the very thing that causes us to misjudge optical illusions. The second idea these theories share is that we live in a three-dimensional world that is projected onto our eyes in two dimensions. Our eyes are nearly flat, and light striking two places on the eye right beside each other may be coming from things very different in distance. We interpret distance and depth from cues other than where the light falls on the eye. This happens even though the light coming to the eye from one object reaches the eye next to where the light coming from another object reaches the eye.

A number of cross-cultural studies challenge our traditional notions about optical illusions, as would be expected should experience contribute to our perceptions. As early as 1905, W. H. R. Rivers (Rivers, 1905) compared the responses to the Mueller-Lyer and horizontal-vertical illusions using groups in England, rural India, and New Guinea. He found that the English people saw the lines in the Mueller-Lyer illusion as being more different in length than did the two other groups. He also found that the Indians and New Guineans were more fooled by the horizontal-vertical illusion than were the people in England. These results surprised Rivers and many other people from Europe and the United States. They believed that the people from India and New Guinea were more primitive and would therefore be more fooled by the illusions than would the more educated and "civilized" people from England. The results showed that the effect of the illusion differed by culture, but there was something besides education involved in how much people were deceived by the illusions. The researchers concluded that culture must have some effect on the way the world is "seen." How this difference in perception comes about has been a source of curiosity ever since.

Both the carpentered world theory and the front-horizontal foreshortening theory can be used to explain the results Rivers obtained. The former, for example, would suggest that most Americans and the English people in Rivers's study are used to seeing things that are rectangular in shape. People in India and New Guinea, however, are more accustomed to rounded and irregular environments. With the Mueller-Lyer illusion, English people would tend to see the figures as squared corners that project in depth toward or away from us. The Indians and New Guineans, on the other hand, live in cultures where less of the environment is human made. They would have less tendency to make the same perceptual mistake. Thus, the people from England made more errors in interpreting the Mueller-Lyer illusion than did the people from India or New Guinea. The front-horizontal foreshortening theory can also account for the cultural differences obtained in Rivers's study. There are fewer buildings to block the vista of distance in India or New Guinea. Thus, the Indians and New Guineans rely more on depth cues than do the English and make more errors in judgments of the horizontal-vertical figure. This is, in fact, what Rivers found.

A third theory has been offered to explain cultural differences in visual perception. The **symbolizing three dimensions in two** theory suggests that in Western cultures we focus more on things on paper than do people in other cultures. In particular, we spend more time learning to interpret pictures than do people in non-Western cultures. Thus, people in New Guinea and India are less likely to be fooled by the Mueller-Lyer illusion because it is more "foreign" to them. They would, however, be more fooled by the horizontal-vertical illusion because it is more representative of their lifestyle (although in this example it is unclear whether the differentiation between the cultures is Western versus non-Western or industrialized versus nonindustrialized).

To ensure that Rivers's findings held for cultures in general, Segall and colleagues (1963, 1966) compared people from 3 industrialized groups to people from 14 nonindustrialized groups on the Mueller-Lyer and the horizontal-vertical illusions. The results showed that the effect of the Mueller-Lyer illusion was stronger for the industrialized groups than for the nonindustrialized groups. On the other hand, the effect of the vertical-horizontal illusion was stronger for the nonindustrialized groups than for the industrialized ones. This supported Rivers's findings.

Segall et al. (1963, 1966) also found some evidence that did not fit with any of the three theories. That is, the effects of the illusions declined and nearly disappeared with older subjects. This presents a problem for all the theories mentioned above. We might expect the effects of the illusions to increase with age because older people have had more time to learn about their environments than younger people. Wagner (1977) examined this problem using different versions of the Ponzo illusion and comparing the performance of people in both rural and urban environments, some of whom continued their education and some of whom did not. One version of the Ponzo illusion was like that in Figure 9.3; another was a picture containing the same configuration of lines embedded in a complete picture. Wagner found that for the simple line drawing the effect of the illusion declined with age for all groups. For the illusion embedded in a picture, he found that the effect of the illusion increased with age, but only for urban people and people who continued their schooling. So here is more direct evidence of the effects of urban environments and schooling on the Mueller-Lyer illusion.

There is also a physical theory that must be considered. Pollack and Silvar (1967) showed that the effects of the Mueller-Lyer illusion are related to the ability to detect contours, and this ability declines with age. They also noted that as people age and are more exposed to sunlight, less light enters the eye, and this may affect people's ability to perceive the lines in the illusion. They also showed that retinal pigmentation is related to contour-detecting ability. Non-European people have more retinal pigmentation and so are less able to detect contours. Thus, Pollack and Silvar (1967) suggested that the cultural differences could be explained by racial differences in retinal pigmentation.

To test whether the racial or the environmental learning theory was more correct, Stewart (1973) noted that both race and environment need to be compared without being mixed together, as was done in the study by Segall and his colleagues. To do this, Stewart tested the effects of the Mueller-Lyer illusion on both black and white children living in one town,

Evanston, Illinois. She found no differences between the two racial groups. She then compared groups of elementary school children in Zambia in environments that ranged from very urban and carpentered to very rural and uncarpentered. She found that the effects of the illusion were dependent on the degree to which the children lived in a carpentered environment. She also found that with increased age the effect declined, suggesting that both learning and heredity played roles in the observed cultural differences.

Hudson (1960) also conducted an interesting study to highlight cultural differences in perception. He had an artist draw pictures similar to those in the Thematic Apperception Test (TAT) that psychologists thought would make Bantu tribe members think of their deep emotions. They were surprised to find that the Bantu often saw the pictures in a very different way than anticipated. The Bantu often did not use relative size as a cue to depth. In Figure 9.4, for example, we tend to see the hunter preparing to throw his spear at the gazelle in the foreground, while an elephant stands on a hill in the background. Many of the Bantu, however, thought the hunter in a similar picture was preparing to stab the baby elephant. In another picture, an orator, who we would see as waving his arms dramatically with a factory in the background, was seen as warming his hands over the tiny chimneys of the factory. Hudson (1960) found that these differences in depth perception were related to both education and exposure to European cultures. In other words, Bantu people who were educated in European schools, or who had more experience with European culture, saw things as Europeans did. Bantu people who had no education and little exposure to Western culture saw the pictures differently.

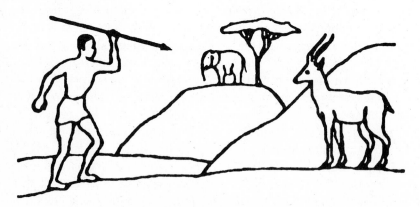

What is the hunter's target? Americans and Europeans would say it is the gazelle in the foreground. The Bantu in Hudson's (1960) research, however, said it was the elephant.

Figure 9.4 Hudson's (1960) picture of depth perception

Cultural differences found in fundamental psychological processes of perception have considerable implications for conflicts that may arise in intercultural interactions. People of different cultures interact with others from different backgrounds and experiences. These experiences, in turn, alter the ways we receive information about our interactions. Yet we operate on that information with little thought or evaluation of the validity of that information, for we have learned ways of interpreting the world that are mostly valid for the culture in which we live. When we cross cultures, either in interaction or in travel, we take those experiences and learned patterns of perception with us, even though they may no longer be valid.

Culture and Cognition

Just as culture influences the way we receive information about the world around us, culture also influences the way we process that information. Psychologists use the term *cognition* to denote all the mental processes we use to transform sensory input into knowledge. These processes involve perception, rational thinking and reasoning, language, memory, problem solving, decision making, and the like. In this section, I will review some of the ways culture affects cognitive processes.

Culture, Categorization, and Concept Formation

One basic mental process is the manner in which people group things together into categories. People **categorize** on the basis of similarities and attach labels (namely, words) to groups of objects perceived to have something in common. In so doing, people create categories of objects that share certain characteristics. In addition, people often decide whether something belongs in a certain group by comparing it to the most common or representative member of that category. For instance, a bean bag chair, a straight-backed dining room chair, and a seat in a theater differ in appearance from one another, but all belong to the basic category "chair." All these things can be grouped together under the label "chair," because all share a common function. When we say "that thing is a chair" in our culture, we mean that the item can and should be used as something for people to sit on (Rosch, 1978). Function is the primary determinant of this category.

Some categories appear to be universal across cultures. Facial expressions that signal basic emotions—happiness, sadness, anger, fear, surprise, and disgust—are placed in the same categories across cultures (see Chapter 12).

Likewise, there is widespread agreement across cultures about which colors are primary and which are secondary. The universality of the way people select and remember colors appears to be largely independent of both culture and language. Regardless of whether people speak a language that has dozens of words for colors or one that distinguishes colors only in terms of whether they are bright or dark, individuals from both cultural extremes group colors around the same primary hues. They also remember primary colors with greater ease when asked to compare and recall colors in an experimental setting. For example, an individual from a culture that has only one word for red/yellow/white will select the same kind of red as the best example of this category as graduate students at Harvard will. Also, both groups of people will remember this particular color of red more easily than they will a shade like lilac or orange pink, despite having a very different set of names for colors (see Chapter 13 for a fuller discussion of color perception and the categorization of colors).

People across cultures also tend to categorize shapes in terms of the best example of basic forms (perfect circles, equilateral triangles, and squares) rather than forming categories for irregular geometrical shapes. These cross-cultural parallels suggest that physiological factors influence the way humans categorize certain basic stimuli. That is, humans seem to be predisposed to prefer certain shapes, colors, and facial expressions.

Research has also shown how cultures differ in categorization. For example, even though a particular category (for example, facial expressions or chairs) may be universal to all cultures, its exact prototype can differ across cultures. Because all people of the world have the same facial morphology (Oster & Ekman, 1979), facial prototypes of emotional expressions will not necessarily differ. However, because the materials used to construct furniture differ across cultures, the prototype of chairs may differ.

One common way to study cultural differences in categorization involves the use of sorting tasks. When presented with pictures that could be grouped either in terms of function, shape, or color, children in Western cultures tend to group by color at younger ages. Then they group by shape and then by function as they grow older (see Bruner, Oliver, & Greenfield, 1966). This means that Western adults tend to put all the tools one group and all the animals in another, rather than grouping all the red things or all the round things together. It had been assumed that this trend was a function of basic human maturation. But given similar sorting tasks, adult Africans showed a strong tendency to group objects by color rather than function (Suchman, 1966; Greenfield, Reich, & Oliver, 1966). This shows that something besides simple maturation must be responsible for the category shifts.

These differences may be due to culture or education. Evans and Segall (1969) attempted to separate the effects of maturation from those of schooling by comparing children and adults in Uganda. Some of the subjects had received formal schooling, while others had not attended school. The researchers gave sorting tasks to all their subjects and found a preference for color grouping most common among people who had little or no formal schooling. However, it is not clear at this point in time whether cultural differences in sorting tasks and categorization are best attributed to differences in cultural heritage or to differences in formal schooling.

Cultural Differences in Memory

Another basic intellectual task we all share is remembering things. We have all agonized over the task of memorizing for tests and noticed the difficulty with which we memorize lists of dates or names or other similar things. Whenever we can, we use memory aids like shopping lists or calendars to help us remember things we are likely to forget.

Many of us have heard the claim that individuals from nonliterate societies develop better memory skills because they don't have the ability to write things down to remember them (Bartlett, 1932). Is it true that our memories are not as good when we habitually use lists as aids in remembering? Ross and Millson (1970) suspected that reliance on an oral tradition might make people better at remembering. They compared the memories of American and Ghanian college students in remembering stories that were read aloud. They found that, generally, the Ghanian students were better than the Americans at remembering the stories. Thus, it seemed that cultures with an oral tradition were better at remembering things. But Cole and his colleagues (Cole, Gay, Glick, & Sharp, 1971) found that nonliterate African subjects did not perform better when they were tested with lists of words instead of with stories. These findings imply that cultural differences in memory as a function of an oral tradition may be limited to meaningful material.

One of the best-known aspects of memory, established by research in the United States, is what is known as the **serial position effect**. This effect suggests that we remember things better if they are either the first (primacy effect) or last (recency effect) thing on a list of things to remember. Interestingly, Cole and Scribner (1974) found no relation between serial position and the likelihood of being remembered in studying the memory of Kpelle tribespeople in Liberia.

Wagner (1980) suggested that the primacy effect is dependent on rehearsal or the silent repetition of things you are trying to remember and that this memory strategy is related to schooling. Wagner compared groups of Moroccan children who had and had not gone to school and found that the primacy effect was much stronger in the children who had been to school.

Wagner suggested that the process of memory has two parts. These include a "hardware" part that is the basic limitation of memory, which does not change across cultures, and a "software" or programming part that has to do with how we go about trying to remember, which is learned. It is the software part that varies across cultures.

The ability to remember unconnected information appears to be influenced not so much by culture but by whether people have attended school. In a classroom setting, children are expected to memorize letters, multiplication tables, and other basic facts. Subjects who have been to school, therefore, have had more practice at memorizing than unschooled individuals. They are also able to apply these skills in test situations that resemble their school experience. A study by Scribner (1974) with educated and uneducated Africans supported this idea; educated Africans were able to recall lists of words to a degree similar to that of American subjects, while uneducated Africans remembered fewer words. It is not clear whether culture or schooling or both contribute to the observed differences.

Culture and Problem Solving

Problem solving refers to the process by which we attempt to discover ways of achieving goals that do not seem readily attainable. Psychologists have tried to isolate the process of problem solving by asking people from different cultures to solve unfamiliar problems in artificial settings. One such experiment (Cole et al., 1971) consisted of instructing American and Liberian subjects on the use of an apparatus containing various buttons, panels, and slots. To open the device and obtain a prize, subjects had to independently combine two different procedures, first pressing the correct button to release a marble, and then inserting the marble into the appropriate slot to open a panel. American subjects under the age of 10 were generally unable to obtain the prize. Older American subjects, however, combined the two steps with ease. Liberian subjects of all ages and educational backgrounds experienced great difficulty solving the problem; less than a third of the adults were successful. One might conclude from this experiment that Americans are better at advanced problem solving than Liberians and that the Liberian culture produces adults who seem to lack a capacity for logical reasoning. However, this experiment may have been biased for the Americans, despite its apparent objectivity. That is, the Americans may have benefited from the hidden advantage of living in a technological society. As such, we are accustomed to mechanical devices; buttons, levers, dials, and slots on machines are common in our daily environment. In some non-Western cultures, people seldom operate machines, and the unfamiliarity of the apparatus may have influenced the outcome by intimidating or bewildering the Liberian subjects. (Remember the first time you ever worked on a computer?)

Cole and his colleagues repeated their experiment with materials familiar to people in Liberia, using a locked box and keys instead of the mechanical contraption. Under this circumstance, the great majority of Liberians solved the problem easily. In the new version of the two-step problem, the Liberian subjects had to remember which key opened the lock on the box and which matchbox container housed the correct key.

The success of the Liberians in solving a two-step problem with a familiar set of materials brings us back to the question of whether the experiment tested their ability to think logically or tested their previous knowledge and experience with locks and keys. In an attempt to clarify this issue, the researchers designed a third experiment, combining elements from both the first and second tests. Liberian and American subjects were again presented with a locked box, but the key that opened the box had to be obtained from the apparatus used in the first experiment. To the surprise of the researchers, the third test produced results similar to the first experiment; while Americans solved the problem with ease, most Liberians were not able to retrieve the key to open the box.

Cole and his colleagues concluded that the ability of the Liberians to reason logically to solve problems depends on context. When presented with problems that employ materials and concepts already familiar to them, Liberians drew logical conclusions effortlessly. When the test situation was alien to them, however, they had difficulty knowing where to begin. In some cases, the problem went beyond confusion; uneducated Liberians appeared to be visibly frightened by the tests that employed the strange apparatus and were reluctant to manipulate it. Although adult Americans did very well in these experiments in comparison to the Liberians, how might average Americans react if placed in a similar experimental situation that required the Americans to use wholly unfamiliar concepts and technology—for example, an experiment requiring American subjects to track animals using smells and the appearance of their footprints.

Another type of problem that has been studied cross-culturally involves syllogisms (for example, all children like candy; Mary is a child; does Mary like candy?). In wide-ranging studies of tribal and nomadic peoples in East and Central Asia, Luria (1976) documented sharp differences in the way people approached these problems. As with other cultural differences in cognition and thought, the ability to provide the correct answer to verbal problems was found to be closely associated with school attendance. Individuals from traditional societies who were illiterate were generally unable to provide answers to syllogisms containing unfamiliar information. Individuals from the same culture and even from the same village who had received a single year of schooling could respond correctly.

Various explanations have been proposed to account for the inability of uneducated people to complete word problems. Luria (1976) concluded that illiterate people actually think differently from those who are educated. According to this hypothesis, logical reasoning is essentially artificial, because it is a skill that must be learned in a westernized school setting. Some studies lend support to this interpretation. Tulviste (1978) asked schoolchildren in Estonia from the ages of 8 to 15 to solve verbal problems and explain their answers. Although the children were able to solve most of the problems correctly, they explained their answers by citing the logical premises of the problem only in areas where they did not have firsthand knowledge. Elsewhere, their answers were justified with appeals to common sense or statements about their personal observations.

Scribner (1979) questioned whether illiterate subjects are truly incapable of thinking logically and looked more closely into the reasons uneducated people fail to give correct responses to verbal problems. When uneducated peasants were asked to explain illogical answers to syllogism problems, they consistently cited evidence that was known to them personally or stated that they didn't know anything about the subject, ignoring the premises given to them. For example, in response to the word problem "all children like candy; Mary is a child; does Mary like candy?" subjects might shrug their shoulders and comment, "How would I know whether Mary likes candy?—I don't even know the child!" or "Maybe she doesn't like candy; I've known children who didn't." These individuals appear to be unable or unwilling to apply concepts of scientific thinking to verbal problems. But this is not because they lack the capacity to reason logically; rather, they do not understand the hypothetical nature of verbal problems or view them with the same degree of importance. People who have been to school have had the experience of answering questions posed by an authority figure who already knows the correct answers. Uneducated people, however, have difficulty understanding the notion that questions need not be requests for information.

Intelligence: Definitions and Concepts

Traditional Definitions of Intelligence in U.S. Psychology

The English word *intelligence* is derived from Latin word *intelligentia,* coined 2000 years ago by the Roman orator Cicero. In the United States, we use the term *intelligence* to refer to a number of different abilities, skills, talents, and knowledge, generally all referring to our mental or cognitive abilities. Thus, we traditionally consider a number of processes to represent intelligence, such as memory (how well and how much we can remember for how long), vocabulary (how many words we know and can use properly), comprehension (how well we can understand a passage or set of ideas or statements), mathematical abilities (addition, subtraction, and so forth), logical reasoning (how well we can understand underlying logic or sequence among events, things, or objects), and the like.

A number of theories have dominated our understanding of intelligence in psychology. Piaget's theory (described in Chapter 5) views intelligence as a reflection of cognitive development through a series of stages, with the highest stage corresponding to abstract reasoning and principles. Spearman (1927) and Thurstone (1938) developed what are known as factor theories of intelligence. These theories view intelligence as a general concept comprised of many subcomponents, or factors, which include verbal or spatial comprehension, word fluency, perceptual speed, and the like. Guilford (1985) built on factor theories to describe intelligence using three dimensions—operation, content, and product—each of which have separate components. Through various combinations of these three dimensions, Guilford suggests that intelligence is actually composed of upwards of 150 separate factors.

While traditional thinking and reasoning abilities have dominated views of intelligence in the past, in recent years psychologists have begun to turn their attention to other aspects of the mind as part of intelligence. For example, interest has increased around the concept of creativity as a part of intelligence. Until very recently, creativity was not considered a part of intelligence per se. Now, however, psychologists are increasingly considering this important human ability as a type of intelligence. Other aspects of intelligence are also coming to the forefront. Gardner and Hatch (1989), for example, suggested that there are really seven different types of intelligences: logical mathematical, linguistic, musical, spatial, bodily kinesthetic, interpersonal, and intrapersonal. According to this scheme, not only are the core components of each of the seven different types of intelligences different but also some example end-states (such as mathematician versus dancer).

Sternberg (1986) has proposed a theory of intelligence that is based on the existence of three separate "subtheories" of intelligence: contextual, experiential, and componential intelligence. Contextual intelligence refers to an individual's ability to adapt to the environment, solving problems in specific situations. Experiential intelligence refers to the ability to formulate new ideas and combine unrelated facts. Componential intelligence refers to the ability to think abstractly, process information, and determine what needs to be done. Sternberg's theory focuses more on the processes that underlie thought than on specific thought outcomes. Because intelligence is defined as process rather than outcome, it has the potential for application across cultures.

Despite the fact that inclusion of these various types of intelligence has added a new dimension of diversity to our definitions of intelligence, traditional mainstream definitions of intelligence still tend to center around cognitive and mental capabilities concerning verbal and mathematical skills.

Cultural Differences in the Meaning and Concept of Intelligence

When considering intelligence in a cross-cultural context, the first thing we need to take into account is the fact that many languages have no word that corresponds to our idea of intelligence. Definitions of intelligence often reflect cultural values. The closest Mandarin equivalent, for instance, is a Chinese character that means "good brain and talented." Chinese people often associate this with traits such as imitation, effort, and social responsibility (Keats, 1982). Such traits do not constitute important elements of the concept of intelligence for most Americans.

Another example is from the Baganda of East Africa. They use the word *obugezi* to refer to a combination of mental and social skills that make a person steady, cautious, and friendly (Wober, 1974). The Djerma-Songhai in West Africa use the term *akkal,* which has an even broader meaning and is a combination of intelligence, know-how, and social skills (Bissilat, Laya, Pierre, & Pidoux, 1967). Still another society, the Baoule, uses the term *n'glouele,* which describes children who are not only mentally alert but also willing to volunteer their services without being asked (Dasen et al., 1985).

Because of the enormous differences in the ways cultures define intelligence, it is difficult to make valid comparisons of the notion of intelligence from one society to another. That is, different cultures value different traits, which comprise their notion of "intelligence." Consequently, there are divergent opinions across cultures concerning which traits are useful in predicting future important behaviors, especially because different cultures value different future behaviors. People in different cultures not only disagree about the very nature of what intelligence is but also have very different attitudes about the proper way to demonstrate their abilities. In mainstream U.S. society, individuals are typically rewarded for displaying knowledge and skills. This same behavior may be considered improper, arrogant, or rude in societies that stress personal relationships, cooperation, and modesty.

These differences are important to cross-cultural studies of intelligence because successful performance on a task of intelligence may require behavior that is considered immodest and arrogant in Culture A (and therefore only reluctantly displayed by members of Culture A) but desirable in Culture B (and therefore readily displayed by members of Culture B). Clearly, such different attitudes to the same behavior could result in inaccurate conclusions being made about differences in intelligence between Culture A and Culture B. As I have shown, it is also difficult to compare intelligence cross-culturally for another reason; namely, because tests of intelligence often rely on knowledge that is particular to a culture. Investigators based in another culture may not know what to test for in the first place.

A test designed for one culture is often not suitable for another, even when the test is carefully translated into a second language. For example, one U.S. intelligence test has the following question: How does a violin resemble a piano? Clearly, this question assumes prior knowledge about violins and pianos, quite a reasonable expectation when it comes to middle-class Americans but not for people from cultures that use other musical instruments.

Much cross-cultural research on intelligence has focused on the issue of testing within multicultural societies where cultural minorities are evaluated with tests designed for a dominant culture. Cross-cultural research extends not only to cultures in different countries but also to subcultures within Western society. In the next section, I will examine some of the problems involved in defining and measuring intelligence cross-culturally.

Cultural Influences on the Measurement of Intelligence

Modern intelligence tests were first developed in the early 1900s for the purpose of identifying mentally retarded children. Intelligence tests provided a way to distinguish children in need of special education from those whose schoolwork suffered for other reasons. In the years that followed, intelligence tests came into widespread use in public schools and other government programs.

But not everyone benefited from the new tests of intelligence. Because such tests relied at least in part on verbal performance and cultural knowledge, immigrants who spoke English poorly and came from different cultural backgrounds were at a disadvantage. For example, when tests of intelligence were administered to immigrants at Ellis Island beginning in 1913, over three-quarters of the Italian, Hungarian, and Jewish immigrants tested as mentally defective. Such low scores for certain immigrant groups provoked a storm of controversy. Some people defended the scientific nature of the new tests, charging that southern European immigrants were not fit to enter the country. Others responded that intelligence tests were biased and did not accurately measure the mental ability of people from different cultures. Thus, less than a decade after their invention, testing people from different cultures became a matter of political controversy.

At the end of the century, this controversy has not yet been laid to rest. The debate surrounding the interpretation of test scores of groups who do not belong to the dominant culture continues today, although the groups of people scoring low on standard tests have changed. The average scores of some minority groups in the United States are 12 to 15 percentage points lower than the average observed for whites. This does not mean that all the individuals in these groups test poorly—high-scoring individuals can also be found in minority subcultures—it simply means that larger percentages of the minority populations score low. In a controversy that has come to be known as the "nature versus nurture" debate, people have differed sharply in their interpretations of these scores. Witness the controversy surrounding the recent publication of *The Bell Curve* (Herrnstein & Murray, 1994), which suggests that differences in intelligence across ethnic and social groups are related to differences in physical endowment. This debate is very important in psychology in general and in cross-cultural psychology in particular.

The nature side of the debate argues that differences in IQ scores between different societies and ethnic groups are due mainly to our inborn nature or heredity. Arthur Jensen (1969, 1980, 1981) is one of the best-known proponents of this position. He believes that about 80% of a person's intelligence is inherited and suggests that biological differences explain the gap between the scores of whites and ethnic minorities in the United States. Jensen argues that special programs for the underprivileged are a waste of money because inborn intellectual deficiencies of ethnic minorities are mostly to blame for their performance on IQ tests.

Studies of twins have provided some evidence for the nature hypothesis. The most important of these studies compared identical twins who grew up in separate homes to fraternal twins raised together (Bouchard & McGue, 1981). If test scores are determined by heredity, identical twins raised apart should have very similar scores. But if environment is primary, the scores of the fraternal twins raised together should be more similar. These twin studies revealed that the scores of identical twins raised in different environments were significantly more alike than those of fraternal twins raised together. However, the scores of identical twins raised apart varied more than those of identical twins raised together. These mixed results have been used by both sides. On the nature side, the results have been interpreted to support the claim that much of intelligence is genetic, while opponents give considerably lower estimates. There is widespread agreement, however, that at least 40% of intelligence can be attributed to heredity (Henderson, 1982; Jencks et al., 1972).

The nurture side of the debate argues that culture and environment fully account for the difference in IQ scores between whites and minorities in the United States. Those who hold this position claim that minorities score lower because most subcultures in this country are economically deprived (Blau,

1981; Wolf, 1965). Advocates of this position have turned to studies showing that IQ scores are strongly related to social class. The average IQ score of poor whites, for instance, is 10 or 20 percentage points lower than the average score of the middle class. The effect of environment over race can be seen most clearly in studies showing that poor whites tested in southern states scored lower than blacks who lived in northern states. It is also possible that between-group differences in intelligence scores are the result of (1) different beliefs about what intelligence is or (2) culturally inappropriate measures of intelligence. What we do know is that intelligence tests are a good predictor of the verbal skills necessary for success in a culture associated with the formalized educational systems of modern industrial societies and increasingly adopted as a model throughout the world. However, such tests may not measure motivation, creativity, talent, or social skills, all of which are important factors in achievement.

Another view held by some cross-cultural psychologists is that intelligence tests do measure true differences between societies but that such differences should not be regarded as deficiencies of one culture as compared with another.

When intelligence tests are used to predict performance (for example, in a job or at school), the issue that many people must deal with concerns the validity of the criterion used to judge the outcome of the test. A test may be perceived as culturally "biased" but still be the best predictor of performance at a certain task. Altering the test to reduce the cultural bias may actually weaken the ability of the test to predict performance. If people are admitted based on faulty data, their overall performance may not be as high as it could have been with the use of the better predictor, although it is the more culturally biased test. If you were in an organization (or business) that needed to base selection on test scores, what would you do?

Perhaps questions of selection should be separated from tests used simply to measure intelligence as end points. Regardless of how we interpret cross-cultural differences in measured intelligence, we should respect the values of other cultures. Indeed, we would be well advised to consider the evaluation of intelligence in another culture according to that culture's own definition of intelligence.

 ## Conclusion

In this chapter, we have examined how culture influences the basic psychological processes of perception, cognition, and intelligence. These influences have profound implications for our understanding of the impact of culture on people and behavior. I remember fondly when I was first introduced to the material concerning cultural influences on visual perceptions and optical illusions. I had never thought that culture, and experience in general, could have the effect that it does on what I thought must be innate, basic properties. When I learned of cultural differences in optical illusions, it gave me a new perspective on the nature of the pervasiveness of culture because of its effect on such basic and fundamental properties of living.

These differences have important ramifications to intercultural interactions and applied settings. If people from different cultural backgrounds can view such things as optical illusions differently, it is no wonder they perceive so much of the rest of the world differently as well. When this information is coupled with information related to other basic psychological processes such as attribution, emotion, and personality, the effect of culture on individual psychology is amazing.

Likewise, issues concerning cultural differences and similarities in definitions and processes of intelligence are not without considerable meaning to various applied settings. Many current curriculum transformation movements in the United States, for example, are based on a particular view and definition of intelligence and cognitive development. It is not uncommon to hear allegations of cultural bias in these types of educational reforms. Indeed, if broad, sweeping educational changes are implemented in the United States without recognition and awareness of deeply embedded cultural differences in the nature and definition of intelligence, we may be actually broadening the gaps that already exist between groups, and increasing, rather than decreasing, intergroup conflict on the basis of "education."

Awareness of cultural differences in intelligence raises difficult questions concerning testing and the use of test scores. Should bias in testing be eliminated at the expense of the predictive validity of the test? This difficult question stands before many educational institutions and business organizations today and is compounded by legal ramifications and the constant threat of litigation. Perhaps we need to give consideration to yet another aspect of intelligence; that is, our attitudes regarding intelligence. A cross-cultural understanding of differences in the definitions and processes of intelligence should help to deepen our appreciation and respect for definitions of intelligence different from our own.

 **Glossary**

blind spot   A spot in our visual field where the optic nerve goes through the layer of receptor cells on its way back toward the brain, creating a lack of sensory receptors in the eye at that location.

carpentered world theory   A theory of perception that suggests that people (such as most Americans) are used to seeing things rectangular in shape; thus, we unconsciously come to expect things to have squared corners.

categorize   The process of classifying objects on the basis of perceived similarities and attaching labels (namely, words) to those classifications.

cognition   The way we process information in our minds once information is received.

front-horizontal foreshortening theory   A theory of perception that suggests that we interpret vertical lines as horizontal lines that exist in the distance. We then interpret the vertical line in the horizontal-vertical illusion as a line extending away into the distance.

optical illusions   Perceptions that involve an apparent discrepancy between how an object looks and what it actually is.

perception   The process of how we perceive and gather information about the world around us.

serial position effect   This effect suggests that we remember things better if they are either the first or last thing on a list of things to remember.

symbolizing three dimensions in two theory   A theory of perception that suggests that in Western cultures we focus more on things on paper than do people in other cultures. In particular, we spend more time learning to interpret pictures than do people in non-Western cultures.

10

Culture and Gender

Cultural Similarities and Differences in Gender Roles

As with so many other aspects of our lives, culture influences all of us in the behaviors associated with being male or female. In the last 20 or 30 years, we have witnessed many changes in the behaviors Americans consider appropriate for males and females. Certainly, American culture is one of the most dynamic in the exploration of sex and gender differences (or similarities). This dynamism has led to a great deal of confusion and conflict, but it has also produced excitement about the changing nature of human relations and culture itself.

While similar changes may be occurring in other cultures, these changes may not be as decisive or as drastic as is the case in American culture. Differences across cultures in the rate of change in appropriate sex or gender roles and behaviors can easily lead to a negative view of those cultures. I have heard many American students and other adults give negative opinions of gender role differentiation in cultures they thought were old-fashioned or dated. It is important to keep in mind that differences between the sexes exist for a reason, and oftentimes those reasons are peculiar to those cultures. We must exercise considerable caution when evaluating other cultures, especially when we do so according to our own standards.

In this chapter, we will examine how culture influences behavior related to sex and gender. Sex and gender differences have been discussed in relation to a variety of different aspects of behavior elsewhere in this book, and this chapter is not meant to be the sole resource concerning cultural influences

203

on sex and gender. Rather, I view this chapter as providing additional information concerning the background and framework for sex and gender differences discussed elsewhere. I will begin this chapter with a brief discussion of the role of the study of sex and gender differences in relation to the study of other cultures.

A Special Note about the History of Studying Sex and Gender in Relation to Culture

The study of culture, especially as it relates to undergraduate education in the United States, owes a lot to the study of sex and gender differences, and vice versa. Beginning 20 or 30 years ago, what is commonly known as the women's movement in the United States helped American academic communities evaluate the treatment and presentation of women in textbooks and research. Many people concluded that most research was conducted using men as subjects, and thus most information presented about "people" in academic textbooks and university courses was based on information gathered from men. This bias with regard to gender differences also existed with regard to what scholars considered important to study, the relative status of different studies and topics, and the probability and outlet for publication. Of course, information presented about people gathered from this biased sample would naturally not be entirely accurate, given that there are many differences (as well as similarities) between men and women in their needs, concerns, wishes, and behaviors. Scholars, researchers, teachers, and students alike began to question what was presented to them as knowledge about people in general.

In the last several decades, we have come a long way toward improving our knowledge about both men and women in the social sciences. Although questioning the imbalance of research on both men and women was difficult, many behavioral and social scientists have responded well to this inequity in our knowledge and practice. Today, studies of gender differences are commonplace in social science research, and textbooks incorporate sex and gender differences as a standard practice when imparting knowledge about people (although the degree to which the presentation of such material is comparable to the message it should provide is still questioned and debated).

We have been witness to the same type of question with regard to cultural norms for women and men. Just as knowledge about women and women's concerns was missing from research and scholarship 30 years ago, knowledge about cultural similarities and differences and cultural diversity had been missing from our scholarship. Much of this gap still exists today.

Many of the same questions are still being raised concerning whether what we are learning in classes and in our laboratories is indeed true for people of all cultures and ethnicities. The answer so far has been "not necessarily." To address this gap, many researchers have made a conscious effort to study behaviors across cultures to learn what is similar across cultures and what is different. The importance we place on the study of culture and gender today owes much of its impetus to similar concerns with regard to the limitations and boundaries of the information and knowledge we have in psychology. The study of both gender and cultural differences has been enhanced because of the emphasis on similarities and differences that they both explore.

Issues Related to Terminology

Before we go much further in our study of cultural influences on sex and gender, we need first to make clear what we mean when we say *sex* and *gender*. Indeed, studying sex and gender similarities and differences has been aided by an increased differentiation of the terminology used to discuss the various issues related to sex and gender.

A number of social scientists have offered a variety of ideas to differentiate among the various terms (for example, Prince, 1985). There seems to be a consensus that **sex** refers to the biological and physiological differences between men and women, with the most obvious being the anatomical differences of the reproductive systems of men and women. The difference in reproductive systems, however, is not the sole difference between men and women; other biological and physiological differences also exist between them.

The term **sex roles** is used to describe the behaviors and patterns of activities men and women may engage in that are directly related to their biological differences and the process of reproduction. One example of a common sex role for females is breastfeeding their infants, a behavior that only women can engage in (Brislin, 1993). The term **sexual identity** is used to describe the degree of awareness and recognition of sex and sex roles an individual may have. Male sexual identity includes "his awareness that he has the potential to impregnate women and knows the necessary behaviors. Female sexual identity includes the woman's awareness of her reproductive potential and her knowledge about behaviors that lead to pregnancy" (p. 287).

In contrast, **gender** refers to the behaviors or patterns of activities that a society or culture deem appropriate for men and women. These behavior patterns may or may not be related to sex and sex roles, although they oftentimes are. For example, traditional gender roles that we all know about or have heard of suggest that males are aggressive and unemotional (with the exception of anger) and that the male should leave the home every day to make a living and be the principal wage earner. Traditional gender roles for females suggest that women are nurturant, caring, and highly emotional and that they should stay at home and take care of the home and children. **Gender role** refers to the degree to which a person adopts the gender-specific and appropriate behaviors ascribed by his or her culture. **Gender identity** refers to the degree to which a person has awareness or recognition that he or she adopts a particular gender role. Finally, **gender stereotypes** refer to the psychological or behavioral characteristics associated typically with men and women.

Of course, these are general categories that help us to classify and understand different issues concerning sex and gender. Not everyone can be pigeonholed into stereotypes according to sex or gender roles, as there are considerable individual differences across people with regard to these roles. In addition, different gender role stereotypes interact with other forms of group membership. African American women, for example, are generally not perceived in the traditional ways described above (Binion, 1990), nor are women who are disabled or who have different sexual preferences. Separating the biological and physiological facts of sex from the behavioral aspects of gender is the first step in understanding differences between males and females. Indeed, it should become clear from this differentiation that we are mostly concerned with gender differences, not sex differences. Culture, as a macro construct, influences our perception of gender differences considerably.

The Influence of Culture on Gender

How can we understand the influence of culture on gender? Clearly, with the distinctions between definitions I have drawn here, a newborn has sex but no gender. Gender is a construct that develops in children as they are socialized in their environments. As children grow older, they learn specific behaviors and patterns of activities appropriate and inappropriate for their sex, and they either adopt or reject those gender roles.

Ensuring that reproduction occurs fulfills men's and women's sex roles. But what happens after that (and before that as well) is entirely dependent on a host of variables. One of these variables is culture. The biological fact and necessity of reproduction, along with other biological and physiological differences between men and women, leads to behavioral differences between men and women. In earlier days, these behavioral differences were no doubt reinforced by the fact that a division of labor was necessary—someone had to look after children while someone else had to find food for the family. No one person could have done it all. Thus, the existence of reproductive differences led to a division of labor advantageous to the family as a unit. These differences, in turn, produced differences in a variety of psychological traits and characteristics, including aggressiveness, nurturance, achievement, and so forth. Berry and his colleagues (1992) have suggested that the model presented in Figure 10.1 describes how cultural practices can affect gender differences in psychological characteristics, and I think it is an excellent springboard for understanding the effects of culture on gender. From my perspective, however, the important thing to remember is that the factors involved in understanding culture and gender that are outlined in Figure 10.1 are not static or unidimensional. Indeed, the entire system is dynamic and interrelated and feeds back on and reinforces itself. As a result, this system is not a linear unit with influences going in a single direction; it acquires a life of its own. And the life of this system is reinforced by the glue we know of as culture.

Consequently, different cultures produce different outcomes in this system. One culture may foster considerable equality between the sexes and relatively few differences between the sexes on cultural practices and psychological characteristics. Another culture may foster considerable differences

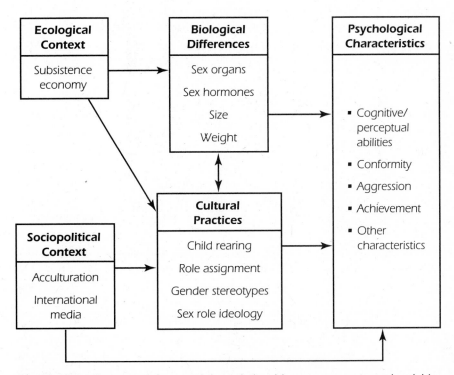

Figure 10.1 Framework for examining relationships among contextual variables and gender differences in behavior.

Source: Cross-Cultural Psychology: Research and Applications, by J. W. Berry, Y. H. Poortinga, M. H. Segall, and P. R. Dasen, p. 58. Copyright © 1992 Cambridge University Press. Reprinted with permission of Cambridge University Press.

between the sexes, their cultural practices related to reproduction, and psychological characteristics associated with sex roles. Some cultures may foster differences between the sexes in one direction (for example, males primary decision maker, females compliant and obedient); another culture may foster differences in the opposite direction.

The important point to remember is that different cultures arrive at varying outcomes even given the same process. Men and women will have gender-specific roles in any society or culture. In learning about gender across cultures, it is important to remember that all cultures encourage particular behavioral differences between the genders; that is, culture helps to define the roles, duties, and responsibilities appropriate for males and females.

Cultural Similarities and Differences in Ascribed Gender Roles and Stereotypes

The number of roles available to males and females is limitless. Some cultures foster a certain gender distinction; other cultures foster other distinctions. We are all familiar with traditional gender role differentiations—the notion that males should be independent, self-reliant, strong, and emotionally detached, while women should be dependent, reliant, weak, nurturant, and emotional. To what degree is this an American or Western cultural phenomenon?

The best-known study of gender stereotypes across cultures is one conducted by Williams and Best (1982). These researchers sampled people in 30 countries, involving almost 3000 individuals with between 52 and 120 respondents per country (Williams & Best, 1982). The study was quite simple and involved the use of a questionnaire known as the Adjective Check List (ACL). The ACL is a list of 300 adjectives. Respondents in each country were asked to decide whether each adjective was more descriptive of a male or of a female. Whether the subjects agreed with the assignment of an adjective to males or females was irrelevant; instead, subjects were asked merely to report the characteristics generally associated with males and females in their culture.

The researchers tallied the data from all individuals. Looking at responses within each culture, Williams and Best (1982) established the criterion that if more than two-thirds of a sample from a country agreed on a particular term for either males or females, there was a consensus within that culture for that general characteristic. Then, looking at responses across the cultures, the researchers decided that if two-thirds of the cultures reached a consensus on the characteristic, there was a cross-cultural consensus on that characteristic to describe males and females. These analyses indicated that there was a high degree of pancultural agreement across all the studied countries in the characteristics associated with men and women. Table 10.1 gives 100 items of the pancultural adjective checklist that Williams and Best (1994) reported for men and women.

The degree of consensus these adjectives received in describing males and females is amazing. In fact, Berry et al. (1992) suggested that "this degree of consensus is so large that it may be appropriate to suggest that the researchers have found a psychological universal when it comes to gender stereotypes" (p. 60). However, Berry et al. (1992) themselves cautioned against making such sweeping generalizations of the data. But the possibility of a universally accepted gender stereotype has interesting ramifications for possible evolutionary similarities across cultures in division of labor between males and females and the psychological characteristics that result from that universal division of labor.

Table 10.1 The 100 Items of the Pancultural Adjective Checklist

Male-Associated		Female-Associated	
Active	Loud	Affected	Modest
Adventurous	Obnoxious	Affectionate	Nervous
Aggressive	Opinionated	Appreciative	Patient
Arrogant	Opportunistic	Cautious	Pleasant
Autocratic	Pleasure-seeking	Changeable	Prudish
Bossy	Precise	Charming	Self-pitying
Capable	Progressive	Complaining	Sensitive
Conceited	Rational	Confused	Sexy
Confident	Realistic	Curious	Shy
Courageous	Reckless	Dependent	Softhearted
Cruel	Resourceful	Dreamy	Sophisticated
Cynical	Rigid	Emotional	Submissive
Determined	Robust	Excitable	Suggestible
Disorderly	Serious	Fault-finding	Talkative
Enterprising	Sharp-witted	Fearful	Timid
Greedy	Show-off	Fickle	Touchy
Hardheaded	Steady	Foolish	Unambitious
Humorous	Stern	Forgiving	Unintelligent
Indifferent	Stingy	Frivolous	Unstable
Individualistic	Stolid	Fussy	Warm
Initiative	Tough	Gentle	Weak
Interests wide	Unfriendly	Imaginative	Worrying
Inventive	Unscrupulous	Kind	Understanding
Lazy	Witty	Mild	Superstitious

Source: "Cross-Cultural Views of Women and Men," by J. E. Williams and D. L. Best. In W. J. Lonner & R. Malpass (Eds.), *Psychology and Culture*, p. 193. Copyright © 1994 Allyn & Bacon. Reprinted by permission.

Williams and Best (1982) conducted a second type of analysis on their data in order to summarize their major findings. They scored the adjectives in each country in terms of favorability, strength, and activity to examine how the adjectives were distributed according to affective or emotional meaning. There was surprising congruence in these analyses; the characteristics associated with men were stronger and more active than those associated with women across all countries. On favorability, however, there were cultural differences, with some countries (such as Japan and South Africa) rating the male characteristics more favorable than female whereas the female characteristics were more favorable in other countries (for example, Italy and Peru).

How are we to interpret these results? It could be that a division of labor for males and females according to reproductive processes produced differences in behaviors that, in turn, produced differences in psychological characteristics. It may be that these psychological characteristics had some evolutionary and adaptive advantages for males and females to fulfill their roles as prescribed by the division of labor. It could be that men and women in all cultures became locked into these set ways, accounting for universal consensus on these descriptors. It could be that men and women become locked into a particular mindset about cultural differences because of perceived social inequality or social forces and indirect communication via mass media and the like. Or these findings could all be a function of the way the research was conducted, using university students as samples in the cultures, which would tend to make the entire sample from the entire experiment more homogeneous than if people were randomly sampled from each culture.

While it is impossible to disentangle these factors from each other to better interpret the findings, it is important to note that Williams and Best themselves collected and analyzed data concerning gender stereotypes from young children and found a considerable degree of agreement between the findings for children and those for university students (Williams & Best, 1990). This would argue against the notion that the original findings were obtained because of a homogeneity in the samples due to selecting university students (but it would not completely eliminate such an argument).

In a follow-up study, Williams and Best (1990) studied judgments about what males and females should be like, what they should do, and so forth. These are not necessarily judgments of gender roles or stereotypes per se; rather, they are judgments of **gender role ideology**. In conducting this study, Williams and Best asked subjects in 14 countries to complete the ACL in relation to what they believe they are, and what they would like to be. The subjects also completed a sex role ideology scale that generated scores between two polar opposites, labeled "traditional" and "egalitarian." The traditional scores tended to describe gender roles that met with the traditional or universal norms found in their earlier research. Egalitarian scores, in contrast, reflected a tendency for less differentiation between males and females on the various psychological characteristics.

The most egalitarian scores were found in the Netherlands, Germany, and Finland; the most traditional ideologies were found in Nigeria, Pakistan, and India. Women tended to have more egalitarian views than the men. Gender differences within each country, however, were relatively small compared to cross-country differences, which were considerable. In particular, countries with relatively high socioeconomic development, a high proportion of Protestant Christians, a low proportion of Muslims, a high percentage of women employed outside the home, a high proportion of women enrolled in universities, and a greater degree of individualism were associated with more egalitarian scores. These findings make sense, as greater affluence and individualistic tendencies tend to produce a culture that allows women increased access to jobs and education, thus blending traditional gender roles.

In addition to studying gender stereotypes and ideologies, Williams and Best (1990) also examined gender differences in self-concept. The same students in the 14 countries described above rated each of the 300 adjectives of the ACL according to whether the adjectives were descriptive of themselves or their ideal self. Responses were scored according to masculinity/femininity as well as in terms of favorability, strength, and activity. When scored according to masculinity/femininity, both self and ideal-self ratings for men were more masculine than were women's ratings, and vice versa, across all countries. However, both men and women in all countries rated the ideal self as more masculine than their self. In effect, they were saying that they wanted to have more traits traditionally associated with males.

When scored according to the three emotional dimensions, male self-concepts tended to be rated stronger than female self-concepts. Moreover, in some countries, the ratings on the three dimensions were relatively similar between men and women, whereas in other countries the ratings were quite divergent. The degree of differentiation among the ratings themselves may be related to other variables; Williams and Best (1990) suggest that such variables may include socioeconomic status, religion, proportion of women employed outside the home, and the like.

Taken as a whole, these studies suggest there is considerable, perhaps even universal, consensus among cultures in terms of what kinds of psychological characteristics describe males and females. But despite these similarities, there are considerable cultural differences in the degree to which each culture believes in these differentiations as an ideal. It may very well be that attitudes and values about gender appropriate roles are changing too fast in today's world and that research findings must be limited to generalizations about the time frame in which the data were collected. Still, it is interesting that there is a discrepancy between what some cultures believe is the ideal and the degree of consensus that exists concerning what is currently true.

Hofstede's Study

In Chapter 6, I discussed research by Hofstede, who studied work-related attitudes across 50 countries. Because his research is relevant to the issue of culture and gender, I will briefly review his study here. Hofstede (1980) conducted a large-scale survey of work-related values in a major, multinational corporation. Based on the data obtained, Hofstede generated four dimensions of differentiation among the cultures in his sample. One of these dimensions was called "masculinity" (MA). This dimension referred to the degree to which a culture will foster, encourage, or maintain differences between males and females. Cultures scoring high on MA tended to endorse items and values thought to be associated with masculinity and male gender roles in the workplace. Japan, Austria, Venezuela, and Italy had the highest MA scores. Cultures scoring low on MA minimized differences between the sexes and genders. Denmark, Netherlands, Norway, and Sweden had the lowest scores.

While Hofstede's study focused entirely on work-related values, the findings he obtained highlight a major point of this chapter—that is, cultures will arrive at different ways of dealing with differences between men and women. The behaviors men and women engage in produce different psychological. outcomes that have direct ramifications for actual life behaviors (such as work-related behaviors). Cultures vary in how they act on these gender differences, with some cultures fostering and encouraging great differences between the genders and other cultures minimizing those differences. It is precisely these cultural differences in gender roles that Hofstede's data on MA speak to.

Other Psychological Gender Differences across Cultures

Culture, biology, gender roles, and gender role ideology all interact to produce differences between the genders on a variety of psychological and behavioral outcomes (review Figure 10.1). That is, the division of labor and actual behaviors males and females engage in as a result of their biological and physiological differences help to produce a different psychology or mindset as well. These psychological differences between genders can be considered a product of the differences between males and females because of the division of labor and behaviors surrounding reproduction.

Just as there will be psychological differences between males and females in any one culture, psychological differences can also be found across cultures. And the degree, direction, or exact nature of those gender differences may differ across cultures. That is, while one culture may foster a certain type of gender difference, another culture may not foster that difference to the same degree. A third culture may foster that difference even more than the first two cultures. Psychological gender differences across cultures are not simply products of biology and culture; they are also important reinforcers of culture, feeding back onto the culture, behaviors, gender roles, and gender role ideologies. In this cyclical fashion, the psychological products of gender differentiation also become a crucial aspect of the culture-behavior-psychology link that exists among a people and their rituals, traditions, and behaviors.

When the cross-cultural literature on psychological differences between the genders is examined, three general areas of difference stand out: perceptual/spatial/cognitive abilities, conformity and obedience, and aggressiveness (Berry et al., 1992). Studies in each of these areas do indeed show that while there is a general difference between genders, the degree of these differences is indeed different across cultures.

Perceptual/Spatial/Cognitive Differences

At least in American society, it is common folklore that males are better at mathematical and spatial reasoning tasks, while females are better at verbal comprehension tasks. An analysis of the scores for males and females on standardized tests in elementary school, college entrance examinations, or graduate school entrance examinations shows some degree of support for these notions, although the difference between males and females seems to be narrowing in recent years. In their review of the literature, Maccoby and Jacklin (1974) also concluded that males tend to do better on spatial tasks and other tasks having a spatial component. Years ago, however, Berry (1966) pointed out that such differences do not appear to exist among males and females of the Inuit culture in Canada. That is, neither males nor females were superior on spatial related tasks. Berry suggested that the gender difference did not exist because "spatial abilities are highly adaptive for both males and females in Inuit society, and both boys and girls have ample training and experience that promote the acquisition of spatial ability" (Berry et al., 1992, p. 65).

Following up on the possibility of cultural differences on this gender difference, Berry (1976) and his colleagues conducted a study in which a block design task was given to males and females in 17 different cultures. A stimulus card depicting a geometric representation of a set of blocks was presented, and the task was to manipulate an actual set of blocks to emulate the design provided. The results were interesting and provocative. While there were indeed a number of cultures in which males did better than females on the task, there also were a considerable number of cultures where females did better than males. In interpreting these data, Berry et al. (1992) suggested that male superiority on the task tended to be found in cultures that were tight (that is, relatively homogeneous), sedentary, and agriculturally based, but that female superiority was found in cultures that were loose, nomadic, and hunting-gathering based. In these latter cultures, the roles ascribed to males and females are relatively flexible, as more members perform a variety of tasks related to the survival of the group.

A similar finding was reported in a meta-analysis of the research literature by Born, Bleichrodt, and Van der Flier (1987). These researchers also reported that while no gender differences in overall intelligence were found, gender differences on various subtests of intelligence did occur. While their findings leave open the question of the exact role of culture on the gender difference, they do show that the differences in the cognitive test scores between males and females are variable across cultures.

Conformity and Obedience

One of the most common gender role stereotypes is that females are more conforming and obedient than are males. This stereotype is no doubt related to the traditional gender roles females and males have acquired, with males traditionally being "head of the household" and making primary decisions over big-ticket items that involve the family. In this traditional viewpoint, females were not to be concerned with such authority and decision-making power; rather, the female role focused on caring for the children and managing the household affairs. In short, females were expected to conform to decisions imposed upon them by males or by society in general.

The degree to which this difference is enacted varies considerably from culture to culture. In Berry's (1976) study, the researchers also obtained an index of the degree to which each person conforms in the 17 cultures included in the sample. Across the 17 cultures, clear variation emerged, and these appeared to be related to the cultural concept of tightness and agriculture reported above for gender differences in spatial reasoning. That is, cultures that were tighter appeared to foster a greater gender difference on conformity, with females being more conformist than males. Tight cultures may require a greater degree of conformity on the part of both males and females to traditional gender roles. In contrast, cultures that were looser fostered less gender difference on conformity, and in some of these cultures, males were found to be more conforming than females. While traditional gender stereotypes of females being more conforming than males appears to have some validity, considerable cross-cultural difference exists in the degree, and in some cases the direction, of this difference.

Aggressiveness

Another common gender stereotype is that males are more aggressive than females. Indeed, there is support for this stereotype in all cultures for which documentation exists (Block, 1983; Brislin, 1993). Males account for a disproportionate amount of violent crime in both industrialized and nonindustrialized societies. The focus in research on this topic has been adolescent males. Several researchers have searched for the biological correlates of aggression. In particular, some researchers have questioned whether increased levels of the hormone testosterone during male adolescence may account for or contribute to increased aggression in males. Increased testosterone levels have been associated with dominance hierarchies in some nonhuman primates, but the human analog is not as clear. On the basis of the evidence available, it appears that hormones may contribute to some degree of aggressiveness, but culture and the environment can certainly act to encourage or discourage its emergence (Berry et al., 1992).

A study by Barry, Josephson, Lauer, and Marshall (1976) is also interesting with regard to aggressiveness. Given that a biological explanation may not be available for aggression, these researchers examined the degree to which cultures foster aggressive tendencies in the socialization of their children. These researchers found a sex-related difference in the degree of teaching about aggressiveness on average across 150 different cultures. Inspection of their data, however, reveals that this average difference is produced by a disproportionate number of high-scoring cultures in which teaching aggression actually occurs. In fact, a large majority of societies did not show a sex-related difference in teaching aggression.

Thus, neither biology nor sex differences in teaching aggressive acts can account for gender differences in aggression observed across cultures. Some researchers (Berry et al., 1992; Segall, Dasen, Berry, & Poortinga, 1990) offer yet another interesting possibility to explain gender differences in aggression across cultures. They suggest that male aggression may be a compensatory mechanism to offset the conflict produced by a young male's identification with a female care provider and his initiation into adulthood as a male. In this model, aggressiveness is viewed as "gender marking" behavior.

Regardless of the actual mechanism that produces gender differences in aggression across cultures, the evidence is clear: while the gender stereotype of aggressiveness may be generally true, considerable differences exist across cultures as well. What is true for one culture may definitely not be true for another.

Ethnicity and Gender

One of the most pressing issues and concerns facing us in the United States today has to do with gender differences across different ethnicities. Just as people in different cultures in different countries and in faraway lands may have different gender roles and expectations, people of different ethnic backgrounds here in the United States have different gender role expectations as well. Many of these gender differences across ethnic lines are rooted in the cultures people of these ethnicities brought with them when they originally came to the United States. But gender differences we observe in the United States today definitely reflect an "American" influence, making gender issues unique in this culture.

There is really very little research on gender differences between African American males and females. The research that exists typically compares African American males and females to European American males and females (which in itself may be a statement about the nature and politics of studying gender, race, and culture in the United States), and the results convey a flavor of the unique differences, struggles, and strengths of African American males and females. African American males are more likely than European American males to live below the poverty line, die at an early age, make less money, be in jail, and be executed for a crime. With regard to psychological processes, African American males are especially adept at body language and nonverbal encoding and decoding and improvised problem solving (Allen & Santrock, 1993).

Research on the concerns of African American females has painted a changing picture over the last 20 years (Hall, Evans, & Selice, 1989). Early research focused almost exclusively on generally negative characteristics and situations. Of late, however, an increasing amount of research has focused on many other psychological aspects of African American females, including self-esteem or achievement. For example, the number of Ph.D.s awarded to African American women increased by 16% between 1977 and 1986 (Allen & Santrock, 1993), indicating some improvement in the accessibility of advanced graduate degrees for African American women and increased motivation to achieve those degrees.

Many Asian American families have carried on traditional gender roles associated with males and females from their original culture. Asian females are often expected to bear the brunt of domestic duties, to raise children, and to be a "good" daughter-in-law. Asian American males are often raised to remain aloof, unemotional, and authoritative, especially concerning familial issues (Sue, 1989). There have been some studies, however, that suggest a loosening of these rigid, traditional gender roles for Asian American males and females. While Asian American males may still appear as a figurative head of a family in public, in reality much decision-making power within the family in private is held by the Asian American female head of the household (Huang & Ying, 1989).

As with Asian American gender roles, the traditional role of the Mexican female was to provide for the children and take care of the home (Comas-Diaz, 1992). Likewise, the role for Mexican American males traditionally dictated a strong expectation of provider for the family. These differences are related to the concept of **machismo**. This concept involves many of the traditional expectations of the male gender role, such as being unemotional, strong, authoritative, aggressive, and masculine (see Table 10.1, p. 209). However, recent research has shown that these gender differences for Mexican American males and females are also on the decrease. Mexican American women are increasingly sharing in decision making in the family, as well as taking on a more direct role in being a provider through work outside the home (Espin, 1993). While adolescent Mexican American males are generally still given more freedom outside the home than are females, gender differences may be decreasing in the contemporary Mexican American family.

Gender role differentiation for Native Americans seems to depend heavily on the patriarchal or matriarchal nature of the tribal culture of origin. In patriarchal tribes, for example, women assume the primary responsibility for the welfare of the children and extended family members. But males of the Mescalero Apache tribe often take responsibility for children when they are with their families (Ryan, 1980). As with the other ethnic groups, the passage of time, increased interaction with people of other cultures and with mainstream American culture, and the movement toward urban areas seems to have influenced changes in these traditional values and expectations for Native American males and females.

Certainly, the picture I have painted for these ethnic groups is not universally true or salient for all males and females of these ethnic groups. Instead, they serve as generalized descriptions of the possible gender roles males and females of these ethnic groups have been socialized with in the past. There are many cultural and ethnic differences even within each of these four major groupings. As time passes and societal trends and cultural mores change, gender roles will also change both between and within each of these ethnic groups. As we are in a state of flux, it is important to remember that people of different ethnic and cultural backgrounds can and will have different gender role expectations despite appearances of overlap and similarity due to the fact that they all live in the same country and are influenced by the same mainstream culture.

Conclusion

Sex refers to the biological and physiological differences between males and females. Sex roles refers to behaviors expected of males and females in relation to their biological differences and reproduction. Gender, however, refers to the psychological and behavioral traits and characteristics cultures carve out using sex differences as a base. Gender roles refer to the degree to which a person adopts the gender-specific and appropriate behaviors ascribed by his or her culture.

Gender roles are different for males and females in all cultures. Some stereotypic notions about gender differences seem to be universal across cultures, such as aggressiveness, strength, and lack of emotionality for males, and weakness, submissiveness, and emotionality for females. Other research, however, has shown that the degree, and in some case the direction, of these differences varies across cultures. That is, not every culture will necessarily harbor the same gender differences in the same way as other cultures.

Examining gender differences in the United States is especially challenging because of the cultural and ethnic diversity within this single country and the influence of interactions with mainstream American culture. While each ethnic group has its own cultural preferences for gender differentiation, some blending of the old with the new, the traditional with the modern appears to be taking place. Without evidence to the contrary, it is probably best to consider the blending as the addition of different cultural repertoires concerning gender differences rather than a subtraction from the old ways.

As we meet people from different cultural backgrounds, we may encounter gender roles that are different from our own. Oftentimes, we feel strongly and negatively about them. While our own feelings are indicative of our own personal outlook on those differences, we must exercise considerable care and caution in imposing our preferences on others. In most cases, people of other cultures feel just as strongly about their own way of living. Still, this is a delicate balancing act for all of us, because there is a fine line between cultural relativity and a social justification for oppression. While the former is a desired state of comprehension, the latter is entirely unacceptable.

 # Glossary

gender   The behaviors or patterns of activities a society or culture deems appropriate for men and women. These behavioral patterns may or may not be related to sex and sex roles, although they oftentimes are.

gender identity   The degree to which a person has awareness of or recognition that he or she has adopted a particular gender role.

gender role   The degree to which a person adopts the gender-specific and appropriate behaviors ascribed by his or her culture.

gender role ideology   Judgments about what gender roles in a particular culture should or ought to be.

gender stereotype   The psychological or behavioral characteristics associated typically with men and women.

machismo   A concept related to Mexican American gender role differentiation that is characterized by many of the traditional expectations of the male gender role, such as being unemotional, strong, authoritative, aggressive, and masculine.

sex   The biological and physiological differences between men and women. The most obvious difference involves the anatomical differences of the reproductive systems for men and women.

sex roles   The behaviors and patterns of activities men and women may engage in that are directly related to their biological differences and the process of reproduction.

sexual identity   The degree of awareness and recognition by an individual of his or her sex and sex roles.

11

Culture and Health

Sociocultural Influences on Health,
Illness, and Health Care Delivery

One major role of education is to improve the lives of the people we touch. Whether through research, service, or provision of primary or secondary health care, we look forward to the day we can adequately diagnose and treat medical diseases, prevent abnormal behavior, and foster positive states of being in balance with others and the environment around us. This is not an easy task; a multitude of forces influence our health and our ability to prevent and treat illness.

As we strive to meet this challenge, the important role of culture in contributing to the etiology, maintenance, and treatment of disease has increasingly become clearer. While our goals for prevention and treatment of disease and maintenance of health may be the same across cultures, cultures vary in their definitions of what is considered "healthy" or "mature" (Tseng & McDermott, 1981). Cultural differences also exist in perceptions of problems and in preferred strategies for coping with problems (Terrell, 1992). Our job is made more difficult because cultural beliefs and practices influence treatment, and they shape both the therapist's and the client's definitions and understandings of the problem (Berry et al., 1992). Traditional approaches to treatment of abnormal behavior may prove insensitive or inappropriate when applied across cultures.

In this chapter, I will delve into the question of how cultural factors influence the development of medical and psychological disorders and attempts to treat them. I will also examine the way cultural differences influence help-seeking, treatment compliance, and issues of responsibility, trust, and self-control over personal health and disease processes. I will begin this chapter by defining exactly what is meant by the word *health*.

Cultural Differences in the Definition of Health

Before we can even begin to look at how culture influences health and disease processes, we need to examine exactly what we mean by *health*. In the United States, our views of health have been heavily influenced by what many call the **medical model** of health and disease. This model views disease as resulting from a specific, identifiable cause originating inside the body. These causes, whether viral, bacterial, or otherwise, are referred to as **pathogens** and can be seen as the root of all physical and medical diseases. Cardiovascular disease, for example, has been linked to specific pathogens such as clotting from lipids and cholesterol.

The medical model of disease has influenced psychology's view of abnormal behavior and psychopathology quite heavily. Traditional psychological approaches, for example, view the origin of abnormal behaviors as residing within the person. These origins may result from lack of gratification or overgratification of basic, instinctual processes (such as suggested by Freudian psychoanalytic theory) or from learned responses (as suggested through classical or operant conditioning).

Inevitably, the traditional medical model of health in both medicine and psychology has had a profound influence on treatment approaches. If specific medical or psychobehavioral pathogens exist within the body of a person, those pathogens themselves must be dealt with when treating disease. Medical treatment as well as traditional psychological approaches focus on making an intervention within a person. Using the traditional medical model, health can be best characterized as *the lack of disease*. If a person remains free of disease, this model or approach would view this person as healthy.

Views of health from other cultures suggest different definitions of health. People of ancient China and Greece, for example, viewed health not only as the absence of negative states but also as the presence of positive ones. Balance between self and nature and across the individual's various roles in life is viewed as an integral part of health in many Asian cultures. This balance can produce a positive state—a synergy of the forces of self, nature, and others—that many call *health*. Alternative views of health that incorporate the presence of positive as well as the absence of negative states are important today in many cultures.

Incorporating balance as a positive aspect of health is not foreign in the United States today. In the last decade or two, we have seen a rising frustration in defining health solely as the absence of disease. Here in the United States, we have become much more aware of how lifestyle factors can contribute not only to the absence of negative states but also to the presence of positive ones. Biobehavioral medicine and health psychology, nonexistent even a few years ago, represent the health care and academic professions' response to a growing need to search for and act upon definitions of health different from those afforded by the traditional medical model. We now know that many of the leading causes of death are directly and indirectly attributable to lifestyle choices and to unhealthy behaviors (Feist & Brannon, 1988). These findings contribute greatly to our increasing knowledge of the impact of behavior on health. Since our behavior is heavily influenced by culture, we must increase our awareness of the link between health, lifestyle, and behavior and seek better ways to understand sociocultural influences on health and disease.

Sociocultural Influences on Physical Health and Medical Disease Processes

When you think about how culture may affect health and disease processes, what often comes to mind is how cultures affect psychological disorders like schizophrenia or depression. Indeed, as you will soon see, cultures do influence the nature of these and other psychological disorders. But psychological health and illness are not the only domains of health that can be affected by culture; physical health and illness are also influenced by culture.

The influence of psychosocial factors on disease processes is one of the most exciting fields of research and study today. Scholars have long been interested in the close relationship between mental and physical health. Research linking Type A personality patterns and cardiovascular disease is a good example of this area of study. Beyond looking at personality differences, however, many scholars and health care practitioners alike have long been interested in the contribution of sociocultural factors to health. Unfortunately, this study has been hindered for many years, probably because we don't know exactly how to study cultures. But some recent studies have pointed out how culture may play a major role in the development and treatment of illness. These studies are important, because they destroy the common notion that physical illness has nothing to do with sociocultural or psychological factors, and vice versa. Indeed, these studies contribute to our combined knowledge of psychological factors on physical disease processes. Changes in lifestyle (for example, diet, smoking, exercise, and alcohol consumption) can be seen as our response to this increasing awareness and recognition of the complex interrelationship among culture, psychology, and medical processes.

Social Isolation and Mortality

The final physical disease process we all experience is death. In earlier research, some studies highlighted the potential negative effects of social isolation and social disadvantage on health and disease (Feist & Brannon, 1988). One of the best-known and influential of these studies is the Alameda County study (Berkman & Syme, 1979), named after the county in which the data were collected and the study conducted. Researchers interviewed almost 7000 individuals to discover their degree of social contact. The final data set used in the study included approximately 4725 people, as some people had to be dropped from the study. Following the initial assessment interview, deaths were monitored over a nine-year period. The results were clear for both men and women: Individuals with the fewest social ties suffered the highest mortality rate, and people with the most social ties had the lowest rate. These findings were valid even when other factors were statistically or methodologically controlled, including the level of physical health reported at the time of the initial questionnaire, the year of death, socioeconomic status, and a number of health-related behaviors (for example, smoking and alcohol consumption). This study was one of the first to clearly delineate the enormous role sociocultural factors may play in the maintenance of physical health and illness.

Cardiovascular Diseases

Cardiovascular disease has received considerable attention from researchers interested in sociocultural and psychological influences on disease. For many years now, researchers have examined how social and psychological factors influence the development and treatment of this disease. Researchers have identified a number of psychological and behavioral factors that appear to influence cardiovascular disease. Perhaps the best known of these factors is the Type A (versus Type B) personality profile (see Friedman & Rosenman, 1974) and its impact on heart disease.

Above and beyond personality factors, however, social and cultural factors also contribute to this disease. Marmot and Syme (1976) studied Japanese Americans, classifying 3809 subjects into groups according to how "traditionally Japanese" they were (that is, spoke Japanese at home, retained traditional

Japanese values and behaviors, and so forth). They found that the group of Japanese Americans who were the "most" Japanese had the lowest incidence of coronary heart disease—levels comparable to Japanese in Japan. The group that was the "least" Japanese had a three to five times greater incidence rate. Moreover, the differences between the groups could not be accounted for by other coronary risk factors.

Triandis and his colleagues (Triandis et al., 1988) took this finding one step further, using the individualism versus collectivism cultural dimension and examining its relationship to heart disease across eight different cultural groups. American Caucasians, the most individualistic of the eight cultural groups compared, had the highest rate of heart attacks; Caucasian Trapist monks, who were the least individualistic, had the lowest rate. Of course, this study is not conclusive as many other variables confound comparisons between Americans and Trapist monks (such as industrialization, class, lifestyle, and so forth). Nevertheless, Triandis et al. (1988) suggested that social support or isolation was the most important factor that explained this relationship, a position congruent with the earlier research on social isolation.

Other Diseases

Triandis et al.'s (1988) study was the first to examine the relationship between cultural differences across different groups of people and the incidence of a particular disease state (heart disease). Research has also been done on other disease states and health-related behaviors, such as cancer, smoking, stress, and pain (see Feist & Brannon, 1988). But no study has examined the relationship between sociocultural factors across different groups of people and the incidence of diseases other than heart disease.

A recent study reported by Matsumoto and Fletcher (1994) has opened the door to this line of study. These researchers obtained the mortality rates of six different medical diseases: infections and parasitic diseases, malignant neoplasms, diseases of the circulatory system, heart diseases, cerebrovascular diseases, and respiratory system diseases. These epidemiological data were taken from the *World Health Statistics Quarterly* (World Health Organization, 1991) and were compiled across 28 different countries widely distributed around the globe, spanning five continents, and representing many different ethnic, cultural, and socioeconomic backgrounds. In addition, incidence rates for each of the diseases were available at five age points for each country, at birth and at ages 1, 15, 45, and 65.

To get cultural data from each country, Matsumoto and Fletcher (1994) used cultural index scores previously obtained by Hofstede (1980, 1983), which I discussed earlier in Chapter 6. Hofstede analyzed questionnaire data about cultural values and practices to large samples in each of these countries and classified their responses according to four cultural tendencies: individualism versus collectivism (IC), power distance (PD), uncertainty avoidance (UA), and masculinity (MA). These cultural index scores were then correlated with the epidemiological data.

The results were quite fascinating and pointed to the importance of culture as a social phenomenon in the development of these disease processes. For example, PD was significantly correlated with rates for infections and parasitic diseases across the five age points. That is, cultures scoring higher on PD (Philippines, Mexico) also had higher rates for infections and parasitic diseases. IC was also significantly correlated with infections and parasitic diseases; individualistic cultures (United States, Australia) had lower rates of these diseases, and collectivistic cultures had higher rates. PD and IC also predicted the incidence of malignant neoplasms, but in the opposite direction. Cultures scoring higher on PD had lower rates of malignant neoplasms. And individualistic cultures had higher rates of malignant neoplasms, while collectivistic cultures had lower rates of these diseases.

PD was predictive of circulatory diseases. Cultures scoring higher on PD had lower rates of these types of diseases. IC and UA were also predictive of these diseases. PD, IC, and UA were all predictive of heart diseases across all five age points. Cultures scoring higher on PD were associated with lower incidences of heart diseases. Cultures scoring higher on UA and IC, however, had greater incidences of heart disease than cultures scoring lower on these dimensions. The findings for IC and heart disease are similar to those of Marmot and Syme (1976) and Triandis et al. (1988) described earlier.

UA, IC, and MA all predicted cerebrovascular diseases. Cultures scoring higher on UA or IC had lower rates of these types of diseases than did cultures scoring lower on this dimension. MA was positively correlated with cerebrovascular diseases, suggesting that cultures that fostered greater gender differences had higher incidences of these types of diseases than cultures that minimized gender differences. Finally, UA was negatively correlated with respiratory diseases. Cultures that were low on UA had higher rates of these diseases, while cultures that were high on UA had lower rates.

Wide economic differences exist across these countries, as well as cultural differences, and it may very well be that these economic differences also contribute to disease, particularly with regard to the availability of treatment, diet, and sanitation. To deal with this possibility, Matsumoto and Fletcher (1994) recomputed the correlations reported above, this time controlling for per capita gross domestic product (GDP) of each country. The predictions for infections and parasitic diseases, circulatory diseases, and heart diseases all survived even when the effects of per capita GDP were accounted for. The predictions for UA and cerebrovascular and respiratory diseases, and MA and cerebrovascular diseases, also survived. Thus, these cultural dimensions predicted disease above and beyond what is accounted for by economic differences among the countries. Only the prediction for malignant neoplasms was not supported, indicating that economic differences among the countries cannot be disentangled from cultural differences in predicting the incidence of neoplasms.

How and why does culture affect medical disease processes? Clearly, research is still in its infancy. But future studies will begin to bridge the gap between culture as a macroconcept and specific medical disease processes in the body. Triandis et al. (1988) suggested that culture plays an important role in mediating stress, which affects health. Matsumoto and Fletcher (1994) suggested that culture influences human emotion and human physiology, particularly with respect to autonomic nervous system activity and the immune system. For example, the prediction linking PD and circulatory and heart diseases may be explained by noting that cultures low on PD tend to minimize status differences among their members. As status and power differences diminish, people are freer to feel and express negative emotions such as anger or hostility to ingroup others. Containing negative emotions may have dramatic consequences for the cardiovascular system, resulting in a relatively higher incidence of circulatory and heart diseases. A study by Ekman, Levenson, and Friesen (1983) documented substantial increases in heart rate associated with angry expressions, which lends further credence to this hypothesis.

Whatever the exact mechanisms, the contribution of culture to physical health and disease is clearer now than ever before. Future research will expand our understanding of how and why this relationship exists.

Sociocultural Influences on Psychological Disorders and Abnormal Behaviors

One of the most active areas of cross-cultural inquiry is the examination of the role of culture in understanding, assessing, and treating abnormal behavior. Several major themes have guided research and thinking in this area of psychology. First and foremost are questions concerning definitions of abnormality—what is abnormal behavior? A second set of questions relates to the expression of abnormal behavior and our ability to detect it when it is expressed (assessment). A third question concerns how we should treat abnormal behavior when it is detected.

These questions have special significance in relation to culture, as culture adds an important dimension to the answers to these questions. Several major themes have characterized cross-cultural approaches to abnormality and treatment (Marsella, 1979). These themes can be expressed in the following questions:

- Do definitions of normality and abnormality vary across cultures, or are there universal standards of abnormality?
- Do cultures vary in rates of abnormal behavior?
- Is abnormal behavior expressed in the same way across cultures, or can we identify culturally distinct patterns of abnormal behavior?

The answers to these questions have gained importance in the last two decades as psychologists and other mental health professionals have questioned the cultural sensitivity of traditional methods of assessing and treating individuals with psychological disorders. Indeed, the answers to these questions have important implications for how we identify and intervene to change abnormal behavior.

In the next section, I will review studies of the prevalence and course of the psychological disorders known as schizophrenia and depression across cultures and discuss some culture-specific disorders. As you will see, culture plays a major role in shaping people's experience of psychological disorder.

Defining Abnormality

Consider the following scenario: A woman is in the midst of a group of people but seems totally unaware of her surroundings. She is talking loudly to no one in particular, often using words and sounds the people around her find unintelligible. When questioned later about her behavior, she reports that she had been possessed by the spirit of an animal and was talking with a man who had recently died.

Some traditional viewpoints. Is this woman's behavior abnormal? When defining abnormal behavior, psychologists usually adopt one of several different types of approaches. One way to define abnormality is by using a statistical approach and applications of criteria of impairment or inefficiency, deviance, and subjective distress. Using a statistical comparison approach, for example, the woman's behavior could be defined as abnormal because its occurrence is rare or infrequent. Being out of touch with your surroundings, having delusions (mistaken beliefs) that you are an animal, and talking with the dead are not common experiences. One of the problems with this approach to abnormality, however, is that not all rare behavior is disordered. Nor is all disordered behavior rare! Composing a concerto or speaking four languages are uncommon behaviors, yet we generally view them as highly desirable. Conversely, drinking to the point of drunkenness occurs quite frequently in the United States (and in many other countries of the world). Nevertheless, drunkenness is widely recognized as a sign of a possible substance abuse disorder.

Another approach for defining abnormality focuses on whether an individual's behavior is associated with impairment or inefficiency when carrying out customary roles. It is hard to imagine the woman I have described carrying out normal day-to-day functions like caring for herself and working while she believes herself to be an animal. In many instances, psychological disorders do involve serious impairments or a reduction in an individual's overall functioning. This, however, is not always the case. Some people suffering from bipolar disorder (manic-depression) report enhanced productivity during manic episodes.

If we examine the woman's behavior in terms of deviance, we might also conclude that it is abnormal since it seems to go against social norms. But, not all behavior that is socially deviant can be considered abnormal or psychologically disordered. For example, many people continue to believe that homosexuality is deviant, although it is no longer classified as a mental disorder (American Psychiatric Association, 1987). Although some in our culture may view homosexuality as abnormal, in other cultures and at various periods in history homosexuality has been widely practiced. Using societal norms as a criterion for abnormality is difficult not only because norms change over time but because they are subjective. What one member of a society or culture considers deviant, another may accept.

Reliance on reports of subjective distress to define abnormal behavior is also problematic. Whether a person experiences distress as a consequence of abnormal behavior may depend on how others treat him or her. For example, if the woman I described is ridiculed, shunned, and viewed as "sick" because of her behavior, she may well experience distress. Conversely, if she is seen as having special powers and is part of an accepting circle, she may not be distressed at all.

Each of these more or less traditional viewpoints for defining abnormality used by psychologists has advantages as well as disadvantages. These issues become even more complex when culture is considered. Definitions of abnormality may vary both within and across cultures.

Cross-cultural viewpoints of abnormality.   Dissatisfaction with traditional definitions has led some cross-cultural scholars to argue that we can understand and identify abnormal behavior only if we take the cultural context into account. This viewpoint suggests that we must apply the principle of **cultural relativism** to abnormality. For example, the woman's behavior might appear disordered if it occurred on a street corner in a large city in the United States. It could, however, appear appropriate and understandable if it occurs in a shamanistic ceremony in which she is serving as healer. Cultures that hold beliefs in supernatural interventions are able to clearly distinguish when trance states and talking with spirits are an acceptable part of a healer's behavioral repertoire and when the same behaviors would be considered a sign of disorder (Murphy, 1976). Examples of such cultures include the Yoruba in Africa and some Eskimo tribes in Alaska.

Some behaviors, particularly those associated with psychosis (for example, delusions, hallucinations), are universally recognized as abnormal (Murphy, 1976). However, some investigators (for example, Kleinman, 1988; Marsella, 1979, 1980) argue that abnormality and normality are culturally determined concepts. These investigators point to the fact that cultures differ in their beliefs and attitudes about abnormal behavior.

Reliance on reports of subjective distress to define abnormal behavior is also problematic when considering abnormality across cultures. There is some indication that cultural groups vary in the degree of distress they report experiencing in association with psychological disorders. Kleinman (1988) describes research indicating that depressed Chinese and African samples report less guilt and shame than do depressed Euro-American and European samples. The Chinese and African samples, however, report more somatic complaints. These findings may reflect a cultural response bias (see discussion in Chapter 4). Some cultural groups may have values that prohibit reporting or focusing on subjective distress, in contrast to Western notions of the importance of self-disclosure.

Whether to accept universal or culturally relative definitions of abnormality is a source of continuing controversy in psychology. This tension can be seen when considering the expression of abnormality across cultures as well.

Schizophrenia.   Schizophrenia is part of a "group of psychotic disorders characterized by gross distortions of reality; withdrawal from social interaction; and disorganization of perception, thought, and emotion" (Carson, Butcher, & Coleman, 1988, p. 322). Some theories concerning the etiology (causes) of schizophrenia give primacy to biological factors (for example, excess dopamine or other biochemical imbalances). Other theories emphasize family dynamics (for example, expression of hostility to ill person). The diathesis-stress model of schizophrenia suggests that individuals with a biological predisposition to the disorder (diathesis) may develop the disorder following exposure to environmental stressors.

The World Health Organization (WHO, 1973, 1979, 1981) sponsored the International Pilot Study of Schizophrenia (IPSS) to compare the prevalence and course of the disorder in several countries: Colombia, Czechoslovakia, Denmark, England, India, Nigeria, the former Soviet Union, Taiwan, and the United States. Following rigorous training in using the research assessment tool, psychiatrists in each of the countries achieved good **reliability** in diagnosing schizophrenia in patients included in the study. As a result, WHO investigators were able to identify a set of symptoms present across all cultures in the schizophrenic samples. These symptoms include lack of insight, auditory and verbal hallucinations, and ideas of reference (assuming one is the center of attention) (Leff, 1977). The WHO studies are widely cited to bolster arguments for the universality of schizophrenia. But, there were some important cross-cultural differences as well. In a finding that took the investigators by surprise, the course of the illness was shown to be easier for patients in developing countries compared to those in highly industrialized countries. Patients in Colombia, India, and Nigeria recovered at faster rates than those in England, the former Soviet Union, or the United States. These differences were attributed to cultural factors such as the presence of extended kin networks and the tendency to return to work in developing countries.

The researchers also noted differences in symptom expression across cultures. Patients in the United States were less likely to demonstrate symptoms of lack of insight and auditory hallucinations than were Danish or Nigerian patients. These findings may be related to cultural differences in values associated with insight and self-awareness, which are highly regarded in the United States, but less well regarded in the other countries. Also, there may have been cultural differences in tolerance for particular symptoms; the Nigerian culture as a whole is more accepting of the presence of voices. Nigerian and Danish patients, however, were more likely to demonstrate catatonia (extreme withdrawal or agitation).

Kleinman (1988) and Leff (1981) discussed some of the methodological problems that plagued the WHO studies. These included an assessment tool that failed to tap culturally unique experiences and expressions of disorder. Kleinman also noted that the samples were made artificially homogeneous because of the selection criteria. He argued that the findings of cross-cultural differences might have been greater still had not the heterogeneity of the sample been reduced.

Other cross-cultural comparisons of rates and expression of schizophrenia (Leff, 1977; Murphy, 1982) have also found evidence of cultural variations in rates and symptomatology. Murphy (1982) found that rates of admissions for schizophrenia are four times higher in Ireland compared to England and Wales. These findings suggested that some features of Irish culture (for example, sharp wit, ambivalence toward individuality) may have accounted for the cultural differences. In an early study of New York psychiatric cases, Opler and Singer (1959) found that Irish American schizophrenic patients were more likely to experience paranoid delusions than were Italian American patients. The authors cited cultural differences in parenting to account for the difference. A study of Japanese schizophrenics (Sue & Morishima, 1982) indicated that they are more likely than Euro-American counterparts to be withdrawn and passive, conforming to cultural values.

Recent studies of schizophrenics have tested the theory that expressed emotion—family communication characterized by hostility and over-involvement—increases the risk of relapse. The expressed emotion construct is important because it suggests that family and social interactions influence the course of schizophrenia. These interactions are in turn influenced by cultural values. Research indicates that expressed emotion predicts relapse in Western samples (Mintz, Mintz, & Goldstein, 1987). Kleinman (1988), however, notes the difficulties in using this construct in other cultures, particularly those that emphasize nonverbal communication. Karno and associates (1987) reported that expressed emotion also predicts relapse in Mexican Americans, but Kleinman (1988) questions whether measures of expressed emotion developed in one cultural context have validity in another.

Reports of cultural differences in diagnosis have also raised questions about the validity of assessment techniques used in cross-cultural comparisons of schizophrenia and other disorders (Kleinman, 1988; Leff, 1977). In a re-analysis of some of the early WHO data, Leff (1977) found that U.S. psychiatrists were more likely to give diagnoses of schizophrenia than were psychiatrists in England, and less likely to give diagnoses of depression. Abebimpe (1981) and Thomas and Sillen (1972) have documented that African Americans are more likely than Euro-Americans to receive diagnoses of schizophrenia rather than depression, even when the symptom picture is the same. Racial bias seems to account for some of the differential pattern (Thomas & Sillen, 1972), and cultural differences in expression of symptomatology may also be important.

Depression.   All of us have experienced moods of depression, sadness, or the blues in our lives. We may have these feelings in response to a death in the family, the breakup of a relationship, falling short of a goal, and the like. The presence of a depressive disorder involves the symptoms of "intense sadness, feelings of futility and worthlessness, and withdrawal from others" (Sue, Sue, & Sue, 1990, p. 325). Depression is often also characterized by physical changes (for example, sleep and appetite disturbances) as well as emotional and behavioral changes (Berry et al., 1992). Like schizophrenia, depression is one of the most common psychological disorders in the United States. In a large-scale study, Myers et al. (1984) found that 3% and 7% of the adult male and female population, respectively, had experienced a depressive disorder in the previous six-month period. Lifetime prevalence rates for depression are also high, sometimes as high as 26% for women and 12% for men (Sue et al., 1990). There is also some evidence to suggest that the incidence rates for depression have risen over the last few decades (Robins et al., 1984).

In cross-cultural studies of depression, variations in expression of symptomatology have been widely documented. Some cultural groups (for example, Nigerians) are less likely to report extreme feelings of worthlessness. Others (for example, Chinese) are more likely to report somatic complaints (Kleinman, 1988). As with schizophrenia, rates of depression also vary from culture to culture (Marsella, 1980).

Leff (1977) argues that cultures vary in terms of their differentiation and communication of emotional terminology and, hence, in how they experience and express depression. Some cultures have few words to convey emotions such as sadness or anger (see Chapter 12 for more on this). Also, cultures locate feeling states in different parts of the body. This may explain why some cultural groups emphasize somatic complaints in the expression of depression. In arguing for a culturally relative definition of depression, Kleinman (1988) writes that

> depression experienced entirely as low back pain and depression experienced entirely as guilt-ridden existential despair are such substantially different forms of illness behavior with distinctive symptoms, patterns of help seeking, and treatment responses that although the disease in each instance may be the same, the illness, not the disease, becomes the determinative factor. And one might well ask, is the disease even the same? (p. 25)

Earlier, Kleinman (1978) argued that depressive disease reflects a biologically based disorder, while depressive illness refers to the personal and social experience of depression. Although Kleinman accepts the idea that depressive disease is universal, he argues that the expression and course of the illness are culturally determined.

Marsella (1979, 1980) also argues for a culturally relative view of depression, saying that depression takes a primarily affective form in cultures with strong objective orientations (that is, which emphasize individualism). In these cultures, feelings of loneliness and isolation dominate the symptom picture. Somatic symptoms such as headaches would be dominant in subjective cultures (those having a more communal structure). Marsella (1979) has also proposed that depressive symptom patterns differ across cultures due to cultural variations in sources of stress as well as in resources for coping with the stress.

Other psychological disorders.   The approach used in the cross-cultural studies of depression and schizophrenia reported here can be characterized as an "etic" one that assumes universally accepted definitions of abnormality and methodology (review Chapter 1 for definitions of *emic* and *etic*). In contrast to this etic approach, there have also been some ethnographic reports of **culture-bound syndromes.** These are forms of abnormal behavior observed only in certain sociocultural milieus. Findings concerning differential rates and courses of the disorder across cultures and of culturally distinct forms of the disorder, suggest the importance of culture in shaping the expression of abnormal behavior. In fact, ethnographic reports of culture-bound syndromes provide perhaps the strongest support for applying cultural relativism to understanding and dealing with abnormality.

Using primarily emic (culture-specific) approaches involving ethnographic examinations of behavior within a specific cultural context, anthropologists and psychiatrists have identified several apparently unique forms of psychological disorder. Some similarities between symptoms of these culture-specific disorders and those recognized across cultures have been observed. The particular pattern of symptoms, however, typically does not fit the diagnostic criteria of psychological disorders recognized in Western classification schemes.

The most widely observed culture-bound syndrome has been identified in several countries in Asia (Malay, Philippines, Thailand). *Amok* is a disorder characterized by sudden rage and homicidal aggression. It is thought to be brought on by stress, sleep deprivation, and alcohol consumption (Carson et al., 1988), and has been observed primarily in males. Several stages of the disorder have been identified, ranging from extreme withdrawal prior to the assaultive behavior to exhaustion and amnesia for the rage. The term *running amok* derives from observations of the disorder.

Witiko (also known as windigo) is a disorder that has been identified in Algonquin Indians in Canada. It involves the belief that the individual has been possessed by the witiko spirit—a man-eating monster. Cannibalistic behavior may result, along with suicidal ideation to avoid acting on the cannibalistic urges (Carson et al., 1988).

Anorexia nervosa is a disorder identified in the West but not observed in Third World countries (Swartz, 1985). The disorder is characterized by a distorted body image, fear of becoming fat, and a serious loss of weight associated with food restraining or purging. Several factors have been cited as possible causes of this disorder. These include a cultural emphasis on thinness as an ideal for women, constricted sex roles, and an individual's fears of being out of control or of taking on adult responsibilities.

Kiev (1972) and Yap (1974) reviewed the literature on these and other culture-bound syndromes, including *latah* (characterized by hysteria and echolalia, observed primarily in women in Malay), *koro* (impotence resulting from fear that the penis is retracting, observed in Southeast Asian men), and *susto* (characterized by depression and apathy thought to reflect "soul loss," observed in Indians of the Andean highlands). Yap (1974) has attempted to organize information concerning culture-bound syndromes into a classification scheme that parallels Western diagnostic schemes. Thus, *latah* and *susto* are viewed as unique cultural expressions of universal primary fear reactions.

Amok is similarly viewed as a unique cultural expression of a universal rage reaction. Yap recognizes that his attempt to subsume culture-bound syndromes into a universal classification scheme may be premature, particularly since Western clinical tools and methods of research may make it difficult to assess culturally diverse expressions of abnormal behavior.

Pfeiffer (1982) has identified four dimensions for understanding culture-bound syndromes. He argues that culture-specific areas of stress may contribute to the syndromes. These areas of stress include family and societal structure and ecological conditions. For example, *koro* might be best understood as resulting from the unique cultural emphasis on potency in certain cultures that emphasize paternal authority. Culture-specific shaping of conduct and interpretations of conduct may also account for the development of culture-bound syndromes. Pfeiffer suggests that cultures may implicitly approve patterns of exceptional behavior as in the case of *amok,* in which aggression against others "broadly follows the patterns of societal expectations" (p. 206). Finally, Pfeiffer argues that how a culture interprets exceptional behavior will be linked to culture-specific interventions. For example, interventions to heal the soul loss associated with *susto* will involve sacrifices carried out by a native healer to appease the earth so that it will return the soul.

Some scholars (for example, Kleinman, 1988; Marsella, 1979; Pfeiffer, 1982) argue that it is impossible to use current Western classification schemes to understand culture-bound syndromes because the latter are experienced from a qualitatively different point of view. They argue that culture shapes the experience of psychological disorder, both in determining the expression of symptoms of universal disorders and in contributing to the emergence of culture-specific disorders. The recognition of the role of culture in shaping abnormal behavior requires that we reexamine the way we assess and treat individuals with psychological disorders.

Cultural Differences in Dealing with Illness

Differences in Health Care and Medical Delivery Systems

In understanding how different cultures deal with medical and psychological illnesses, we first need to recognize the differences that exist in health care systems. The recognition of the role of culture in health care systems is also important to our discussions of health care reform in our own country. Different countries and cultures have developed their own, unique ways of dealing with health care. Undoubtedly, a number of factors contribute to the exact type of health care delivery system that exists in each country. These factors include social and economic development, technological advances and availability, and the influence of neighboring and collaborating countries. Social trends also contribute to health care delivery services, including urbanization, industrialization, governmental structure, international trade laws and practices, demographic changes, demands for privatization, and public expenditures.

Worldwide, there are four major categories of national health systems: entrepreneurial, welfare-oriented, comprehensive, and socialist (Roemer, 1993). Within each of these four major types of health care systems, there are major differences among countries in terms of their economic level. For instance, the United States is an example of a country with a relatively high economic level that uses an entrepreneurial system of health care, characterized by a substantial private industry influence covering individuals as well as groups. The Philippines and Ghana, however, also use an entrepreneurial system of health care but have relatively moderate and low economic levels. France, Brazil, and Burma are examples of high, moderate, and low economy countries, respectively, that utilize welfare-oriented health systems. Likewise, Sweden, Costa Rica, and Sri Lanka utilize comprehensive health care, and the former Soviet Union, Cuba, and China utilize socialist health systems.

One factor that has not been considered much in terms of compatibility with national health care systems is culture. A quick review of the countries listed here will demonstrate that major cultural differences exist among the countries and that these cultural differences are related to the type of national health care policies in each country. It makes sense for an entrepreneurial system to be used in the United States, for example, because of the highly individualistic nature of American culture. Likewise, it makes sense that socialist systems of health care are utilized in China and Cuba, given their collectivistic, communal nature. However, cultural influences cannot be separated from the other factors that contribute to national health care. In particular, the complex interaction among culture, economy, technology, and government exemplifies how intertwined social aspects of culture are inseparable from social institutions, and vice versa.

Differences in Psychotherapy and Psychological Assessment

Assessment of abnormal behavior involves identifying and describing an individual's symptoms "within the context of his or her overall level of functioning and environment" (Carson et al., 1988, p. 531). The tools and methods of assessment should be sensitive to cultural and other environmental influences on behavior and functioning. The literature on standard assessment techniques, however, indicates that there may be problems of bias or insensitivity when psychological tests and methods developed in one cultural context are used to assess behavior in a different context. I will briefly review the literature on assessment and treatment across cultures, paying attention to models proposed to address cultural issues in assessment and treatment.

Cross-cultural assessment of abnormal behavior.   Traditional tools of clinical assessment in psychology are based on a standard definition of abnormality and use a standard set of classification criteria for evaluating problematic behavior. Therefore, the tools may have little meaning in cultures with varying definitions, however well translated into the native language; and they may mask or fail to capture culturally specific expressions of disorder (Marsella, 1979). The assessment problems encountered in studying schizophrenia and depression across cultures illustrate the limitations of traditional assessment methods.

The Present State Examination (PSE), for example, was used to diagnose schizophrenia in the WHO studies described earlier. Leff (1986) commented on the ethnocentric bias of procedures such as the PSE and the Cornell Medical Index. In a psychiatric survey of the Yoruba in Nigeria, investigators had to supplement the PSE to include culture-specific complaints such as feeling "an expanded head and goose flesh."

Standard diagnostic instruments to measure depressive disorder may also miss important cultural expressions of the disorder in Africans (Beiser, 1985) and Native Americans (Manson, Shore, & Bloom, 1985). In an extensive study of depression among Native Americans (Manson & Shore, 1981; Manson et al., 1985), the American Indian Depression Schedule (AIDS) was developed to assess and diagnose depressive illness. The investigators found that depression among the Hopi includes symptoms not measured by standard measures of depression such as the Diagnostic Interview Schedule (DIS) and the Schedule for Affective Disorders and Schizophrenia (SADS). These measures, based on diagnostic criteria found in the *Diagnostic and Statistical Manual of Mental Disorders* (APA, 1987), failed to capture the short but acute dysphoric moods sometimes reported by the Hopi (Manson et al., 1985).

Several researchers (Higginbotham, 1979; Lonner & Ibrahim, 1989; Marsella, 1979) have offered guidelines for developing measures to use in cross-cultural assessment of abnormal behavior. They suggest that sensitive assessment methods examine social-cultural norms of healthy adjustment as well as culturally based definitions of abnormality. Higginbotham (1979) also suggests the importance of examining culturally sanctioned systems of healing and their influence on abnormal behavior. There is evidence that people whose problems match cultural categories of abnormality are more likely to seek folk healers (Leff, 1986). Failure to examine **indigenous healing systems** would overlook some expressions of disorder. Assessment of culturally sanctioned systems of cure should also enhance planning for treatment strategies, one of the primary goals of traditional assessment (Carson et al., 1988).

Treatment of abnormal behavior across diverse cultures in the United States.   In the last two decades, a growing literature has indicated that culturally diverse clients may be under- or inappropriately served by traditional treatment methods. In a pioneering study of ethnic differences in response to standard mental health services in the Seattle area, Sue (1977) found lower rates of utilization of services for Asian Americans and Native Americans compared to Euro-Americans and African Americans. More dramatically, he found that all the groups except Euro-Americans had high dropout rates and relatively poorer treatment outcomes. A later study in the Los Angeles area produced similar findings (Sue, 1991). Sue (1977; Sue & Zane, 1987) concluded that low utilization and high attrition rates were due to the cultural insensitivity of standard treatment methods.

In efforts to fashion more culturally sensitive services, Sue and others (Comas-Diaz & Jacobsen, 1991; Higginbotham, 1979; Sue & Zane, 1987; Tseng & McDermott, 1981) suggest that treatment methods should be modified to improve their fit with the worldviews and experiences of culturally diverse clients. For example, psychoanalytic approaches are derived from a worldview that assumes that unconscious conflicts (probably sexual) give rise to abnormal behavior. This worldview may reflect the experience of the well-to-do Austrian women Freud treated and based many of his theoretical assumptions on. However, a therapeutic approach based on such a worldview may prove inappropriate with cultures that attribute abnormality either to natural factors (for example, physical problems or being out of harmony with the environment) or supernatural causes (for example, spirit possession). Cultural systems of cure and healing may be effective precisely because they operate within a particular culture's worldview (Tseng & McDermott, 1981). For example, a spiritual ceremony performed by a native shaman (priest or healer) might prove to be a more effective treatment of the culture-bound syndrome of susto than the cognitive behavioral approach typically used in the United States.

A large body of research on preferences for therapeutic approaches in ethnically different populations in the United States indicates that non–Euro-American clients tend to prefer action-oriented therapy to nondirective approaches like psychoanalytic or humanistic therapy (Sue & Zane, 1987). There is also some indication that culturally diverse clients prefer to see therapists who are similar in terms of cultural background and gender. But more recent research indicates that similarity of worldviews and attitudes to treatment between client and therapist may be more important than ethnic similarity (Atkinson, Ponce, & Martinez, 1984). Acculturation status may also determine client responses to treatment (Atkinson, Casa, & Abreu, 1992). Culture-sensitive counselors have been rated as being more credible and competent to conduct treatment across cultures by African Americans (Atkinson, Furlong, & Poston, 1986), Asian Americans (Gim, Atkinson, & Kim, 1991), and Mexican Americans (Atkinson et al., 1992).

Several authors (for example, Higginbotham, 1979; Sue, Akutsu, & Higashi, 1985; Sue & Zane, 1987; Tseng & McDermott, 1981) have outlined the competencies and knowledge base necessary for therapists to conduct sensitive and effective treatment across cultures. Sue et al. (1985) suggest that the culturally sensitive therapist will have acquired (1) knowledge of diverse cultures and lifestyles, (2) skill and comfort in using innovative treatment methods, and (3) actual experience working with culturally diverse clients. It is also critically important for the culturally sensitive therapist to be aware of his or her own cultural background and its influences on definitions and perceptions of abnormal behavior. Furthermore, the therapist must be aware of how cultural beliefs and experiences influence the course of treatment. Comas-Diaz and Jacobsen (1991) have outlined several ways in which ethnocultural factors may shape therapy, including the elicitation of strong transference reactions on the part of the client (unconscious projections onto the therapist) and barriers to empathy on the part of the therapist (understanding of another's experience).

Treatment of abnormal behavior in other cultures.   A focus in recent discussions of cross-cultural treatment of abnormal behavior has been culture-specific interventions. Several culture-specific forms of treatment have been identified in the literature, including *naikan* and *morita* therapy in Japan, and *espiritismo* practiced among some Puerto Ricans. These approaches are generally very "foreign" to many Americans. *Naikan* therapy, for example, involves a "process of continuous meditation based upon highly structured instruction in self-observation and self-reflection" (Murase, 1986, p. 389). Patients are usually placed in a small sitting area and practice their meditations from early in the morning (5:30 A.M. or so) until the evening (9:00 P.M. or so). Interviewers come every 90 minutes to discuss progress, usually for about five minutes. Patients are instructed to examine themselves severely, much like a prosecutor would examine an accused prisoner.

Prince (1980) argues that what is common to treatment across cultures is the mobilization of healing forces within the client. Several others (for example, Torrey, 1972; Tseng & McDermott, 1981) have also attempted to determine universal features of culture-specific systems of treatment. Although there may well be universal elements underlying systems of cure, culture-specific systems alone appear to address the unique definitions and expressions of abnormal behavior in a given culture.

Other Aspects Related to Culture and Health

Up to this point, I have focused on cultural differences in the definition of health, cultural influences on physical and psychological health and disorder, and national and cultural differences in the treatment and assessment of disease. But other aspects of culture also have an impact on our understanding of cultural influences on health. These include cultural differences in attitudes and values about seeking help, complying with treatment, and about the etiology of disease, which directly affect feelings of personal responsibility and control over health and disease. Unfortunately, despite the importance of these other areas of culture in relation to disease and health care, research has been slow to investigate exactly the extent to which these differences may exist and how and why they exist. This is no doubt related to the fact that we are only now becoming aware of the importance of sociocultural differences when developing treatment and intervention programs for medical and psychological problems.

A recent study by Matsumoto and his colleagues (Matsumoto et al., 1994) highlights the importance of furthering our understanding of cultural influences in these areas. These researchers recruited Japanese and Japanese American women over the age of 55 living in the San Francisco Bay Area to participate in a study of the attitudes and values related to the medical disorder osteoporosis and its treatment. Osteoporosis is a disease of the bones that results in the gradual weakening of the bones through a decrease in bone density. It can be a particularly devastating disease for older women of European or Asian descent. The research included a rather comprehensive battery, including a complete medical history, an assessment of risk factors particular to osteoporosis, an attitudes survey about the disease, and a health care issues assessment. In addition, a subsample of the women were assessed for their bone mineral density (BMD) levels.

While there were some amazing findings in all the data, especially interesting results were found with regard to cultural differences in the attitudes survey and the health care issues assessment. The entire sample of women was divided into two groups. One group was born and raised in the United States and spoke English as their primary language. The other group was born and raised in Japan and spoke Japanese as their primary language. When asked about the types of problems they would have if they were diagnosed with osteoporosis, more Japanese than American women reported problems with finances and with finding help. The major concern for American women was "other" problems, including problems of mobility. This is an especially interesting finding, because mobility is such a central element in fostering individualism, which is more characteristic of the United States than Japan. When asked what kinds of problems they would have if they had to take care of someone with osteoporosis, more Japanese women reported problems with not enough time. American women again reported "other" problems involving their physical abilities.

The researchers also asked about the types of support services the women would want to have available if they were diagnosed with osteoporosis. More Japanese women reported that they wanted institutions, temporary homes, rehabilitation centers, nursing homes, information services, social service organizations, and organizations to find help. The American women, however, reported wanting "other" services such as medical care.

More American women knew what osteoporosis is. More Japanese women, however, reported that it was of major concern to them and that they would view it very negatively if diagnosed. Also, more American than Japanese women reported that people other than friends or family would care for them if diagnosed. If diagnosed with osteoporosis, Japanese women were more likely to attribute the cause of the illness to fate, chance, or luck. American women, however, were more likely to attribute the illness to diet. Interestingly, there were no differences between the groups in degree of personal responsibility or control, nor in the number of women who specifically asked for osteoporosis examinations, or in their feelings about estrogen therapy.

A final striking finding was that more Japanese women reported that they would comply with invasive treatment, even though fewer Japanese women had positive feelings about their physicians or reported that they trusted their physicians. This type of finding speaks to the power of culture to influence issues regarding treatment compliance and physician trust. Even though the Japanese women had fewer positive feelings about and trust toward their physicians, they would have been more likely to comply with invasive medical treatment. This is related to the Japanese culture's emphasis on compliance with authority and suggests that the relationship between interpersonal trust and compliance with authority figures in the Japanese culture is not the same as it is here in the United States.

These types of findings strongly suggest that we reexamine our notions about power and trust when dealing with intercultural physician-patient relationships in future practice and research. This relationship is already fraught with potential pitfalls and dangers of abuse. Without this reexamination, we may open the door further to even greater problems.

Conclusion

Many factors contribute to health and disease processes. While we are well aware of the effects of the environment, diet, direct health-related behaviors (smoking, alcohol consumption, and so forth), health care availability, and the like, culture is also a major factor. Understanding the role culture plays in the development of disease, whether medical or psychological, will take us a long way toward developing ways of preventing disease in the future. As research uncovers the possible negative consequences of cultural tendencies, we can also look to an understanding of cultural influences to help us treat people of different cultures better than we have in the past.

Recognition of the role of culture in influencing the definition and expression of health suggests that we must modify our methods of assessing and treating disease. To develop adequate assessment strategies, knowledge of culturally based definitions of health and disease must be taken into account. Awareness of culture-specific systems of healing is also necessary to develop effective methods of both assessment and treatment. Research indicates that culturally sensitive assessment and treatment methods are vital to improving our ability to appropriately and effectively meet the medical and mental health needs of culturally diverse populations, both in the United States and globally.

 # Glossary

cultural relativism   A viewpoint that suggests that the unique aspects of a particular culture need to be considered when understanding and identifying behavior.

culture-bound syndromes   Forms of abnormal behavior observed only in certain sociocultural milieus.

indigenous healing systems   Healing systems particular to a certain culture and not found elsewhere.

medical model   A model of health that views disease as resulting from a specific, identifiable cause originating inside the body.

pathogen   In the medical model, a cause of disease, whether viral, bacterial, or otherwise; the root of all physical and medical diseases.

reliability   A concept in psychometrics that has to do with the degree of consistency in measurement. Measures and assessment techniques shown to be reliable give consistent results across time, person, and measure.

12

The Diversity of Human Feeling

Cultural Similarities and Differences in the Expression, Perception, and Experience of Emotion

The Importance of Emotions in Our Lives

It is difficult to imagine life without emotion, devoid of feeling. We treasure our feelings—the joy we feel at a ball game, the pleasure of the touch of a loved one, the fun we have with our friends having a night out, seeing a movie, or visiting a nightclub. Even our negative or unpleasant feelings are important: the sadness when we are apart from our loved ones, the death of a family member, the anger we feel when violated, the fear that overcomes us in a scary unknown situation, and the guilt or shame we feel toward others when our sins are made public. Emotions color our life experiences. They inform us of who we are, what our relationships with others are like, and how to behave. Emotions give meaning to events. Without emotions, those events would be mere facts of our lives.

Emotions separate us from computers and other machines. Technology advances have brought machines that are increasingly capable of recreating much of our own complex thought processes. Computers now handle much of own work more efficiently than humans can. But no matter how much a computer can accomplish, no technology can make a computer *feel* as we feel—have *emotions* as we have them. (Not yet, anyway!)

Feelings and emotions may be the most important aspect of our lives. All people of all cultures have them, and all must learn to deal with them, to attribute some degree of value and worth to them. Life around us may appear to be focused on development of technological capabilities for artificial intelligence and critical thinking and reasoning skills. But our emotions hold the key to make it all happen.

The world of emotion underscores the great diversity among people. How we package emotion, what we call it, how much importance we give it, how we express and perceive it, and how we feel it—these are questions that all people and all cultures answer differently. The different answers each person and each culture have to these questions contribute substantially to the great diversity that we see and, more importantly, feel among people of different lands and nations. In this chapter, I will explore the nature of those differences—the diversity in human feeling and emotion across cultures. Many studies on human emotion in psychology, sociology, and anthropology from many different parts of the world inform us about those differences as well as the similarities. Throughout this book, I have approached learning about other cultures by first evaluating our own, and this chapter is no different. Thus, we begin our journey on cultural differences in human emotion with an understanding of how emotions are viewed in our own American culture and why this is so.

Emotions from a Mainstream American Perspective

Emotions in Everyday American Life

In the United States, we place a premium on our feelings. We all recognize that each of us is unique and that we have our own, individual feelings about the things, events, situations, and people around us. We consciously try to be aware of our feelings, to be "in touch" with them, as we say. To be in touch with our feelings and to understand the world around us emotionally is to be a mature adult in our society.

We place a heavy importance and value on feelings and emotions throughout the life span. We cherish our feelings as adults, and we actively try to recognize the feelings of our children and of other young ones around us. It is not uncommon for parents to ask their young children how they feel about their swimming lessons, or piano lessons or their teachers at school, or the broccoli on their plates. Parents often give much weight to the feelings of their children in making decisions that affect them. "If Johnny doesn't want to do it, we shouldn't make him do it" is a common sentiment among parents in the United States. Indeed, children's emotions are afforded almost the same status as the emotions of adults and the older generations.

Much therapeutic work in psychology centers around human emotions. The goal of individual psychotherapy systems is often to get people to become more aware of their feelings and emotions and to accept them. Much psychotherapeutic work is focused on helping individuals freely express the feelings and emotions they may have bottled up inside. In group therapy, the emphasis is on communicating your feelings toward others in the group and listening and accepting the expressions of feeling of others. This emphasis is also prevalent in work groups outside of strict psychotherapy. Industrial and organizational interventions are common, and much time, effort, and energy are spent establishing better lines of communication among employees and recognizing the feelings and emotions of individuals.

How our society values and structures our feelings and emotions is directly related to the values that our American culture fosters. In the United States, rugged individualism has been a cornerstone of our dominant culture, and part of that rugged individualism means that we recognize and value the unique aspects of each and every person. Diversity of feelings and emotions are part of this package; in fact, it may be the most important part in identifying individuals because emotions are highly personalized and individual themselves. Children are valued as separate entities, and their feelings are valued. When we "fix" something through psychotherapeutic intervention, the therapist often tries to help the client discover his or her emotions and express them.

Emotions as Viewed by American Psychologists

Even the study of emotions in American science has this flavor or twist. The earliest American psychologist attributed with an important theory of emotion was William James. In the second volume of his *Principles of Psychology* (1890), James suggested that emotions occurred as a result of our behavioral reaction to a stimulus that produced that reaction. For example, if we saw a bear, we would run away from it, and we would then interpret our running and breathing and the other visceral changes of our body as an emotion we would label *fear*. Another scholar, C. Lange, wrote about a theory of emotion very similar to James's at about the same time (1887). Thus, this theory is called the James/Lange theory of emotion.

Various other theories about emotion have been proffered since James's. Cannon (1927), for example, argued that autonomic arousal was too slow to account for changes in emotional experience. Instead, he and Bard argued that emotional experience resulted from direct stimulation of brain centers in the cortex that produced the conscious experience of emotion (Bard & Mountcastle, 1948). Thus, we feel fear when we see the bear because of the stimulation of certain brain centers that trigger that reaction. In this view, our running and breathing occurred as a result of that fear, not as precursors to it.

In the early 1960s, a very influential United States study on emotion was published by Schachter and Singer (1962). Based on their study, they suggested that emotional experiences depend solely on the individual's interpretation of the environment in which he or she is being aroused. According to this theory, emotions are not differentiated physiologically. Instead, what is important in the production of emotional experience is how you interpret the events around yourself. Emotion is labeling the arousal or behavior in that situation.

Some of the most important theories about emotion in the U.S. have to do with its expression rather than its experience. These theories are often presented in introductory psychology textbooks today and are part of a regular curriculum on the psychology of emotions in universities across the United States. Tomkins's theory, for example, was one of the most influential theories about emotional expression and is often credited with having spurred much of the subsequent research in this field. Tomkins (1962, 1963) suggested that emotions are evolutionarily adaptive and that their expression is biologically innate and universal to all people of all cultures and races. After publication of his theory, Tomkins joined forces with psychologists Paul Ekman (1972) and Carroll Izard (1971) to conduct a series of studies showing that at least six facial expressions of emotion are panculturally universal— anger, disgust, fear, happiness, sadness, and surprise. I will return to these studies and their findings later in the chapter.

Despite the apparent differences among these theories about emotion, there are striking similarities across them as well. These similarities are directly related to our own American culture, which has "guided" the way American scientists (and our students) have learned about emotion. For example, there is considerable similarity across these theories in their implied view of emotion. All suggest an important role for the **subjective experience of emotion**—that is, experiencing our inner feelings. The James/Lange, Cannon/Bard, and Schacter/Singer theories all attempt to explain the nature of that subjective, inner state we call emotion. They all view that subjective feeling as an emotion, but they all came up with different ways to explain how it occurs.

Evolutionary theories based on emotional expressions, such as those by Tomkins, Ekman, and Izard, also posit a central role to inner feelings, but by default. That is, by focusing on the expression of emotion, their work implies that something is being expressed—emotion. Because emotional expressions are outward displays of inner experience, these theories by default see internal, subjective experience as an important part of emotion (if not the most important part).

Another common theme across emotion theories is the importance of emotion labeling—what we call an emotion. The James/Lange, Cannon/Bard, and Schachter/Singer theories all suggest that the labeling process is an important and integral part of emotion. Evolutionary theories of emotion are, for the most part, based on studies relying on labeling facial expressions of emotion as evidence for universality. These similarities—the focus on inner, subjective experience and the importance of labeling—are cornerstones of the way American scientists and laypersons alike speak of and understand emotion. In American culture, we define emotions for ourselves in these two important ways. This focus on the introspective, subjective feeling of emotion is important to us and helps us place primary importance on emotion in our lives, whether as children or adults, caregiver or care receiver, or whatever roles we play. Being in touch with our feelings, finding ways to express them, and recognizing that others have different feelings and that that is okay are all ways our culture has molded emotions for us. And these are exactly the ways American scientists have sought to understand them.

This view of emotions probably makes good, intuitive sense to many of us. But this way of understanding emotion may be a particularly Western or, even more specifically, American way of understanding emotions. Not all cultures view emotions this way. While "sincere" and "mature" people in the United States may express their emotions to themselves and to others honestly and with forthright candor, these very same people may very well be viewed as "dishonest," untrustworthy," and "immature" in another culture. Why? Because different cultures mold the world of emotion and human feelings differently for their members. What is true for us in this culture is not necessarily true for the people of another culture.

The Concept of Emotions from a Cross-Cultural Perspective

Cultural Similarities and Differences in the Concept of Emotion

Even before we look at how people of different cultures express, perceive, and feel emotions, we should first look at whether the word *emotion* even means the same thing to all people of all cultural backgrounds. We often fall into the trap of thinking that people all over the world mean the same things when they speak of emotion. If people of all cultures meant the exact same thing every time they spoke of emotion, we could speak with a certain degree of certainty of similarities or differences in expression or perception or feelings. But if people of different cultures refer to different things when they speak of emotion, even if they used words that translated into *approximately* the same things, then these differences would inform us that we are starting from different bases when discussing emotion.

Fortunately, many studies have been conducted in the fields of anthropology and psychology to address this important issue. Indeed, the sheer number of studies and the amount of information about emotion in these various social science disciplines speaks to the importance of emotion in human life and the recognition of that importance by scholars. Ethnographic approaches—the in-depth immersion and study of single cultures on their own merits that originates from anthropology—are especially useful in helping to uncover how different cultures define and understand the concept we call *emotion*. A few years ago, Russell (1991) reviewed much of the cross-cultural and anthropological literature on emotion concepts and pointed out many ways cultures do indeed differ, sometimes considerably, in their definitions and understanding of emotion. His excellent review of this topic provides a strong basis for discussion of this question.

The concept and definition of emotion.   First of all, as Russell (1991) pointed out, not all cultures have a word that corresponds to our word *emotion*. Levy (1973, 1983) has suggested that Tahitians do not have a word for emotion. Lutz (1980, as reported in Russell, 1991; Lutz, 1983) also suggested that the Ifaluks of Micronesia do not have a word for emotion. The fact that some cultures do not even have a word that corresponds to our word *emotion* is important; consider what the *nonexistence* of this word means to their cultures. Clearly, in these cultures, the concept of emotion is different from that of our own culture. Perhaps it is not as important to these cultures as it is to ours. Or perhaps what we know of as emotion is labeled differently, in an untranslatable sort of way, and refers to something other than internal, subjective feelings. In this case, too, our concept of emotion would be quite different from the concept of emotion for those cultures.

But most cultures of the world do have a word or concept for what we call *emotion*. Brandt and Boucher's study (1986) examined the concepts of depression in eight different cultures. The languages studied included Indonesian, Japanese, Korean, Malaysian, Spanish, and Sinhalese. Each of the languages had a word for emotion, suggesting the cross-cultural existence of the concept of emotion. But even if a culture has a word for emotion, that culture's word may have different connotations, and thus different meanings, than our English word *emotion*. For example, Matsuyama, Hama, Kawamura, and Mine (1978) analyzed emotional words from the Japanese language, which included some words that are typically considered emotions (for example, *angry, sad*). Some words were included, however, that we Americans might question as to whether they denote emotion (for example, *considerate, lucky*). Samoans do not have a word for emotion but do have a word (*lagona*) that refers to feelings and sensations (Gerber, 1975, as reported in Russell, 1991).

We can conclude, therefore, that not all cultures of the world have a word or concept for what we label *emotion* in English. Even among those cultures that do have a word for emotion, those words may not mean the same thing as the English word *emotion*. These studies certainly point to the fact that the class of events—expressions, perceptions, feelings, situations—that we call emotion in our culture does not represent the same class of phenomena in other cultures.

Categorizating or labeling emotion.   People in different cultures also categorize or label emotions differently. Some English words, such as *anger, joy, sadness, liking,* and *loving,* have equivalents in different languages and cultures. But many English words have no equivalent in another culture, and emotion words in other languages may have no exact English equivalent.

The German language contains the word *schadenfreude*, which refers to pleasure derived from another's misfortunes. There is no exact English translation for this word. The Japanese language contains words such as *itoshii, ijirashii,* and *amae.* These also have no exact English translation (longing for an absent loved one, a feeling associated with seeing someone praiseworthy overcoming an obstacle, and dependence, respectively). Conversely, some African languages have a word that covers what English suggests are two emotions—anger and sadness (Leff, 1973). Likewise, Lutz (1980) suggests that the Ifaluk word *song* can be described sometimes as anger and sometimes as sadness. And some English words have no equivalents in other languages. The English words *terror, horror, dread, apprehension,* and *timidity* are all referred to by the single word *gurakadj* in Gidjingali, an Australian aboriginal language (Hiatt, 1978). This aboriginal word also refers to the English concepts of shame and fear. *Frustration* may be a word with no exact equivalent in Arabic languages (Russell, 1991).

Just because a culture may not have a word for something that we consider an emotion certainly does not mean that people of those cultures do not have those feelings. The fact that there is no exact equivalent in some Arabic languages for our word *frustration* does not mean that people of these cultures do not get or feel frustrated. Similarly, just because our English language does not have a translation equivalent for the German word *schadenfreude* does not mean that people in the United States do not sometimes derive pleasure from someone else's misfortunes (not you or I, however!). Certainly, in the world of subjective, emotional feeling, there must be considerable overlap in the emotions we feel, regardless of whether different cultures and languages have translation equivalents for those feeling states or not.

The fact that translation differences exist in the exact meaning and labeling of different emotional states across languages and cultures does suggest that different cultures divide their world of emotion differently. The fact that German culture, for example, contains the word *schadenfreude* must mean that identification of that feeling state or situation has some importance in that language and culture that it does not share with American culture or the English language. The same can be said of English words that find no exact translation equivalent in other languages. The types of words that different cultures use to identify and label the emotion worlds of their members gives us yet another clue about the way different cultures structure and mold the emotional experiences of their people. Not only are the concepts of emotion culture bound but the ways each culture attempts to frame and label its emotion world are also culture bound.

The location of emotion.   To Americans, perhaps the single most important aspect of emotions is the inner, subjective experience of emotion. In the United States, it seems most natural that our feelings take precedence over all other aspects of emotion. But the importance we place on inner feelings and the importance of **introspection** (that is, looking inside yourself) may be culture bound in American psychology. Other cultures can and do view emotions as originating or residing elsewhere.

Emotion words in the languages of several Oceanic peoples, such as the Samoans (Gerber, 1975), Pintupi aborigines (Myers, 1979), and Solomon Islanders (White, 1980), are statements about relationships among people or between people and events. Likewise, Riesman (1977) suggests that the African Fulani's concept of *semteende*, which is commonly translated as shame or embarrassment, refers more to a situation than to a feeling. That is, if the situation is appropriate to *semteende*, then someone is feeling it, regardless of what any one individual actually feels (Russell, 1991).

In the United States, we place matters of emotion and inner feelings in the heart. Even among cultures that locate emotions within the body, cultures differ in that exact location. The Japanese identify many of their emotions in the *hara*—the gut or abdomen. The Chewong of Malay group feelings and thoughts in the liver (Howell, 1981). Levy (1984) suggests that Tahitians locate emotions as arising from the intestines. Lutz (1982) suggests that the closest Ifaluk word to the English word *emotion* was *niferash*, which she translated as "our insides."

That different cultures locate emotions in different places informs us that emotions are understood differently and have different meanings for different peoples. Locating emotions in the heart is convenient and important for us in American culture, as it speaks to the importance of our feelings as something that is truly unique to ourselves, that no one else can share. By identifying emotion with the heart, we identify it with the most important biological organ necessary for survival. The fact that other cultures identify and locate emotions outside the body, such as in social relationships with others, speaks to the importance of relationships to these cultures as opposed to the individualism common to our own culture.

Cultural differences in the meaning of emotions to people and to behavior. All the differences we have discussed in the concept and meaning of emotion, labeling specific emotions, and the location of emotion point to differences in the ways different cultures attribute meanings to emotional experiences. In the United States, emotions have enormous personal meaning, perhaps because Americans typically view inner, subjective feelings as the major defining characteristic of emotion. Once emotions are defined in such a way, a major role of emotion is to inform oneself about the self. Our self-definitions, the ways we define and identify ourselves, are informed by our emotions, and they are personal, private, inner experiences.

Cultures differ in the role or meaning of emotions. Many cultures, for example, consider emotions as statements of the relationship between people and their environment, be it things in the environment or social relationships with other people. Emotions for both the Ifaluks of Micronesia (Lutz, 1982) and the Tahitians (Levy, 1984) denote statements of social relationships and the physical environment. The Japanese concept of *amae*, a central emotion in Japanese culture, specifies an interdependent relationship between two people. The very concept, definition, understanding, and meaning of emotion to people of different cultures is different from what we are accustomed to here in the United States. Certainly, when talking to someone about our feelings, we cannot simply make the assumption that others will understand us in the way we expect, even though we are speaking of something as "basic" as human emotion. And we certainly cannot assume that we know what someone else is feeling, and what it all means, just on the basis of knowing about emotions from our own limited, American perspective.

Views of emotion as social constructions and with social meaning have not been totally absent in American psychology (for example, Averill, 1980; Kemper, 1978), but they have received considerably less attention in mainstream, academic psychology than views that center on the introspection of subjective feeling states. As our world becomes increasingly more diverse, perhaps there will soon be a time when American social science embraces thoughts, ideas, and research on emotions from a social and cultural perspective.

Cultural Similarities and Differences in Emotional Expression

Many of us have interacted with people from different cultural backgrounds and have experienced uncertainty about how best to interpret the expressions of someone from another culture. At the same time, we often wonder whether our own expressions are being interpreted in the way we intend. Although we see signs of emotional expressions that are similar to ours in people from very diverse backgrounds, more often than not we see many differences as well.

Over the years, many scientists in both psychology and anthropology have attempted to address the question of just how much cultures are similar or different in their emotional expressions. Most studies have focused on facial expressions of emotion, although some studies have looked at the voice as well. Collectively, these studies demonstrate how facial expressions of emotion have both universal and culturally specific aspects.

The Universality of Facial Expressions of Emotion

Much of the impetus for cross-cultural research on facial expressions of emotion stems from the writing of Charles Darwin. Many people are familiar with Darwin's theory of evolution, outlined in his work *On the Origin of Species* (1859). Darwin suggested that humans had evolved from other, more primitive animals, such as apes and chimpanzees, and that our behaviors exist today because they have proven evolutionarily adaptive. In an accompanying volume, *The Expression of Emotion in Man and Animals* (1872), Darwin suggested that facial expressions of emotion, like other behaviors, were biologically innate and evolutionarily adaptive. Humans, Darwin argued, expressed emotions in their faces in exactly the same ways around the world, regardless of race or culture. Moreover, those facial expressions could also be seen across species, such as in gorillas.

During the early to mid-1900s, several studies were conducted to test Darwin's ideas concerning the universality of emotional expressions (for example, Triandis & Lambert, 1958; Vinacke, 1949; Vinacke & Fong, 1955). Unfortunately, many of them had methodological problems that made drawing conclusions based on them difficult (see Ekman, Friesen, & Ellsworth, 1972, for a review). At the same time, prominent anthropologists such as Margaret Mead and Ray Birdwhistell argued that facial expressions of emotion could not be universal; instead, these scholars suggested that facial expressions of emotion had to be learned, much like a language (Ekman, Friesen, & Ellsworth, 1972). Just as different cultures had different languages, they also had different facial expressions of emotion.

It was not until the 1960s, when psychologists Paul Ekman and Wallace Friesen (Ekman, 1972) and, independently, Carroll Izard (1971) conducted the first set of methodologically sound studies, that this debate was laid to rest. Spurred on by the work of Sylvan Tomkins (1962, 1963), these researchers conducted a series of studies now called the **universality studies**. Since their original publication, the findings have been replicated in many different studies in many different countries and cultures by other investigators, ensuring the robustness of their work.

Universality of facial expressions of emotion was first shown in simple judgment studies. In conjunction with Tomkins, these researchers selected photographs of facial expressions of emotion they thought portrayed universally recognizable emotions. Ekman and Friesen (Ekman, 1972) showed these photographs to observers in five different countries (the United States, Argentina, Brazil, Chile, and Japan) and asked the observers to label each of the expressions. The data revealed a level of agreement across all observers in each of the cultures in the interpretation of six emotions—anger, disgust, fear, happiness, sadness, and surprise. Izard (1971) conducted a similar study in other cultures and obtained similar results. One problem with these studies, however, was that all of the cultures included in the research were industrialized and relatively modern. It was possible, therefore, that the observers in each of the cultures could have *learned* how to interpret the facial expressions in the photographs. The fact that each of the cultures shared mass media— television, movies, magazines, and so forth—made this a distinct possibility.

To address this concern, Ekman, Sorenson, and Friesen (1969) conducted similar studies in two preliterate tribes of New Guinea. When the tribe members were asked to identify the emotions in the photographs they were shown, the data were amazingly similar to that obtained in literate, industrialized societies. But the researchers went a step further, asking different tribe members to show on their faces what they would look like if they experienced the different emotions. Photographs of these expressions were brought back to the United States and shown to American observers, none of whom had ever seen the tribe members from New Guinea. When asked to label the emotions shown on the tribe members' faces, the data were again similar to that found in previous studies.

This research involved judgment of emotion from still photographs of posed, not spontaneous, faces. There was still a question as to whether people actually display those expressions on their faces when they experience emotion. To address this question, Ekman (1972) and Friesen (1972) conducted a study in the United States and Japan, asking American and Japanese subjects to view highly stressful stimuli as their facial reactions were videotaped without their awareness. Later analysis of the video records indicated that Americans and Japanese did indeed show exactly the same types of facial expressions at the same points in time. Here again was evidence for the universality of facial expressions of emotion.

By this time, the evidence supporting the universality of facial expressions of emotion had accumulated considerably. Many other studies conducted by other investigators in different cultures have repeated these findings. Thus, it does seem that a small set of emotions—anger, disgust, fear, happiness, sadness, and surprise—are universally expressed and recognized, regardless of race or culture. The most recent research on this topic, in fact, has shown that a seventh expression, that of contempt, is also universal (Ekman & Friesen, 1986; Ekman & Heider, 1988; Matsumoto, 1992). Figure 12.1 shows these seven universal facial expressions of emotion.

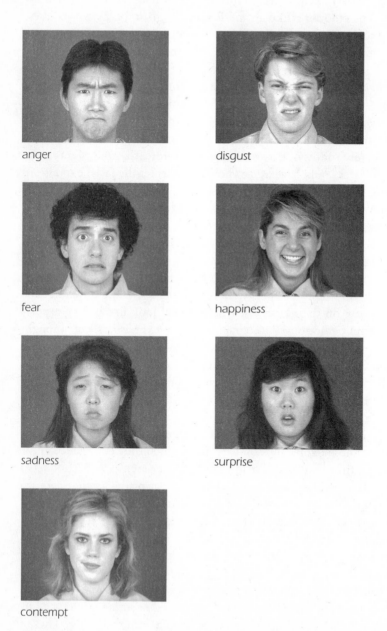

anger

disgust

fear

happiness

sadness

surprise

contempt

Figure 12.1 The seven universal facial expressions of emotion

Cultural Differences in Facial Expressions: Display Rules

Original display rule research.   The fact that a small set of facial expressions of emotion is universally expressed and recognized is often difficult for people to believe, especially those who have extensive contact with people from different cultures and whose personal experiences say otherwise. Certainly, these findings run against what scholars typically believed about facial expressions until only a few decades ago. How is it that our everyday experiences, and the experiences of well-known scholars such as Margaret Mead, can lead us to believe that the emotional expressions of people of different cultures differ like language, when the findings from so many studies say otherwise? Ekman and Friesen pondered this question many years ago and came up with the concept of **cultural display rules** to account for this discrepancy. Cultures differ, they reasoned, in the rules they have governing how these universal emotions can be expressed. These rules center on the appropriateness of displaying each of these emotions in particular social circumstances. These rules are learned early, and they dictate how the universal emotional expressions should be modified according to social situation. By the time of adulthood, these rules are automatic, having been very well practiced.

Ekman (1972) and Friesen (1972) designed a study to document the existence of these cultural display rules to produce cultural differences in emotional expressions. In the study described earlier, American and Japanese subjects were asked to view highly stressful films while their facial reactions were videotaped. That experiment actually had two conditions; the one described above was the first condition, in which subjects viewed the stimuli by themselves in a laboratory room. In a second condition, an older, higher status experimenter came into the room and asked the subjects to watch the films again. They did so, but this time while sitting in the presence of the experimenter, who observed the subjects as they watched the films. Their facial reactions were again videotaped. Analysis of the videotapes showed that the Americans in general continued to show negative feelings of disgust, fear, sadness, and anger. The Japanese, however, invariably *smiled* in these instances. These findings show how universal, biologically innate emotional expressions interact with culturally defined rules of display to produce appropriate emotional expressions in interaction. In the first condition, display rules did not operate, resulting in the Americans and the Japanese exhibiting the same expressions. In the second condition, display rules were operative, forcing the Japanese to smile in order not to offend the experimenter, despite their obvious negative feelings. These findings are especially impressive when you consider that it was the very same subjects in the second condition that produced differences as it was in the first condition that produced similarities.

Thus, it appears that our facial expressions of emotion are under the dual influence of universal, biologically innate factors and culturally specific, learned, display rules (see Figure 12.2). When an emotion is triggered, a message is sent to the facial affect program (Ekman, 1972), which stores the prototypic facial configuration information for each of the universal emotions. At the same time, however, a message is sent to the area of the brain storing learned, cultural display rules. The resulting output (that is, facial ex-

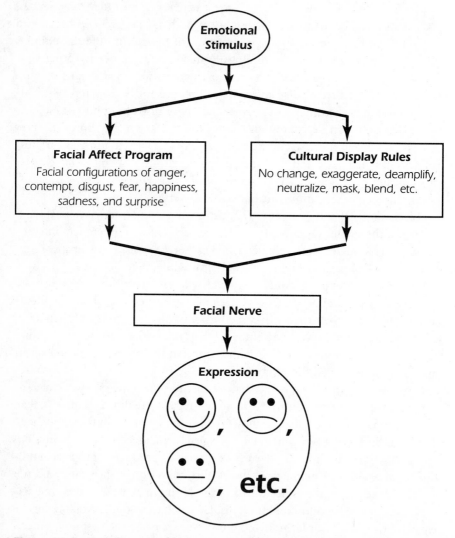

Figure 12.2 The neurocultural theory of emotional expression
Source: Adapted from P. Ekman, "Universals and Cultural Differences in Facial Expression of Emotion," in J. Cole (ed.), *Nebraska Symposium of Motivation, 1971,* vol. 19 (Lincoln, NE: University of Nebraska Press, 1972).

pression) represents the joint influence of both factors. When display rules do not modify an expression, the universal facial expression of emotion will be displayed. Depending on social circumstance, however, display rules may act to neutralize, amplify, deamplify, qualify, or mask the universal expression.

More recent research on display rules.   A number of more recent studies on cultural display rules has expanded the findings of the original study. In one of these (Matsumoto & Hearn, 1991), participants in the United States, Poland, and Hungary viewed each of the six universal emotions and rated how appropriate it would be to display them in three different social situations. The situations were (1) by yourself, (2) with others considered as "ingroup" members (for example, close friends, family members), and (3) with others considered "outgroup" (for example, in public, with casual acquaintances). The Poles and Hungarians reported that it was less appropriate to display negative emotions in ingroups and more appropriate to display positive emotions. The Poles and the Hungarians also reported that it was more appropriate to display negative emotions to outgroups. Americans, in contrast, were more likely to display negative emotions to ingroup members and positive emotions to outgroup members. Compared to Americans, the Poles also reported that the display of negative emotions was less appropriate even when they were alone.

One recent study examined ethnic differences in display rules within the United States (Matsumoto, 1993). American subjects were self-classified into one of four major ethnic categories: Caucasian, black, Asian, and Latino. These participants viewed the universal facial expressions of emotion and rated the appropriateness of displaying them in different social situations. The findings showed that Caucasians rated contempt as more appropriate than Asians, disgust as more appropriate than blacks and Latinos, fear as more appropriate than Latinos, and sadness as more appropriate than blacks and Asians. In addition, Caucasians rated the expression of emotions in public and with children as more appropriate than Latinos, with casual acquaintances as more appropriate than blacks, Asians, and Latinos, and with lower status others as more appropriate than blacks or Latinos. Interestingly, however, in another part of the experiment, blacks reported expressing anger more often than Caucasians, Asians, and Latinos.

These recent studies also point to ways people of different cultures, both in different countries and within the United States, use the universal facial expressions of emotion differently, depending on social situations. These studies show that culture exerts considerable influence over our emotional expressions via culturally learned display rules. Given that most interactions among people are social by definition, we should expect that cultural differences via display rules are operative most, if not all, of the time. To understand the emotional expressions of people of different cultures, we must first understand what universal bases underlie those expressions, and second, what kinds of cultural display rules are operating when we interact with them.

Cultural Similarity and Diversity in Other Aspects of Emotion

Perceiving Emotions

Do cultures influence the ways we perceive the emotions of others? On one hand, the fact that some facial expressions of emotion are universal suggests that all people, regardless of culture or race, perceive emotions in exactly the same ways. On the other hand, the existence of cultural display rules suggests that people of different cultures learn different ways to perceive emotions in others. A number of studies have been conducted on this topic over the years, and they suggest that, like emotional expression, the perception of emotion also has universal, pancultural elements as well as culturally specific aspects.

The universality of emotion recognition.   Much of the research showing that facial expressions of emotion can be universally recognized comes from the judgment studies reported earlier documenting the universal expression of emotion. When shown photographs of the universal facial emotions, observers in all countries and cultures studied agreed on what emotion was being portrayed in the expressions, at quite high levels across cultures (Ekman, 1972; Ekman & Friesen, 1971; Ekman, Sorenson, & Friesen, 1969; Izard, 1971).

Many studies conducted since then have repeated the original findings (see Matsumoto, Wallbott, & Scherer, 1987, for a review). In one of the more recent studies, Ekman et al. (1987) asked observers in ten different cultures to view photographs depicting each of the six universal emotions. The judges not only labeled each emotion by selecting an emotion word from a predetermined list but also rated how intensely they perceived the emotion to be expressed. The judges in all ten cultures agreed on what emotion was being displayed, highlighting the universality of recognition. In addition, observers in each culture gave the strongest intensity ratings to the emotions that corresponded with the facial expressions they were judging. The findings from these studies have shown unequivocally that people of all cultures can recognize the universal facial expressions of emotion.

Cultural differences in emotion perception.   Despite the fact that facial expressions of emotion can be universally recognized, a number of recent studies have shown ways people of different cultures can differ from each other in their perceptions. One of the first studies to show that cultures differed in their perceptions was Ekman et al.'s (1987) study. In that study, although each of the cultures gave the universal emotion the highest intensity rating, the observers in the ten cultures differed as to exactly *how strongly* they rated the expression. Some cultures rated some emotions very strongly, while other cultures did not. Follow-up tests conducted by Ekman et al. (1987) showed that Asian cultures rated the emotions less intensely than did non-Asian cultures. In a later study, Matsumoto and Ekman (1989) replicated these findings and showed that the Asian cultures rated the faces less strongly than did American observers, regardless of whether they viewed an Asian or a Caucasian face.

People of different ethnic backgrounds within the United States also appear to perceive emotions differently. In Matsumoto's (1993) study of Caucasian, black, Asian, and Latino observers, participants viewed examples of the universal facial expressions of emotion and made a scalar rating of how intensely they perceived each face. Blacks tended to perceive anger and fear more intensely than Asians; disgust more intensely than Caucasians and Asians; Caucasian faces more intensely than did Caucasians and Asians; and female expressions more intensely than did Asians. Latinos also perceived fear more intensely than Asians.

Culture also influences the labeling of emotion. As mentioned earlier, there is general agreement across cultures on which emotions are being displayed in a facial expression; indeed, this is the basis of universality. But there is some variability in the *level* of agreement across cultures (Matsumoto, 1989, 1992). For example, even though most of the judges in Indonesia, Japan, France, Brazil, and the United States may agree that a face expresses an emotion (for example, fear), there are differences across the cultures in exactly what percent of the judges in each culture agree on that judgment (90% of the judges in the United States, Brazil, and France may label the expression as fear, whereas only 70% of the judges in Japan and Indonesia may label it as fear).

Other studies tell us how culture affects the perception and interpretation of emotion. One study showed cultural differences between American and Japanese children as young as 3 years in labeling emotions from nonverbal vocal cues (Matsumoto & Kishimoto, 1983). Other studies have reported cultural differences in the interpretation of other nonverbal behaviors, such as postures (Kudoh & Matsumoto, 1985; Matsumoto & Kudoh, 1987). Finally, a small number of studies suggest that people perceive emotions more accurately when judging others of the same race as themselves, as opposed to judging others of different races (Shimoda, Argyle, & Ricci Bitti, 1978; Wolfgang & Cohen, 1988).

How do cultures influence the perception and interpretation of emotion? Some scholars believe that cultures have rules that govern the perception of emotion, much like rules that govern their expression (that is, display rules). Rules governing the interpretation and perception of emotion are called **decoding rules** (Buck, 1984). These are learned, culturally based rules that shape how people of each culture view and interpret the emotional expressions of others. Like display rules, these rules are learned early in life and sufficiently well so that we are not totally conscious of their influence. Our judgments and interpretations of the emotional expressions of others are under the dual influence of a universal, pancultural element and a learned, culturally specific decoding rules aspect (see Figure 12.3).

Decoding rules are a cultural filter that affects how we perceive the emotional expressions of others. Because these rules are learned early in life, they are very well practiced by adulthood. They operate when we interact with others, and because they are so well practiced we don't know that they're there.

Experiencing Emotions

When people of different cultures feel an emotion, do they experience it in the same or different ways? This question has been addressed in the last few years by several major research programs that collectively have involved thousands of respondents in more than 30 different countries and cultures around the world (Scherer, Summerfield, & Wallbott, 1986; Wallbott & Scherer, 1986). Participants were asked such questions as how long they experienced the emotions, how strongly, how often they occurred, what brought them about (**emotion antecedents**), what they thought about the antecedents (cognitive evaluations of the antecedents), and any physiological changes they may have noticed in themselves. As with much of the research described in this chapter, these studies also show that culture affects the experience of emotions.

The frequency, intensity, and duration of emotion.   Although it is easy to believe that people around the world experience different emotions at about the same frequency, they do not. Scherer, Matsumoto, Wallbott, and Kudoh (1988) tested differences between Europeans, Americans, and Japanese on the frequency of their emotional experiences. The Japanese reported experienc-

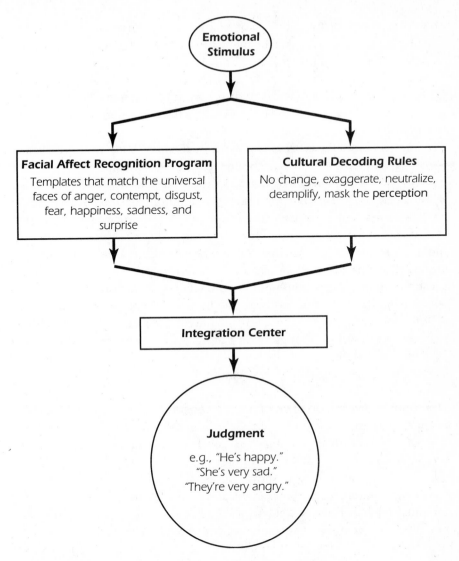

Figure 12.3 A neurocultural theory of emotional perception

ing all emotions—joy, sadness, fear, and anger—more often than did either the Americans or the Europeans. The Americans, in turn, reported experiencing joy and anger more often than did the Europeans. People from different cultures also reported that they experienced their emotions at different strengths and for different lengths of time. Americans reported feeling their emotions for longer durations and at greater intensities than did the Europeans or the Japanese.

The antecedents of emotion.   For many years, scholars have wondered whether emotions are triggered by the same or different types of events across cultures. Some writers (for example, Boucher, 1979) have suggested that the antecedents of emotion have to be similar across cultures because emotions themselves are universal. Recent studies, however, suggest considerable cultural differences in not only the types of events that trigger emotions but also the *degree* to which they bring forth emotions.

Cultural events, the birth of a new family member, body-centered "basic pleasures," and achievement-related situations were more important antecedents of joy for Europeans and Americans than for the Japanese. Death of family members or close friends, physical separation from loved ones, and world news were more frequent triggers of sadness for the Europeans and Americans than for the Japanese. Problems in relationships, however, produced more sadness for the Japanese than for Americans or Europeans. Strangers and achievement-related situations elicited more fear for Americans, while novel situations, traffic, and relationships were more frequent elicitors of fear for the Japanese. Finally, situations involving strangers were more frequent elicitors of anger for the Japanese but not for the Americans or Europeans. Situations involving relationships brought about more anger for Americans than for Japanese. These findings make it clear that the same type of situation or event will not necessarily trigger the same emotion in people across cultures.

The cognitive evaluation of emotion antecedents.   How do people in different cultures think about or evaluate the events that trigger their emotions? Do emotions and their eliciting situations have commonalities across cultures? Or do people in different cultures think about emotion antecedents differently? Research findings show considerable cultural differences in the ways people in different cultures evaluate emotion-eliciting situations (Matsumoto, Kudoh, Scherer, & Wallbott, 1988). For example, cultural differences in self-esteem were noted as resulting from emotion-eliciting events; emotions had a more positive effect on self-esteem and self-confidence for Americans than they did for the Japanese. There were also cultural differences in attributions of causality of emotions, with Americans attributing the cause of sadness-producing events to others, and Japanese attributing the cause of sadness to themselves. Americans are also more likely to attribute the causes of joy, fear, and shame to other people, whereas the Japanese tend to attribute the causes of these emotions to chance or fate. Japanese believe more than Americans do that no action or behavior is necessary after an emotion is elicited. For emotions such as fear, more Americans than Japanese believe they can do something to influence the situation positively. For anger and disgust, more Americans believe they are powerless and dominated by the event and its consequences. For shame and guilt, more Japanese than Americans pretended that nothing had happened and tried to think of something else.

These findings clearly show that people of different cultures think differently about the events and situations that trigger their emotions. The findings also show that emotions have different effects on self-esteem, confidence, and behavior. We cannot take for granted that emotions mean the same thing for all people, or that they will be thought about in the same ways.

The physiological sensations of emotion.   No study has tested cultural differences in actual physiological reactions associated with emotion, but several studies have tested cultural differences in physiological sensations and behavioral reactions *reported* by people of different cultures (Matsumoto et al., 1988; Scherer et al., 1988). These studies demonstrate interesting differences in the ways people of different cultures experience their emotions physiologically.

Japanese respondents on the whole reported fewer hand and arm gestures, whole body movements, and vocal and facial reactions to the emotions than did Americans or Europeans. Americans reported the highest degree of expressivity in both facial and vocal reactions. Americans and Europeans also reported many more physiological sensations than did the Japanese. These sensations included changes in temperature (becoming flushed, hot), cardiovascular changes (heart racing, pulse changing), and gastric disturbances (stomach problems).

We can safely conclude that cultural backgrounds substantially affect our subjective experiences of emotion in many ways. From the types of events that trigger emotion to the ways our bodies react to these events, culture plays a large role in helping to mold and create our experiences.

Conclusion

Emotions, the most private, personal, and arguably the most important aspects of our lives, give life events meaning. They tell us what we like and what we don't, what is good and bad for us. They enrich our lives, giving color and meaning to events and the world around us. They tell us who we are and how we are faring with others. Emotion is the invisible glue that binds us with the rest of the world, whether it be events around us or people. Emotions play such a central role in our lives that no wonder culture, as that invisible shaper of experiences, shapes and molds our emotional world around us. Although we may be born with certain innate abilities, such as the capacity to express and perceive emotions in our faces and to feel emotions, culture helps to shape when, where, and how we can express, perceive, and feel those emotions. Culture creates the meaning of emotions for us, whether we understand our emotions as a totally personal, private, and individual experience or as an interpersonal, public, collective experience with others.

As scientists continue to explore the roles and contributions of culture to human emotion, we will undoubtedly uncover more and more bases by which culture influences this basic human process. Theories incorporating culture have already begun to infiltrate the scientific world of emotion (for example, Matsumoto, 1991) and will continue to have an impact on research and science on emotions for years to come. Future research promises increases in not only the number but also the complexity of findings. The sociocultural diversity of people across the world and within our own country ensures that this increase will occur.

If nothing else, at least emotions are a universal process that binds all peoples together, regardless of race, culture, ethnicity, or gender. As we continue our study of human feelings and emotions across cultures, perhaps it is most important to recognize how these boundaries mold our emotions. Although we all have emotions, they mean different things to different people and are experienced, expressed, and perceived in different ways. One of our first tasks in learning about emotions across cultures is to recognize and respect those differences. But an equally important task is to recognize our similarities as well.

Glossary

cultural display rules   Culturally prescribed rules that govern how universal emotions can be expressed. These rules center on the appropriateness of displaying emotion, depending on social circumstances. Learned by people early in their lives, they dictate how the universal emotional expressions should be modified according to social situation. By adulthood, these rules are quite automatic, having been very well practiced.

decoding rules   Rules that govern the interpretation and perception of emotion. These are learned, culturally based rules that shape how people of each culture view and interpret the emotional expressions of others.

emotion antecedents   The events or situations that elicit an emotion.

introspection   The process of looking inside yourself.

subjective experience of emotion   An individual's inner feelings or experiences of an emotion.

universality studies   A series of studies conducted by Ekman and Friesen and Izard that demonstrated the pancultural universality of facial expressions of emotion.

13

Culture and Language

The Relationship Between Culture,
Language, and Worldview

One of the most important aspects of our behavior is our ability to communicate with others. Communication is important in our everyday lives, but it is also important for the development, maintenance, and transmission of culture. The definition of culture includes communication of cultural attitudes, values, and beliefs from one generation to the next. Thus, communication plays a special role in our understanding of culture and cultural influences on behavior.

When we think of communication in general, the first and perhaps most salient aspect of communication that comes to mind is verbal language. Words and language play a major role in our communication processes. Our verbal language, whether English or French or German or Chinese or Indonesian, is extremely important to our ability to communicate. People place great emphasis on the words we use and how we use them. Mastery of verbal language is an important part of any successful communication, and we all tend to make judgments of people based on their level of mastery of their particular language. Of course, verbal language is not the only aspect of communication. Another large and important world of communication is nonverbal communication, including facial expressions, tone of voice, posture, dress, distance, and the like. All of these nonverbal behaviors are discussed more fully in Chapter 14.

In this chapter, I will focus on the relationship between culture and language. Culture and language share an intimate relationship. Culture influences the structure and functional use of language, and as such, language can be thought of as the result or manifestation of culture. Language also influences and reinforces our cultural values and worldview, thus feeding back onto them. The cyclical nature of the relationship between culture and language suggests that no complete understanding of culture can be obtained without understanding the language, and vice versa. In this chapter, we will explore the relationship between culture and the structure of language. Then, we will examine an important line of reasoning in cross-cultural psychology and anthropology known as the Sapir-Whorf hypothesis. This hypothesis suggests that language helps to structure our worldview and is crucial to the culture-language relationship. We will look at the special case of bilingualism as it affects behavior and personality and examine cultural similarities and differences in language acquisition. I will begin with some basic reflections about culture and language.

Some Thoughts about Culture and Language

Language is a very interesting part of our lives. Language can be thought of as a manifestation and product of a culture. American English, its words and how we use them, is a reflection of American culture. Surely, if we examine the structure and function of American English, we will see many parallels to important aspects of American culture. Likewise, this is true for any language and culture we examine.

Examining languages across cultures is an important and valuable exercise. It serves as a bridge to understanding other cultures, and it helps us gain a better understanding and appreciation of our own culture. Many of us have heard that the Eskimo language contains more words for snow than exist in the English language. Whorf (1956) was the first to point this out; he indicated that the Eskimo language actually has three words for snow while the English language contains a single word, *snow*, to describe all three types of Eskimo snow. Many words in other cultures and languages do not exist in the English language. In Chapter 12, many words were introduced describing emotional states that exist in other cultures but not in American English. The German word *schadenfreude* is one.

When we translate a word in English into its literal equivalent in another language, we often think the words mean the same. While it is most certainly the case that many words have generally the same meanings, it is also true that many words in different languages have different nuances and connotations than what we would expect in American English. Even common words for breaking, cutting, eating, and drinking can have entirely different connotations and nuances and will be used in different contexts in other cultures (Suzuki, 1978). Moreover, the associations people of different cultures have to the same word may be different. When considering the relationship between words in your own language and the same translation equivalents in another, it is probably best not to consider those translations as exact equivalents. If we take into account all the meanings of a word, it would be very difficult to find words in different languages that have exactly the same meaning, nuance, connotation, and associations, even if they are translation equivalents.

These observations make it clear that people of different cultures structure the world around them differently, at least in the language they use to describe that world. Of course, this is not only true when comparing different languages across cultures but also when comparing different people within the same culture who speak the same language. Two people using the same language can, and often do, use the same words with different meanings and in different ways. Language differences within a culture also contribute to possible conflicts within a culture. But the differences in language structure and use within a culture are probably less than those between cultures.

It is clear that people of different cultures "slice up" their worlds differently via their languages, but are these differences so pervasive that they also see the same things differently? Do Americans and Eskimos actually see, think, and feel about snow differently? Or do they see exactly the same thing but just categorize it differently? Studies examining this and related questions suggest that language reflects a genuine difference in overall worldview and is not just a matter of categorization.

Culture and the Structure of Language: The Case of Self- and Other-Referents

The relationship between culture and language can be seen in many different aspects of language, including its structure and function. In this section, I will describe how one aspect of language, self-referents, exemplifies the cyclical relationship between language and culture. In American English, we generally use one of two words, and their derivatives, to describe ourselves when talking to others—*I* and *we*. We use these words irrespective of whom we are talking to or what we are talking about. If we are talking to a university professor, we use the word *I* to refer to ourselves. If we are talking to our parents, we use the same word *I*. And we use the same word *I* when referring to ourselves with friends, family, neighbors, acquaintances, bosses, or subordinates. The word *I* is an extremely useful word for referring to ourselves in the American English language. Likewise, we generally use a single word in English to refer to another person—*you*. In conversation with our parents, bosses, friends, lovers, strangers, and just about anyone, we say "you" or one of its derivatives to refer to the other person directly. Like *I, you* is another extremely useful word in English.

The Japanese language may be the most extreme opposite to American English in terms of self-referents. Japanese certainly has linguistic equivalents of the English words *I* and *we* (for example, *watashi* and *watashi-tachi*, respectively). But these words are used much less frequently in the Japanese language. Likewise, the Japanese language has linguistic equivalents of the English *you* (for example, *anata*). But there is a vast difference between the English and Japanese languages with regard to self- and other-referents. In Japanese, what you call yourself and others is totally dependent on the relationship between you and the other person. Often, the decision about what is appropriate to call yourself and another person is dependent on the status differential between the two people. For example, if you are of a higher status than the other person, in Japan you would refer to yourself by position or role rather than by the English equivalent of *I*. In Japan, teachers use the word *teacher* to refer to themselves when talking to students. Doctors may use the term *doctor,* and parents use the word *mother* or *father* when referring to themselves when speaking to their children.

In the Japanese language, if you are of a lower status than the person to whom you are speaking, you refer to yourself via a pronoun equivalent of *I*. There are several pronoun equivalents of *I* in Japanese, such as *watashi*, *watakushi*, *boku*, and *ore*. The use of these different terms for *I* depends on your sex (women cannot say *boku* or *ore*), degree of politeness, and degree of familiarity with the other person. When speaking to someone of higher status, for example, people generally use *watashi* to refer to themselves. When speaking to friends or colleagues, men usually refer to themselves as *boku* or *ore*.

Likewise, if you are speaking to someone of higher status, you generally refer to that person by role or title. When speaking to your teachers, you refer to them as *teacher,* even when talking directly with them. You would call your boss by his or her title, such as *section chief* or *president*. You would definitely not use a personal pronoun such as our English *you* in referring to a person of higher status. When referring to a person of lower status, you would generally use a personal pronoun or the person's actual name. Like personal pronouns for *I*, the Japanese language contains several pronouns for *you*. These include *anata*, *omae*, and *kimi*. Again, the appropriate use of each depends on the relationship; generally, *omae* and *kimi* are used when referring to someone of lower status than you or to someone very familiar and intimate with you. Indeed, the Japanese language system of self- and other-referents is very complicated, especially when compared to American English (see Figure 13.1).

The difference between the English and Japanese languages reflects important cultural differences between the two cultures as well. In the Japanese culture, language, mannerisms, and other aspects of behavior must be modified according to the relationship and context under which the communication is occurring. The most important dimensions along which behavior and language are differentiated in Japan are status and group orientation. All aspects of behavior differ depending on whether one person is higher or lower in status than the other person in the conversation. Also, behavior and

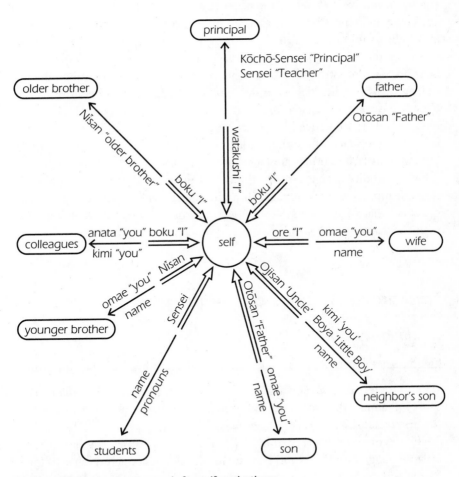

Figure 13.1 Japanese words for self and others

Source: Words in Context by Takao Suzuki, published by Kodansha International Ltd. Copyright © 1973 by Takao Suzuki. English translation copyright © 1978 by Kodansha International Ltd. Reprinted by permission. All rights reserved.

language differ depending on whether the other person is a member of your ingroup or not. Thus, the appropriate choice of self- and other-referents in the Japanese language reflects important aspects of Japanese culture.

Self- and other-referents in American English also reflect important aspects of the American culture. American culture in general places less emphasis on status differences between people, or whether the person with whom you are interacting is an ingroup member or not. American culture views each and every individual as a separate, unique, and independent person. Because American culture views individuals as important, not context or status, people are people are people, regardless of when or where we are talking with them. Thus, we can use *I* to refer to ourselves in almost any conversation, and *you* to refer to the other person.

These differences reflect important differences between cultures, and they also help to reinforce culture. By using the complex system of self- and other-referents in the Japanese language, a person's system of thought and behavior becomes structured over time to reflect the culture. Through the use of language, an individual is transformed into an agent of the culture. As this occurs, the feelings, associations, connotations, and nuances of language influence and are influenced by the culture. Over time, an individual embodies the very essence of culture via language. This is true for Japanese as well as English as well as other languages of other cultures.

Many studies have examined the components of language and the direct relationship between language, thought, and behavior. These studies also speak to what I have been describing and form the basis for what is known as the Sapir-Whorf hypothesis.

Traditional Theories of Language

Language Features

Linguists have typically tried to describe language using five critical features:

1. The **lexicon**, or vocabulary, refers to the words contained in a language. For example, the words *tree, eat, how,* and *slowly* are each part of the English lexicon.
2. The **syntax and grammar** of a language refer to the system of rules governing word forms and how words should be strung together to form meaningful utterances. For example, English has a grammatical rule that says we add *s* to the end of many words to indicate plurality (*cat* becomes *cats*). And English has a syntactic rule that we place adjectives before most nouns, not after (for example, small dog, not dog small).

3. **Phonology** refers to the system of rules governing how words should sound (pronunciation) in a given language. For instance, in English, we don't pronounce *new* the same as *sew*.
4. **Semantics** refers to what words mean. *Table* refers to a physical object that has four legs and has a flat horizontal surface.
5. **Pragmatics** refers to the system of rules governing how language is used and understood in given social contexts. For example, the statement "it is cold" could be interpreted as a request to close a window or as a statement of fact about the temperature. How it's interpreted may depend on the social and environmental context.

Linguists use two other concepts to help explain the structure of language. **Phonemes** are the smallest and most basic units of *sound* in a language, and **morphemes** are the smallest and most basic units of *meaning* in a language. Accordingly, phonemes form the base of a language hierarchy, in which language gains in increasing complexity as sounds gain meaning, which in turn produces words, which are strung together in phrases and, finally, sentences.

One of the most important and long-lasting debates in studies of language and behavior is over the relationship between the kind of language we speak and the kinds of thought processes we have. This is often referred to as the **Sapir-Whorf hypothesis**. It is particularly important to the cross-cultural study of language because each culture is associated with a given language as a vehicle for its expression. How does culture influence language? And how does language influence culture?

The Sapir-Whorf Hypothesis

The Sapir-Whorf hypothesis suggests that speakers of different languages think differently, and they do so because of the differences in their languages. Because different cultures typically have different languages, the Sapir-Whorf hypothesis is especially important for understanding cultural differences (and similarities) in thought and behavior as a function of language.

Before we examine this question further, let's reflect for just a moment on exactly what this issue is about and its potential implications. If the Sapir-Whorf hypothesis is correct, it suggests that people of different cultures think differently, just by the very nature, structure, and function of their language. Their thought processes, their associations, their ways of interpreting the world—even the same events we perceive—may be different because they speak a different language and this language has helped shape their thought patterns. This hypothesis also suggests that people who speak more than one language may actually have different thought patterns when speaking different languages.

Many studies have looked at language cognition issues since Edward Sapir and Benjamin Whorf proposed their hypothesis earlier this century. These are often referred to as studies of the Sapir–Whorf hypothesis, as if there were only one such hypothesis. Actually, there are several different Sapir–Whorf hypotheses. In 1960, Joshua Fishman published a comprehensive breakdown of the most important ways the Sapir–Whorf hypothesis has been discussed (see Table 13.1). In his description, these different approaches are ordered in increasing levels of complexity. Two factors determine the level at which a given version of the hypothesis might fall. The first factor relates to the particular aspect of language that is of interest, for example, the lexicon or the grammar. The second factor relates to the cognitive behavior of the speakers of a given language, for example, cultural themes or nonlinguistic data such as a decision-making task. Of the four levels, Level 1 is the least complex; Level 4 is the most complex. Both Levels 3 and 4 are actually closer to Whorf's original ideas in that they concern the grammar or syntax of language as opposed to its lexicon. In reviewing the literature on the Sapir–Whorf hypothesis, it is extremely important to keep in mind exactly which level of the hypothesis is being tested.

Table 13.1   Fishman's Sapir-Whorf Hypothesis Schema

Data of Language Characteristics	Data of Cognitive Behavior	
	Linguistic Data	Nonlinguistic Data
Lexical/Semantic	Level 1*	Level 2
Grammatical	Level 3	Level 4**

* Least sophisticated
** Most sophisticated

Cross-Cultural Research on the Sapir-Whorf Hypothesis

In one of the earliest language studies, Carroll and Casagrande (1958) compared Navajo and English speakers. They examined the relationship between the system of shape classification in the Navajo language and the amount of attention children pay to shape when classifying objects. The Navajo language has the interesting grammatical feature that certain verbs of handling (for example, "to pick up," "to drop") require special linguistic forms depending on what kind of object is being handled. There are 11 such linguistic forms describing different shapes. For example, there is a form for round spherical objects, one for round thin objects, one for long flexible things, and so forth.

Carroll and Casagrande (1958) noted how much more complex this linguistic feature is in Navajo than it is in English. They suggested that such linguistic features might play a role in influencing cognitive processes. In their experiment, they compared Navajo- and English-dominant children to see how often they used shape, form, or type of material to categorize objects. The Navajo-dominant children were significantly more likely to carry out this task on the basis of shape than were the English-dominant children. In that same study, Carroll and Casagrande (1958) also reported that the performance of low-income African American English-speaking children was similar to that of the Anglo children. This is particularly important since the African American children, unlike the white children, were not accustomed to blocks and form-board toys. The researchers' finding provided evidence supporting the idea that the language we speak may influence the kind of thoughts we have. This suggests that language may act in a mediating role; that is, where prior nonlinguistic experience does not intervene, language may determine the ways children conceive of some aspects of their world. Language seems to be one of several factors that can influence the way we think.

Carroll and Casagrande's study is one of the few to investigate the Sapir-Whorf hypothesis at Fishman's Level 3 or 4. In contrast, a considerable amount of research compares lexical differences and linguistic behavior (Fishman's Level 1) or nonlinguistic behavior (Fishman's Level 2). Most of this research is at Level 2, which typically has compared lexical differences with nonlinguistic behaviors. When such comparisons have shown differences, language is assumed to have caused these differences.

Sapir-Whorf and the language of color.   Most of the early work in this area focused on color perception. The position of many investigators was stated clearly more than 30 years ago:

> The continuous gradation of color which exists in nature is represented in language by a series of discrete categories. . . . There is nothing inherent either in the spectrum or the human perception of it which would compel its division in this way. The specific method of division is part of the structure of English. (Gleason, 1961, p. 4)

Studies of language and color perception have typically looked at how colors are categorized and how they are named in different languages. Brown and Lenneberg (1954) found a positive relationship between the codability of a color and the accuracy with which a color could be remembered in a memory task. In their study, codability was defined as how well speakers of English agreed on a name for a given color, the length of the name, and the time taken to name a color. If we describe this experiment in terms of Fishman's outline of the Sapir–Whorf hypothesis, color is the nonlinguistic domain, memory is the nonlinguistic behavior, and semantic aspects of language are the linguistic behaviors. Brown and Lenneberg's results lent support to the Sapir–Whorf hypothesis.

Berlin and Kay (1969) examined 78 languages and found that 11 basic color terms form a universal hierarchy. Some languages, like English and German, use all 11 terms, while others, like the Dani (New Guinea), use as few as two. Further, they noticed there was an evolutionary order in which languages encode these universal categories. For example, if a language is known to have three color terms, we know the three terms describe black, white, and red. This hierarchy of color names in human language is a follows:

1. All languages contain terms for white and black.
2. If a language contains three terms, it also contains a term for red.
3. If a language contains four terms, it also contains a term for either green or yellow (but not both).
4. If a language contains five terms, it contains terms for both green and yellow.
5. If a language contains six terms, it also contains a term for blue.
6. If a language contains seven terms, it also contains a term for brown.
7. If a language contains eight or more terms, it also contains a term for purple, pink, orange, gray, or some combination or these.

To test such claims as Gleason's, Berlin and Kay (1969) undertook a study of the distribution of color terms in 20 languages. They asked international university students in the United States to list the "basic" color terms in each of their native languages. They then asked these foreign students to identify from an array of glass color chips the most typical or best examples of a basic color term the researchers specified. Berlin and Kay (1969) found a limited number of basic color terms in any language. They also found that the color chips chosen as best examples of these basic terms tended to fall in clusters they termed *focal points*. In languages that had a basic term for bluish colors, the best example of the color was found to be the same "focal blue" for speakers of all the languages. Berlin and Kay's findings suggested that people in different cultures perceive colors in much the same way despite radical differences in their languages. Many people began to doubt the validity of the Sapir–Whorf hypothesis, because it didn't seem to apply in the perceptual domain of color.

Berlin and Kay's findings were later confirmed by a series of experiments conducted by Rosch. In her experiments, Rosch (for example, 1973) set out to test just how culturally universal these focal points were. She compared two languages that differed markedly in the number of basic color terms: English, with multiple color terms, and Dani, which has only two color terms. Dani is the language spoken by a stone-age tribe living in the highlands of Irian Jaya, Indonesian New Guinea. One color term, *mili,* was found to include both "dark" and "cold" colors (for example, black, green, and blue), while the second color term, *mola,* included both "light" and "warm" colors (for example, white, red, and yellow). Rosch also explored the relationship between language and memory. She argued that if the Whorfian position were correct, Dani's lack of a rich color lexicon would inhibit Dani speakers' ability to discriminate and remember colors. As it happened, Heider and Oliver (1972) found that Dani speakers did not confuse color categories any more than did speakers of English. Nor did Dani speakers perform differently from English speakers on memory tasks.

The way we perceive color is determined to a significant degree by our biological makeup and, in particular, our biological visual system. This system is the same across human cultures. De Valois and his associates (De Valois, Abramov, & Jacobs, 1966; De Valois & Jacobs, 1968) studied a species of monkey with a visual system similar to that of humans. They suggested that we have cells that are only stimulated by two colors (red + green, and blue + yellow) and that, at any given moment, these cells can only be stimulated by one of these two colors. For example, our red + green cells can respond to red or to green, but not to both simultaneously. This is rather interesting because many people have noticed that while it is possible to mix red and green, it is not possible for humans to perceive such combinations in the same way we perceive a mixture of blue and green as turquoise or a mixture of red and blue as purple. Thus, "reddish green" is a perceptual as well as a semantic impossibility.

It's clear that our biology is very important in how we perceive colors. Given this situation, it would be surprising to find language-based differences in color perception. But we cannot dismiss the Sapir-Whorf hypothesis just because language seems to have little influence on the way we perceive colors. Indeed, if we look at other areas of human behavior, we find significant evidence to support the Sapir-Whorf hypothesis.

Sapir-Whorf and the language of causality. One area of human behavior that appears susceptible to Whorfian effects is that of causality, or how we explain the reasons things happen the way they do. Niyekawa-Howard (1968) studied the relationship between Japanese grammar and Japanese perceptions of what causes events to happen. Traditionally, Japanese has an interesting passive form. This grammatical form includes the following meaning: Because the subject of the sentence "was caused to" take the action expressed by the main verb, he is not responsible for the act nor the outcome. Of course, we can convey this information in English but only by using cumbersome extra words and phrases. In contrast, such meaning is conveyed by this Japanese passive form in a subtle way. Niyekawa-Howard found that because of the frequency with which native speakers of Japanese are confronted with this passive form, they are more likely than English speakers to attribute responsibility to others even when the outcome is positive.

Sapir-Whorf and other aspects of language. More evidence to support the Sapir-Whorf hypothesis was obtained by Bloom's (1981) study reporting that Chinese speakers were less likely than English speakers to give hypothetical interpretations to a hypothetical story. He interpreted these results as constituting strong evidence for the structure of language as a mediator of cognitive processes because English and Chinese differ in how they convey hypothetical meaning. For example, in English, we do this by using the subjunctive tense (if I were you, not if I am you). Chinese has no subjunctive in the sense of a mandatory marking in each verb (the grammatical Chinese equivalent of the above English example would roughly be translated "be if I am you"). Although Au (1983, 1984) has contested Bloom's interpretation of his data, Bloom's study remains as evidence for the importance of the link between language grammar and human cognition.

Yet another source of support for the Sapir-Whorf hypothesis is Kay and Kempton's (1984) finding that at least some differences in cognition depend on differences in linguistic structure. They compared the thought processes of speakers of English with those of speakers of Tarahumara, a language indigenous to the Yucatán peninsula in Mexico that does not distinguish between blue and green. They had subjects complete two nonlinguistic tasks, both of which involved choosing from a number of color chips the color that was the "most different" from the others. They found that color discrimination was better when subjects could use a naming strategy, demonstrating clearly that linguistic differences can affect the performance of a nonlinguistic task.

In summary, the best-studied area is lexical differences between languages. The lexicon seems to be only minimally related to our thought processes, which may account for some skepticism about the Sapir-Whorf hypothesis. A less well-studied area, that of syntactic and grammatical differences between languages, seems to provide stronger evidence for the claim that language influences cognition. Perhaps the strongest evidence will be found in future studies of how the pragmatic systems of different languages influence speakers' thought processes. Take the case of Javanese, for example. This Indonesian language has an elaborate system of forms of address depending on the social status, age, and sex of the person being spoken to. Does speaking the Javanese language influence Javanese people to be more precise in their thinking about social and status differences between people than speakers of English are? Japanese has a similarly complex system of honorifics. Hunt and Agnoli (1991) suggest that such a "Whorfian" process might be operating with Japanese speakers as compared with speakers of English.

In this section, I have referred to the Sapir-Whorf hypothesis as it might relate to monolingual speakers of a given language. This is primarily because most, if not all, of the research on this issue has been limited to a comparison of monolingual populations. What might the Sapir-Whorf hypothesis imply about the behavior of bilingual or multilingual populations? One implication might be that the behavior of bilingual individuals would depend on the language that is in current use. This is not strictly a "Whorfian" issue, because it does not necessarily imply that it is any aspect of a bilingual's two languages that causes language-related changes in bilingual behavior (such as their lexical, syntactic/grammatical, semantic, phonological, or pragmatic systems). It is simply that when we learn a language we learn it in the context of a culture. When bilingual immigrants learn two languages, they often do so in the context of two cultures. So the point here is simply that each language may access a different set of cultural values.

Language and Behavior:
The Special Case of Bilingualism

Earlier in this century, many Americans thought that knowledge of more than one language should be avoided. It was commonly believed that humans have limited "room" to store language; if you learn "too much" language, you take "space" away from other functions such as intelligence. We now know that such notions are wrong; there is no evidence that bilinguals do worse on intellectual (or other) tasks. On the contrary, there is evidence that knowledge of more than one language may improve cognitive flexibility.

Until now, I have referred to "speakers of a language" as if most people speak just one language. Despite the cultural diversity in the United States, we might easily assume both that this is true and that bilingualism is primarily a minority issue. In fact, on a global level, the opposite is true; monolinguals are a minority. The majority of the inhabitants of our global village speak more than one language.

Besides being an issue of considerable global importance, the United States has a large (and growing) number of people who regularly use both English and another language. In many cases this "other" language is their native tongue. Many of these people have come to this country from elsewhere. Such bilingual immigrants pose an especially interesting issue in terms of the psychology of language, because their two languages are often associated with two different cultural systems. Moreover, many bilinguals report that they think and feel differently depending on their current linguistic context. This may be thought of as having a different sense of self, depending on which language is being used.

Can we assume that bilinguals have access, through their two languages, to two culturally different modes of thought? If so, does this imply the existence of two different personalities within the same individual, each associated with one of the bilingual's two languages? Ervin (1964) compared responses from a sample of English and French bilinguals to pictures from the Thematic Apperception Test (a common test used in many cross-cultural studies). The subjects told their stories in response to the pictures once in English and then another time in French. Ervin found that subjects demonstrated more aggression, autonomy, and withdrawal in French than they did in English, and only females demonstrated a greater need for achievement in English than in French. In Ervin's view, these differences were due to the higher value French culture places on verbal prowess in the former case and to greater sex role differences in the latter case.

What about immigrants to the United States? How might the issue of bilingualism and personality be important? Consider this example: a Chinese-English bilingual raised in a monolingual, Chinese-speaking home and who learned English naturalistically only after migrating to the United States from China at 8 years of age. She is a 20-year-old college student, lives with her parents, and has used Chinese as the only language in the home. English is used at school and with most of her peers. We might predict that when using Chinese she would be likely to behave in ways appropriate to Chinese cultural norms in the home. In English, however, she might be more likely to behave in ways that are shifted away from the Chinese norm to that of the Anglo-American norm. A "Whorfian" view might account for such language-related behavioral differences in terms of the pragmatic systems of Chinese and English (as well as other linguistic differences). There are at least two other explanations for the mechanisms that underlie such language-related shifts in personality. These are called the culture–affiliation hypothesis and the minority group–affiliation hypothesis.

The **culture–affiliation hypothesis** is simply that immigrant bilinguals will tend to affiliate themselves with the values and beliefs of the culture associated with the language in which they are currently operating. When the language is switched, so are the cultural values with which they affiliate. The **minority group–affiliation hypothesis**, in contrast, suggests that immigrant bilinguals will tend to self-identify as members of an ethnic minority group and adopt the behavioral stereotypes of the majority culture about their minority as their own when they are operating in the language associated with their minority group. Where such stereotypes are accurate, the minority group–affiliation hypothesis will make the same predictions as does the culture-affiliation hypothesis. That is, when interacting in their first language, people will behave in ways more typical of their culture as well as being more consistent with majority culture stereotypes of that culture. Given that we expect differences in behavior depending on language context, we would also expect differences in personality in linguistic contexts.

Hull (1987) and Dinges and Hull (1992) reported studies in which this prediction was tested. They reasoned that if any such differences were to be found, they would be most evident among a population of immigrant bilinguals. Such bilinguals are believed to have two clearly distinct cultural affiliations, accessible through the language in which much of this cultural knowledge was learned or is associated. In these studies, Chinese-English and Korean-English immigrant bilinguals were given the California Psychological Inventory (CPI), a widely used personality test. It's a particularly good test for this type of study as it has been translated into many different languages and used in cross-cultural research over many years.

The immigrant bilinguals completed the CPI twice, once in their native language and once in English. The central question was: Would a dual self or dual personality emerge, showing up as between-language, within-group differences in CPI scores? The answer was a resounding "yes." In other words, these bilinguals presented different personalities depending on whether they were responding in English (their second language) or in their native language. In a second study, Hull (1990a, 1990b) confirmed these earlier findings using a different measure of personality.

Some evidence also suggests that our perceptions of others are dependent on the language we speak when making those judgments. Matsumoto and Assar (1992) asked bilingual observers in India to view a set of 40 different facial expressions of emotion. The observers were asked to judge which emotion was being portrayed in the faces, and how intensely. The observers made these judgments twice, separated a week apart, once in English, and a second time in Hindi. The results showed that judgments of which emotion was being portrayed were more accurate when the judgments were made in English. But the emotions were perceived more intensely when the ratings were made in Hindi. The bottom line of this study is that the same people, viewing the same facial expressions, made different judgments of those expressions depending on which language they used to make those judgments.

The research I have described demonstrates how much language and culture are intertwined with each other. It also demonstrates the importance of language in everyday experience. These findings also help to dispel the misconception that the existence of two personalities within an individual means that such individuals are suffering from a mental disorder. Such a situation is clearly a natural and healthy part of the bilingual/bicultural experience.

Another important question concerns the extent to which the processes of language acquisition are innate (and thus culturally universal), and the extent to which such processes are learned (and thus vary from culture to culture). This question concerns language acquisition, to which I now turn.

Language Acquisition

We do not yet have a clear answer to the question of the degree to which the processes of language acquisition are innate or learned. The evidence to date suggests that some aspects of language acquistion are learned, while others are innate. How do we learn language? A common myth in many cultures is that children learn their native language by imitating the sounds that they hear in their natural environment. We now know that imitation is not an important strategy in learning language. In fact children are far more sophisticated in their learning strategies than we used to believe.

In a now-famous study in the 1950s, Jean Berko (Berko, 1958; Berko-Gleason, 1989) showed very cleverly that rather than simply imitating what they hear, children generate hypotheses about language and then test these hypotheses. This hypothesis generation and testing is a crucial strategy by which children around the world learn their native language. It appears to be a universal strategy for learning language. Berko (1958) showed American children a picture of an imaginary creature. She told them that the picture was of "a wug" (an imaginary creature she invented for this experiment). She then showed the same children a picture of two such imaginary creatures and asked them what they saw: "Now there are two ——!" Most of the children filled in the blank by saying "wugs." Since the word *wugs* is not an English word and one that they had never encountered before, this shows very clearly that these children could not have used imitation to produce the word *wugs*. In order to answer "wugs," they had to have prior knowledge of the rule of English grammar that we often add *s* to nouns to indicate plurality.

Sometimes children's knowledge of grammatical rules causes them to appear to be "backsliding" in their language development. Many parents have been dismayed when their children, who previously used the correct form of the verb "to go," begin to use an incorrect form they may never have used before. For example, after using the standard past tense form "went" in a sentence such as "I went to school," children may suddenly begin to say "I goed to school." Anxious parents may regard such apparent regression as evidence of a learning disability. More often than not, nothing could be further from the truth. The children first learned the form "went" through simple imitation without learning anything about the rules of English grammar. Then later on, when their linguistic understanding became more sophisticated, they learned the English grammatical rule of adding *ed* to the end of verbs to make them past tense. Using the form "goed" instead of went shows a higher level of linguistic development because the children are applying a grammatical rule rather than simply imitating a word they have heard. Further in the children's development, they will learn the exceptions to rules previously learned, such as this irregular past tense form, went. The point is that knowing a grammatical rule and applying it creatively in new situations shows much greater cognitive sophistication than mere imitation, and it is a universal language learning strategy.

People in different cultures have different beliefs about how children learn language. Cultures also differ in the way they behave toward children learning language. The Kaluli of Papua New Guinea believe that children need carefully controlled explicit instruction in both the forms of language and in conversation skills (Schieffelin, 1981, 1990; Schieffelin & Ochs, 1986). They believe children won't learn language and conversational skills unless they are taught to do so explicitly. The Kaluli act on these beliefs and teach their children how to conduct conversations.

Samoan adults typically believe that children's early attempts at language have no meaning and in any case that children have nothing to say that is of any importance to adults. Because of these beliefs, Samoan adults don't engage their children in formal language training; nor do they typically engage in conversation with children. In fact, it is the language of elder siblings that Samoan children are mostly exposed to rather than the language of adults (Ochs, 1988; Ochs & Schieffelin, 1979, 1983).

In the United States, there is a curious discrepancy between what adults believe and their actions. On one hand, most adults believe children need explicit instruction from caretakers to learn English properly. On the other hand, most American parents actually pay attention to what children are saying (that is, the content) rather than how they are saying it (that is, the grammar or syntax) (Chomsky, 1965, 1967, 1969).

Such differences in cultural beliefs and practices with regard to language learning are fascinating. What is even more fascinating, however, is that in all cultures, regardless of any such beliefs or practices, children learn their native language fluently with or without help from adults. This implies that humans have some universal and innate ability to learn language. Chomsky, a renowned linguist, proposed precisely this. According to Chomsky (1967), humans possess a **language aquisition device** (LAD). He argued that it is this

LAD that enables all normal children to learn language fluently. Although there is no direct evidence of the existence of Chomsky's LAD, it is currently one of the best explanations we have for the fact that all normal children learn their native languages fluently regardless of wide differences in the environments in which they do so.

Further evidence to support the existence of a language acquisition device comes from cross-cultural research on pidgin and creole speakers. Bickerton (1981), at the University of Hawaii, studied a number of pidgin speakers and their development into creole speakers. Many of the linguistic features found in several unrelated creole languages were not present in any of the source languages from which the original pidgin developed. Where might such features come from? Bickerton suggested that the only plausible explanation for the existence of such features in creole speakers who have had no contact with other creole speakers who share those features is that such features are preprogrammed or hard-wired in humans as part of our LAD.

It is clear that people of different cultures harbor different opinions and attitudes about language acquisition, but it is not clear whether the exact processes of language learning are different across cultures. With the lack of evidence to the contrary, Chomsky's notion of a universal LAD that enables children to learn languages appears to be the best explanation for language acquisition. Future research may test the limits of the LAD by exploring exactly how this process occurs. Then, perhaps we can uncover some ways in which cultural differences in attitudes and opinions about language learning affect the learning process in specific cultures.

 ## Conclusion

Language is the principal means by which we communicate with each other and store information. Language is also the principal means by which each generation receives its cultural inheritance from the previous generation. Indeed, without language, culture as we know it would not exist at all. So it should come as no surprise that language is of particular interest to cross-cultural researchers.

Languages differ enormously from one another, and these differences are related to important differences in the customs and behaviors of the cultures in which those languages reside. Although there has been some skepticism about the strength of the Sapir-Whorf hypothesis, a closer examination of the cross-cultural research testing it tends to support some versions. Language also plays an important and predictive role in the personalities of multilingual people. Finally, although the processes by which we learn language appear to be universal, cultures clearly differ in their attitudes and opinions about language acquisition. It is not yet clear how these attitudes and opinions influence language learning.

Language acquisition is an important aspect of the study of language because it helps us understand much broader issues of human behavior. By discovering which acquisition processes are universal and which are specific to single cultures, we can better address to what extent our behavior is innate (biologically determined) or learned (culturally determined).

Understanding how language is acquired is also important for practical reasons: As the world moves increasingly to what has been called a global village (that is, greater interdependence among nations), knowledge of more than one language has become a vital tool in understanding and communicating with people of other cultures. This is true both within a pluralistic, multicultural society such as the United States as well as between people living in different nations. No matter how important multilingualism is now, the future suggests that it will become even more important.

The importance of learning about language and the relationship between language, culture, and behavior cannot be emphasized enough, especially for students in the United States. Americans are notoriously ignorant of languages other than English, and this ignorance is often accompanied by an ethnocentric view rejecting the need to learn, understand, and appreciate other languages, customs, and cultures. The fact that Americans are the most monolingual of all peoples of the world, that language is intimately tied to culture, and that multilingualism is associated with an appreciation of different cultures suggests that Americans may actually be the most ethnocentric of all people as well. Recognition of the special relationships between language, culture, and behavior cannot be emphasized enough for students in the United States. Our ignorance of languages other than English, and the unfortunate ethnocentrism that often accompanies this ignorance, may be the root of our future downfall. For many of us who have little exposure to these issues in our everyday lives, now is the time to begin our study of language and culture for a better understanding of the partners in our global village.

Glossary

culture-affiliation hypothesis   The hypothesis that immigrant bilinguals will tend to affiliate themselves with the values and beliefs of the culture associated with the language in which they are currently operating. When the language is switched, so are the cultural values with which they affiliate.

language aquisition device   Proposed by Chomsky, it is the mechanism thought to account for the development of language in children.

lexicon   The words contained in a language, the vocabulary.

minority group–affiliation hypothesis   The hypothesis that immigrant bilinguals will tend to self-identify as members of an ethnic minority group and adopt the behavioral stereotypes of the majority culture about their minority as their own when they are operating in the language associated with their minority group.

morphemes   The smallest and most basic units of meaning in a language.

phonemes   The smallest and most basic units of sound in a language.

phonology   The system of rules governing how words should sound (pronunciation, "accent") in a given language.

pragmatics   Refers to the system of rules governing the how language is used and understood in given social contexts.

Sapir-Whorf hypothesis   A hypothesis that suggests that speakers of different languages think differently and that they do so because of the differences in their languages.

semantics   What words mean.

syntax and grammar   The system of rules governing word forms and how words should be strung together to form meaningful utterances.

14

Culture and Communication

The Nonverbal Dimension

"Control your gestures. Keep your hands at your sides. The Japanese find big arm movements threatening. Speak slowly. Keep your voice calm and even."
Sean Connery to Wesley Snipes in the movie *Rising Sun*

What Are Nonverbal Behaviors?

When people think about communication, they generally think about language. But language is just one part of communication. In fact, it may be the smallest component of communication. We use many other vehicles of expression to communicate our thoughts, feelings, desires, and wishes to others. These other vehicles are not language; that is, they are not words or sentences. In short, they are not verbal. They are nonverbal. In the broadest sense, **nonverbal behaviors** are all the behaviors that occur during communication other than words. Facial expressions are examples of nonverbal behaviors. The movements of our hands, arms, and legs are nonverbal behaviors. Our postures are nonverbal behaviors. Even characteristics of our voices above and beyond the words we speak are nonverbal behaviors. Indeed, the term *nonverbal behaviors* captures a whole range of behaviors associated with communication, including behaviors we typically associate with active expressivity, such as facial expressions, gestures, posture, and voice characteristics. But there is a whole world of more subtle behaviors associated with nonverbal behavior and communication as well. These include the use of space and interpersonal distance, gaze behavior and visual attention, the use of time, the type of clothing we wear, and the type of architectural structures we have and use around us.

All these different types of behavior fall under the general category of nonverbal behaviors. When you stop to think of all the different things that are actually occurring when people communicate with each other, it is mind-boggling. People come to an interaction in a certain place that is bounded by how they have structured it physically. They come to that interaction with a certain appearance. They space themselves from one another at certain distances. They adopt certain postures when interacting. They gesture and use hand movements to illustrate what they are saying. Their faces may become animated or reserved. Their voices may become excited or suppressed. Indeed, when communication is occurring, the actual words and language used are only a small part of the entire package of events and behaviors that constitute communication. It is no wonder that several studies have reported that only a small fraction of the meaning people get in an interaction is based on the words that were spoken. In fact, most of the messages conveyed and perceived in interactions are nonverbal (for example, Mehrabian, 1981).

Classifying Nonverbal Behaviors

Many different types of behaviors can be classified as nonverbal. It may be useful to think about each different type (for example, facial expressions, voice, gestures, postures) as a different channel of communication. Each channel conveys its own set of data or information during communication. But what types of information are communicated along these various channels? Several writers (for example, Efron, 1941; Ekman & Friesen, 1969) have attempted to classify the different types of behaviors that any channel can engage in. While each classification scheme has merits and disadvantages, Ekman and Friesen's (1969) scheme may be particularly useful to us in understanding cultural influences on nonverbal behaviors.

In Ekman and Friesen's (1969) scheme, nonverbal behaviors can be classified into five major categories: illustrators, adaptors/manipulators, emblems, emotion, and regulators. **Illustrators** are nonverbal behaviors we use to highlight aspects of the words we speak. They illustrate visually what the words are trying to say symbolically. Many people, for example, use their hands in gesture to illustrate or highlight their speech. Many times the gestures are used solely to highlight characteristics of the voice or to convey how excited the person is about the message or to describe the actual content of the message. You may notice that when violinist Itzhak Perlman strikes a high note, he raises his brows. When he plays a low one, his brows lower. Perhaps the same behaviors occur when Placido Domingo or Pavaroti sing the opera.

Adaptors/manipulators are nonverbal behaviors we engage in to help our bodies adapt to the environment around us. Scratching an itch, picking our noses, biting our lips, and rubbing our eyes are all examples of adaptive behavior. While these behaviors may not be important in communication, they are important in our everyday lives (try not scratching an itch sometime), and all cultures develop rules of etiquette and manners concerning adaptors.

Emblems are nonverbal behaviors that convey a message by themselves. They do not have to occur during a conversation, although they often do. When they occur, they convey a message just as a word, phrase, or sentence does. There are many emblems in our society: raising your brows, pushing your lower lip up, pulling your lip corners down, and shaking your head from side to side. In the United States, this generally means that you question the validity of what is being said. Of course, there are simpler and more direct emblems, such as nodding the head to mean yes, shaking the head to mean no, and the good old finger. As you can probably guess, many emblems are culture specific, and issues of cultural differences in nonverbal behaviors will be examined later in this chapter. Look at the now relatively famous picture of American servicemen taken captive in 1968 (Figure 14.1). This picture was shot by the Koreans and sent back to the United States supposedly to show that the servicemen were in good care. If you look closely, however, you will notice that several servicemen are giving the "finger." This was a clear emblematic indication to Americans viewing the photo that everything was *not* all right with them.

Emotion is yet another message conveyed by nonverbal behaviors. In Chapter 12, I discussed how one type of nonverbal behavior, facial expressions, conveys information about emotion and how that information is universal and culture-specific. The face is the most studied channel of nonverbal behavior with respect to emotion, probably because of its ability to signal discrete, specific emotional states on a moment-to-moment basis. In this chapter, I will only deal with emotional messages related to other forms of nonverbal behaviors.

Finally, **regulators** are nonverbal behaviors we engage in to regulate the flow of speech during a conversation. We use our faces quite often to signal we are done or waiting or even inviting someone else to speak. Our tone of voice also regulates speech, informing others when we are finished speaking. In many cultures, gaze and visual attention regulate speech, as do gestures inviting others to chime in.

Figure 14.1 These American servicemen were taken captive when North Korea seized the U.S. ship *Pueblo* in 1968. Can you find the emblem displayed by some of these men?

Not only are there many different channels of nonverbal behaviors, but each channel can convey many different types of messages. It is ironic that so much information is conveyed by these nonverbal behaviors, yet we spend relatively little time paying any attention to them or thinking about them when we consider issues of communication. Indeed, these nonverbal behaviors are vital to communication and often provide the basis for successful communication, intercultural or otherwise, even though they are often unconscious and automatic.

Verbal and Nonverbal Behaviors in Communication

Communication does not occur in a vacuum. Communication occurs in a specific context. People have certain biases, and words are couched in a particular framework, coupled with facial expressions, gestures, postures, and such. When we interact with someone or a group of people, the amount of information transmitted from one person to the next is unbelievably large. We may think that the only part or the main part of communication is the words being spoken. Indeed, we attend to the words and the language that is used. Our formal educational experiences, from elementary school on up, center around language—words, grammar, spelling, and punctuation. We spend much of our time thinking about just the right words to use to express ourselves—our ideas, our thoughts, our opinions. We think about just the right thing to say to our boyfriends and girlfriends, business associates, acquaintances, work colleagues, or the police. We concentrate on the words and language when we speak.

But the words we use in interaction and conversation are only one part of the *entire* communication process. Our verbal language channel is just one of many communication channels activated when we communicate. All our behaviors and gestures—in short, our nonverbal behaviors—form important channels of communication as well. The only difference is that we do not think about them as much or as consciously as we think about the words we use or the language we speak. And we do not think about them as much when we listen to others speak. But just because we do not attend to them consciously does not mean they are not important. Indeed, these nonverbal behaviors are very important.

Nonverbal behavior can highlight or accent information. Nonverbal behaviors accent our emotional states. They convey how excited we are or whether we are angry, upset, or happy. Nonverbal behaviors convey information about the content of what we are talking about. Nonverbal behaviors tell us when it is time to speak and time to listen. We can get conflicting messages from nonverbal behaviors. The words coming out of someone's mouth may tell you one thing, but their nonverbal behaviors (for example., tone of voice, gaze) may tell you something else. Someone may say, "I love you" with words but communicate "not really" with nonverbal behaviors.

In short, communication is an intricate, complicated process with many different channels open for message transmission and many different messages being transmitted. During interaction, we all do amazing things. We take all the information we are receiving and synthesize it somehow to make sense out of it. While much conscious energy is spent understanding and interpreting the words and the language we and others use in interaction, most of how we learn to read and interpret the important nonverbal dimension is unconscious and automatic. No one ever taught us how to do this. We receive nonverbal messages, process them, make sense out of it all, and put that information together with the verbal messages we receive via language. We do this automatically, refining this skill from infancy through adulthood. We don't attend classes in nonverbal behavior, yet the amount of information conveyed nonverbally in communication is enormous.

Our ability to be fluent in nonverbal as well as verbal language is quite amazing. All of our education about nonverbal behaviors is informal not formal, on the streets not in the classrooms. Yet all of us learn the rules by which our society and culture dictate we engage in nonverbal behaviors and interpret them. They are a silent language but are no less important than the spoken language we are accustomed to using.

Culture, Nonverbal Behaviors, and Communication

Just as spoken languages differ from one culture to the next, so does unspoken, nonverbal behaviors. People of all cultures learn to use nonverbal behaviors—facial expressions, gestures, distance, gaze, and postures—as part of their communication repertoire, but people in each culture learn to use them in very specific ways. All humans are born with the capacity to form all types of sounds; culture dictates how we shape and mold those sounds into particular languages. In this same way, culture shapes and molds nonverbal behaviors into each culture's nonverbal language.

Consider, for example, our American culture. We all have a certain way of dressing for school or for business. When we speak to someone, we look them straight in the eye. Our faces and gestures often become animated, highlighting specific, important parts of our speech. We learn to sit or stand at a certain distance when we interact, depending on with whom we are interacting and the specific context or situation in which that interaction is occurring. We learn how to signal when we are finished speaking and when we want to continue speaking. In short, we learn a very specific, American system of nonverbal behaviors to aid in our communication process, just as we have learned American English as a verbal language.

When we interact with people from our own culture, they have generally learned the same system or language of nonverbal behaviors. They will most likely follow the same rules of dress, manner, appearance, distance, tone of voice, facial expressions, gestures, and postures. When we interact with longtime friends, for example, we know what that system is (even though we may not be able to verbalize it!), and we can interact with them successfully, being unambiguous with regard to the content of the message or its intent.

The same is true for our families. Our family members generally "speak" the same nonverbal language we do. After all, it is from these families that we learned our nonverbal language. When we interact with them, there are relatively fewer instances when we are unable to read or correctly interpret the meaning of the nonverbal signals we receive from all the various nonverbal channels.

The power of culture can be seen when we interact with people from our own culture who may be totally unfamiliar to us. When we meet someone for the first time, at a party, a business engagement, on the street, or in the theater, we can usually engage in some kind of conversation where we can successfully interpret the nonverbal messages being conveyed. Their nonverbal behaviors may be coy, flirtatious, or annoying—just about anything.

The point is that we have all learned the same rules of making and interpreting nonverbal behaviors. When we see a certain action or behavior, we have learned how to interpret it, according to an implicit and informal set of guidelines dictated by our culture-specific nonverbal language. When the rules by which someone is engaging in nonverbal behaviors and language are the same as the rules by which another person is interpreting those behaviors, everything is fine. Interaction comes off smoothly and successfully, with little ambiguity about intent or message.

Now consider a situation where you are interacting with someone from a different culture. People from another culture bring with them their own verbal language. A person from Israel, for example, will bring the ability to speak Hebrew. A person from India will bring the ability to speak Hindi or a provincial dialect of India. But beyond the culture-specific verbal language they bring with them, they also bring a culture-specific nonverbal language. Thus, people from Israel will bring with them the Israeli- or Jewish-specific language of nonverbal behaviors; people from India will bring with them the India-specific language of nonverbal behaviors. When you stop to think about it, there are really two languages occurring in all types of interactions—one verbal and one nonverbal.

People from different cultures have their own rules for engaging in nonverbal behaviors. These rules may be quite different from the rules you or I may be fluent in. These rules may dictate that different behaviors are enacted to get a certain point across or to accent a specific point. These rules may mean that the same behavior can actually carry quite different meanings.

Just as people from different cultures have their own rules for engaging in nonverbal behaviors, they have their own rules for interpreting the nonverbal behaviors of others. Obviously, they will have learned to associate certain behaviors with certain meanings and these associations or relationships are all dependent on their culture and its rules.

When we interact with people from a different culture, most of the time we try to attend most closely to the verbal language. But nonverbal language is also occurring. Just because we don't attend to it consciously as much does not mean that it is not occurring. Nonverbal language continues, like verbal language. The unconscious filters and processes we have learned so we can automatically interpret the nonverbal behaviors of people from our own culture are also occurring; they do not stop.

The problem in intercultural communication is that these nonverbal languages are silent. Our interpretational processes are unconscious and automatic. We may not attend to them very much, but messages are being transmitted. More often than not, the nonverbal language of people of a different culture is different from what we are accustomed to. After interacting with people from another culture, it is not uncommon to wonder whether you really "got" what was meant. Oftentimes we leave these situations feeling like we may have missed something. These feelings arise because our unconscious system of nonverbal communication is having difficulty interpreting the nonverbal behaviors of the people from a different culture. Something just doesn't "feel" right. You leave these interactions with an aftertaste that leaves you thinking.

Problems occur in the opposite direction as well. People often interpret certain types of behaviors positively when, in fact, they are not meant to be positive at all. Consider, for example, the Japanese head nodding and the use of the word *hai*. The best translation of this word in English is "yes." But in Japanese this word does not necessarily mean yes. It may mean yes, but it can also mean maybe, or even no. It is often used as a speech regulator, informing the speaker that the listener is listening. It can be a signal of deference to authority. This word and the nonverbal behaviors associated with it (head nod) most definitely do not have the same meaning in Japanese as they do in English. Yet many business and government negotiations have faltered on the interpretation of exactly this behavior, with Americans believing that the Japanese have agreed to something and that the deal is closed. The Japanese, however, may merely be signaling that they are listening. This type of cultural difference is the source of many interpersonal conflicts between spouses and lovers as well.

When we interact with people who have different nonverbal languages, we often form negative impressions of them. In the United States, we all learn to interact with people at a certain distance. When you interact with someone you do not know very well and this person places himself close enough to you so you feel his breath when he speaks, you will probably feel quite uncomfortable and try to adjust the distance. He will follow. You will adjust again. He will follow again. You will probably want to get out of that interaction as soon as possible. When you do, you will think that the person was rude or without manners. Many Arab and Middle Eastern cultures foster what we Americans would consider too close interpersonal spacing during interactions and this can be unsettling.

Or consider the opposite scenario. You are interacting with someone who stands quite far away from you, farther than you think would be normal under the circumstances. When you try to get closer, she moves further away. You move up again; she moves back again. Afterwards, you will probably think she had a negative impression of you and didn't really want to interact with you.

We make these interpretations because we are trying to match observed behavior with our own rules for what those behaviors should mean. If the people described above were indeed from your own culture and operated according to the same rules, you would probably be correct in your interpretations. But what if those people were from a different culture and operate under different rules? Then your negative impressions and interpretations of their behaviors may be totally off base. Yet you have them, and you leave feeling bad about the interaction, probably not wanting to interact any more. They probably feel the same way.

Nonverbal behaviors are just like a second language, albeit a silent, unspoken language. Just as cultures develop spoken, verbal languages, they also develop unspoken, nonverbal languages. These nonverbal languages are just as important, if not more so, to the overall communication process. If we are to get a handle on cultural similarities and differences in communication, we obviously need to pay more attention to cultural differences in these silent, nonverbal languages.

Cultural Differences in Nonverbal Behaviors

If you were to take a trip to another country or had visitors from another country coming to stay with you or you just wanted to learn another language, what might you do? One of the things you might consider is going to your local bookstore, finding the reference or language section, and searching through the various types of language learning books or dictionaries for sale for your particular language of interest. You'd search through some of the alternatives that were for sale, find one you like, and buy it. With dictionary in hand, you would be able to look up words or phrases you want to say. When someone speaks to you in that language, you can look up what they were saying to you or have them find the passage and point it out to you.

Wouldn't it be great if dictionaries existed for the silent, nonverbal languages of the world as well? There could be a book or videotape reference containing all the possible nonverbal behaviors in a certain language and their translation in English and the American nonverbal system. If we saw some behaviors or noticed a certain expression when interacting with someone from another culture, we could look it up and find out what it might mean instead of trying to interpret those behaviors according to our own, implicit, nonverbal language dictionary.

Fortunately, there has been a considerable amount of research on nonverbal behaviors and how cultures differ in the use of them. This research has spanned a number of topics and types of nonverbal behaviors, including gaze and visual behavior, interpersonal space and proxemics, gestures, postures, nonverbal vocal cues, facial expressions, the use of time, clothing, touch, and even smell. Studies in each of these various areas have produced a wealth of information about the complexity and importance of nonverbal behaviors in interpersonal communication and interaction.

In the remainder of this chapter, I will focus on three specific nonverbal behaviors—gaze and visual attention, interpersonal space, and gestures. I selected these topics for several reasons. First of all, there is a substantial base of cross-cultural research in each of these areas to inform us of how culture influences these aspects of the communication process. Also, these are primary areas of concern and interest in interpersonal interaction episodes and have the greatest relevance to our understanding and appreciation of cultural differences in communication styles. One other major channel of nonverbal behavior, facial expressions, has been described more fully in Chapter 12 in relation to communication of emotional messages. While the face is one of the primary nonverbal signal channels, I mention it here only periodically because it is covered in greater depth in that chapter.

Gaze and Visual Behavior

In learning about cultures and how they influence human behavior, from time to time it is useful to look at research findings not with humans but with animals that have relevance to our understanding of possible universal and culture-specific aspects of behavior. If we reviewed research on nonhuman primates (for example, apes, chimpanzees, gorillas) and found that these animals engaged in many behaviors similar to those of humans, we would certainly begin to wonder if those behaviors might have evolutionary or biological bases. At the very least, these studies would help us gain a broad perspective of the nature of our behaviors and how much they are influenced by culture.

This is especially true of research on gaze and visual attention. A considerable number of studies on gaze and visual behaviors in nonhuman primates force us to think about whether some of our behaviors may be "built into" our behavioral systems. Researchers as early as the 1960s, for example, showed how mutual gazing between animals, especially staring, is a primary and important component of aggressive and threatening displays. The relationship between staring and aggression has been observed in male baboons, gorillas, rhesus and bonnet macaques, and old world monkeys and apes (Altman, 1962; Hall & Devore, 1965; Hinde & Rowell, 1962; Schaller, 1963, 1964; Simonds, 1965; van Hooff, 1967).

This type of research formed much of the basis of our knowledge about what is known as **attention structures** in animal societies. An attention structure is an organized pattern that dictates which animals can look at others, and vice versa. Attention structures appear to be highly related to dominance hierarchies in animal societies. In general, comparative research on nonhuman primates has shown that animals with lower status and power in a group pay more attention to higher status animals and adjust their behaviors accordingly.

Let's switch our attention temporarily back to humans. Have you ever played a game of staring? This game has several different names, depending on the time period and geographic area of the United States in question, but it involves two interactants staring at each other with a blank or neutral face. The game proceeds until one of the two people looks away, starts laughing, or generally breaks off the stare. The one who breaks off the stare is the loser.

This game exemplifies some of the dominance, status, and power themes associated with gaze and found in the animal literature. In animal research, it has been shown that animals, too, have a dominance or power struggle that involves mutual glaring or staring at each other (Fehr & Exline, 1987). The power struggle between two animals will end when one of the animals backs off and breaks the gaze. We seem to have a taboo against these types of direct stares, as if our cultures produce rules by which we can curb or control such displays of aggression or dominance.

Dominance and aggression, however, are not the only messages that gazing gives. Some writers (for example, Argyle & Cook, 1976) have suggested that gazing can also signal affiliation or nurturance. Phrases in English such as "gazing into someone's eyes" or "getting lost in one's eyes" seem to capture this aspect of gaze as well. Fehr and Exline (1987) suggest that the affiliative aspects of gazing may have their roots in infancy, because infants are very attentive, via gaze, to adults, as adults are their source of care and protection.

It is not unusual to think that cultures should come up with rules concerning gazing and visual attention. Both aggression and affiliation are behavioral tendencies that are important for group stability and maintenance. Each culture derives its own set of rules concerning gazing and visual attention to ensure that its members are affiliated while at the same time curbing aggressive tendencies.

Cross-cultural research on gazing in humans has also produced some very interesting findings. Several studies have shown that people from Arabic cultures gaze much longer and more directly at their partners than

Americans do (Hall, 1963; Watson & Graves, 1966). Watson (1970) studied visual attention patterns in 30 different countries and separated the countries according to whether they were a "contact" culture (that is, those that facilitated physical touch or contact during interaction) or a "noncontact" culture. Watson found that people in contact cultures engaged in more gazing than did people of noncontact cultures. In addition, people from contact cultures had more direct orientations when interacting with others, less distance, and more touching.

When a person does not look at us as much as we are used to normally when interacting, it seems to be common to all people to make some negative attributions about that behavior. For example, we may believe that the other person is not interested in us or in our conversation. We may believe that the other person does not want to be here or wants to break off the conversation. I have often heard how many Americans get frustrated and perplexed when interacting with people from some Asian cultures, because it seems as if the people from Asian cultures do not look directly at the other person when interacting. We may feel negatively about this person, wondering if they feel angry at us or are not interested romantically or are lying. It is important to keep this in the proper perspective, however. Watson and Hall both mention that many people from Arabic cultures get annoyed when interacting with Americans, probably because the Americans tend to gaze less than the Arabs are used to. This is a two-way street!

Even within the United States, there are differences in gaze and visual behavior between different groups of Americans. A number of studies have shown that African Americans tend to gaze less directly than do European Americans when interacting with someone (Exline, Jones, & Maciorowski, 1977; LaFrance & Mayo, 1976). In studies of interethnic interactions, Fehr (1977, 1981) studied African American and European American mixed and same ethnicity interactions and found that the African Americans gazed less directly, repeating the findings of other researchers. Fehr also found, moreover, that the participants tended to prefer people who gazed at about the same amounts as they were typically accustomed to, regardless of ethnicity.

Studies from nonhuman primates, across human cultures, and within our own culture all indicate that gaze is an important aspect of social and interactive behavior. When we encounter people who gaze differently than we are used to, we often come away from those interactions with negative or questioning feelings about our relationship with the other person or about that person. If the other person does not gaze as much as we are accustomed, we tend to make negative attributions about that person's interest in us or in the conversation. If the other person gazes too much, we feel that person is too aggressive or domineering in some way.

These attributions only occur if we use the rules of interpretation we are accustomed to. If the person with whom we are interacting is from another culture, operating with another set of rules, our interpretations of that gaze behavior may actually be wrong. What if the other person is not looking at you directly out of deference or appreciation for your status or power? While looking a person straight in the eye has some roots in our American culture, other cultures may not have these roots but still exhibit this behavior more strongly than we do.

Interpersonal Space and Proxemics

Space is another extremely important dimension of nonverbal behavior that we often take for granted. How we use space can send important messages about power, status, and dominance. This is true for people in interactions as well as in their own private spaces. Have you ever noticed how some of the more powerful people in a company or organization seem to have spaces that are the most remote and difficult to access? The people with the most power in an organization usually have the nicest spaces, and certainly some of the largest spaces. Even within a certain floor the people with the most power seem to have the corner spaces, with a view to the outside world and limited access to their space from the inside. People with less power are accessible by everyone from all directions; people with more power are relatively inaccessible.

Like gaze and visual behavior, space is an important nonverbal dimension in animals and nonhuman primates. Animal societies, humans included, seem to come up with rules about how to use space optimally given space restrictions and other limitations placed on them for survival. Hall (1978) reports that deer, gulls, and pelicans have ordered rules about spacing in their colonies. Calhoun (1950) conducted a study with 150 rats and found that the rats seemed to settle "naturally" into 12 groups of approximately 12 rats each, given a certain amount of space in which to live.

The rules we develop in relation to interpersonal spacing are highly dependent on the space resources we have available to us. The rules we develop, in turn, have dramatic effects on the rules of social interaction, appropriateness, and politeness that we must subsequently adopt to survive, given the size of the population and space available for them (population density). These rules form the basis for what become our cultural rules about interpersonal space. Also, these rules feed off the space and population density, which in turn feed off the rules, forming a circular, self-renewing cycle.

Americans, like people from other cultures and countries, have developed rules governing the use of interpersonal space. Hall (1978) specifies four different levels of interpersonal space use depending on social relationship type. The closest type of relationship, intimate relationships, are characterized by interpersonal spaces of between 0 and $1\frac{1}{2}$ feet. Personal relationships are generally characterized by distances of $1\frac{1}{2}$ feet to 4 feet. Social consultive relationships are generally characterized by distances between 4 and 8 to 10 feet. Relationships that involve distances greater than 10 feet are generally considered public relationships.

This is a general guide to interpersonal distances in the United States for Americans, but other cultures will definite different distances for these same relationships. Indeed, cross-cultural research on interpersonal distance and space has shown exactly that. Watson and Graves (1966) studied pairs of male students from Arab cultures and compared their use of space against the use of space of similar male pairs of American students. They found that Arab males tended to sit closer to each other, with more direct, confrontational types of body orientations. They had greater eye contact and tended to speak in louder voices than did the Americans. Hall (1963, 1966), in fact, concluded that people from Arab cultures generally learn to interact with others at distances close enough to feel the other person's breath.

Other cross-cultural studies show how people of different cultures learn to use space differently in interpersonal contexts. Forston and Larson (1968) cited anecdotal evidence of how students with Latin American backgrounds tended to interact more closely than did students of European backgrounds. Noesjirwan (1977, 1978) reported that Indonesian subjects tended to sit closer than did the Australian subjects in the studies. Shuter (1977) reported that Italians interacted more closely than did either Germans or Americans. Shuter (1976) also reported that people from Colombia generally interacted at closer distances than did the subjects from Costa Rica.

It is no wonder that we can come away from interpersonal interactions with people of different cultural backgrounds feeling quite negatively about them. For example, if we Americans were to interact with someone from a culture (such as an Arab culture) who learned to interact much more closely than we were accustomed, we would probably be quite put off by this. If this person were a casual acquaintance, we would probably interact with this person at a distance comfortable to us, say, 4 to 5 feet. But, this person may want to get right up to our face and talk. As this happened, we would probably try to back up, adjusting to the closing gap. That person would probably keep coming on. We might feel as if we were being stalked! We may think, "How dare this person talk to me as if he were an intimate friend of mine!" We may leave feeling quite offended, when in fact that person may have just been trying to interact at the distance he has learned is appropriate for your type of relationship.

The opposite can and does occur. For example, a man might want to get closer to someone, trying to gauge whether she has a romantic interest in him. She may be from a culture that dictates more space between people, even in intimate, romantic relationships, than he is accustomed to. She may sit farther from him than he would like, but it actually may be closer to him than is appropriate for her. He would interpret that she doesn't feel anything for him. She, on the other hand, may feel that she is getting too involved!

Differences in the rules we all have concerning the use of space in interpersonal contexts can pose major problems in intercultural communication situations. Like other nonverbal behaviors, our use of space and our interpretation of the use of space around us often happens automatically and unconsciously. We have internalized these unspoken cultural rules and act on them automatically. And just as we operate on them automatically, people from all other cultures do so as well. But their rules may be different from ours, and we need to take these differences into account when understanding and interacting with people of different cultures.

Gestures

Say you met someone in class whom you were attracted to. One day, you worked up enough courage to go up to him or her and ask for a date. You are busy making conversation, kind of fumbling around with your words, hands, and books. Finally, you pop the question—will he or she go out with you tonight? He or she nods. You're about ready to jump through the ceiling with excitement. But you'd better control yourself, you think to yourself, and make arrangements to see him or her later. He or she nods again. You go away calm, cool, and oh so collected. Later that night, you show up to pick up your date, but your date is not there. Your date left word with a roommate that he or she won't be there. What happened?

Well, if your date were an American using an American gesture (head nod), then something would be definitely strange. But if your date were from another culture—where nodding the head means no, and shaking the head means yes—then he or she was telling you no all along! While people of most cultures seem to nod their heads when meaning yes and shake their heads when meaning no, there are some cultures (for example, some parts of Greece and Turkey) where the people do exactly the opposite (Ekman, Friesen, & Bear, 1984; Kendon, 1987).

Gestures are movements of the body, usually the hands, that are generally reflective of thought or feeling. Like language, gestures are culture-specific and differ in each culture. But when we use them, especially in intercultural contexts, we don't readily think about the fact that they may have a different meaning to someone else. Being unaware of these differences can definitely cause problems. At the very least, you might miss out on some dates.

Many cultures emphasize differences in the use of gestures as illustrators. Remember that illustrators are actions that highlight or accent speech or speech content. Some cultures (for example, Jewish, Italian) encourage their members to be very expressive in their gestures and mannerisms when speaking. Other cultures (for example, Japan, Thailand) encourage their members to be more reserved in using gestures as illustrators. It is amazing how we become accustomed to our cultural norms and expectations concerning gestures. In cultures that encourage gestures as illustrators (what Kendon, 1987, would call "gesticulation"), people think nothing of it when interacting with people who seem to flail about, using large hand movements (and hopefully some safe distance!) when talking to others. In fact, people of these cultures would probably think something was wrong when they interact with people from more reserved cultures. Conversely, people from more reserved cultures may think something is strange when they interact with gesturally expressive people. They may actually feel threatened or overwhelmed when interacting with these people.

The possibility of unnecessary intercultural conflict is large. We can come away from intercultural communication situations with quite negative feelings about the people we were interacting with or about the conversation topic. These feelings may generalize into detrimental stereotypes about all people of that culture. All this may occur solely on the basis of cultural differences in gestures, gesticulations, and other nonverbal aspects of communication.

Most cultures have quite an elaborate system of emblematic gestures. Remember, emblems are gestures and movements that have a total meaning by themselves. The "finger," thumbs up, A-OK, head nods and shakes, and the V sign are all examples of emblems we use in the United States. Shrugging your shoulders and raising both hands, palms up, is yet another emblematic gesture signaling uncertainty or ignorance about something. We take these emblematic gestures for granted. But there are many stories of travelers from the United States getting into trouble using American gestures in other countries, where the gestures have different meanings. While traveling in some parts of Europe, for example, you don't want to use the A-OK sign. While you might mean to say that "everything's okay," in some parts of Europe it is a rude or vulgar gesture, often interpreted as an invitation for sex (Ekman et al., 1984). In some other parts of Europe, it might mean that "you're nothing." Pointing your index finger toward your head and temple area in the United States signals that you are smart. In some parts of Europe and Asia, however, it means that you are stupid.

The "V for victory" sign with the index and middle fingers is another example of cultural differences in gestures. This gesture was commonly used in the United States to mean victory, and it has caught on in other countries as well. It is said that some members of the Greek and American military may have insulted former British Prime Minister Winston Churchill when they gave that sign with the palm facing backward instead of forward. Facing backward, it is a common English insult equivalent to our American saying "up yours." The original V for victory sign is signaled with the palm facing outward. But you wouldn't want to do that in Greece, because it is an abbreviated form of an insult in Greece. The gesture evolved in Greece from a practice of people throwing garbage and dirt from the streets toward criminals as they were paraded through the streets.

Japanese often signify that someone is angry by raising the index fingers of both hands, in a pointing fashion, toward the sides of their heads, pointing up. In Brazil and other South American countries, however, this signifies that one wants sex (is horny). Imagine what would happen if a Japanese person were trying to tell someone from Brazil that someone else is angry and the Brazilian interpreted the signal to mean the Japanese person is horny!

These are just a few of the many different types of gestures used around the world, and the differences in their meaning and interpretation. Some scholars have attempted to catalogue in great detail the use of gestures in various different cultures. Many of these resources are in book form (for example, Ekman et al., 1984; Kendon, 1987; Morris, Collett, Marsh, & O'Shaughnessy, 1980), and there is at least one videotape on the market that demonstrates differences in the meaning and use of gestures in different cultures (Archer, 1991).

 ## Conclusion

In this chapter, I have discussed in depth only three types of nonverbal behaviors and how cultures may influence them: gaze and visual attention, interpersonal space and distance, and gestures. There are many other channels and types of nonverbal behaviors. I chose these three areas because of the wealth of cross-cultural research on these topics and because of their impact on the communication process. Indeed, the world of nonverbal behaviors is as complex and varied as that of verbal language. The contribution of nonverbal behavior to the total communication process is no longer debated in the social sciences. This contribution is large indeed.

Unfortunately, despite the degree to which nonverbal behaviors contribute to communication, we often take them for granted. We are so learned at sending and receiving nonverbal messages and signals that as adults we do this unconsciously and automatically. We receive no formal training on how to send or receive these communications correctly and accurately as we do for formal language training. We learn spelling, grammar, punctuation, reading, and writing from grade school, but there is no equivalent formal education system for nonverbal behaviors.

Nonverbal behaviors are just as much a language as any other. Just as languages differ from culture to culture, so do nonverbal languages of each culture. We are all fully aware that verbal languages are different from one culture to the next. That is why we do not hesitate to purchase language reference dictionaries to help us understand different languages. But when it comes to the nonverbal arena, we often take it for granted that our systems of communicating nonverbally are all the same. This is a mistake.

Understanding cultural differences in nonverbal behavior is the first step in the process of truly appreciating cultural differences in communication. To study intercultural communication solely from the standpoint of verbal language will result in the exclusion of an important process of communication.

Can formal training in nonverbal behavior interpretation help intercultural communication processes and outcomes? While only a few studies on this topic have been published to date, their findings are indeed suggestive of the positive impact of nonverbal skills training. Collett (1971), for example, trained English subjects to engage in more visual attentive types of behaviors when engaging with subjects from Arabic cultures. In later ratings, Arabic subjects preferred interacting with English subjects who had received training better than they did with English subjects who had not received training. Yet other English subjects could not discriminate which English people had been trained and which had not. Garratt, Baxter, and Rozelle (1981) trained police officers to engage in gaze and visual attentive behavior patterns that were similar to those found with African Americans in previous studies. The police officers then used these patterns when interviewing male African American undergraduate subjects. The subjects invariably rated the trained officers more favorably than the untrained officers.

These studies do suggest the feasibility and value of training programs for nonverbal behavior. Still, the real task left to those of us who study culture and cultural differences is to recognize the profound influence nonverbal behaviors play in the communication process and then realize how our own cultural background influences the ways we engage and interpret the nonverbal world around us. While these processes are usually unconscious and automatic, that doesn't mean we can't improve on them to be more flexible and inclusive of different cultural systems of behavior.

 Glossary

adaptors/manipulators   Nonverbal behaviors we engage in to help our bodies adapt to the environment around us.

attention structures   An organized pattern that dictates which animals can look at others, and vice versa. These structures appear to be highly related to dominance hierarchies in animal societies.

emblems   Nonverbal behaviors that convey a message by themselves.

gestures   Movements of the body, usually the hands, that are generally reflective of thought or feeling.

illustrators   Those nonverbal behaviors used to highlight aspects of the words we speak.

nonverbal behaviors   All the behaviors that occur during communication other than words, such as facial expressions; the movements of hands, arms, and legs; posture; characteristics of our voices above and beyond the words we speak; space; gaze; clothing; and so forth.

regulators   Nonverbal behaviors we engage in to regulate the flow of speech during a conversation.

15

Conclusion

Culture itself is invisible, but its influence on our lives is enormous. Culture influences the language we speak, our perceptions of the world around us, our behaviors and attitudes, the structures of our homes, our system of education, government, and our health. Across the many topics covered in this book, culture plays a major, albeit sometimes silent and invisible, role in determining how we act and how we perceive the actions of others.

When we study cultural differences, it is easy to get lost in the mass of "facts" about those differences. The facts acquired from cross-cultural research in psychology, anthropology, and other disciplines would indeed fill the volumes of an encyclopedia on cultural differences. It would be interesting to have such an encyclopedia—a Farmer's Almanac of Culture, if you will—to help us understand the breadth and scope of culture's influence on our lives.

But even when we are surrounded by all those differences, or perhaps *especially* when we are surrounded by those differences, we must not forget that there are important similarities as well. The study of human behavior across cultures informs us of those similarities as well as the differences. Our nature being what it is, however, we are most fascinated by differences and oftentimes ignore similarities across cultures and among people.

Several aspects of our lives appear to be panculturally universal. Some processes of perception (for example, of color) are universal as are some types of cognition and thinking skills and strategies. Processes of language acquisition may be universal as is the expression of emotions in the face.

Moreover, beyond the similarities we find in behaviors, there are important similarities in our underlying intentions, motives, and feelings. When people come together in interaction to form relationships—in business, school, love, and the like—it has been my experience that few people come with malicious intent. Instead, people bring with them good intentions and motives. It is the behavioral manifestations of these intentions and motives, however, that often differ across cultures and that we observe. We get caught up in these differences in the behaviors and forget to think about the underlying intentions of those behaviors.

As we learn more and more about both cultural similarities and differences, we need to touch base with the reasons we study cultures in the first place. Without revisiting our motivations, the mass of facts about both similarities and differences will remain just that, a mass of facts. We need a way to take those facts and use them—to allow those facts to become means to an end and not an end in and of themselves. When we revisit our motivations, we should quickly come back to the fact that the ultimate reason we study culture is to improve our lives and our relationships with others in an increasingly diverse world. This goal should be the primary reason we study culture and its influence on human behavior. If we are not able to take the information gathered so far and use it in some productive way, the great opportunity provided by this information will slip through our hands and be wasted.

How can you approach this final task? One way would be to create that Farmer's Almanac in your mind, documenting the cultural similarities and differences found in specific cultures and building your own reference title so you can retrieve it at any time. This is a formidable task, as there is so much about culture to learn and so little time, energy, and storage space available. Despite the difficulties, however, this approach is not without merit. While it might be impossible to gain a deep appreciation of many cultures using this approach, many of us who spend extended periods of time immersed in different cultures—through travels, business, homestay programs, and the like—can and do build this almanac, albeit unconsciously. Moreover, the strength of this approach lies both in increasing our capacity to be culturally relative in relation to others and in guiding our behavior in daily interactions with people from diverse backgrounds.

Guidelines to Improve Cross-Cultural Relationships

In the final section of this chapter, I present seven guidelines I feel will help us improve relationships with others in the future. These guidelines are not universal in the sense that they have been "proven" by cross-cultural research.

Instead, they are my feeble attempt at taking all the information presented in this book and my experience and the experiences of others interacting with people of different backgrounds and synthesizing this information into a coherent set of guidelines that I have found useful. Others may have their own guidelines, and those may be at variance with mine. I offer these not as my end-all prescription for successful human relations but as a platform to launch meaningful discussions with others about this important topic. Whether people agree or disagree with these guidelines is a question secondary to the more important issue of their contribution to our ability to talk about these emotionally charged issues.

Recognize That Culture Is a Psychological Construct

I have focused on a definition of culture as a psychological construct emphasizing the subjective (Triandis, 1972) rather than objective aspects of culture. I believe it is these subjective aspects of culture existing in out minds as mental blueprints or programming that are most important to understanding the contribution of culture to human behavior. Culture refers to the degree to which a group of people share attitudes, values, beliefs, and behaviors. It is communicated from one generation to the next. As such, culture is a functional entity—one you cannot see but only infer from observations of human behavior.

Culture is not race. Being born of a particular race does not mean that you automatically harbor the cultural values associated with that race. Culture is not nationality. Being a citizen of a country does not mean that you automatically adopt the culture associated with that country. Culture is not birthplace. Being born in a certain place does not automatically mean that you harbor the culture of your birthplace.

When we think of intercultural relations and cultural diversity, both within the United States and abroad, we mostly think of differences according to race, ethnicity, or nationality. Yet I have not used these terms and concepts in this book. The lack of a focus on race, ethnicity, and nationality is a function of my view that the important aspect about people is their underlying psychological culture, not the color of their skin or the citizenship on their passport.

Some people may interpret my position as suggesting that race, nationality, and other personal characteristics are not important. That is not true. Future cross-cultural research and thinking in this area must meet the formidable challenge of integrating these concepts with psychological definitions of culture to examine their joint influence and interactive effects on human behaviors. In adopting the approach I took in this book, I hoped to highlight the important role of subjective, psychological culture in producing similarities and differences in behaviors and to bring a fresh way of thinking to old and nagging problems.

As we learn more about what culture is and is not, we need to recognize the fuzzy nature of the definition culture, based in function rather than biology or geopolitics. By recognizing that culture is a psychological construct—our learned, mental programming—we can avoid the use of race and nationality in understanding cultural differences among people. Defining culture as a meaningful psychological construct also allows us to consider the remaining guidelines.

Recognize Individual Differences within a Culture

Defining culture as a sociopsychological construct is not enough. With a functional definition of culture, we need to recognize individual differences within cultures. Within any culture, people differ according to how strongly they adhere to or comply with the values, standards, and mores of that culture. While some people may be true representatives of their culture, others may not be as adequately described by the culture. Yet they are all members of the culture. Even within our own individualistic American culture we can find people who harbor considerable collectivistic cultural values. Describing all individuals within this cultural group as individualistic ignores actual cultural differences that exist among individual members.

Recognizing that there are individual differences within cultures helps us develop flexibility in our ethnocentrism and stereotypes. One of the keys to improving intergroup and interpersonal relationships is to develop a healthy flexibility with regard to ethnocentrism and stereotypes. Recognizing individual differences in culture and how these differences are related to behaviors is one of the first steps to eliminating reliance on negative and detrimental stereotypes.

Understand Our Own Filters and Ethnocentrism

We are not always aware of our own cultural filters as we perceive, think about, and interpret events around us and the behavior of others. We are not always aware of the cultural bases of our behaviors and actions. Many of the ways we see the world (worldview) are fundamentally different from the way others see the world.

One important first step in gaining an understanding of cultural influences on behavior is to recognize that we have our own filters for perception and bases for behavior. We need to stop and think about how our own cultural upbringing contributed to how we interact with the world and with others. One arena where this comparison comes to the forefront is when we travel outside our culture. By clashing with the cultures of others, we are forced to think about differences in cognition and behavior. In doing so, we may come to a better understanding of our own filters and biases.

Allow for the Possibility That Conflicts Are Cultural

One fallacy that exists in cross-cultural study is the assumption that if you study cultures, there will be no intercultural conflicts. This is not the case. In interacting with others, conflicts and misunderstandings will undoubtedly occur. Unfortunately, all too often we are too quick to attribute the cause of the conflict or misunderstanding to some kind of fault or shortcoming in the other person or with the other person's culture. Oftentimes, because we have a limited understanding of culture based on race or nationality, we make negative attributions about that race or nationality, when in fact the differences arose because of culture, not race or nationality.

With a better understanding of cultural influences on behavior, we can allow for the possibility that many conflicts and misunderstandings are due to cultural differences. By doing so, we avoid personalizing the source of conflict and misunderstanding in our interactions and focus on the reasons the misunderstanding may have arisen in the first place. Of course, some conflicts do arise because of personal differences, ignorance, stupidity, or close-mindedness. But we can allow that culture may be a contributing factor and give people the benefit of the doubt.

Recognize That Cultural Differences Are Legitimate

Simply allowing for conflicts and misunderstandings to be attributed to culture is not enough. Indeed, we need to recognize and respect legitimate differences between our cultural upbringing and that of others. This is often a very difficult task because our perception of transgressions to our own culturally appropriate ways of behaving are typically seen as "bad" or "wrong" in our own cultural context, and it is easy to label the same behaviors of others as "bad" or "wrong." But a person from another culture may view those same behaviors as "good" or "acceptable" or "normal." In fact, behaviors that seem bad or ignorant or stupid to us may in fact be performed by a person of sincerity and trustworthiness. No matter how much we want to label it as bad or ignorant or stupid, the other person's cultural ways and values and beliefs have just as much legitimacy to them as ours have to us. A step in the right direction is to respect that legitimacy and that difference and find a way to work from that level of respect.

Have Tolerance, Be Patient, and Presume Good Intent

How can we find ways to work things out? Where do we go, once we recognize that conflicts arise because of differences in culture and that cultural differences in others are legitimate? One answer lies in examining how we traditionally deal with these conflicts.

American culture is based on a considerable amount of preservation of an individualistic sense of self. In finding ways to maintain self-integrity, we unfortunately often attribute negative characteristics to others, lashing out at others immediately when we feel our cultural norms have been violated. This style of making attributions and understanding the world around us is related to our individualistic American culture. It is neither bad nor good; it is just the way things are.

When we are too quick to attribute negative characteristics to others, we deny the possibility that their intent may have been good and that it was only the behavioral manifestations of that good intent that we were at odds with. By being tolerant of transgressions and presuming good intent in intercultural interaction, we allow that possibility to exist. If all participants of that interaction practice tolerance and presume good intent, we will be able to operate on the level of psychological culture discussed throughout this book and find ways explore and react to underlying intent rather than focusing solely on behaviors we find offensive.

Learn More about Cultural Influences on Behavior

As we turn toward the future, we must continue to learn how culture influences human behavior. By recognizing the importance of culture on behavior, we face an incredible challenge and opportunity. The diverse world that faces us, not only in the United States but also relative to our interdependence on others in our global village, provides a rich and complex arena for human behavior. Psychology has yet to explore this arena fully. These challenges bring new opportunities and new hopes, not only for science but also for people and their lives.

As we come in contact with people of different cultures from around the world, either through our own travels or through theirs, we are exposed to many different ways culture manifests itself in behavior. As our understanding grows, we will come to appreciate even more the important role culture plays, not only in providing us with a way to live but also in helping us meet the challenges of survival successfully and with integrity. Changes in culture will continue to occur; culture is not a static, fixed entity. We know that cultures change over time; the changes we witness today in Europe, Russia, Asia, and even within our own country speak to this fact. These changes ensure that there will never be a shortage of things to learn about cultural influences on human behavior. The important thing is that we have to want to learn it.

In Knowing Others, We Will Come to Know Ourselves

I hope I have been able to convey to you that human behavior is too rich and complex to be "captured" by understanding the world through the eyes of a single culture. One of the major goals of this book has been to examine how culture influences our behaviors and our lives and to challenge the many truths of our cultural world. Many cross-cultural studies in the literature speak to this breadth, and to this need.

In challenging the "traditional," we cannot and should not disregard its importance or the work that produced that knowledge. Indeed, to disregard that material or the work that produced it would be insensitive and that has no place in academic work. But we have much more to learn, and as time progresses the need to learn increases. Improvements in communications technologies bring previously distant points on the globe closer and closer together to further enmesh us in the global village. The opening of national borders and the infusion of people from all walks of life and cultures in our workplaces and in our families ensures that cross-cultural issues will remain a high priority in the years to come.

Can we keep up? Further cross-cultural research will help uncover universal and culture-specific aspects of human behavior. Scholars will increasingly have to include culture as a major determinant in theories of human behavior, and researchers will include culture as a variable in their studies. As new information is uncovered, we will undoubtedly improve our thinking about the nature of culture and cultural influences on the behavior of others. In knowing others, we will come to know ourselves.

References

Abebimpe, V. R. (1981). Overview: White norms and psychiatric diagnosis of black patients. *American Journal of Psychiatry, 139,* 888–891.

Acioly, N. M., & Schliemann, A. D. (1986). *Intuitive mathematics and schooling in understanding a lottery game.* Paper presented at the Tenth PME Conference, London.

Adamopoulos, J. (1991). The emergence of interpersonal behavior. In S. Ting-Toomey & F. Korzenny (Eds.), *Cross-cultural interpersonal communication* (pp. 155–270). Newbury Park, CA: Sage.

Ainsworth, M. D., Blehar, M. C., Waters, E., & Wall, S. (1978). *Patterns of attachment: A psychological study of the strange situation.* Hillsdale, NJ: Erlbaum.

Albright, L., Kenny, D. A., & Malloy, T. E. (1988). Consensus in personality judgments at zero acquaintance. *Journal of Personality and Social Psychology, 55,* 387–395.

Allen, L., & Santrock, J. W. (1993). *Psychology: The context of behavior.* Dubuque, IA: Brown & Benchmark.

Altman, I., & Taylor, D. A. (1973). *Social penetration: The development of interpersonal relationships.* New York: Holt, Rinehart, & Winston.

Altman, S. A. (1962). A field study of the sociobiology of rhesus monkeys, *Macacca mulatta. Annals of the New York Academy of Sciences, 102,* 338–435.

American Psychiatric Association. (1987). *Diagnostic and statistical manual of mental disorders* (3rd ed.). [DSM-III-R]. Washington, DC: author.

Archer, D. (Producer and director). (1991). *A world of gestures: Culture and nonverbal communication* [Videotape]. Berkeley: University of California Extension Center for Media and Independent Learning.

Argyle, M., & Cook, M. (1976). *Gaze and mutual gaze.* Cambridge, England: Cambridge University Press.

Argyle, M., Henderson, M., Bond, M. H., Iizuka, Y., & Contarello, A. (1986). Cross-cultural variations in relationship rules. *International Journal of Psychology, 21,* 287–315.

Asch, S. E. (1951). Effects of group pressure upon the modification and distortion of judgments. In H. Guetzkow (Ed.), *Groups, leadership and men: Research in human relations* (pp. 177–190). Pittsburgh: Carnegie Press.

Asch, S. E. (1955). Opinions and social pressures. *Scientific American, 193,* 31–35.

Asch, S. E. (1956). Studies of independence and conformity: A minority of one against a unanimous majority. *Psychological Monographs, 70*(9, Whole No. 416).

Atkinson, D. R., Casa, A., & Abreu, J. (1992). Mexican American acculturation, counselor ethnicity and cultural sensitivity, and perceived counselor competence. *American Psychologist, 39,* 515–520.

Atkinson, D. R., Furlong, M. J., & Poston, W. C. (1986). Afro-American preferences for counselor characteristics. *Journal of Counseling Psychology, 33,* 326–330.

Atkinson, D. R., Ponce, F. Q., & Martinez, F. M. (1984). Effects of ethnic, sex, and attitude similarity on counselor credibility. *Journal of Counseling Psychology, 31,* 588–590.

Atkinson, J. W. (1964). *An introduction to motivation.* Princeton, NJ: Van Nostrand Reinhold.

Au, T. K. (1983). Chinese and English counterfactuals: The Sapir-Whorf hypothesis revisited. *Cognition, 15,* 155–187.

Au, T. K. (1984). Counterfactuals: In reply to Alfred Bloom. *Cognition, 17,* 289–302.

Averill, J. R. (1980). Emotion and anxiety: Sociocultural, biological, and psychological determinants. In A. O. Rorty (Ed.), *Explaining emotions* (pp. 37–72). Berkeley: University of California Press.

Baddeley, A. D., & Hitch, G. (1974). Working memory. In G. Bower (Ed.), *Recent advances in learning and motivating.* New York: Academic Press.

Bahrick, H. P., & Hall, L. K. (1991). Lifetime maintenance of high school mathematics content. *Journal of Experimental Psychology: General, 120,* 20–33.

Bard, P., & Mountcastle, V. B. (1948). Some forebrain mechanisms involved in the expression of rage with special reference to suppression of angry behavior. *Research Publications of the Association for Research on Nervous and Mental Disease, 27,* 362-404.

Barry, H. (1980). Description and uses of the Human Relations Area Files. In H. C. Triandis & J. W. Berry (Eds.), *Handbook of cross-cultural psychology, Vol. 2: Methodology* (pp. 445–478). Boston: Allyn & Bacon.

Barry, H., Josephson, L., Lauer, E., & Marshall, C. (1976). Agents and techniques for child training. *Ethnology, 16,* 191–230.

Bartlett, F. C. (1932). *Remembering.* Cambridge, England: Cambridge University Press.

Baumrind, D. (1971). Current patterns of parental authority. *Developmental Psychology Monograph, 4* (No. 1, Pt. 2).

Beiser, M. (1985). A study of depression among traditional Africans, urban North Americans, and Southeast Asian refugees. In A. Kleinman & B. Good (Eds.),

Culture and depression. Studies in the anthropology and cross-cultural psychiatry of affect and disorder (pp. 272–298). Berkeley: University of California.

Benedict, R. (1946). *The crysanthemum and the sword.* Boston: Houghton Mifflin.

Berkman, L. F., & Syme, S. L. (1979). Social networks, host resistance, and mortality: A nine-year follow-up study of Alameda County residents. *American Journal of Epidemiology, 109,* 186–204.

Berko, J. (1958). The child's learning of English morphology. *Word, 14,* 150–177.

Berko-Gleason, J. (Ed.). (1989). *The development of language* (2nd ed.). Columbus, OH: C. E. Merrill.

Berlin, B., & Kay, P. (1969). *Basic color terms: Their universality and evolution.* Berkeley: University of California Press.

Bernal, M. (1994, August). *The development of ethnic awareness.* Paper presented at the Annual Convention of the American Psychological Association, Los Angeles, CA.

Berry, D. S., & McArthur, L. Z. (1985). Some components and consequences of a babyface. *Journal of Personality and Social Psychology, 48,* 312–323.

Berry, D. S., & McArthur, L. Z. (1986). Perceiving character in faces: The impact of age-related craniofacial changes in social perception. *Psychological Bulletin, 100,* 3–18.

Berry, J. W. (1966). Temne and Eskimo perceptual skills. *International Journal of Psychology, 1,* 207–229.

Berry, J. W. (1969). On cross-cultural comparability. *International Journal of Psychology, 4,* 119–128.

Berry, J. W. (1976). Sex differences in behavior and cultural complexity. *Indian Journal of Psychology, 51,* 89–97.

Berry, J. W., Poortinga, Y. H., Segall, M. H., & Dasen, P. R. (1992). *Cross-cultural psychology: Research and applications.* New York: Cambridge University Press.

Berscheid, E. (1988). Some comments on love's anatomy: Or, whatever happened to old-fashioned lust? In R. J. Sternberg & M. L. Barnes (Eds.), *Anatomy of love.* New Haven, CT: Yale University Press.

Berscheid, E., & Walster, E. (1978). *Interpersonal attraction.* Reading, MA: Addison-Wesley.

Betancourt, H., & Lopez, S. W. (1993). The study of culture, ethnicity, and race in American psychology. *American Psychologist, 48,* 629–637.

Bickerton, D. (1981). *The roots of language.* Ann Arbor, MI: Karoma Publishers.

Binion, V. J. (1990). Psychological androgyny: A black female perspective. *Sex Roles, 22,* 487–507.

Bissilat, J., Laya, D., Pierre, E., & Pidoux, C. (1967). La notion de lakkal dans la culture Djerma-Songhai [The concept of lakkal in Djerma-Songhai culture]. *Psychopathologie Africaine, 3,* 207–264.

Blau, Z. S. (1981). *Black children—white children: Competence, socialization, and social structure.* New York: Free Press.

Block, J. (1983). Differential premises arising from differential socialization of the sexes: Some conjectures. *Child Development, 54,* 1335–1354.

Bloom, A. H. (1981). *The linguistic shaping of thought: A study in the impact of language on thinking in China and the West.* Hillsdale, NJ: Erlbaum.

Bochner, S. (1982). *Cultures in contact: Studies in cross-cultural interaction.* Oxford, England: Pergamon.

Bond, M. H. (1986). *The psychology of the Chinese people.* New York: Oxford University Press.

Bond, M. H., & Forgas, J. P. (1984). Linking person perception to behavior intention across cultures: The role of cultural collectivism. *Journal of Cross-Cultural Psychology, 15,* 337–352.

Bond, M. H., Leung, K., & Wan, K. C. (1982). The social impact of self-effacing attributions: The Chinese case. *Journal of Social Psychology, 118,* 157–166.

Bond, M. H., & Tak-Sing, C. (1983). College students' spontaneous self concept: The effect of culture among respondents in Hong Kong, Japan, and the United States. *Journal of Cross-Cultural Psychology, 14,* 153–171.

Bond, M. H., & Wang, S. (1983). China: Aggressive behavior and the problems of mainstreaming order and harmony. In A. P. Goldstein & M. H. Segall (Eds.), *Aggression in global perspective* (pp. 58–74). New York: Pergamon.

Born, M., Bleichrodt, N., & Van der Flier, H. (1987). Cross-cultural comparison of sex-related differences on intelligence tests: A meta-analysis. *Journal of Cross-Cultural Psychology, 18,* 283–314.

Bouchard, T. J., Jr., & McGue, M. (1981). Familial studies of intelligence: A review. *Science, 212,* 1055–1059.

Boucher, J. D. (1979). Culture and emotion. In A. J. Marsella, R. G. Tharpl, & T. V. Ciborowski (Eds.), *Perspectives on cross-cultural psychology* (pp. 159–178). San Diego, CA: Academic Press.

Boucher, J. D., Landis, D., & Clark, K. A. (1987). *Ethnic conflict: International perspectives.* Newbury Park, CA: Sage.

Bowlby, J. (1969). *Attachment and loss, Vol. 1: Attachment.* New York: Basic Books.

Bradley, G. W. (1978). Self-serving biases in the attribution process: A re-examination of the fact or fiction question. *Journal of Personality and Social Psychology, 35,* 56–71.

Brandt, M. E., & Boucher, J. D. (1986). Concepts of depression in emotion lexicons of eight cultures. *International Journal of Intercultural Relations, 10,* 321–346.

Brehm, S. S. (1985). *Intimate relationships.* New York: Random House.

Brewer, M. B., & Campbell, D. T. (1976). *Ethnocentrism and intergroup attitudes.* New York: Wiley.

Brewer, M. B., & Kramer, R. M. (1985). The psychology of intergroup attitudes and behavior. *Annual Review of Psychology, 36,* 219–243.

Brislin, R. (1970). Back translation for cross-cultural research. *Journal of Cross-Cultural Psychology, 1,* 185–216.

Brislin, R. (1993). *Understanding culture's influence on behavior.* Fort Worth, TX: Harcourt Brace Jovanovich.

Brislin, R., & Hui, C. H. (1992). The preparation of managers for overseas assignments: The case of China. In O. Shenkar & N. L. Kelley (Eds.), *International business in China.* London: Routledge.

Bronstein, P. A., & Paludi, M. (1988). The introductory psychology course from a broader human perspective. In P. A. Bronstein & K. Quina (Eds.), *Teaching a psychology of people: Resources for gender and sociocultural awareness* (pp. 21–36). Washington, DC: American Psychological Association.

Brown, R., & Lenneberg, E. (1954). A study in language and cognition. *Journal of Abnormal and Social Psychology, 49,* 454–462.

Bruner, J. S., Oliver, R. R., & Greenfield, P. M. (1966). *Studies in cognitive growth.* New York: Wiley.

Buck, E. B., Newton, B. J., & Muramatsu, Y. (1984). Independence and obedience in the U. S. and Japan. *International Journal of Intercultural Relations, 8,* 279–300.

Buck, R. (1984). *The communication of emotion.* New York: Guilford Press.

Burger, J. M., & Hemans, L. T. (1988). Desire for control and the use of attribution processes. *Journal of Personality, 56,* 531–546.

Burgos, N. M., & Diaz-Perez, Y. I. (1986). An explanation of human sexuality in the Puerto Rican culture. Special issue: Human sexuality, ethnoculture, and social work. *Journal of Social Work and Human Sexuality, 4,* 135–150.

Buss, D. M. (1988). The evolution of human intrasexual competition: Tactics of mate attraction. *Journal of Personality and Social Psychology, 54,* 616–628.

Buss, D. M. (1989). Sex differences in human mate preferences: Evolutionary hypotheses tested in 37 cultures. *Behavioral and Brain Sciences, 12,* 1–49.

Byrne, D., & Murnen, S. K. (1988). Maintaining loving relationships. In R. J. Sternberg & M. L. Barnes (Eds.), *The psychology of love.* New Haven, CT: Yale University Press.

Calhoun, J. B. (1950). The study of wild animals under controlled conditions. *Annals of the New York Academy of Sciences, 51,* 113–122.

Cannon, W. B. (1927). The James-Lange theory of emotions: A critical examination and an alternative theory. *American Journal of Psychology, 39,* 106–124.

Carroll, J. B., & Casagrande, J. B. (1958). The function of language classifications in behavior. In E. E. Maccoby, T. M. Newcomb, & E. L. Hartley (Eds.), *Readings in social psychology* (pp. 18–31). New York: Holt.

Carson, R. C., Butcher, J. N., & Coleman, J. C. (1988). *Abnormal psychology and modern life* (8th ed.). Glenview, IL: Scott, Foresman.

Cashmore, J. A., & Goodnow, J. J. (1986). Influences on Australian parents' values: Ethnicity versus sociometric status. *Journal of Cross-Cultural Psychology, 17,* 441–454.

Cederblad, M. (1988). Behavioural disorders in children from different cultures. *Acta Psychiatrica Scandinavia Supplementum, 344,* 85–92.

Chinese Culture Connection. (1987). Chinese values and the search for culture-free dimensions of culture. *Journal of Cross-Cultural Psychology, 18,* 143–164.

Chisholm, J. (1983). *Navajo infancy.* New York: Aldine.

Chomsky, N. (1965). *Aspects of the theory of syntax.* Cambridge, MA: MIT Press.

Chomsky, N. (1967). *Current issues in linguistic theory.* The Hague: Mouton.

Chomsky, N. (1969). *Deep structure, surface structure, and semantic interpretation.* Bloomington: Indiana University Linguistics Club.

Cole, M., Gay, J., Glick, J. A., & Sharp, D. W. (1971). *The cultural context of learning and thinking: An exploration in experimental anthropology.* New York: Basic Books.

Cole, M., & Scribner, S. (1974). *Culture and thought: A psychological introduction.* New York: Wiley.

Collett, P. (1971). On training Englishmen in the non-verbal behavior of Arabs: An experiment in inter-cultural communication. *International Journal of Psychology, 6,* 209–215.

Comas-Diaz, L. (1992). The future of psychotherapy with ethnic minorities *Psychotherapy, 29,* 88–94.

Comas-Diaz, L., & Jacobsen, F. M. (1991). Ethnocultural transference and counter-transference in the therapeutic dyad. *American Journal of Orthospsychiatry, 61,* 392–402.

Cousins, S. D. (1989). Culture and self-perception in Japan and the United States. *Journal of Personality and Social Psychology, 56,* 124–131.

Crittenden, K. S. (1991). Asian self-effacement or feminine modesty? Attributional patterns of women university students in Taiwan. *Gender and Society, 5,* 98–117.

Darwin, C. (1872). *The expression of emotion in man and animals.* London: John Murray.

Dasen, P. R. (1975). Concrete operational development in three cultures. *Journal of Cross-Cultural Psychology, 6,* 156–172.

Dasen, P. R. (1982). Cross-cultural aspects of Piaget's theory: The competence-performance model. In L. L. Adler (Ed.), *Cross-cultural research at issue.* New York: Academic Press.

Dasen, P. R., Dembele, B., Ettien, K., Kabran, L., Kamagate, D., Koffi, D. A., & N'Guessean, A. (1985). N'glouele, l'intelligence chez les Baoule [N'glouele: Intelligence among the Ivory Coast Baoule]. *Archives of Psychologie, 53,* 293–324.

Dasen, P. R., Lavallee, M., & Retschitzki, J. (1979). Training conservation of quantity (liquids) in West African (Baoule) children. *International Journal of Psychology, 14,* 57–68.

Dasen, P. R., Ngini, L., & Lavallee, M. (1979). Cross-cultural training studies of concrete operations. In L. Eckensberger, Y. Poortinga, & W. Lonner (Eds.), *Cross-cultural contributions to psychology* (pp. 94–104). Amsterdam: Swets & Zeitlinger.

Deck, L. P. (1968). Buying brains by the inch. *Journal of College and University Personnel Associations, 19,* 33–37.

DePaulo, B. M., Stone, J., & Lassiter, G. D. (1985). Deceiving and detecting deceit. In B. R. Schlenker (Ed.), *The self and social life* (pp. 323–370). New York: McGraw-Hill.

De Valois, R. L., Abramov, I., & Jacobs, G. H. (1966). Analysis of response patterns of LGN cells. *Journal of the Optical Society of America, 56,* 966–977.

De Valois, R. L., & Jacobs, G. H. (1968). Primate color vision. *Science, 162,* 533–540.

Dinges, N. G., & Hull, P. (1992). Personality, culture, and international studies. In D. Lieberman (Ed.), *Revealing the world: An interdisciplinary reader for international studies.* Dubuque, IA: Kendall-Hunt.

Dion, K. K. (1986). Stereotyping based on physical attractiveness: Issues and conceptual perspectives. In C. P. Herman, M. P. Zanna, & E. T. Higgins (Eds.), *Ontario symposium on personality and social psychology* (Vol. 3). Hillsdale, NJ: Erlbaum.

Doi, K. (1982). Two dimensional theory of achievement motivation. *Japanese Journal of Psychology, 52,* 344–350.

Doi, K. (1985). The relation between the two dimensions of achievement motivation and personality of male university students. *Japanese Journal of Psychology, 56,* 107–110.

Doi, T. (1973). *The anatomy of dependence.* Tokyo: Kodansha.

Duda, J. L., & Allison, M. T. (1989). The attributional theory of achievement motivation: Cross-cultural considerations. *International Journal of Intercultural Relations, 13,* 37–55.

Durkheim, E. (1938/1964). *The rules of sociological method.* Reprint. London: The Free Press of Glenscoe.

Durrett, M. E., Otaki, M., & Richards, P. (1984). Attachment and mothers' perception of support from the father. *Journal of the International Society for the Study of Behavioral Development, 7,* 167–176.

Dyal, J. A. (1984). Cross-cultural research with the locus of control construct. In H. M. Lefcourt (Ed.), *Research with the locus of control construct* (Vol. 3), (pp. 209–306). New York: Academic Press.

Earley, P. C. (1989). Social loafing and collectivism: A comparison of the United States and the People's Republic of China. *Administrative Science Quarterly, 34,* 565–581.

Efron, D. (1941). *Gesture and environment.* New York: King's Crown.

Ekman, P. (1972). Universal and cultural differences in facial expression of emotion. In J. R. Cole (Ed.), *Nebraska symposium on motivation, 1971* (pp. 207–283). Lincoln: University of Nebraska Press.

Ekman, P., & Friesen, W. V. (1969). The repertoire of nonverbal behavior: Categories, origins, usage, and coding. *Semiotica, 1,* 49–98.

Ekman, P., & Friesen, W. V. (1971). Constants across cultures in the face and emotion. *Journal of Personality and Social Psychology, 17,* 124–129.

Ekman, P., & Friesen, W. V. (1986). A new pan-cultural expression of emotion. *Motivation and Emotion, 10,* 159–168.

Ekman, P., Friesen, W. V., & Bear, J. (1984, May). International language of gestures. *Psychology Today,* pp. 64–69.

Ekman, P., Friesen, W. V., & Ellsworth, P (1972). *Emotion in the human face.* New York: Garland.

Ekman, P., Friesen, W. V., O'Sullivan, M., Chan, A., Diacoyanni-Tarlatzis, I., Heider, K., Krause, R., LeCompte, W. A., Pitcairn, T., Ricci-Bitti, P. E., Scherer, K., Tomita, M., & Tzavaras, A. (1987). Universals and cultural differences in the judgment of facial expressions of emotion. *Journal of Personality and Social Psychology, 53,* 712–717.

Ekman, P., & Heider, K. G. (1988). The universality of a contempt expression: A replication. *Motivation and Emotion, 12,* 17–22.

Ekman, P., Levenson, R., & Friesen, W. V. (1983). Autonomic nervous system activity distinguishes among emotions. *Science, 221,* 1208–1210.

Ekman, P., Sorenson, E. R., & Friesen, W. V. (1969). Pan-cultural elements in facial displays of emotion. *Science, 164,* 86–94.

El-Islam, M. F. (1983). Cultural change and intergenerational relationships in Arabian families. *International Journal of Family Psychiatry, 4,* 321–329.

Erikson, E. H. (1950). *Childhood and society.* New York: Norton.

Erikson, E. H. (1963). *Childhood and society* (2nd ed.). New York: Norton.

Ervin, S. M. (1964). Language and TAT content in bilinguals. *Journal of Abnormal and Social Psychology, 68,* 500–507.

Espin, O. M. (1993). Feminist theory: Not for or by white women only. *Counseling Psychologist, 21,* 103–108.

Evans, J. L., & Segall, M. H. (1969). Learning to classify by color and function: A study of concept discovery by Ganda children. *Journal of Social Psychology, 77,* 35–55.

Exline, R. V., Jones, P., & Maciorowski, K. (1977). *Race, affiliative-conflict theory and mutual visual attention during conversation.* Paper presented at the American Psychological Association meeting in San Francisco.

Fehr, B. J. (1977). *Visual interactions in same and interracial dyads.* Unpublished master's thesis, University of Delaware.

Fehr, B. J. (1981). *The communication of evaluation through the use of interpersonal gaze in same and interracial female dyads.* Unpublished doctoral dissertation, University of Delaware.

Fehr, B. J., & Exline, R. V. (1987). Social visual interaction: A conceptual and literature review. In A. W. Siegman & S. Feldstein (Eds.), *Nonverbal behavior and communication* (2nd ed.) (pp. 225–326). Hillsdale, NJ: Erlbaum.

Feist, J., & Brannon, L. (1988). *Health psychology: An introduction to behavior and health.* Belmont, CA: Wadsworth.

Ferrante, J. (1992). *Sociology: A global perspective.* Belmont, CA: Wadsworth.

Festinger, L., Schachter, S., & Back, K. (1950). *Social pressures in informal groups: A study of human factors in housing.* New York: Harper.

Fishman, J. A. (1960). A systematization of the Whorfian hypothesis. *Behavioral Science, 5,* 323-339.

Forgas, J. P., Furnham, A., & Frey, D. (1989). Cross-national differences in attributions of wealth and economic success. *Journal of Social Psychology, 129,* 643–657.

Forston, R. F., & Larson, C. U. (1968). The dynamics of space: An experimental study in proxemic behavior among Latin Americans and North Americans. *Journal of Communication, 18,* 109–116.

Franklin, Y. (1992). *Communication and marital satisfaction in Japanese and Caucasian American intermarried couples.* Unpublished doctoral dissertation, California Institute of Integral Studies, San Francisco.

Freedman, D. (1974). *Human infancy: An evolutionary perspective.* Hillsdale, NJ: Erlbaum.

Friedman, M., & Rosenman, R. H. (1974). *Type A behavior and your heart.* New York: Knopf.

Friesen, W. V. (1972). *Cultural differences in facial expressions in a social situation: An experimental test of the concept of display rules.* Unpublished doctoral dissertation, University of California, San Francisco.

Fromm, E. (1941). *Escape from freedom.* New York: Farrar & Rinehart.

Furnham, A. F. (1984). Value systems and anomie in three cultures. *International Journal of Psychology, 19,* 565–579.

Gabrenya, W. K., Jr., Wang, Y., & Latane, B. (1985). Social loafing on an optimizing task: Cross-cultural differences among Chinese and Americans. *Journal of Cross-Cultural Psychology, 16,* 223–242.

Garcia Coll, C. T. (1990). Developmental outcomes of minority infants: A process oriented look at our beginnings. *Child Development, 61,* 270–289.

Garcia Coll, C. T., Sepkoski, C., & Lester, B. M. (1981). Cultural and biomedical correlates of neonatal behavior. *Developmental Psychobiology, 14,* 147–154.

Gardner, H., & Hatch, T. (1989). Multiple intelligences go to school: Educational implications of the theory of multiple intelligences. *Educational Researcher, 18,* 4–10.

Garratt, G. A., Baxter, J. C., & Rozelle, R. M. (1981). Training university police in black-American nonverbal behaviors. *Journal of Social Psychology, 113,* 217–229.

Geertz, C. (1975). From the natives point of view: On the nature of anthropological understanding. *American Scientist, 63,* 47–53.

Georgas, J. (1989). Changing family values in Greece: From collectivist to individualist. *Journal of Cross-Cultural Psychology, 20,* 80–91.

Georgas, J. (1991). Intrafamily acculturation of values in Greece. *Journal of Cross-Cultural Psychology, 22,* 445–457.

Gerber, E. (1975). *The cultural patterning of emotions in Samoa.* Unpublished doctoral dissertation, University of California, San Diego.

Gilligan, C. (1982). *In a different voice: Psychological theory and women's development.* Cambridge, MA: Harvard University Press.

Gim, R. H., Atkinson, D. R., & Kim, S. J. (1991). Asian-American acculturation, counselor ethnicity and cultural sensitivity, and ratings of counselors. *Journal of Counseling Psychology, 38,* 57–62.

Gladwin, H., & Gladwin, C. (1971). Estimating market conditions and profit expectations of fish sellers at Cape Coast, Ghana. In G. Dalton (Ed.), *Studies in economic anthropology. Anthropological Studies No. 7* (pp. 122–143). Washington, DC: American Anthropological Association.

Gladwin, T. (1970). *East is a big bird: Navigation and logic on Puluwat Atoll.* Cambridge, MA: Harvard University Press.

Gleason, H. A. (1961). *An introduction to descriptive linguistics.* New York: Holt, Rinehart & Winston.

Goody, J. R. (1968). *Literacy in traditional societies.* Cambridge, England: Cambridge University Press.

Goody, J. R. (1977). *The domestication of the savage mind.* Cambridge, England: Cambridge University Press.

Graham, S. (1984). Communicating sympathy and anger to Black and White children: The cognitive (attributional) consequences of affective cues. *Journal of Personality and Social Psychology, 47,* 40–54.

Graham, S., & Long, A. (1986). Race, class, and the attributional process. *Journal of Educational Psychology, 78,* 4–13.

Greenfield, P. M., Reich, L. C., & Oliver, R. R. (1966). On culture and equivalence II. In J. S. Bruner, R. R. Oliver, & P. M. Greenfield (Eds.), *Studies in cognitive growth* (pp. 270–318). New York: Wiley.

Grossmann, K., Grossmann, K. E., Spangler, S., Suess, G., & Unzner, L. (1985). Maternal sensitivity and newborn attachment orientation responses as related to quality of attachment in northern Germany. In I. Bretherton & E. Waters (Eds.), *Growing points of attachment theory. Monographs of the Society of Research in Child Development, 50* (1–2 Serial No. 209).

Gudykunst, W. B., Gao, G., Schmidt, K. L., Nishida, T., Bond, M. H., Leung, K., Wang, G., & Barraclough, R. A. (1992). The influence of individualism-collectivism, self-monitoring, and predicted-outcome value communication in in-group and outgroup relationships. *Journal of Cross-Cultural Psychology, 23,* 196–213.

Gudykunst, W. B., & Ting-Toomey, S. (1988). Culture and affective communication. Special Issue: Communication and affect. *American Behavioral Scientist, 31,* 384–400.

Guilford, J. P. (1985). The structure of intellect model. In B. B. Wolman (Ed.), *Handbook of intelligence: Theories, measurements, and applications.* New York: Wiley.

Hadiyono, J. E. P., & Hahn, M. W. (1985). Personality differences and sex similarities in American and Indonesian college students. *Journal of Social Psychology, 125,* 703–708.

Hall, C. C. I., Evans, B. J., & Selice, S. (Eds.). (1989). *Black females in the United States: A bibliography from 1967 to 1987.* Washington, DC: American Psychological Association.

Hall, E. T. (1963). A system for the notation of proxemic behavior. *American Anthropologist, 65,* 1003–1026.

Hall, E. T. (1966). *The hidden dimension.* New York: Doubleday.

Hall, J. A. (1978). Gender effects in decoding nonverbal cues. *Psychological Bulletin, 85,* 845–857.

Hall, K. R. L., & Devore, I. (1965). Baboon social behavior. In I. Devore (Ed.), *Primate behavior.* New York: Holt, Rinehart & Winston.

Hall, V. C., Howe, A., Merkel, S., & Lederman, N. (1986). Behavior, motivation, and achievement in desegregated junior high school science classes. *Journal of Educational Psychology, 78,* 108–115.

Hamilton, V. L., Blumenfeld, P. C., Akoh, H., & Miura, K. (1991). Group and gender in Japanese and American elementary classrooms. *Journal of Cross-Cultural Psychology, 22,* 317–346.

Harkins, S. G. (1987). Social loafing and social facilitation. *Journal of Experimental Social Psychology, 23,* 1–18.

Harkins, S. G., & Petty, R. E. (1982). Effects of task difficulty and task uniqueness on social loafing. *Journal of Personality and Social Psychology, 43,* 1214–1229.

Harlow, H. F., & Harlow, M. K. (1969). Effects of various mother-infant relationships on rhesus monkey behavior. In B. M. Foss (Ed.), *Determinants of infant behavior* (Vol. 4). London: Methuen.

Harrison, A. O., Wilson, M. N., Pine, C. J., Chan, S. Q., & Buriel, R. (1990). Family ecologies of ethnic minority children. *Child Development, 61,* 347–362.

Hatfield, E. (1988). Passionate and companionate love. In R. J. Sternberg & M. L. Barnes (Eds.), *The psychology of love* (pp. 191–217). New Haven, CT: Yale University Press.

Hau, K., & Salili, F. (1991). Structure and semantic differential placement of specific causes: Academic causal attributions by Chinese students in Hong Kong. *International Journal of Psychology, 26,* 175–193.

Heider, E. R., & Oliver, D. (1972) The structure of the color space in naming and memory for two languages. *Cognitive Psychology, 3,* 337–354.

Helgeson, V. S., Shaver, P., & Dyer, M. (1987). Prototypes of intimacy and distance in same-sex and opposite-sex relationships. *Journal of Social and Personal Relationships, 4,* 195–233.

Henderson, N. D. (1982). Human behavior genetics. *Annual Review of Psychology, 33,* 403–440.

Hendrick, C., & Hendrick, S. (1983). *Liking, loving, and relating.* Pacific Grove, CA: Brooks/Cole.

Herrnstein, R. J., & Murray, C. (1994). *The bell curve: Intelligence and class structure in American life.* New York: Free Press.

Hiatt, L. R. (1978). Classification of the emotions. In L. R. Hiatt (Ed.), *Australian aboriginal concepts* (pp. 182–187). Princeton, NJ: Humanities Press.

Higginbotham, H. N. (1979). Culture and mental health services. In A. J. Marsella, G. DeVos, & F. L. K. Hsu (Eds.), *Perspectives on cross-cultural psychology* (pp. 307–332). New York: Academic Press.

Hinde, R. A., & Rowell, T. E. (1962). Communication by posture and facial expressions in the rhesus monkey (*Macaca mulatta*). *Proceedings of the Zoological Society of London, 138,* 1–21.

Hippler, A. E. (1980). Editorial. *International Association of Cross-Cultural Psychology Newsletter, 14,* 2–3.

Hofstede, G. (1980). *Culture's consequences: International differences in work-related values.* Beverly Hills, CA: Sage.

Hofstede, G. (1983). Dimensions of national cultures in fifty countries and three regions. In J. B. Deregowski, S. Dziurawiec, & R. C. Annis (Eds.), *Expiscations in cross-cultural psychology* (pp. 335–355). Lisse: Swets & Zeitlinger.

Hofstede, G. (1984). *Culture's consequences: International differences in work-related values.* Newbury Park, CA: Sage.

Hofstede, G., & Bond, M. (1988). Confucius & economic growth: New trends in culture's consequences. *Organizational Dynamics, 16*(4), 4–21.

Hollander, E. (1985). Leadership and power. In G. Lindzey & E. Aaronson (Eds.), *The handbook of social psychology* (3d ed.), (Vol. 2), (pp. 485–537). New York: Random House.

Howell, S. (1981). Rules not words. In P. Heelas & A. Lock (Eds.), *Indigenous psychologies: The anthropology of the self* (pp. 133–143). San Diego, CA: Academic Press.

Huang, L. N., & Ying, Y. (1989). Japanese children and adolescents. In J. T. Gibbs & L. N. Huang (Eds.), *Children of color.* San Francisco: Jossey-Bass.

Hudson, W. (1960). Pictorial depth perception in subcultural groups in Africa. *Journal of Social Psychology, 52,* 183–208.

Hui, C. H. (1984). *Individualism-collectivism: Theory, measurement, and its relation to reward allocation.* Unpublished doctoral dissertation, University of Illinois.

Hui, C. H. (1988). Measurement of individualism-collectivism. *Journal of Research in Personality, 22,* 17–36.

Hui, C. H., & Triandis, H. C. (1986). Individualism-collectivism: A study of cross cultural researchers. *Journal of Cross-Cultural Psychology, 17,* 225–248.

Hull, P. V. (1987). Bilingualism: *Two languages, two personalities? Resources in education, educational resources clearinghouse on education.* Ann Arbor: University of Michigan Press.

Hull, P. V. (1990a). *Bilingualism: Two languages, two personalities?* Unpublished doctoral dissertation, University of California, Berkeley.

Hull, P. V. (1990b, August). *Bilingualism and language choice.* Paper presented at the Annual Convention of the American Psychological Association, Boston.

Hunt, E., & Agnoli, F. (1991). The Whorfian hypothesis: A cognitive psychology perspective. *Psychological Review, 98,* 377–389.

Husen, T. (1967). *International study of achievement in mathematics.* New York: Wiley.

Ineichen, B. (1979). The social geography of marriage. In M. Cook & G. Wilson (Eds.), *Love and attraction.* New York: Pergamon Press.

Izard, C. E. (1971). *The face of emotion.* New York: Appleton-Century-Crofts.

Jackson, J. M., & Williams, K. D. (1985). Social loafing on difficult tasks: Working collectively can improve performance. *Journal of Personality and Social Psychology, 49,* 937–942.

James, W. (1890). *The principles of psychology* (Vol. 2). New York: Holt.

Jencks, C., Smith, M., Acland, H., Bane, M. J., Cohen, D., Gintis, H., Heyns, B., & Michaelson, S. (1972). *Inequality: A reassessment of the effect of family and schooling in America.* New York: Harper & Row.

Jensen, A. R. (1969). How much can we boost IQ and scholastic achievement? *Harvard Educational Review, 39,* 1–123.

Jensen, A. R. (1980). *Bias in mental testing.* New York: Free Press.

Jensen, A. R. (1981). *Straight talk about mental tests.* London: Methuen.

John, O. (1989). The BFI-54. Unpublished test, Institute of Personality and Social Research, Department of Psychology, University of California, Berkeley.

Jones, E. E., & Harris, V. A. (1967). The attribution of attitudes. *Journal of Experimental Social Psychology, 3,* 1–24.

Jones, E. E., & Nisbett, R. E. (1971). The actor and the observer: Divergent perceptions of the causes of behavior. In E. E. Jones, D. E. Kanouse, H. H. Kelley, R. E. Nisbett, S. Valins, & B. Weiner (Eds.), *Attribution: Perceiving the causes of behavior* (pp. 79–94) Morristown, NJ: General Learning Press.

Joseph, R. A., Markus, H. R., & Tafarodi, R. W. (1992). Gender differences in the source of self-esteem. *Journal of Personality and Social Psychology, 63,* 1017–1028.

Karno, M., Jenkins, J. H., De la Silva, A., Sanatana, F., Telles, C., Lopez, S., & Mintz, J. (1987). Expressed emotion and schizophrenic outcome among Mexican-American families. *Journal of Nervous and Mental Disease, 175,* 145–151.

Kashima, Y., & Triandis, H. C. (1986). The self-serving bias in attributions as a coping strategy: A cross-cultural study. *Journal of Cross-Cultural Psychology, 17,* 83–97.

Kay, P., & Kempton, W. (1984). What is the Sapir-Whorf hypothesis? *American Anthropologist, 86,* 65–89.

Keats, D. M. (1982). Cultural bases of concepts of intelligence: A Chinese versus Australian comparison. In P. Sukontasarp, N. Yongsiri, P. Intasuwan, N. Jotiban, & C. Suvannathat (Eds.), *Proceedings of the Second Asian Workshop on Child and Adolescent Development* (pp. 67–75). Bangkok: Burapasilpa Press.

Kelley, H. H. (1967). Attributional theory in social psychology. *Nebraska Symposium on Motivation, 15,* 192–241.

Kelley, H. H. (1973). The processes of causal attribution. *American Psychologist, 28,* 107–128.

Kemper, T. (1978). *A social interactional theory of emotions.* New York: Wiley.

Kendon, A. (1967). Some functions of gaze-direction in social interaction. *Acta Psychologica, 26,* 22–63.

Kendon, A. (1987). On gesture: Its complementary relationship with speech. In A. W. Siegman & S. Feldstein (Eds.), *Nonverbal behavior and communication* (pp. 65–97). Hillsdale, NJ: Erlbaum.

Kiev, A. (1972). *Transcultural psychiatry.* New York: Free Press.

Kitayama, S., & Markus, H. R. (in press, a). A cultural perspective to self-conscious emotions. In J. P. Tangney & K. Fisher (Eds.), *Shame, guilt, embarrassment, and pride: Empirical studies of self-conscious emotions.* New York: Guilford Press.

Kitayama, S., & Markus, H. R. (in press, b). Culture and self: Implications for internationalizing psychology. In J. D'Arms, R. G. Hastie, & H. K. Jacobson (Eds.). *Becoming more international and global: Challenges for American higher education.* Ann Arbor: University of Michigan Press.

Kitayama, S., Markus, H. R., Kurokawa, M., & Negishi, K. (1993). *Social orientation of emotions: Cross-cultural evidence and implications.* Unpublished manuscript. University of Oregon.

Kitayama, S., Markus, H. R., & Matsumoto, H. (1995). Culture, self, and emotion: A cultural perspective on "self-conscious" emotions. In J. P. Tangney & K. Fisher (Eds.), *Self-conscious emotions: The psychology of shame, guilt, embarrassment, and pride* (pp. 439–464). New York: Guilford Press.

Kleinman, A. (1978). Culture and depression. *Culture and Medical Psychiatry, 2,* 295–296.

Kleinman, A. (1988). *Rethinking psychiatry: From cultural category to personal experience.* New York: Free Press.

Kluckholn, F., & Strodtbeck, F. (1961). *Variations in value orientations.* Evanston, IL: Row, Peterson.

Kohlberg, L. (1976). Moral stages and moralization: The cognitive-developmental approach. In J. Lickona (Ed.), *Moral development behavior: Theory, research and social issues.* New York: Holt, Rinehart & Winston.

Kohlberg, L. (1984). *The psychology of moral development: The nature and validity of moral stages* (Vol. 2). New York: Harper & Row.

Kroeber, A. L., & Kluckholn, C. (1952). *Culture: A critical review of concepts and definitions* (Vol. 47, No. 1). Cambridge, MA: Peabody Museum.

Kudoh, T., & Matsumoto, D. (1985). A cross-cultural examination of the semantic dimensions of body postures. *Journal of Personality and Social Psychology, 48,* 1440–1446.

LaFrance, M., & Mayo, C. (1976). Racial differences in gaze behavior during conversations: Two systematic observational studies. *Journal of Personality and Social Psychology, 33*(5), 547–552.

Lammers, C. J., & Hickson, D. J. (Eds.).(1979). *Organizations alike and unlike: International and interinstitutional studies in the sociology of organizations.* London: Routledge & Kegan Paul.

Lange, C. (1887). *Ueber Gemuthsbewegungen.* Leipzig: Theodor Thomas.

Latane, B. (1981). The psychology of social impact. *American Psychologist, 36,* 343–356.

Latane, B., Williams, K., & Harkins, S. (1979). Many hands make light the work: The causes and consequences of social loafing. *Journal of Personality and Social Psychology, 37,* 322–332.

Laurendeau–Bendavid, M. (1977). Culture, schooling, and cognitive development: A comparative study of children in French Canada and Rwanda. In P. R. Dasen (Ed.), *Piagetian psychology: Cross-cultural contributions* (pp. 123–168). New York: Gardner/Wiley.

Laurent, A. (1978). *Matrix organizations and Latin cultures.* Working Paper 78–28. Brussels: European Institute for Advanced Studies in Management.

Lazarus, R. S. (1991). *Emotion and adaptation.* New York: Oxford University Press.

Lee, H. O., & Boster, F. J. (1992). Collectivism-individualism in perceptions of speech rate: A cross-cultural comparison. *Journal of Cross-Cultural Psychology, 23,* 377–388.

Leff, J. (1973). Culture and the differentiation of emotional states. *British Journal of Psychiatry, 123,* 299–306.

Leff, J. (1977). International variations in the diagnosis of psychiatric illness. *British Journal of Psychiatry, 131,* 329–338.

Leff, J. (1981). *Psychiatry around the globe: A transcultural view.* New York: Dekker.

Leff, J. (1986). The epidemiology of mental illness. In J. L. Cox (Ed.), *Transcultural psychiatry* (pp. 23–36). London: Croom Helm.

Leung, K. (1988). Some determinants of conflict avoidance. *Journal of Cross-Cultural Psychology, 19,* 125–136.

Levine, R. A. (1977). Child rearing as cultural adaptation. In P. H. Leiderman, S. R. Tulkin, & A. Rosenfeld (Eds.), *Culture and infancy* (pp. 15–27). New York: Academic Press.

Levy, R. I. (1973). *Tahitians.* Chicago: University of Chicago Press.

Levy, R. I. (1983). Introduction: Self and emotion. *Ethos, 11,* 128–134.

Levy, R. I. (1984). The emotions in comparative perspective. In K. Scherer & P. Ekman (Eds.), *Approaches to emotion* (pp. 397–412). Hillsdale, NJ: Erlbaum.

Levy-Bruhl, L. (1910). *Les fonctions mentales dans les societes inferieures.* Paris: Alcan. (Trans: 1928, *How natives think.* London: Allen & Unwin.)

Levy-Bruhl, L. (1922). *Mentaliete primitive.* Paris: Alcan. (Trans. 1923, *Primitive mentality.* London: Allen & Unwin.)

Levy-Bruhl, L. (1949). *Les camets de Lucien Levy-Bruhl.* [The notebooks of Lucien Levy-Bruhl.] Paris: Press Universitaires de France.

Lively, W. J., & Bromley, D. B. (1973). *Person perception in childhood and adolescence.* London: Wiley.

Lonner, W. J., & Ibrahim, F. A. (1989). Assessment in cross-cultural counseling. In P. B. Pedersen, J. Dragus, W. Lonner, & J. E. Trimble (Eds.), *Counseling across cultures* (3rd ed.), (pp. 299–334). Honolulu: University of Hawaii.

Luria, A. R. (1976). *Cognitive development: Its cultural and social foundations.* (M. Lopes & L. Solotaroff, trans.). Cambridge, MA: Harvard University Press (original work published 1974).

Lutz, C. (1980). *Emotion words and emotional development on Ifaluk Atoll.* Unpublished doctoral dissertation, Harvard University.

Lutz, C. (1982). The domain of emotion words in Ifaluk. *American Ethnologist, 9,* 113–128.

Lutz, C. (1983). Parental goals, ethnopsychology, and the development of emotional meaning. *Ethos, 11,* 246–262.

Lutz, C. (1988). *Unnatural emotions: Everyday sentiments on a Micronesian atoll and their challenge to Western theory.* Chicago: University of Chicago Press.

Maccoby, E. E., & Jacklin, C. N. (1974). *The psychology of sex differences.* Stanford, CA: Stanford University Press.

Maccoby, E. E., & Martin, J. A. (1983). Socialization in the context of the family: Parent-child interaction. In E. M. Hetherington (Ed.), *Handbook of child psychology, Vol. 4: Socialization, personality, and social development* (4th ed.), (pp. 1–101). New York: Wiley.

Maehr, M., & Nicholls, J. (1980). Culture and achievement motivation: A second look. In N. Warren (Ed.), *Studies in cross-cultural psychology* (Vol. 2), (pp. 221–267). London: Academic Press.

Malpass, R. (1993, August). *A discussion of the ICAI.* Symposium presented at the Annual Convention of the American Psychological Association, Toronto, Canada.

Manson, S. M., & Shore, J. H. (1981). Psychiatric epidemological research among American Indian and Alaska Natives: Some methodological issues. *White Cloud Journal, 2,* 48–56.

Manson, S. M., Shore, J. H., & Bloom, J. D. (1985). The depressive experience in American Indian communities: A challenge for psychiatric theory and diagnosis. In A. Kleinman & B. Good (Eds.), *Culture and depression: Studies in the anthropology and cross-cultural psychiatry of affect and disorder* (pp. 331–368). Berkeley: University of California Press.

Markus, H. R. (1977). Self-schemata and processing information about the self. *Journal of Personality and Social Psychology, 35,* 63–78.

Markus, H. R., & Kitayama, S. (1991a). Cultural variation in self-concept. In G. R. Goethals & J. Strauss (Eds.), *Multidisciplinary perspectives on the self.* New York: Springer-Verlag.

Markus, H. R., & Kitayama, S. (1991b). Culture and the self: Implications for cognition, emotion, and motivation. *Psychological Review, 98,* 224–253.

Markus, H. R., & Zajonc, R. (1985). The cognitive perspective in social psychology. In G. Lindzey & E. Aaronson (Eds.), *Handbook of social psychology* (3d ed.), (Vol. 1), (pp. 137–230). New York: Random House.

Marmot, M. G., & Syme, S. L (1976). Acculturation and coronary heart disease in Japanese Americans. *American Journal of Epidemiology, 104,* 225–247.

Marsella, A. J. (1979). Cross-cultural studies of mental disorders. In A. J. Marsella, G. DeVos, & F. L. K. Hsu (Eds.), *Perspectives on cross-cultural psychology* (pp. 233–262). New York: Academic Press.

Marsella, A. J. (1980). Depressive experience and disorder across cultures. In H. C. Triandis & J. Draguns (Eds.), *Handbook of cross-cultural psychology, Vol. 6: Psychopathology* (pp. 237–289). Boston: Allyn & Bacon.

Martyn-Johns, T. A. (1977). Cultural conditioning of views of authority and its effect on the business decision-making process with special reference to Java. In Y. H. Poortinga (Ed.), *Basic problems in cross-cultural psychology* (pp. 344–352). Lisse: Swets and Zeitlinger.

Matsumoto, D. (1989). Cultural influences on the perception of emotion. *Journal of Cross-Cultural Psychology, 20,* 92–105.

Matsumoto, D. (1991). Cultural influences on facial expressions of emotion. *Southern Communication Journal, 56,* 128–137.

Matsumoto, D. (1992). American-Japanese cultural differences in the recognition of universal facial expressions. *Journal of Cross-Cultural Psychology, 23,* 72–84.

Matsumoto, D. (1993). Ethnic differences in affect intensity, emotion judgments, display rule attitudes, and self-reported emotional expression in an American sample. *Motivation and Emotion, 17*(2), 107–123.

Matsumoto, D. (1994). *Cultural influences on research methods and statistics.* Pacific Grove, CA: Brooks/Cole.

Matsumoto, D., & Assar, M. (1992). The effects of language on judgments of universal facial expressions of emotion. *Journal of Nonverbal Behavior, 16,* 85–99.

Matsumoto, D., & Ekman, P. (1989). American-Japanese cultural differences in intensity ratings of facial expressions of emotion. *Motivation and Emotion, 13,* 143–157.

Matsumoto, D., & Fletcher, D. (1994). *Cultural influences on disease.* Manuscript submitted for publication.

Matsumoto, D., & Hearn, V. (1991). *Culture and emotion: Display rule differences between the United States, Poland, and Hungary.* Manuscript submitted for publication.

Matsumoto, D., & Kishimoto, H. (1983). Developmental characteristics in judgments of emotion from nonverbal vocal cues. *International Journal of Intercultural Relations, 7,* 415–424.

Matsumoto, D., & Kudoh, T. (1987). Cultural similarities and differences in the semantic dimensions of body postures. *Journal of Nonverbal Behavior, 11,* 166–179.

Matsumoto, D., & Kudoh, T. (1993). American-Japanese cultural differences in attributions of personality based on smiles. *Journal of Nonverbal Behavior, 17*(4), 231–243.

Matsumoto, D., Kudoh, T., Scherer, K., & Wallbott, H. (1988). Emotion antecedents and reactions in the U.S. and Japan. *Journal of Cross-Cultural Psychology, 19,* 267–286.

Matsumoto, D., Pun, K. K., Nakatani, M., Kadowaki, D., Weissman, M., McCarter, L., Fletcher, D., & Takeuchi, S. (1994). *Cultural differences in attitudes and concerns about osteoporosis in older Japanese and Japanese-American women: Differential implications for patient management.* Manuscript submitted for publication.

Matsumoto, D., Wallbott, H. G., & Scherer, K. R. (1987). Emotions in intercultural communication. In M. K. Asante & W. B. Gudykunst (Eds.), *Handbook of international and cultural communication.* Newbury Park, CA: Sage.

Matsumoto, D., Weissman, M., Preston, K., & Brown, B. (1995). *Context-specific measurement of individualism-collectivism on the individual level: The IC Assessment Inventory (ICAI).* Manuscript submitted for publication.

Matsuyama, Y., Hama, H., Kawamura, Y., & Mine, H. (1978). Analysis of emotional words. *The Japanese Journal of Psychology, 49,* 229–232.

McClelland, D. C. (1961). *The achieving society.* Princeton, NJ: Van Nostrand.

McCrae, R. R., & Costa, P. T. (1987). Validation of the five-factor model of personality across instruments and observers. *Journal of Personality and Social Psychology, 52,* 81–90.

Mead, M. (1961). *Cooperation and competition among primitive people.* Boston: Beacon Press.

Mehrabian, A. (1981). *Silent messages: Implication of emotions and attitudes* (2nd ed.). Belmont, CA: Wadsworth.

Messick, D. M., & Mackie, D. M. (1989). Intergroup relations. *Annual Review of Psychology, 40,* 45–81.

Milgram, S. (1974). *Obedience to authority.* New York: Harper & Row.

Miller, J. G. (1984). Culture and the development of everyday social explanation. *Journal of Personality and Social Psychology, 46,* 961–978.

Miller, J. G., & Bersoff, D. M. (1992). Culture and moral judgment: How are conflicts between justice and interpersonal responsibilities resolved? *Journal of Personality and Social Psychology, 62,* 541–554.

Mintz, J., Mintz, L., & Goldstein, M. (1987). Expressed emotion and relapse in first episodes of schizophrenia. *British Journal of Psychiatry, 151,* 314–320.

Miyake, K., Chen, S., & Campos, J. J. (1985). Infant temperament, mother's mode of interaction, and attachment in Japan. An interim report. In I. Bretherton & E. Waters (Eds.), *Growing points of attachment theory. Monographs of the Society of Research in Child Development, 50* (1–2, Serial No. 209).

Moghaddam, F. M., Ditto, B., & Taylor, D. M. (1990). Attitudes and attributions related to psychological symptomatology in Indian immigrant women. *Journal of Cross-Cultural Psychology, 21,* 335–350.

Morelli, G. A., Oppenheim, D., Rogoff, B., & Goldsmith, D. (1992). Cultural variations in infant sleeping arrangements: Questions of independence. *Developmental Psychology, 28,* 604–613.

Morgan, L. H. (1877). *Ancient society: Or, researches in the line of human progress from savagery through barbarism to civilization.* Chicago: C. H. Kerr.

Morris, D., Collett, P., Marsh, P., & O'Shaughnessy, M. (1980). *Gestures: Their origins and distribution.* New York: Scarborough.

Mulder, M. (1976). Reduction of power differences in practice: The power distance reduction theory and its applications. In G. Hofstede & M. S. Kassem (Eds.), *European contributions to organize theory* (pp. 79–94). Assen, Netherlands: Van Gorcum.

Mulder, M. (1977). *The daily power game.* Leyden, Netherlands: Martinus.

Murase, T. (1986). Naikan therapy. In T. S. Lebra & W. P. Lebra (Eds.), *Japanese culture and behavior* (pp. 388–398). Honolulu: University of Hawaii Press.

Murdock, G. P., Ford, C. S., & Hudson, A. E. (1971). *Outline of cultural materials* (4th ed.). New Haven, CT: Human Relations Area Files.

Murphy, H. B. M. (1982). Culture and schizophrenia. In I. Al-Issa (Ed.), *Culture and psychopathology* (pp. 221–249). Baltimore, MD: University Park Press.

Murphy, J. M. (1976). Psychiatric labeling in cross-cultural perspective. *Science, 191,* 1019–1028.

Myers, D. (1987). *Social psychology* (2nd ed.). New York: McGraw-Hill.

Myers, F. R. (1979). Emotions and the self: A theory of personhood and political order among Pintupi aborigines. *Ethos, 7,* 343–370.

Myers, J. K., Weissman, M. M., Tischler, G. L., Holzer, C. E., Leaf, P. J., Orvaschel, H., Anthony, J. C., Boyd, J. H., Burke, J. D., Kramer, M., & Stolzman, R. (1984). Six month prevalence of psychiatric disorders in three communities: 1980 to 1982. *Archives of General Psychiatry, 41,* 959–967.

Niyekawa-Howard, A. M. (1968). *A study of second language learning: The influence of first language on perception, cognition, and second language learning: A test of the Whorfian hypothesis.* Washington, DC: U.S. Dept. of Health, Education, and Welfare, Office of Education, Bureau of Research.

Noesjirwan, J. (1977). Contrasting cultural patterns of interpersonal closeness in doctors' waiting rooms in Sydney and Jakarta. *Journal of Cross-Cultural Psychology, 8,* 357–368.

Noesjirwan, J. (1978). A laboratory study of proxemic patterns of Indonesians and Australians. *British Journal of Social and Clinical Psychology, 17,* 333–334.

O'Reilly, C. A. (1989). Corporations, culture, and commitment: Motivation and social control in organizations. *California Management Review, 31,* 9–25.

O'Reilly, C. A., Chatman, J., & Caldwell, D. F. (1991). People and organizational culture: A profile-comparison approach to assessing person-organization fit. *Academy of Management Journal, 34,* 487–516.

Ochs, E. (1988). *Culture and language development: Language acquisition and language socialization in a Samoan village.* Cambridge, England: Cambridge University Press.

Ochs, E., & Schieffelin, B. B. (Eds.). (1979). *Developmental pragmatics.* New York: Academic Press.

Ochs, E., & Schieffelin, B. B. (1983). *Acquiring conversational competence.* London & Boston: Routledge & Kegan Paul.

Ogbu, J. U. (1981). Origins of human competence: A cultural-ecological perspective. *Child Development, 52,* 413–429.

Okamoto, K. (1993). *Nihonjin no YES wa Naze No Ka? (Why is a Japanese yes a no?).* Tokyo, Japan: PHP Research Laboratory.

Opler, M. K., & Singer, J. L. (1959). Ethnic differences in behavior and psychopathology. *International Journal of Social Psychiatry, 2,* 11–23.

Oster, H., & Ekman, P. (1979). Facial expressions of emotion. *Annual Reviews of Psychology, 30,* 527–554.

Patzer, G. L. (1985). *The physical attractiveness phenomena.* New York: Plenum Press.

Pelto, P. J. (1968, April). The differences between "tight" and "loose" societies. *Transaction,* pp. 37–40.

Pe-Pua, R. (1989). Pagtatanong-Tanong: A cross-cultural research method. *International Journal of Intercultural Relations, 13,* 147–163.

Pfeiffer, W. M. (1982). Culture-bound syndromes. In I. Al-Issa (Ed.), *Culture and psychopathology* (pp. 201–218). Baltimore, MD: University Park Press.

Piaget, J. (1952). *The origins of intelligence in children.* New York: International Universities Press.

Pike, K. L. (1954). *Language in relation to a unified theory of the structure of human behavior, Pt. 1* (Preliminary ed.). Glendale, CA: Summer Institute of Linguistics.

Pollack, R. H., & Silvar, S. D. (1967). Magnitude of the Mueller-Lyer illusion in children as a function of the pigmentation of the fundus oculi. *Psychonomic Science, 8,* 83–84.

Prince, R. (1980). Variations in psychotherapeutic procedures. In H. C. Triandis & J. Draguns (Eds.), *Handbook of cross-cultural psychology, Vol. 6: Psychopathology* (pp. 291–349). Boston: Allyn & Bacon.

Prince, V. (1985). Sex, gender, and semantics. *Journal of Sex Research, 21,* 92–96.

Punetha, D., Giles, H., & Young, L. (1987). Ethnicity and immigrant values: Religion and language choice. *Journal of Language and Social Psychology, 6*, 229–241.

Riesman, P. (1977). *Freedom in Fulani social life: An introspective ethnography* (M. Fuller, Trans.). Chicago: University of Chicago Press. (Original work published 1974.)

Rivers, W. H. R. (1905). Observations on the senses of the Todas. *British Journal of Psychology, 1*, 321–396.

Robbins, S. R. (1987). *Organization theory: Structure, design and applications.* Englewood Cliffs, NJ: Prentice-Hall.

Robins, L. N., Helzer, J. E., Weissman, M. M., Ovraschel, H., Gruenberg, E., Burke, J. D., & Reiger, D. (1984). Lifetime prevalence of specific psychiatric disorders in three sites. *Archives of General Psychiatry, 41*, 949–958.

Roemer, M. I. (1993). *National health systems of the world: The issues* (Vol. 2). New York: Oxford University Press.

Rohner, R. P. (1984). Toward a conception of culture for cross-cultural psychology. *Journal of Cross-Cultural Psychology, 15*, 111–138.

Romero, G. J., & Garza, R. T. (1986). Attributes for the occupational success/failure of ethnic minority and nonminority women. *Sex Roles, 14*, 445–452.

Rosch, E. (1973). On the internal structure of perceptual categories. In T. E. Moore (Ed.), *Cognitive development and the acquisition of language* (pp. 111–144). San Diego, CA: Academic Press.

Rosch, E. (1978). Principles of categorization. In E. Rosch & B. B. Lloyd (Eds.), *Cognition and categorization* (pp. 28–48). Hillsdale, NJ: Erlbaum.

Ross, B. M., & Millson, C. (1970). Repeated memory of oral prose in Ghana and New York. *International Journal of Psychology, 5*, 173–181.

Ross, J., & Ferris, K. R. (1981). Interpersonal attraction and organizational outcome: A field experiment. *Administrative Science Quarterly, 26*, 617–632.

Ross, L. (1977). The intuitive psychologist and his shortcomings: Distortions in the attribution process. In L. Berkowitz (Ed.), *Advances in experimental social psychology* (Vol. 10), (pp. 174–221). New York: Academic Press.

Rotter, J. B. (1954). *Social learning and clinical psychology.* Englewood Cliffs NJ: Prentice-Hall.

Rotter, J. B. (1966). Generalized expectancies for internal versus external control of reinforcement. *Psychological Monographs, 80* (Whole No. 609).

Russell, J. A. (1991). Culture and the categorization of emotions. *Psychological Bulletin, 110*, 426–450.

Ryan, R. A. (1980). Strengths of the American Indian family: State of the art. In F. Hoffman (Ed.), *The American Indian family: Strength and stresses.* Isleta, NM: American Indian Social Research and Development Association.

Sagi, A., Lamb, M. E., Lewkowicz, K. S., Shoham, R., Dvir, R., & Estes, D. (1985). Security of infant-mother, -father, and metapelet attachments among kibbutz reared Israeli children. In I. Bretherton & E. Waters (Eds.), *Growing point in attachment theory. Monographs of the Society for Research in Child Development, 50* (1-2 Serial No. 209).

Schachter, S., & Singer, S. S. (1962). Cognitive, social and physiological determinants of emotional state. *Psychological Review, 69*, 379–399.

Schaller, G. (1963). *The mountain gorilla.* Chicago: University of Chicago Press.

Schaller, G. (1964). *The year of the gorilla.* Chicago: University of Chicago Press.

Scherer, K. R., Matsumoto, D., Wallbott, H., & Kudoh, T. (1988). Emotional experience in cultural context: A comparison between Europe, Japan, and the USA. In K. Scherer (Ed.), *Facets of emotion: Recent research* (pp. 5–30). Hillsdale, NJ: Erlbaum.

Scherer, K. R., Summerfield, A., & Wallbott, H. (1986). Cross-national research on antecedents and components of emotion: A progress report. *Social Science Information, 22,* 355–385.

Schieffelin, B. B. (1981). *How Kaluli children learn what to say, what to do, and how to feel: An ethnographic study of the development of communicative competence.* Unpublished doctoral dissertation, University of California, San Diego.

Schieffelin, B. B. (1990). *The give and take of everyday life: Language socialization of Kaluli children.* New York: Cambridge University Press.

Schieffelin, B. B., & Ochs, E. (Eds.). (1986). *Language socialization across cultures.* Cambridge, England: Cambridge University Press.

Schwartz, S. (1990). Individualism-collectivism: Critique and proposed refinements. *Journal of Cross-Cultural Psychology, 21,* 139–157.

Schwartz, S., & Bilsky, W. (1987). Toward a universal psychological structure of human values. *Journal of Personality and Social Psychology, 53,* 550–562.

Scribner, S. (1974). Developmental aspects of categorized recall in a West African society. *Cognitive Psychology, 6,* 475–494.

Scribner, S. (1979). Modes of thinking and ways of speaking: Culture and logic reconsidered. In I. O. Freedle (Ed.), *New directions in discourse processing* (pp. 223–243). Norwood, NJ: Able.

Segall, M. H. (1979). *Cross-cultural psychology: Human behavior in global perspective.* Pacific Grove, CA: Brooks/Cole.

Segall, M. H., Campbell, D. T., & Hersokovits, J. (1963). Cultural differences in the perception of geometric illusions. *Sciences, 193,* 769–771.

Segall, M. H., Campbell, D. T., & Hersokovits, J. (1966). *The influence of culture on visual perception.* Indianapolis: Bobbs-Merrill.

Segall, M. H., Dasen, P. R., Berry, J. W., & Poortinga, Y. H. (1990). *Human behavior in global perspective: An introduction to cross-cultural psychology.* New York: Pergamon Press.

Shayer, M., Demetriou, A., & Perez, M. (1988). The structure and scaling of concrete operational thought: Three studies in four countries and only one story. *Genetic Psychology Monographs, 114,* 307–376.

Shea, J. D. (1985). Studies of cognitive development in Papua New Guinea. *International Journal of Psychology, 20,* 33–61.

Shepperd, J., & Wright, R. (1989). Individual contributions to a collective effort: An incentive analysis. *Personality and Social Psychology Bulletin, 15,* 141–149.

Shimoda, K., Argyle, M., & Ricci Bitti, P. (1978). The intercultural recognition of facial expressions of emotion. *European Journal of Social Psychology, 8,* 169–179.

Shirakashi, S. (1985). Social loafing of Japanese students. *Hiroshima Forum for Psychology, 10,* 35–40.

Shuter, R. (1976). Proxemics and tactility in Latin America. *Journal of Communication, 26,* 46–52.

Shuter, R. (1977). A field study of nonverbal communication in Germany, Italy, and the United States. *Communication Monographs, 44,* 298–305.

Shweder, R. A., & Bourne, E. J. (1984). Does the concept of the person vary cross-culturally? In R. A. Shweder & R. A LeVine (Eds.), *Culture theory: Essays on mind, self, and emotion* (pp. 158–199). Cambridge, England: Cambridge University Press.

Shweder, R. A., Mahapatra, M., & Miller, J. G. (1987). Culture and moral development. In J. Kagan & S. Lamb (Eds.), *The emergence of morality in young children.* Chicago: University of Chicago Press.

Simmons, C. H., vomKolke, A., & Shimizu, H. (1986). Attitudes toward romantic love among American, German and Japanese students. *Journal of Social Psychology, 126,* 327–336.

Simonds, P. E. (1965). The bonnet macaque in South India. In I. DeVore (Ed.), *Primate behavior: Field studies of monkeys and apes* (pp. 175–196). New York: Holt, Rinehart & Winston.

Sinha, J. (1980). *The nurturant task leader.* New Delhi, India: Sage.

Snarey, J. R. (1985). Cross-cultural universality of social development: A critical review of Kohlbergian research. *Psychological Bulletin, 97,* 202–232.

Snyder, C. R., & Higgins, R. L. (1988). Excuses: Their effective role in the negotiation of reality. *Psychological Bulletin, 104,* 23–35.

Song, M. J., & Ginsburg, H. P. (1987). The development of informal and formal mathematical thinking in Korean and U. S. children. *Child Development, 58,* 1286–1296.

Sow, I. (1977). *Psychiatrie dynamique africaine.* Paris: Payot.

Sow, I. (1978). *Les structures anthropologiques de la folie en Afrique noire.* Paris: Payot.

Sowell, T. (1983). *The economics and politics of race.* New York: Quill.

Spearman, C. E. (1927). *The abilities of man.* New York: Macmillan.

Spencer, H. (1876). *Principles of sociology.* New York: D. Appleton.

Steele, S. (1990). *The content of our character: A new vision of race in America.* New York: Harper Collins

Steinberg, S. (1989). *The ethnic myth: Race, ethnicity, and class in America.* Boston: Beacon Press.

Sternberg, R. J. (1986). *Intelligence applied: Understanding and increasing your intellectual skills.* New York: Harcourt Brace Jovanovich.

Sternberg, R. J. (1988). Triangulating love. In R. J. Sternberg & M. L. Barnes (Eds.), *The psychology of love* (pp. 119–138). New Haven, CT: Yale University Press.

Stevenson, H. W., Lee, S. Y., & Stigler, S. Y. (1986). *Beliefs and achievements: A study in Japan, Taiwan, and the United States.* Unpublished manuscript.

Stewart, V. (1973). Tests of the "carpentered world" hypothesis by race and environment in American and Zambia. *International Journal of Psychology, 8,* 83–94.

Stigler, J. W., & Baranes, R. (1988). Culture and mathematics learning. In E. Rothkpof (Ed.), *Review of Research in Education* (Vol. 15), (pp. 253–306). Washington DC: American Educational Research Association.

Stigler, J. W., Lee, S., & Stevenson, H. W. (1986). Digit memory in Chinese and English: Evidence for a temporally limited store. *Cognition, 23,* 1–20.

Stropes-Roe, M., & Cochrane, R. (1990). The child-rearing values of Asian and British parents and young people: An inter-ethnic and inter-generational comparison in the evolution of Kohn's 13 qualities. *British Journal of Social Psychology, 29,* 149–160.

Stryker, S. (1986). Identity theory: Developments and extensions. In K. Tardley & T. Honess (Eds.), *Self and identity* (pp. 89–107). New York: Wiley.

Suchman, R. G. (1966). Cultural differences in children's color and form perception. *Journal of Social Psychology, 70,* 3–10.

Sue, D., Sue, D., & Sue, S. (1990). *Understanding abnormal behavior* (3rd ed.). Boston: Houghton Mifflin.

Sue, S. (1977). Community mental health services to minority groups: Some optimism, some pessimism. *American Psychologist, 32,* 616–624.

Sue, S. (1989). Foreword. In J. T. Gibbs & L. N. Huang (Eds.), *Children of color.* San Francisco: Jossey-Bass.

Sue, S. (1991, August). *Ethnicity and mental health: Research and policy issues.* Invited address presented at the Annual Meeting of the American Psychological Association, San Francisco.

Sue, S., Akutsu, P. D., & Higashi, C. (1985). Training issues in conducting therapy with ethnic-minority-group clients. In P. Pedersen (Ed.), *Handbook of cross-cultural counseling and therapy.* New York: Greenwood Press.

Sue, S., & Morishima, J. K. (1982). *The mental health of Asian Americans.* San Francisco: Jossey-Bass.

Sue, S., & Zane, N. (1987). The role of culture and cultural techniques in psychotherapy: A reformation. *American Psychologist, 42,* 37–45.

Super, C. M., & Harkness, S. (1986). The developmental niche: A conceptualization at the interface of child and culture. *International Journal of Behavioural Development, 9,* 545–569.

Super, C. M., & Harkness, S. (1994). The developmental niche. In W. Lonner & R. Malpass (Eds.), *Psychology and culture* (pp. 95–99). Boston: Allyn & Bacon.

Suzuki, T. (1978). *Japanese and the Japanese.* Tokyo: Kodansha.

Swartz, L. (1985). Anorexia nervosa as a culture-bound syndrome. *Social Science and Medicine, 20,* 725–730.

Tajfel, H. (1982). Social psychology of intergroup relations. *Annual Review of Psychology, 33,* 1–39.

Taylor, J. (1992). *Paved with good intentions: The failure of race relations in contemporary America.* New York: Carroll & Graf.

Terrell, M. D. (1992, August). *Stress, coping, ethnic identity and college adjustment.* Paper presented at the Annual Meeting of the American Psychological Association, Washington, D.C.

Thomas, A., & Chess, S. (1977). *Temperament and development.* New York: Brunner/Mazel.

Thomas, A., & Sillen, S. (1972). *Racism and psychiatry.* New York: Brunner/Mazel.

Thornton, B. (1984). Defensive attribution of responsibility: Evidence for an arousal-based motivational bias. *Journal of Personality and Social Psychology, 46,* 721–734.

Thurstone, L. L. (1938). *Primary mental abilities.* Chicago: University of Chicago Press.

Ting-Toomey, S. (1991). Intimacy expressions in three cultures: France, Japan, and the United States. *International Journal of Intercultural Relations, 15,* 29–46.

Tom, D., & Cooper, H. (1986). The effect of student background on teacher performance attributions: Evidence for counterdefensive patterns and low expectancy cycles. *Basic and Applied Social Psychology, 7,* 53–62.

Tomkins, S. S. (1962). *Affect, imagery, and consciousness, Vol. 1: The positive affects.* New York: Springer.

Tomkins, S. S. (1963). *Affect, imagery, and consciousness, Vol. 2: The positive affects.* New York: Springer.

Torrey, E. F. (1972). *The mind game: Witchdoctors and psychiatrists.* New York: Emerson Hall.

Trankina, F. J. (1983). Clinical issues and techniques in working with Hispanic children and their families. In G. J. Powell (Ed.), *The psychological development of minority group children* (pp. 307–329). New York: Brunner/Mazel.

Triandis, H. C. (1972). *The analysis of subjective culture.* New York: Wiley.

Triandis, H. C. (1989). The self and social behavior in differing cultural contexts. *Psychological Review, 96,* 506–520.

Triandis, H. C. (1992, February). *Individualism and collectivism as a cultural syndrome.* Paper presented at the Annual Convention of the Society for Cross-Cultural Researchers, Santa Fe, NM.

Triandis, H. C. (1994). *Culture and social behavior.* New York: McGraw-Hill.

Triandis, H. C., Bontempo, R., Betancourt, H., Bond, M., Leung, K., Brenes, A., Georgas, J., Hui, C. H., Marin, G., Setiadi, B., Sinha, J. B., Verma, J., Spangenberg, J., Touzard, H., & de Montonollin, G. (1986). The measurement aspects of individualism and collectivism across cultures. *Australian Journal of Psychology, 38,* 257–267.

Triandis, H. C., Bontempo, R., Villareal, M. J., Asai, M., & Lucca, N. (1988). Individualism and collectivism: Cross-cultural perspectives on self-ingroup relationships. *Journal of Personality and Social Psychology, 4,* 323–338.

Triandis, H. C., & Lambert, W. W. (1958). A restatement and test of Schlosberg's theory of emotion with two kinds of subjects from Greece. *Journal of Abnormal and Social Psychology, 56,* 321–328.

Triandis, H. C., Leung, K., Villareal, M., & Clack, F. (1985). Allocentric versus idiocentric tendencies: Convergent and discriminate validation. *Journal of Research in Personality, 19,* 395–415.

Triandis, H. C., McCusker, C., & Hui, C. H. (1990). Multimethod probes of individualism and collectivism. *Journal of Personality and Social Psychology, 59,* 1006–1020.

Tronick, E. Z., Morelli, G. A., & Ivey, P. K. (1992). The Efe forager infant and toddlers pattern of social relationships: Multiple and simultaneous. *Developmental Psychology, 28,* 568–577.

Tseng, W., & McDermott, J. F. (1981). *Culture, mind and therapy: An introduction to cultural psychiatry.* New York: Brunner/Mazel.

Tulviste, P. (1978). On the origins of the theoretic syllogistic reasoning in culture and in the child. *Acta at commentationes Universitatis Tortuensis, 4,* 3–22.

Tylor, E. B. (1865). *Researches into the early history of mankind and development of civilization.* London: John Murray.

U. S. Bureau of the Census. (1985). Persons of Spanish origin in the United States: March 1985. *Current Population Reports* (Series P-20, No. 403). Washington, DC: Government Printing Office.

van Hooff, J. A. R. A. M. (1967). The facial displays of the catarrhine monkeys and apes. In D. Morris (Ed.), *Primate ethology* (pp. 7–68). London: Weidenfeld and Nicolson.

Vinacke, W. E. (1949). The judgment of facial expressions by three national-racial groups in Hawaii: I. Caucasian faces. *Journal of Personality, 17,* 407–429.

Vinacke, W. E., & Fong, R. W. (1955). The judgment of facial expressions by three national-racial groups in Hawaii: II. Oriental faces. *Journal of Social Psychology, 41,* 184–195.

Vontress, C. E. (1991). Traditional healing in Africa: Implications for cross-cultural counseling. *Counseling and Development, 70,* 242–249.

Wagner, D. A. (1977). Ontogeny of the Ponzo illusion: Effects of age, schooling and environment. *International Journal of Psychology, 12,* 161–176.

Wagner, D. A. (1980). Culture and memory development. In H. Triandis & A. Heron (Eds.), *Handbook of cross-cultural psychology, Vol. 4: Developmental psychology.* Boston: Allyn & Bacon.

Walker, L. J. (1984). Sex differences in the development of moral reasoning: A critical review. *Child Development, 57,* 522–526.

Wallbott, H., & Scherer, K. (1986). How universal and specific is emotional experience? Evidence from 27 countries on five continents. *Social Science Information, 25,* 763–795.

Wallbott, H., & Scherer, K. (1988). Emotion and economic development: Data and speculations concerning the relationship between emotional experience and socioeconomic factors. *European Journal of Social Psychology, 18,* 267–273.

Watson, D. (1982). The actor and the observer: How are their perceptions of causality divergent? *Psychological Bulletin, 92,* 682–700.

Watson, O. M. (1970). *Proxemic behavior: A cross-cultural study.* The Hague: Mouton.

Watson, O. M., & Graves, T. D. (1966). Quantitative research in proxemic behavior. *American Anthropologist, 68,* 971–985.

Weiner, B. (1974). *Achievement motivation and attribution theory.* Morristown, NJ: General Learning Press.

Weiner, B., Frieze, I., Kukla, A., Reed, L., Rest, S., & Rosenbaum, R. M. (1972). Perceiving the causes of success and failure. In E. E. Jones, D. E. Kanouse, H. H. Kelley, R. E. Nesbett, S. Valins, & B. Weiner (Eds.), *Perceiving the causes of behavior.* Morristown, NJ: General Learning Press.

Weldon, E., & Gargano, G. M. (1988). Cognitive loafing: The effects of accountability and shared responsibility on cognitive effort. *Personality and Social Psychology Bulletin, 14,* 159–171.

White, G. M. (1980). Conceptual universals in interpersonal language. *American Anthropologist, 88,* 759–781.

Whorf, B. L. (1956). *Language, thought and reality* (J. Carroll, Ed.). Cambridge, MA: MIT Press.

Wierzbicka, A. (1986). Human emotions: Universal or culture-specific? *American Anthropologist, 88,* 584–594.

Williams, J., & Best, D. (1982). *Measuring sex stereotypes: A thirty-nation study.* Beverly Hills, CA: Sage.

Williams, J., & Best, D. (1990). *Measuring sex stereotypes: A multination study.* Beverly Hills, CA: Sage.

Williams, J., & Best, D. (1994). Cross-cultural views of women and men. In W. Lonner & R. Malpass (Eds.), *Psychology and culture*. Boston: Allyn & Bacon.

Wober, M. (1974). Toward an understanding of the Kiganda concept of intelligence. In J. W. Berry & P. R. Dasen (Eds.), *Culture and cognition* (pp. 261–280). London: Methuen.

Wolf, R. M. (1965). The measurement of environments. In C. W. Harris (Ed.), *Proceedings of the 1964 Invited Conference on Testing Problems*. Princeton, NJ: Educational Testing Service.

Wolfgang, A., & Cohen, M. (1988). Sensitivity of Canadians, Latin Americans, Ethiopians, and Israelis to interracial facial expressions of emotions. *International Journal of Intercultural Relations, 12*, 1–13.

Wong, P. T. P., Derlaga, V. J., & Colson, W. (1988). The effects of race on expectancies and performance and attributions. *Canadian Journal of Behavioral Science, 20*, 29–39.

World Health Organization. (1973). *Report of the International Pilot Study of Schizophrenia, Vol. 1*. Geneva: Author.

World Health Organization. (1979). *Schizophrenia: An international follow-up study*. New York: Wiley.

World Health Organization. (1981). *Current state of diagnosis and classification in the mental health field*. Geneva: Author.

World Health Organization (1991). *World health statistics quarterly*. Geneva: Author.

Wylie, R. C. (1979). *The self concept, Vol. 2: Theory and research on selected topics*. Lincoln: University of Nebraska Press.

Yamaguchi, S., Okamoto, K., & Oka, T. (1985). Effects of coactor's presence: Social loafing and social facilitation. *Japanese Psychological Research, 27*, 215–222.

Yamamoto, J., & Kubota, M. (1983). The Japanese-American family. In G. J. Powell (Ed.), *The psychological development of minority group children* (pp. 307–329). New York: Brunner/Mazel.

Yang, K. S. (1982). Causal attributions of academic success and failure and their affective consequences. *Chinese Journal of Psychology* [Taiwan], *24*, 65–83. (The abstract only is in English.)

Yap, P. M. (1974). *Comparative psychiatry. A theoretical framework*. Toronto: University of Toronto.

Yee, A. H., Fairchild, H. H., Weizman, F., & Wyatt. G. E. (1993). Addressing psychology's problem with race. *American Psychologist, 48*, 1132–1140.

Yu, E. S. H. (1974). Achievement motive, familism, and hsiao: A replication of McClellend-Winterbottom studies. *Dissertation Abstracts International, 35*, 593A (University Microfilms No. 74–14, 942).

Zaccaro, S. J. (1984). The role of task attractiveness. *Personality and Social Psychology Bulletin, 10*, 99–106.

Zuckerman, M. (1990). Some dubious premises in research and theory on racial differences. *American Psychologist, 45*, 1297–1303.

Name Index

Subject Index